RESEARCHING POWER, ELITES AND LEADERSHIP

SAGE has been part of the global academic community since 1965, supporting high quality research and learning that transforms society and our understanding of individuals, groups and cultures. SAGE is the independent, innovative, natural home for authors, editors and societies who share our commitment and passion for the social sciences.

Find out more at: **www.sagepublications.com**

RESEARCHING POWER, ELITES AND LEADERSHIP

CHRISTOPHER WILLIAMS

Los Angeles | London | New Delhi
Singapore | Washington DC

Los Angeles | London | New Delhi
Singapore | Washington DC

SAGE Publications Ltd
1 Oliver's Yard
55 City Road
London EC1Y 1SP

SAGE Publications Inc.
2455 Teller Road
Thousand Oaks, California 91320

SAGE Publications India Pvt Ltd
B 1/I 1 Mohan Cooperative Industrial Area
Mathura Road
New Delhi 110 044

SAGE Publications Asia-Pacific Pte Ltd
3 Church Street
#10-04 Samsung Hub
Singapore 049483

Editor: Jai Seaman
Editorial assistant: Anna Horvai
Production editor: Rachel Burrows
Marketing manager: Ben Griffin-Sherwood
Cover design: Jennifer Crisp
Typeset by: C&M Digitals (P) Ltd, Chennai, India
Printed by: MPG Books Group, Bodmin, Cornwall

Library of Congress Control Number: 2011941492

British Library Cataloguing in Publication data

A catalogue record for this book is available from
the British Library

MIX
Paper from
responsible sources
FSC
www.fsc.org   FSC® C018575

ISBN 978-0-85702-428-2
ISBN 978-0-85702-429-9 (pbk)

CONTENTS

Full contents   vi
List of figures   ix
About the author   xii
Acknowledgements   xiii
List of abbreviations   xv

Introduction   1

PART ONE: UNDERSTANDING   **19**

1   Origins   21
2   Theory   54

PART TWO: DOING   **89**

3   Literature   91
4   Planning   111
5   Frameworks   136
6   Data   153

PART THREE: USING   **183**

7   Analysis   185
8   Outcomes   211

Appendices   223
Glossary   245
Internet sources   254
References   261
Index   311

FULL CONTENTS

List of figures   ix
About the author   xii
Acknowledgements   xiii
List of abbreviations   xv

Introduction   **1**
Why research powerful people?   1
Who the book is for   9
Key concepts   10
How the book was researched   12
A quick guide to the book   14
The chapters   15

PART ONE: UNDERSTANDING   **19**

1   Origins   **21**
1.1   Anthropology   22
1.2   History   30
1.3   Philosophy   41
1.4   Up-system research   46

2   Theory   **54**
2.1   Power   58
2.2   Elites   63
2.3   Leadership   68
2.4   Populace   77
2.5   Critique   81

PART TWO: DOING   **89**

3   Literature   **91**
3.1   Searching   92

3.2 Reviewing   94
3.3 Topics   99

4   Planning   **111**
4.1 Design   112
4.2 Focus   114
4.3 Problematization   119
4.4 Definitions   121
4.5 Access   124
4.6 Integrity   128

5   Frameworks   **136**
5.1 Direct   137
5.2 Indirect   139
5.3 Networks and systems   145

6   Data   **153**
6.1 Sources   156
6.2 Selection   175
6.3 Testing   176

PART THREE: USING   **183**

7   Analysis   **185**
7.1 Comparison   186
7.2 Causation   190
7.3 Consistency   195
7.4 Contra-arguments   200
7.5 Common sense   202
7.6 Critical Process Analysis   204
7.7 Conceptualization   207

8   Outcomes   **211**
8.1 Reporting   212
8.2 Presentation   215
8.3 Influencing change   217

Appendices – Tools and templates for research planning   **223**
1 Mapping a case study within a conceptual framework   225
2 Linking the elements of a research study   226
3 A basic research design   227
4 A basic Gantt chart   229
5 Achieving focus at, or across, specific levels   230

6   Systematic links from topic to data collection   231
7   Making distinctions between elite and leadership roles   233
8   Explaining the focus of a study   234
9   Standard research frameworks   235
10   Relating basic questions to frameworks and information sources   239
11   Comparing journalistic and academic approaches to access   241
12   Instruments to implement power   242
13   The structure of a press release   244

Glossary   245
Internet sources   254
References   261
Index   311

LIST OF FIGURES

INTRODUCTION

0.1	Egyptian dynasties – Seti	2
0.2	Egyptian dynasties – Mubarak	2
0.3	The Kuwait 'Not to Forget Museum'	4
0.4	Epitaph to Francis Walsingham, spymaster to Queen Elizabeth I	5
0.5	Heroes and hero worship	6
0.6	The King's speech	7
0.7	Interviewing for PhD research	8
0.8	Admiral Yi Sun-shin and the 'turtle ship'	9
0.9	The conceptual framework used in this book	13

CHAPTER 1

1.1	Ethnography of Egyptian elites (1835)	26
1.2	The Chieftainess of Mohilla	27
1.3	Images of Lokele Chiefs, Congo, 1930 and 1911	29
1.4	The Narmer Palette (3000BC)	31
1.5	The Annals of Thutmosis III in Karnak (c.1570–1320BC)	32
1.6	The rise and fall of elites (Ibn Khaldun, 1377)	39
1.7	Lists	48
1.8	Lineage charts	49
1.9	Typologies and hierarchies	50
1.10	Methodological contributions from early up-system research	51
1.11	Questions and concepts	52

CHAPTER 2

2.1	The delusion of grand theories, John Gray	55
2.2	A null ontological hypothesis	56

2.3   The epistemology of "Iraq's Weapons of Mass Destruction"   57
2.4   The sources of power, Michael Mann   59
2.5   Rules for robots   63
2.6   Are leaders born or made? Nelson Mandela   70
2.7   How leaders fail – cumulative lock-in   75
2.8   Questions, considerations and sources   84

CHAPTER 3

3.1   Operation Northwoods   93
3.2   Extract from the summary of a literature review   96
3.3   Questioning the 'halo effect' of elite sources   98
3.4   Reconceptualizing the abuse of power – 'state crime'   100
3.5   Memorials to abuse of power   102
3.6   Perceptions of political leaders by South Korean children, age 9–10.
      Draw and tell method – 'Good and bad Presidents'   104
3.7   Elites abandoning the planet – perceptions by Chinese children   109

CHAPTER 4

4.1   Literal responses to unclear questions   114
4.2   Action-oriented research   116
4.3   Problem-oriented purposes and rationale   117
4.4   Academic support for research 'rationale'   118
4.5   Conceptualizing a cross-cultural study of leadership   123
4.6   The persona of the interviewer   126
4.7   Impartiality   128
4.8   Confidentiality   131

CHAPTER 5

5.1   Collaborative research   141
5.2   Sam Hinga Norman at the Special Court for Sierra Leone   142
5.3   Power structures   148
5.4   Basic network analysis – cultural and commercial interlocks of CEOs   149

CHAPTER 6

6.1 Secondary analysis – a trend from annual data 155
6.2 Satire – The Fate of The Monopolists and Dance at Fidler's Green 160
6.3 The wider role of interviews 162
6.4 An interview with Abdul Salam A. Majali, former Prime Minister
of Jordan 164
6.5 Yun-joo Lee interviewing Arab and Korean leaders 167
6.6 Images of Korean elites 172
6.7 Backdrops as data 173
6.8 Testimony evidence 178
6.9 Accuracy 179

CHAPTER 7

7.1 Aggregate data based on ratification of international agreements (Global
Leadership Responsibility Index) 188
7.2 A framework for analysing aphorisms in political discourse 189
7.3 Mapping local elites for military intelligence analysis 189
7.4 A radar chart 190
7.5 Causation or coincidence? 192
7.6 Political consistency 197
7.7 Iranian banknotes 199
7.8 Critical Process Analysis (CPA) 205
7.9 Testing a theory – pig-crushing 208
7.10 Interviewing perpetrators – theorizing State 209

CHAPTER 8

8.1 The use of a Venn diagram to explain the confusing terminology
associated with the 'British Isles' 216
8.2 Researching abuse of power among South African
street-working children 217
8.3 Effective use of research 218
8.4 Achieving change – dialogue with decision-makers 220

ABOUT THE AUTHOR

Christopher Williams (AGSM, Cert Ed, PhD, FRSA) is based at the Centre for International Education and Research (CIER), University of Birmingham UK, and has also held posts at the universities of Bristol, Cambridge, Cairo, London and the United Nations University Leadership Academy. He has lived in Egypt, Jordan and South Africa, and worked in many countries including India, Thailand, Turkey, Korea, Japan and China. He has carried out research in Afghanistan for the European Commission, Liberia for Oxfam, South Asia for UNICEF, Lebanon for the US government and Palestine for UNESCO.

He has presented research about abuse of power at the British House of Commons, British military academy Sandhurst, UN Palais des Nations and World Health Organization (Geneva). In 2005 he was a keynote speaker at the UNESCO/United Nations University Global Seminar on 'Cultural diversity in a globalizing world' at Jeju 'peace' University (Korea).

His books include *Leadership Accountability in a Globalizing World* (Palgrave Macmillan), *Leaders of Integrity: Ethics and a Code for Global Leadership* (United Nations University Leadership Academy), *Environmental Victims New Risks, New Injustice* (Earthscan), *Invisible Victims: Crime and Abuse against People with Learning Disabilities* (Jessica Kingsley), *Terminus Brain: The Environmental Threat to Human Intelligence* (Cassell and Klett Cotter), and a series of interviews with UN leaders. Other writing includes, 'The minds of leaders: de-linking war and violence', 'Education and human survival', and 'Educating world leaders' (Club of Budapest). He has written for the *Korea Herald* and *China Daily*, and discussed his work on BBC TV and radio.

Originally he was a professional trumpeter.

Author contact: chrisunula@yahoo.com

ACKNOWLEDGEMENTS

Thanks to:

- those who have met and shared their professional experience and insights including:

  Konadu Acheampony (UNU, authority on traditional Ashante leadership), Lord Alton of Liverpool (UK All Party Parliamentary Group for North Korea), Gro Harlem Brundtland (Director-General WHO), Edwina Currie MP, Barbara Demick (*Los Angeles Times*), Jill Evans MEP (Plaid Cymru, Wales), Vigdis Finnbogadottir (former president of Iceland), Dr Kennedy Graham MP (Green Party, NZ), Penny Green (*International State Crime Initiative*, King's College, London), Subhash Kashyap (former Secretary General, Lok Sabha, India), Jill Kruger (Department of Anthropology, University of South Africa), Abdelsalam al-Majali (former Prime Minister of Jordan), Countess of Mar (House of Lords), Ingrid Massage (Research Support Unit, Amnesty International), the late Yehudi Menuhin and staff at his music school, Mike Moore (Director-General WTO), Mo Mowlam MP (Cabinet Minister), Ambassadors to North Korea, Juan Somavia (Director-General ILO), Thorvald Stoltenberg (former UNHCR), Brian Walker (former director, Oxfam), Masami Yagiu (community leader, Dowa minority, Japan), Farzaneh Yazdani (Oxford Brookes University). Also staff at the UK Foreign & Commonwealth Office, Geneva Press Club, police departments, banks, courts, telecommunications companies, medical and civil service regulators, ministries and embassies in Lebanon, Afghanistan, Geneva and Jordan, and many others who responded to calls for information.

- groups that facilitated forums for discussion within:

  Nagoya University (Japan), Dongseo University (Korea), Sichuan University, UNESCO World Heritage Institute (China), Afghanistan ministries and international agencies (*European Commission*), Lebanese ministries and UN agencies (US Department of Labor), UNEP and GIWEH (Geneva), Global Security Programme (Cambridge University, Gwyn Prins), House of Commons (Preparing for Peace meeting, Tim Farron MP, and the All Party Group on Disability), United Nations University Leadership Academy (Jordan), Royal Military Academy Sandhurst, the International Business School (Isle of Man), the ESRC seminar 'Studying elites' (Manchester Business School) and London Tent City University (TUC).

- colleagues who provided invaluable research assistance for the *Researching Powerful People* project, knowledge of diverse fields and original material, including:

  Natasha Macnab (University of Birmingham), Sun-young Park (global studies, Dongseo University), Won-joo Suh (museum studies, Chung-Ang University, Korea), Yu Jin Lee (head, overseas reporter team, *Datalink*), and Yun-joo Lee (UN/WIPO, former UNULA) who permitted the use of illustrations from her exemplary PhD. And those who made possible field-work in Korea and Geneva, including Gyeongee Province education directorate (Korea), the World Forum on Youth Studies, United Nations University Leadership Academy, and Geneva Institute for Environment and Health.

- staff at SAGE Publications who provided pertinent professional advice, editorial work and production support:

  Patrick Brindle, David Hodge, Jai Seaman, Anna Horvai, Rachel Burrows and others.

LIST OF ABBREVIATIONS

AI	Amnesty International
AU	African Union
BC	Before Christianity
BP	British Petroleum
c.	circa - about
C	chapter in this book
CEO	Chief Executive Officer
CIA	Central Intelligence Agency
CIS	Commonwealth of Independent States (Former Soviet Republics)
CPA	Critical Process Analysis
d.	died
EU	European Union
FIFA	Fédération Internationale de Football Association (International Federation of Association Football)
FOI	Freedom of Information
GDP	Gross Domestic Product
GIWEH	Geneva Institute of Environment and Health
GM	Genetically Modified
GPS	Global Positioning System
HQ	Headquarters
HRW	Human Rights Watch
ICC	International Criminal Court
ICJ	International Court of Justice
ICRC	International Committee of the Red Cross
ICT	Information and Communications Technology
ILO	International Labour Organization
INGO	International Non-Government Organization
ISCI	International State Crime Initiative, King's College, London
IT	Information Technology
NGO	Non Government Organization
NZ	New Zealand
OECD	Organization for Economic Co-operation and Development

OED	*Oxford English Dictionary*
OIC	Organization of the Islamic Conference
PA	Personal Assistant
R&D	Research and Development
TNC	Trans-National Company
UN	United Nations
UNEP	United Nations Environment Programme
UNHCR	United Nations High Commissioner for Refugees
UNU	United Nations University
UNULA	United Nations University Leadership Academy
WHO	World Health Organization (UN)
WIPO	World Intellectual Property Organization
WMD	Weapons of Mass Destruction
WTO	World Trade Organization

INTRODUCTION

Never before have so few, by their actions and inactions, had the power of life and death over so many of the species … Study the colonizers rather than the colonized, the culture of power rather than the culture of the powerless, the culture of affluence rather than the culture of poverty. (Laura Nader, 1972)[1]

WHY RESEARCH POWERFUL PEOPLE?

Powerful people are the cause and cure of social problems. They may be inefficient or abuse their power, or create positive change and social progress. Yet the familiar focus for studying social problems is **down-system** – people who are poor, vulnerable, oppressed or powerless.[2] As anthropologist Laura Nader argued in the 1970s (above), 'studying up' is important.[3] Anthropologists had a long experience of studying traditional leaders and elites in settings such as Africa and South America. And they evolved this approach to study other forms of 'up', from government officials[4] to gang leaders.[5] Sudhir Venkatesh extended the idea of 'participant observation' when, as a 23-year-old sociology student at Chicago University, he joined a gang to collect data used in his book *Gang Leader for a Day*.[6]

But Nader did not mean that 'studying up' replaces 'studying down' or 'studying sideways'. She was arguing that that 'up' is an important complementary perspective.[7] While studying 'down' in relation to a disadvantaged group, such as street-working children,[8] it may be helpful to study similar 'sideways' groups, such as homeless adults. But it is also relevant to look 'up' at the factory owners who exploit the children, the educationists who try to help them, the political processes that cause their problems, and the police who abuse them (Figure 8.2).

There are many reasons for doing **up-system** research. The oldest is to demonstrate **legitimacy** (C1.2).[9] Since the King lists of the Egyptian Pharaohs, powerful people have tried to affirm their **status** on the questionable basis of "borrowed power" through researching and glorifying their ancestors and **superiors** (Figure 0.1). More recently, the former president of Egypt, Hosni Mubarak tried to mimic the ancient Egyptian tradition, until the 'April 6th Movement' (Arab Spring) of 2011 brought an end to his neo-dynastic ambitions (see Figure 0.2). And that change happened because ordinary

Seti, his son Ramesses II and the Abydos King List. Temple of Seti I, Abydos.
King lists, researched by court historians, adorned Egyptian temples and other public places, to 'borrow power' from ancestors to create legitimacy.

FIGURE 0.1   Egyptian dynasties – Seti

Source: Sutherland, B.J. (1903) *Encyclopaedia Biblica*. Toronto: Morang.

Analysing the 'backdrop' used by powerful people in their offices provides useful insights into how they want, or need, to 'borrow power' to create legitimacy. The power of (then) Egyptian President Hosni Mubarak was evident in the office of the president of Al-Azhar University, Ahmad Omar Hashem, in 2003. But Hashem also displayed Islamic texts prominently.

FIGURE 0.2   Egyptian dynasties – Mubarak

Source: Lee, Yun-joo (2010) 'Leadership and development in South Korea and Egypt: the significance of cultural shifts', unpublished PhD thesis, School of Oriental and Asian Studies, University of London.

Egyptians had become aware of how their political leaders were behaving, through research by academics, journalists, labour movements and human rights organizations.

Legitimacy was then related to research about **accountability**.[10] Early scholars – in China, Greece, India and Egypt – tried to devise ethical standards for the use of power, although they rarely had the courage to find out if powerful people followed these standards. Practical accountability is now central to studies in investigative research, media and political science. In 1985 a UN Declaration about victims affirmed that international systems and nation states should recognise 'Victims of abuse of power':

> 18. 'Victims' means persons who, individually or collectively, have suffered harm, including physical or mental injury, emotional suffering, economic loss or substantial impairment of their fundamental rights, through acts or omissions that do not yet constitute violations of national criminal laws but of internationally recognized norms relating to human rights.

> 19. States should consider incorporating into the national law norms proscribing abuses of power and providing remedies to victims of such abuses. In particular, such remedies should include restitution and/or compensation, and necessary material, medical, psychological and social assistance and support.

> 20. States should consider negotiating multilateral international treaties relating to victims, as defined in paragraph 18.

> 21. States should periodically review existing legislation and practices to ensure their responsiveness to changing circumstances, should enact and enforce, if necessary, legislation proscribing acts that constitute serious abuses of political or economic power, as well as promoting policies and mechanisms for the prevention of such acts, and should develop and make readily available appropriate rights and remedies for victims of such acts.

Although a Declaration cannot be enforced, it has influence. Subsequent initiatives have reflected this UN ethic, for example the founding of the *International Criminal Court* (ICC), the UN *Corruption Convention* (2003), and adaptations of these initiatives into national legislation. In parallel, researchers within NGOs such as *Amnesty International* and *Human Rights Watch*, and academic endeavours such as the *International State Crime Initiative* (ISCI) at King's College London, have fuelled political change with high quality research about abuse of power. Cultural initiatives - museums, monuments, literature, and performing arts – create accountability through researching, documenting and building a public understanding of the abuse of power which lasts beyond immediate events (Figure 0.3).

A third aspect also has a long history – **intelligence** gathering.[11] This occurs in the contexts of diplomacy, commerce, military and other security endeavours. The aim of spying is to gain a strategic advantage by understanding the power and leadership of oppositional groups. The idea is often traced back to the Chinese military strategist, Sun Tzu (722–481BC), who even provided a set of research questions, such as 'Which of the

Long-term accountability marked by a memorial of the Iraq invasion of Kuwait at the 'Not to Forget Museum'.
Photo: Author, 2009.

FIGURE 0.3   The Kuwait 'Not to Forget Museum'

two generals has most ability?' (C1.2).[12] In the Hindu text, *Arthashastra* ('The science of politics'), Chanakya (c. 350–283BC) also discusses spies, including the use of women and children.[13] The work of Francis Walsingham (1532–90), spymaster for Queen Elizabeth I, is a remarkable example of counter-espionage and deceit, involving cryptographers (code breakers), a network of 'intelligencers' and false letters hidden in beer barrels which eventually led to the execution of Mary Queen of Scots. An epitaph by his grave in St Paul's Cathedral (London) records his deeds (Figure 0.4).[14] There is much to be learned from comparing techniques used for professional intelligence gathering and academic research.[15] In commercial contexts, present-day intelligence activities range from those of head-hunting companies to elite dating agencies such as *WorldwideElite* in Zurich, where vetting methods include checking ID documents, education references, CVs, company profiles, divorce decrees and financial status.

> C onfounding Foes which wrought our Jeopardie.
> I n foreign Countries their Intents he knew
> S uch was his Zeal to do his Country good,
> W hen Dangers would by Enemies enſue,
> A s well as they themſelves he underſtood.

FIGURE 0.4 Epitaph to Francis Walsingham, spymaster to Queen Elizabeth I

Source: St Paul's Cathedral. John Hackett (1757) *Select and Remarkable Epitaphs*. London: Osborne and Shipton. p. 135.

Studies of the **characteristics** of exceptional people, to provide the knowledge to inform others who aspire to the same status, are more familiar. Thomas Carlyle's *On Heroes, Hero Worship and the Heroic in History* (1841) is an early example (Figure 0.5). The title epitomizes the ethos of many subsequent texts within 'leadership studies', which try to package research in the form of materials that can readily be applied to leadership training (C2.3), and also of the more recent 'celebrity studies'. On a sophisticated level, Howard Gardener's *Leading Minds: An Anatomy of Leadership*[16] provides a psychological assessment of the biographies of famous people, and his *Creating Minds: An Anatomy of Creativity Seen Through the Lives of Freud, Einstein, Picasso, Stravinsky, Eliot, Graham and Gandhi* specifically explored creative elites.[17] There are constant arguments about the degree to which leadership and celebrity can be learned and taught, and this discussion is clouded because research can be influenced by the financial 'utility' rewards of teaching people to be powerful (C2.5).

A related aspect is less well explored – developing **empathy** (but not necessarily sympathy) with powerful people. This can include extremes such as holocaust denial and politicized revisionism, and companies that provide services for elites. But it also embodies genuine differences of opinion. The *Yasakuni Shrine* in Tokyo is seen by some as glorifying recent war criminals, and by others as honouring elite heroes who have defended Japan throughout its history. Understanding and empathizing with the overwhelming challenges that certain powerful people face, and perhaps encouraging support and assistance, can be very productive. Leaders in countries facing severe problems, such as Haiti and Tuvalu, benefit greatly from international understanding which might translate into appropriate assistance or protection. Even outsider leaders, such as terrorists, sometimes need support to present their point of view at diplomatic meetings. They may lack negotiation skills, and will be encouraged to engage in meetings, and participate better, if they are given assistance. This needs to be based on understanding the strengths, weaknesses, emotions and ideology of those people,[18] and is seen as increasingly relevant in diplomacy research.[19] Historical and biographical research for films and books can also entail empathetic understanding. Aleksandr Sokurov's film, *The Sun* (2005), provides a sympathetic portrayal of the wartime Japanese Emperor Hirohito, depicting him as an intellectual who was manipulated by his political leaders.

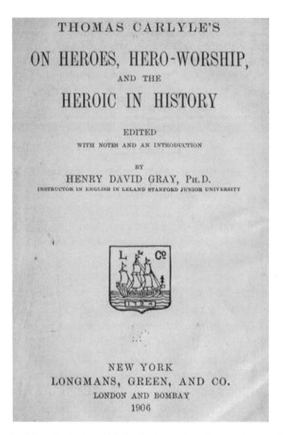

Thomas Carlyle described the physical and intellectual qualities of powerful men in 1841 – a forerunner of modern 'leadership studies'.

FIGURE 0.5 Heroes and hero worship

Movies such as *The King's Speech* (2010) show that an elite life is not always easy, in this case telling how King George VI worked to overcome a speech impediment. The use of modern information technologies can help with analyses for, and of, historical films like this (Figure 0.6).

Up-system research often requires the development of methodologies, sometimes to suit a single interviewee. Researchers should keep in mind that this can represent a contribution to knowledge, and can be presented as an original outcome of a dissertation, thesis, journal article or funding proposal. Sometimes methodological testing and development can be the main or sole purpose of a piece of research. The need to develop methodology should be seen as an opportunity, not an irritation. 'Crowdsourcing' is a recent and innovative aspect of civil society research about the accountability of powerful people (C5.2). From 2008, a campaign about corrupt expenses claims by MPs, by the British newspaper *The Guardian*, led to the use of the *Freedom of Information Act* (C3.1) to gain access to thousands of relevant documents which were made available for the public

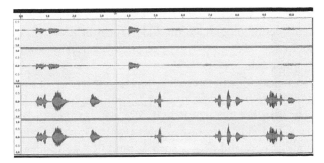

The upper half shows the BBC recording of the broadcast by King George VI in 1939, depicting the long hesitations because of his speech impediment. The lower half shows the version by actor Colin Firth, in the film The *King's Speech* in 2010. The film version has no long pauses, which suggests that the film-makers thought that modern audiences would not tolerate the original very slow pace.

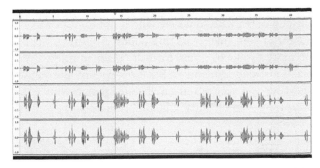

The long hesitations have been edited out, which permits a direct comparison of the speech patterns for the same phrases. Actors can use such techniques to hone their performance, and researchers can analyse famous speeches to teach speechmaking skills.

FIGURE 0.6 The King's speech

Source: drewswalkabout (2011) 'The King's Speech' *Vs the Original/real King George VI War Time Speech*. Available at: www.youtube.com/watch?v=vh1iohLPEEg

to investigate. Many convictions for fraud followed, and a website provides the tools for searching a mass of relevant documents.[20]

Methodological contributions often remain significant far longer than other research outcomes. Present-day Egyptologists are still using the 'King lists' compiled by the royal historians of the Pharaohs (Figure 0.1). Nineteenth-century archaeologists would not have predicted that the methods they were developing to research the bodies of kings and queens, who died millennia earlier, would come to be used by forensic anthropologists employed by UN courts to prove the war crimes committed by despotic leaders in this century. They would not have predicted that their grid system for recording archaeological sites could be applied to photos of the 'backdrops' of present-day leaders (Figure 6.7). When Chinese strategist Sun Tzu described his methods for assessing military leaders in *The Art of War*, he certainly would not have guessed that the book would be bought by American business leaders in airport bookshops 2500 years later. It is arguable that up-system methodologies are the oldest form of research, certainly predating enlightenment sociology.[21] New up-system research is certainly contributing to a very long tradition of methodology (C1).

A central problem of up-system research is how to gain 'access' to powerful people, but there are many innovative ways to address this (C4.5). Improved ICT increasingly permits simple and effective 'distance research' (C5.2). For example there is a mass of data, including transcripts and videos, from the *International Criminal Court* (ICC), tribunals, public examinations of powerful people such as the UK Iraq Inquiry (Figure 5.2), and *Wikileaks*. Interviewing famous people can appear frightening, but again there are many simple ways to evolve a formal discussion into a more revealing encounter (C6.1.2). Simply asking, "What advice would you give someone like me if I hoped to get a job like yours?" can double the length of an interview. Powerful people like giving advice.

Interviewing needs great adaptability, not least being sensitive to cultural norms (Figure 6.5). Settings can range from a cold formal discussion in a diplomatic meeting room, to a friendly cup of tea with someone who is not only an expert in their field, but has surprising interest in your own work and country. Informal opportunistic meetings can sometimes be more productive than formally planned interviews (Figure 6.5). But long experience and a strong academic reputation are not always the best persona for interviewers. Appearing as a young and intelligent listener, who asks interesting questions and is eager to learn, can be equally helpful (Figure 0.7).

Thomas A. Bartlett, President of the American University in Cairo, Egypt and Yun-joo Lee (2003) 'He was my first interviewee in Egypt, so I was very nervous. But he was very warm and friendly. And the moment he knew that I was Korean, he started to talk about Korea because he had worked there in the 1950s. This made me feel very comfortable. He could help with both my case studies, from a neutral, analytical perspective. It was like a great supervision session!'

FIGURE 0.7   Interviewing for PhD research

Source: Lee, Yun-joo (2010) 'Leadership and development in South Korea and Egypt: The significance of cultural shifts', unpublished PhD thesis, School of Oriental and Asian Studies, University of London.

WHO THIS BOOK IS FOR

Up-system research is very diverse, yet those working within specific traditions and disciplines often do not realize or appreciate the wide range of people doing similar research that has common problems and solutions. Interest groups include academics, students, leadership trainers, commercial researchers and 'head hunters', civil society organizations, journalists, investigators, media researchers and public officials. The approaches are also relevant to ordinary people seeking up-system redress, for example citizens mistreated by police, constituents holding MPs to account, unions checking managers, and others who want to assess if power is being used correctly.

As the apparent difficulties of researching powerful people can seem daunting, very simple approaches are included throughout this book. Anyone can start doing up-system research by analysing the banknotes in their pocket (Figure 7.7). These commonly depict national elites that a country wants to show off. A little more investigation can sometimes uncover fascinating stories beyond the images on the notes. When Chung Ju-yung, founder of the *Hyundai* group, went to London in 1971 to get a loan to start a shipyard, bank managers did not take him seriously, saying that Korea had no industrial tradition. He showed them a banknote depicting the Korean 'turtle ship', which was built in the sixteenth century. These ships had five types of cannon, including a dragon head at the front that could also shoot fire. They had armoured metal decks, iron spikes to deter boarders, and were part submerged – a proto-submarine. Chung pointed out that this was about 300 years before Britain had used metal for cladding ships in 1860 (Figure 0.8). He got his loan, and one of the most successful engineering companies in the world was born.

This book facilitates cross-disciplinary thinking and encourages a critical stance. Powerful people do not always give straight answers, but it is also important to be critical of the whole 'paradigm' of up-system research, which itself can be a form of power (C2.5) and sometimes an abuse of power (C1.1). But powerful people can also be vulnerable, and

Chung Ju-yung, head of Hyundai, used a Korean banknote showing the technologically advanced 'turtle ship' deployed by Admiral Yi Sun-shin (1545–98), to impress British bankers.

FIGURE 0.8 Admiral Yi Sun-shin and the 'turtle ship'

so can their families and associates, and they usually deserve the same ethical standards that would be applied in other forms of research (C4.6). The approaches to up-system research are diverse, and extend standard academic methods to embrace other perspectives. These include police and journalistic investigatory strategies, intelligence techniques deployed by diplomats and military analysts, reconstruction methods used by archaeologists, and meta-methods that are familiar to IT experts. These professional methods are often ignored by academics, yet they are sound, well-tested and practical. Increasingly there is overlap between professional and academic spheres. The book is therefore based on research across many different fields, in many countries, and can potentially interest a wide range of people who may not know that they may be interested.

KEY CONCEPTS

> ### RESEARCH
>
> An investigation directed to the discovery of some fact by careful study of a subject. (*OED*)

> ### METHOD
>
> A way of doing anything, especially according to a regular plan. A special form of procedure adopted in any branch of mental activity, whether for exposition or for investigation. (*OED*)

> ### METHODOLOGY
>
> The science of method. A treatise or dissertation on method. (*OED*)

In the past, studies of power, elites and leadership have usually been framed as distinct and separate areas of interest, with different theories and methodological approaches. But in practice the methods have much in common. This book brings these perspectives together, for the first time, and (borrowing Nader's injunction to 'study up') the term 'up-system' research is used to describe this general perspective. Methods books do not use terms consistently, and so methodologies need to provide conceptual frameworks and clarify terminology. This section and Figure 0.9 explain how the basic concepts are used throughout this book, and Appendix 1 shows how a case study can be mapped using this framework.

Elite studies usually concern select groups at the top of a hierarchical relationship with those within a non-specific **populace**. A distinction is often made between political and non-political elites.[22] Historically, elite status has often been **ascribed** – allocated at birth. **Leadership studies** usually concern specific up-system individuals and their relationship with specific down-system **followers** to achieve specific aims. Leadership status is often **achieved** through personal endeavour. Elite and leading organizations – TNCs, banks and UN organizations – can be conceptualized similarly, as can countries such as those in the OECD or OIC. The **hegemonic** leadership of countries, such as China or Germany, requires other countries to position themselves in relation to that power, and transnational forms of hegemony are now evident.[23] **Political** studies consider systems, parties and constituents, which is a distinct field.[24] This book only covers politicians as individuals in terms of political leadership (C2.3) and biographical research.

Research about powerful people is therefore likely to be conceptualized in terms of elite *or* leadership studies, but this is not clear-cut. Not least, who are the leaders or elites, who defines them as such and how are they defined?[25] Might those concerned agree or not with this description? Within one place or domain, the role of elite and leader may coexist, and power relationships can be circumstantial. In an expensive private school, pupils from royal families may be seen as elites, but senior teachers are the leaders and may have arbitrary power to punish those elites. Power sometimes arises because of a capacity gap between people. If the research site is a care-home for older people, low-paid care workers can represent leaders who have immense power over those in their care who may be wealthy elites. People who have the role of elite in one place or domain may be among the **masses** in others. Similarly, someone who has the role of a leader in one place or domain may be a follower in another. Business elites and leaders will probably not also be sports elites and leaders at the gym. A tribal warrior chief from Northern Nigeria would, on the Northern line of the London underground, just be one of the crowd, and in an emergency led by the train staff.

Powerful or influential people may be conceptualized as both elites and leaders – members of the US Senate, the Saudi Royal family, fighter pilots or the Taliban. They might change between being elites and leaders. The virtuoso pianist and composer, Paderewski, also managed to be a prime minister of Poland and Ambassador to the League of Nations, signing the Treaty of Versailles. Ronald Reagan, the actor, became Governor of California and then President of America. Arnold Schwarzenegger, body-builder, actor, businessman, similarly became Governor of California. Therefore the same person – for example, Princess Diana – may be an elite in one study – "The British **monarchy**" – and a leader in another – "Leading the changing attitudes to HIV/AIDS". Individuals may become leaders because they are elites, as have the royals throughout history, or achieve elite status through leadership, for instance a military hero who started as an ordinary soldier. People may become elites and leaders simply because they grow old, as with village or religious elders. Some studies of "leadership groups" could also be termed "elite studies", for example about the chief executives of transnational companies.[26] A study about a particular place or domain could be conceptualized to consider both elites and leaders, although this is not common. In some circumstances it may be more appropriate to talk of **leadership roles** or **elite roles** rather than 'leaders' or 'elites'. Deciding how to conceptualize a study is therefore crucial (C4.4, Appendices

1 and 7). In the future, perhaps there will be more interest in the interaction between elite and leadership roles – how powerful individuals use their two personas to create and maintain their power. Ayatollah Khomeini is an interesting example (Appendix 1).

Elite and leadership groups are often themselves internally **stratified** or **hierarchical**,[27] and so are the populace or followers. Understanding these hierarchies is crucial when trying to analyse individuals within them. Political leaders may have remarkably little power within their own parties or legislative chambers. A member of the 'masses' or the 'followers' may have a lot of power if leading thousands of protestors or strikers. Together, all actors constitute a definable **population**, and they all inhabit a geographical **place**, such as a country or factory, which can be framed as a research **site**. They may also represent a **domain** of endeavour – commerce, arts, sport[28] – within which they may exhibit exceptional ability or '**genius**'.[29] A domain could also be a social institution – religion, politics, family, military, education. So a study might be defined in terms such as, "The reputation of elite sports clubs in Paris" or "Power relations among religious leaders in Pakistan".

The common factor unifying these approaches to research is that all up-system actors have some form of **power** (C2.1) – an 'ability to act upon or affect something strongly' (*OED*) – which is exercised through a mix of **influence** and **coercion** – "carrot and stick". Elites may have obvious power in the form of wealth and social networks, or less tangibly through originality or virtuosity within a creative domain such as music. A leader will have power expressed through the **control** of followers. **Mass communications** permit those up-system to inform, influence and **control** those down-system (C2.4). All power is based on some form of **legitimate authority** – an accepted and/or successful claim to power (C2.1).[30] The discussion of power in relation to elites and leaders tends to be about groups, organizations and individuals, but power is also discussed at the level of nation states,[31] regions, international systems such as the UN,[32] globally,[33] or in terms of specific theoretical stances such as feminism[34] and disability rights.[35] Power is also evident in interpersonal relations, but the focus of this book is the power of the few over the many.

HOW THE BOOK WAS RESEARCHED

Curiously, authors of methodology books rarely describe their own methods. This book is based on the obvious question – how have powerful people been researched in the past and present? The *Researching Powerful People* project stemmed from work at the UN University Leadership Academy, interviewing UN leaders.[36] Academic and professional researchers in the fields of elite and leadership studies were circulated, asking for examples of innovative methods, and the usual database and library searches provided further information. Relevant illustrative material was identified in theses and dissertations, and elites and leaders were asked their views on being researched. Novel approaches were tested on up-system entities such as telecommunications companies, banks, professional regulators, police, government departments and line managers. Innovatory up-system approaches were coded, categorized and organized under new terminology where necessary, to systemize new research frameworks (C5), data collection techniques (C6) and analytical methods (C7). Initial findings were discussed at forums in Japan, Korea, China, Geneva

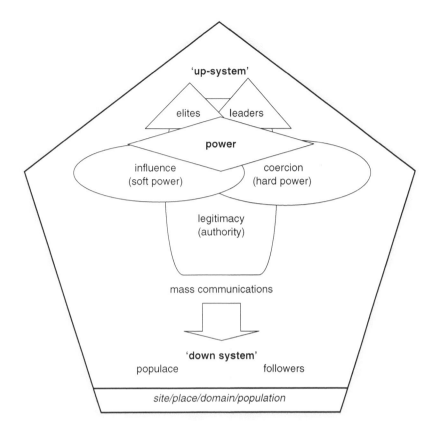

'up-system'

elites | leaders

power

influence
(soft power)

coercion
(hard power)

legitimacy
(authority)

mass communications

'**down system**'

populace | followers

site/place/domain/population

FIGURE 0.9 The conceptual framework used in this book

and UK. An historical perspective (C1) came from a reconstruction of past endeavours in the light of contemporary up-system research. Much of what is presented as recent methodology has been around a long time, albeit under different terminology (C1).

Field work in South Korea provided an East-meets-West perspective that is thought-provoking, and shows how a case study can contribute to broader understandings. Korea is now seen as a country of up-system extremes – typical and atypical cases – encompassing the closed communist elites in the North and the global capitalist elites in the South.[37] But this is not new. The peninsular has previously been divided into two or three warring countries. It has an interesting history of leadership innovation and research, including the unique methodology of the Choson 'annals' which assessed Korean rulers for 472 years (C1.2). King Sejong the Great (1397–1450) invented the rain gauge and public flood markers, because the country suffers severe storms, which 'crowdsourced' the ability to collect data about rainfall and floods.[38] He also replaced the Chinese script with the simple Hangeul alphabet, which permitted the masses to read and write. Acts like these represented the democratization of power well before Kim Dae-jung formally introduced **democracy**.

In the twentieth century Korea has changed from being the 'hermit kingdom' with a rigid social class system (Figure 6.4), suffered brutal colonial rule and ongoing war (Figure 3.1) and evolved from autocratic **dictatorships** to democracy.[39] Yun-joo Lee points out that all but one of South Korea's post-World War II presidents has been in prison. Korea's young people have been fearless resistance and democracy movement leaders, including "Korea's Joan of Arc", Kwan Sun Yu, who was killed by Japanese occupying forces age 16. Since World War II, the country's commercial and political leaders have brought it from being the second poorest country in the world to eleventh richest. The country has strived to host elite international gatherings including the Olympics, Asian games, Winter Olympics and G20, and has produced world class sports stars, internationally recognized classical musicians, and the young celebrities of K-Pop.[40] Korea has also produced international leaders for the WHO, FIFA, ICC and *Rotary International*, and a Secretary General of the UN. How did that trajectory happen, how can this distinct experience be researched, and what are the lessons for leaders in other countries? [41]

A QUICK GUIDE TO THIS BOOK

Methodology books appear linear and logical, but real research is circular, chaotic and often crazy. This book is structured in a start-to-finish way, for easy reference, but it is not intended as a step-by-step instruction manual. It explains a wide range of research frameworks and methods, and proposes how to view them critically. But it does not advocate a particular perspective. Chapters provide basic explanations of relevant methodologies, and link these to relevant international sources and examples. But discussions of general methods and technical details that are well explained in many other methodology books are not repeated here.

Key concepts are in **bold**, and the Glossary provides definitions of terminology in relation to power. Topics, names of organizations and counter-intuitive ideas are indicated by *italics* (as well as being used for emphasis). Explanations and examples are usually presented directly, or indicated by brackets or dashes – to avoid repeating 'for example', 'for instance', 'e.g.', and 'i.e.'. Double "quote marks" show illustrative words and phrases, and terms that should be understood very critically. Definitions at the start of sections and chapters are from the *Oxford English Dictionary*. References to other chapters in the book are shown in brackets – (C5.6). Further relevant sources can be accessed through the superscript numbers.[95, 68] Appendices provide templates and tools for planning and teaching, and a list of internet sources provides quick access to a wide range of relevant materials.

Although the main elements of a research project are presented in separate chapters, outlined below, it is important that there are logical connections across all stages – "threads" that connect all elements of a study from start to finish and beyond. Appendix 2 provides an example of how a study can initially be planned in relation to a linked understanding of the chapters in the book.

THE CHAPTERS

Part One: Understanding

Chapter 1 provides an overview of the *origins* of researching powerful people, within the disciplines of anthropology, history and philosophy. This helps to identify the key questions and concepts that have interested researchers for many centuries, and to recognize the basic tools for systemizing this form of research. This is the first time that a comprehensive history of up-system research methodology has been compiled. It derives from examples of what we would now call 'leadership' and 'elite studies', but these have been presented under a range of different headings across 4000 years. It is arguable that up-system research is one of the oldest forms of social research. Understanding the origins of up-system research provides the basis for understanding a wealth of relevant theory then described in Chapter 2.

Chapter 2 covers the main *theories* of research about power, elites and leadership. The start is to understand the significance of ontology and epistemology, and that this is not complicated. These are explained and exemplified in relation to relevant issues such as the existence of gods, and how we know about the mass fear that may stem from terrorist or authoritarian leadership. This is the first time that these four areas of theory have been presented together, and leads to a conclusion that they may be viewed more holistically in the future. A particular omission in previous texts is the consideration of power together with understandings of those who are the subjects of the exercise of power – masses, crowds, populace, followers. Marx represents a notable exception. The chapter outlines the practical strengths and weaknesses of a wide range of conceptual discussion, as a basis for selecting theoretical stances that are appropriate to a research problem. A critical view suggests that leadership theory may be more questionable than theory arising from studies of elites and power because, as a 'paradigm', it has a 'utility' function to provide material for leadership training, and is therefore constructed primarily to fulfil that purpose. This critique is rarely expressed, for obvious reasons.

Part Two: Doing

Chapter 3 describes the starting point for doing the research – searching and critically reviewing relevant *literature*, to ensure that the research is sound and significant. How can keywords be identified, material organized, dubious information detected and gaps in knowledge identified? The problem for any up-system researcher is information extremes. There may be very little information available about the subjects of the study, and the information that is collected therefore becomes over-valued – an "exclusive quote" may be little more than a passing thought in the mind of the elite who said it. Alternatively, there may be too much information, but it is sanitized and is just a repetition of official rhetoric. Finding a "gap" in the literature, *which realistically may be filled through research*, is not easy. The chapter therefore ends by suggesting topics that are likely to be innovative because they have been marginalized or not perceived as potential research areas, and discusses new methodologies and conceptualizations, including evolutionary psychology and the emergence of global elites.

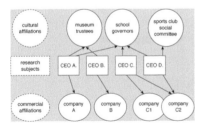

Chapter 4 explains how to *plan* a study. A research design is a provisional "map" that may evolve as methods are thoroughly explored and implemented. Powerful people are often hard to access, and so this needs to be feasible and effective. Access needs to be planned early in a study, and alternatives considered before problems arise. Plans rarely work out as planned. Ethical and legal aspects need to be assessed carefully, to ensure the integrity of a study. Badly judged research designs can cause bias and irresolvable problems and, with powerful people, serious legal problems. As most social research is down-system, there has been little formalization of the unique ethics of up-system research, and this chapter provides the basis for others to develop this aspect further. Up-system study raises many distinct problems for research ethics, not least, can unethical methods be justified to investigate unethical conduct by powerful people, and if so why and how?

Chapter 5 considers and develops research *frameworks*, the general approaches to a research project. Many of these are new for an academic textbook, because up-system research is widely used in professional contexts such as military intelligence. Because 'access' is a significant problem, distinctions are made between direct face-to-face research, indirect research that need not entail face-to-face contact, and studies that analyse groups and relationships rather than individual actions – network and systems analysis. Specific up-system frameworks are discussed, including investigatory methods, legitimacy research and intelligence gathering. And new frameworks are developed, including crowdsourcing, distance research and reconstructive techniques. As with ethics (above), the past emphasis on down-system research means that there are opportunities for considerable innovations in the frameworks for researching powerful people.

Chapter 6 describes relevant *data collection* methods – how can evidence be gathered from texts, people, objects and buildings? In particular, how can the challenges of interviewing powerful people be addressed? Many easily available data sources are often overlooked. It is not always necessary to meet powerful people face-to-face to find out a lot about them. Webcasts, online historical archives and social networking sites provide a wealth of new data that can be accessed and analysed anywhere via a laptop. Up-system research requires the innovative development of multi-methods, for example applying archaeological methods to the 'backdrops' in the offices of powerful people. Once collected, data is then tested and perhaps subjected to some initial analysis to create findings. Findings may be used to inform decision-makers directly, by others for analysis, or for further analysis by the researcher (C7).

Part Three: Using

Chapter 7 utilizes the findings for further *analysis* and explains the significance of comparison. It considers how to argue causation, the distinct role of assessing consistency in up-system studies and the conundrum of applying common sense to assess the plausibility of conclusions. A new framework, Critical Process Analysis (CPA), provides a comprehensive way to manage and critically assess up-system data, which accommodates the relevant frameworks and methods, and helps to address many of the problems of researching powerful people. This encourages the 'reverse engineering' and 'reconstruction' of data about up-system processes, and counterfactual analysis, to check if those involved really did what they claimed they did. Up-system processes are not always as straightforward as they seem. Was a new "equity policy" really to improve equity, or to provide an excuse for firing people who challenge the system? The chapter concludes by considering how analysis leads to conceptualization and theory, and particularly the difficulty of making micro data fit within macro frameworks.

Sudo University Press Office   23.4 2012

PRESS RELEASE

Leaders are better at cheating

New research finds that 90 percent of men with high leadership skills
are also good at cheating.

Last month many MPs were found to have misused their expense
accounts. Yesterday Professor Ivan Ego from the *Centre for the
Psychology of Power* (CPP), Sudo University, provided an explanation.
His recent study found that male students who are above average on
the Leadership Potential Scale were also better at deception skills.

Chapter 8 describes differing approaches to using the *outcomes* of a research study. These include writing up or reporting research for academic or professional audiences, presenting findings effectively and how to influence political and social change. Finding a 'space' to negotiate change is central. Research is a very expensive activity, and it can only be justified if there are clear benefits which exceed the cost of the endeavour. Good outcomes are not always dramatic, but there should clearly be some form of new understanding, practical or intellectual. Put crudely, any research must pass the "so what?" test.

Up-system research can be demanding, daunting, demeaning and dangerous. But it can also create the basis for significant social change. Well-evidenced investigations may support a good leader or bring down a bad one. Meticulous study of archives can help a writer decide whether a film should present elites as benevolent or corrupt. The study of political speech-making can help to teach young leaders to give good speeches or avoid making bad ones. Effective intelligence gathering can create a strategic advantage for a company or effective action plans for human rights NGOs. Whatever the specific purpose, the general outcome hopefully will reflect the eighteenth-century Quaker duty – to '*Speak truth to power*'.

KEY READING

Beck, U. (2008) *Power in the Global Age*. Cambridge: Polity.

Gardener, H. (1995) *Leading Minds: An Anatomy of Leadership*. New York: Basic Books.

Hertz, R. and Imber, J.B. (eds) (1995) *Studying Elites Using Qualitative Methods*. London: Sage.

Jost, J.T. and Major, B. (eds) (2001) *The Psychology of Legitimacy: Emerging Perspectives on Ideology, Justice, and Intergroup relations*. New York: Cambridge University Press.

Klenke, K. (2008) *Qualitative Research in the Study of Leadership*. London: Elsevier.

Nader, L. (1972) 'Up the anthropologist', in D.H. Hymes (ed.), *Reinventing Anthropology*. New York: Pantheon Books. pp. 284–311.

Taylor, P. (2011) *Talking to Terrorists: A Personal Journey from the IRA to Al Qaeda*. London: Harper Press.

Williams, C. (2006) *Leadership Accountability in a Globalizing World*. London: Palgrave Macmillan.

PART ONE

UNDERSTANDING

Chapter 1 – Up-system research uses a very wide range of research methods, and some of these have existed for 4000 years. So it is helpful to understand the *origins* of researching powerful people, the systems of analysis that have been used, and the questions and concepts that have interested researchers throughout history.

Chapter 2 – From these origins, many *theories* have emerged. There are three main areas – elite and leadership studies, and the aspect common to both, power. But powerful people function in relation to people who have less power, and therefore understanding the populace and followers is also relevant.

1

ORIGINS

1.1   ANTHROPOLOGY
1.2   HISTORY
1.3   PHILOSOPHY
1.4   UP-SYSTEM RESEARCH

There is a Scottish joke about a powerful landowner who found a tramp camping on his land, and ordered him to leave. But the tramp asked the landowner,

"Why is this land yours?"

"Because I inherited it from my father", was the landowner's reply.

"And how did he get it?" asked the tramp.

"He inherited it from *his* father" said the landowner.

This pattern of questioning continued back into history, until the landowner remembered a famous ancestor. Hoping to stop the argument, he said,

"And this man owned this land because a thousand years ago he fought a battle right here, and won it."

The tramp said,

"I see. So I'll gladly fight you for this little bit, right here, right now. Put up your fists."

Claims to power are often very questionable when properly researched. It is easier to claim authority on the basis of myths that cannot be proved, than on facts that can. This is a good reason for understanding the origins of up-system research, especially its weaknesses.

This chapter helps to avoid "reinventing the wheel" – a surprising amount of methodology and theory that is presented as new has been around a long time. The chapter is structured in relation to traditional methodological approaches, which also indicate how elites and leadership have evolved across 5000 years. But the purpose is to identify how powerful people have been researched, not to provide a comprehensive analysis of how power has been used. *Anthropologists* have investigated how power is gained and maintained in small-scale non–industrial communities, and suggest what happens when communities have no elites (C1.1). *Historical*, archaeological and biographical studies of powerful people reveal information about elite lifestyles and ruling ideologies (C1.2), which created the evidence for philosophical arguments about the *ethics* of ruling and rulers (C1.3).

1.1 ANTHROPOLOGY

> **ANTHROPOLOGY**
>
> The science of mankind. (*OED*)

Anthropologists usually study "others" – small-scale social groups that are different from their own. This has often included documenting the conduct of diverse elites and leaders, and 'up'-system research became more formalized in the 1970s.[1] Ethnography – direct observation and recording – has been central, and this often involved participant observation – observation through becoming part of the group being studied. But this study of others was often itself a way for dominant peoples to rationalize and misuse their power, particularly in colonial settings.

Anthropologists conclude that **anarchical** (non-hierarchical) and **acephalous** (headless) systems of governance have been rare. But the absence of identifiable leaders does not necessarily mean the absence of leadership, which may be transient and situational. The Bronze Age buildings in Crete show no signs of Kings or Queens, but leadership may still have been 'performed'[2] through rituals and festivals which left no artefacts or architecture. Seemingly leaderless societies are usually small-scale hunter–gatherer groups,[3] or recent ideological movements such as Israeli Kibbutz dwellers and the anarchists in Catalonia.[4] An apparent absence of leadership can sometimes be seen within terrorist groups,[5] organizations based on humility such as the Quakers, or protest movements such as the 'leaderless revolution' that ousted Egyptian President Mubarak in 2011.[6] In the 1940s, a study of 40 'chiefless' tribes of the Nuer society of Southern Sudan, found that decisions were few and usually taken at family and interpersonal levels. Major disagreements between men were settled by duels to the death.[7] Leaderless systems seem fragile and unworkable in large societies. The significant recent example is

Somalia, which dismantled its government in 1991.[8] This supports an obvious conclusion, which was the basis of classical elite theory (C2.2). Hierarchies are found in almost all systems.[9] Elites and leaders seem intrinsic to the survival of most societies as we now know them, and the elite theorists argued that understanding powerful people is therefore a basis for understanding human civilization.

Studies of small-scale **tribal** communities provide indications of how systems of power operated in early societies.[10] Greco-Roman writers detailed tribal life surrounding the European city states of that time, and more recent anthropologists have continued this form of study. But it is misleading to assume that descriptions of more recent so-called "pre-literate" and "pre-industrial" societies intrinsically also explain pre-historic and other early human communities. The context is very different, and tribes adapt to modern demands – present-day Mescalero Apaches now use their former *Inn of the Mountain Gods* for tourism and gambling. However, understanding how small-scale societies use power can provide insights into the underlying structures of power in larger societies. A basic distinction explains how power arises. There are formalized systems of authority within which power is usually **ascribed** or inherited. In parallel, there are usually agreements about how power is **achieved** through warfare or hunting skills, intellectual prowess or artistic excellence.[11] The latter is less often noted in the literature because it is harder to detect. Many powerful people use a blend of both forms of legitimization.

Gerontocracies legitimized an ascribed elite status for elders. Whether or not older people were the most suited to rule, the system had the benefit of being simple and hard to challenge.[12] The main function of elders was settling disputes.[13] They were usually judges rather than political leaders. **Necrocracies** are governments still working according to the rules of a dead former leader, such as present-day North Korea and Iran. In 1977, anthropologist Margaret Mead was prescient of a significant change arising from technology. She identifies a shift from 'postfigurative' relationships in which the elders teach and dominate, to 'cofigurative' in which **peer** learning and power becomes accepted, towards 'prefigurative' where the young teach and often have power over their elders.[14]

Clan **lineages** (genealogical systems) are used to demonstrate that only those from certain **aristocracies** or **nobilities**,[15] within **class** or **caste** hierarchies, can inherit the right to power,[16] as in the Indian caste system.[17] Anthropology has contributed robust methods for studying **kinship,** stemming from the work of Lewis Morgan (1818–1881), who determined systems of kinship such as 'Hawaiian', 'Sudanese' and 'Eskimo'. Both Karl Marx and Engels used Morgan's work to argue how elites appropriated property.[18] Understanding language is central.[19] Even in modern English a simple term such as 'sister' can mean sibling, any female relative, nun, nurse, and a feminist, trades union or Muslim colleague.

In more elaborate **chieftaincies** the chiefs use simple "traditions"[20] to affirm their power and avoid manual labour.[21] Often they became, invented or discovered gods who they claimed to understand, and this legitimized their status.[22] They assumed the right to communicate with their gods by carrying out certain rituals for which they demanded tribute from the commoners.[23] The gods made existence eternal, and eternity created the threat of eternal torture in the afterlife for anyone who disobeyed the gods and therefore their earthly chiefs.[24] Sometimes colonial rulers appropriated the role of the spiritual gods.[25] The "medicine men" and "witch doctors" were the precursors of modern "spiritual leaders", who lend reciprocal support to the military and political leaders. Ancient chiefs seemingly used burial rituals to establish land rights through creating tombs in strategic places. Families could then be persuaded to defend the tombs of their ancestors, the gods who looked after them and this "sacred" land. This often entailed fighting against other tribes to defend the land which, by convenient coincidence, entailed fighting to defend the chiefs.

Once people start to believe in gods whose existence cannot be proven, it is easy for powerful people to get them to believe in other things without proof, not least that earthly kings are also godly kings. The Japanese Shinto religion was originally based on a simple belief that natural forces – earthquakes, volcanoes, tsunamis – were earthly manifestations of transient power from spiritual entities. People were persuaded to anthropomorphize these natural forces – to view them as having human-like qualities such as the ability to understand prayer. Shinto had no revelatory scriptures, **doctrine** or afterlife, and had no written records until the Chinese script arrived. But it was easily usurped by other religions – Buddhism and Christianity – and conflated with earthy power – the Imperial family, and eventually the Mejie fascists from 1860. God Kings dominated many countries,[26] including Europe, from Alexandria the Great to England's Charles I. Even in modern socialist countries powerful **regimes** legitimize themselves with godly personas. In North Korea, Kim Il-sung has been designated as the "eternal president" since his death.

Theories of leadership that are often assumed to be recent have been described in the anthropological literature for many years. Notions of **legitimacy** occur in the form of relationships with environment,[27] divine rights[28] or because of the popular support, as suggested by the Shona saying *Ishe vanhu* (there cannot be a king without subjects).[29] In his study of the Fon (chiefs) in the Cameroon, Kaberry reports that they would often say, 'What is Fon without people? I am in the hands of my people'. Traditional tribal sayings reflect what was subsequently termed the 'transactional'[30] nature of leader–follower relations and represent a form of democracy – 'The Fon rules the people, but the people hold the Fon'.[31] Traditional chieftaincies have modified themselves to coexist with modern governments. In Africa, state politicians now use traditional networks to legitimize their own power.[32] A typology explaining power relationships within the *Akan* of Ghana shows that traditional offices of the paramount chief (*Omanhene*) remain, but have evolved. The 'warrior' (*Tofuhene*) now looks after the chief's companies, and when taking power the chief still takes a very young 'stool wife' but now the marriage is usually symbolic (Figure 1.9).[33]

The roots of anthropology are often traced back to a Persian scholar, Abū Rayhān Bīrūnī (973–1048), sometimes called 'the first anthropologist',[34] who extended his work on scientific methods to devise systematic approaches to studying other peoples. Using what would now be called participant observation, he studied Hinduism, particularly the Brahmin high caste people in the Indian subcontinent. He learned local languages, analysed original documents, and observed power relationships between castes and classes.[35] In his *Indica* he concluded:

> No one will deny that in questions of historic authenticity hearsay does not equal eyewitness; for in the latter the eye of the observer apprehends the substance of that which is observed, both in the time when and in the place where it exists … hearsay has its peculiar drawbacks, [but the] object of eye-witness can only be actual momentary existence, whilst hearsay comprehends alike the present, the past and the future.[36]

His findings contributed to comparative studies of religion, including religious elites in the Middle East and South Asia.

The subsequent nineteenth century European researchers did not all focus on small-scale chieftainship societies. An English lexicologist and engraver, E.W. Lane, who was studying Arabic in Cairo, produced a meticulous ethnographic study of *An Account of the Manners and Customs of the Modern Egyptians* in 1835. He provides a detailed account of government, but also of the elites – men and women 'of the higher and middle orders' and those of 'the lower orders'. The comprehensive nature of the account, and its detailed illustrations, show how the two groups interacted with one another through commerce, values, religion, recreation and superstition. Lane's skills as a linguist and engraver gave him the ability to produce an impressive record, but they also gave him a *persona* which he used to overcome a central problem of elite research – access (C4.5). He was able to observe and discuss the detailed daily life of a wide range of people (Figure 1.1). But his methodology raises ethical questions (C4.6), such as the use of deception. He explained that, 'Many husbands of the middle classes, and some of the higher orders, freely talk of the affairs of the harem with one *who professes to agree with them in their general moral sentiments* … ' (italics added).[37] Later he used his sister to infiltrate women's bathhouses and harems. The outcome was another book in 1842, *The Englishwoman in Egypt*. This book raises ethical questions about the recognition of research assistants. The name of Lane's sister, Sophia Lane Poole, does not appear in the book, and he alters her words to present himself as author, for instance 'my brother' becomes 'I'.[38]

Anthropologists who relied on colonial records sometimes wrongly assumed that all chiefs were men because they, and the colonial administrators, could not identify gender from local names. An engraving of *The Chieftainess of Mohilla* in the Comoros Islands, from 1890,[39] shows that pictures can sometimes be more reliable than texts, and lend themselves to ongoing interpretation (Figure 1.2). The Islamic, perhaps Iranian *shirazi*, influence seems evident. Her dress is clearly better than that of her attendants, but does the strange face covering – not a standard hejab, burka or niqab – symbolize repression or power? The identity of the chieftainess is preserved, but the eyes can clearly see and the mouth can speak. The two attendants have darker skin than the chieftainess, which often indicated lower status, and there seems no prohibition about showing their faces. Perhaps black servants were not seen as real women with evident sexuality.

A Lady in the dress worn in private

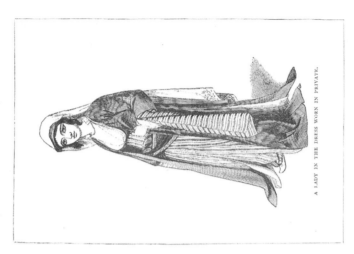

A LADY IN THE DRESS WORN IN PRIVATE.

Men of the Middle and Higher Classes

MEN OF THE MIDDLE AND HIGHER CLASSES.

If he have no regular business to employ him, the Egyptian spends the greater part of the day in riding, paying visits, or making purchases; or in smoking and sipping coffee and chatting with a friend at home; or he passes an hour or more in the morning enjoying the luxuries of a public bath. At noon, he has again to say prayers...Directly after midday (if he has not taken a late breakfast), he eats a light dinner; then takes a pipe and a cup of coffee, and, in hot weather, usually indulges himself with a nap. Often he retires to recline in the hareem; where a wife or female slave watches over his repose, or rubs the soles of his feet with her hands. On such occasions, and at other times when he wishes to enjoy privacy, every person who comes to pay him a visit is told, by the servant, that he is in the hareem; and no friend expects him to be called thence, unless on very urgent business… (p144)

FIGURE 1.1 Ethnography of Egyptian elites (1835)

Source: E.W. Lane, *An Account of the Manners and Customs of the Modern Egyptians* (1835)

FIGURE 1.2 The Chieftainess of Mohilla

Source: Robert Brown (1890) *Peoples of the World*

Colonial administrators often left 'elaborately researched pre-colonial histories of the chiefdoms ... full of equally elaborate chiefly genealogies,'[40] as a means to understand and control "native" peoples. The European missionaries also had unique access to study indigenous elites, but their motives were often duplicitous. In *At the Back of the Black Man's Mind or Notes on the Kingly office in West Africa* (1906), Dennet provides useful descriptions of the 'election' and 'coronation' of 'a king in the Kongo', and a whole chapter analyses, 'The philosophy at the back of the black man's mind in table form'. But he explains the rationale: 'Rotten and degenerate as an African Kingdom may have become, its only hope of regeneration rests in the purification of the kingly office and of the ancient system of government attached to it'.[41]

Also from Congo, Smith's *In Yakusu: The Very Heart of Africa* (c.1911) details the plight of a Lokele chief who ended up in prison, but concludes, 'One fervently hopes that, having become subject to his earthly ruler through painful experience, he may learn to submit himself gladly to the keeping of the Shepherd and Bishop of our souls.' Smith's final chapter addresses a very good question for elite research – what are their 'aims and ambitions'? But the motivation is not academic: 'It must be the supreme aim of the missionary to find points of contact, else he will never gain that beginning of interest which will win him many an adult convert'.[42] A later photo of

Lokele chiefs from 1930 presents a "traditional" image. The caption explains that the men are in their 'gala dresses', and that 'the leopard's teeth in their necklaces are supposed to protect them from the leopards that infest the district'. The small print on the photo states, 'By permission of the Minister of Colonies, Belgium'. The photo was originally from the Belgian record of indigenous power networks in the Congo. Presenting the "primitive" stereotype of indigenous elites helped colonial rulers and missionaries to legitimize their occupation and power. In contrast, a photo of a Lokele chief in Smith's *Yakusu*, 20 years earlier in 1911, shows a chief wearing European-style dress, perhaps to demonstrate the "civilizing" influence of the missionaries (Figure 1.3). The historical context is that of Belgium's King Leopold II who made himself supreme ruler of the Congo from 1878 to 1909, and in the process of exploiting the country he was responsible for the death of millions of people. He used the amputation of hands as a punishment for minor wrongdoing, often of children who did not collect enough rubber. It is said a ton of amputated hands were collected daily, and used as a measure of the enforcement of Leopold's polices.[43]

When a researcher analyses "others", there is an inferred comparison with a home culture that is often assumed to represent the norm and to be morally correct. An important ethical and methodological lesson from anthropology is that comparative methodology, and analytical assumptions, need to be made explicit. Otherwise studies simply become a collection of value-judgements such as this from Smith, about a Lokele chief, Saidi:

> He is a fine figure of a man as he stands before you. In many ways he is one of God's fine creatures. He has his points marking good breeding just as white folk have. Notice the long, tapering fingers, the delicate inflection of the voice when speaking, and the respectful attitude he adopts towards his superiors. But I have to call him crafty. He has a turn for diplomacy which all the better class natives inherit. He is deep and crooked in his dealings, and to his discomfort he is finding that those who deal crookedly get worse and worse into engagement. Unhappily, too, for Saidi, he exercises authority over a people who are cantankerous, heady, high-minded, fickle, gay and obstinate to a degree threatening the possibility of order and discipline … [44]

Whatever its failings, the tradition of anthropology inspired Laura Nader to propose, in the 1960s, that scholars should 'reinvent anthropology' through 'studying up'.[45] Anthropology now embraces theories of power,[46] elite studies[47] and forensic perspectives.[48] This has included investigating terrorist bombings, and mass graves in Rwanda, former Yugoslavia and Iraq to provide evidence of war crimes by despotic leaders. A 2010 study of rape by militias in Democratic Republic of the Congo found that respondents explained power in terms of commanders being 'like fathers', and as a fusion of Christianity and witchcraft.[49]

Source: The Ministry of Colonies, Belgium, 1930.

Source: Smith, H. Sutton (c.1911) *Yakusu: The Very Heart of Africa*. London: Marshall. p. 29.

FIGURE 1.3 Images of Lokele Chiefs, Congo, 1930 and 1911

1.2 HISTORY

> **HISTORY**
>
> A written narrative consisting of a continuous methodical record, in order of time, of important or public events, especially those connected to a particular country, people, or individual. (*OED*)

> History ... deals with ... the different ways by which one group of human beings achieves superiority over another. It deals with royal authority and the dynasties that result, and with the various ranks that exist within them. (Ibn Khaldun, 1377)[50]

Images and texts about ancient elites pervade tombs, temples, castles and palaces throughout the world, as images and texts about present-day elites pervade the internet. In general, "Great men" were history, because "Great men" constructed history (C2.3). Whether fact or fiction, history has provided the bases for questionable claims to power and land, and continues to do so.

The purpose of historical research should not just be to create a good record of the past, but to assess what that tells us about the present and possible future. A visit to any castle provides a central example. Records and objects show that defence and security have been of paramount importance to elites and leaders throughout the world. But the intent was usually to organize the people to protect the powerful not, as is often claimed, the powerful to protect the people. That deception continues to be evident in the use of power in present-day governmental, terrorist, religious, financial and other spheres.

Museums contain a wealth of data about powerful people,[51] and interpretations are always evolving. The Narmer Palette (3000BC) – sometimes termed the 'first historical document in the world'[52] – is not just a simple portrait. It shows the King wearing the White Crown of Upper Egypt on one side and the Red Crown of Lower Egypt on the other. It may document events leading to the unification of the country, or be a symbolic attempt to establish the King's power and legitimacy (Figure 1.4). Whatever the intent, the tablet amounts to a political tract, which could be held and read like a Tablet PC. During the same era, hieroglyphics for leadership (*seshemet*), leader (*seshemu*) and follower (*shemsu*) appeared.

Recent analyses of objects that have attracted little attention in museum collections for centuries also show that inconvenient truths were often sidelined.[53] The Egyptian King, Taharqo (700BC), has been presented for millennia as part of a long lineage of Egyptian pharaohs – the 25th dynasty. Yet a sphinx in the British Museum shows that Taharqo was from Kush (now Northern Sudan), and was black African. The sphinx shows that Taharqo legitimized and maintained his power by adopting Egyptian customs and symbols, while also maintaining his southern identity. This evidence that Egypt was

FIGURE 1.4   The Narmer Palette (3000BC)

Source: Quibell, B.A. (1900) *Hierakonpolis: Plates of Discoveries*. London: Bernard Quaritch

ruled from Kush for 150 years, and that the king was black, did not fit the narrative that subsequent Egyptian rulers wanted to promote about their region.

Museum objects often provide clues about the research methodologies used by powerful people, although that aspect is not always obvious. Rulers needed to research their subjects. The first use of writing was probably to permit administrators to record and manage growing urban populations. A tablet from Mesopotamia, of about 3000BC, depicts words and numbers to ration beer.[54] The Emperors of the Chinese Xia Dynasty (c.2070–1600BC) seemingly counted and categorized their populations. The first Egyptian **census** probably happened around 3340BC and 3050BC, and embodied a basic demographic methodology to find out how many men were suitable for military service and who should pay taxes. This Egyptian system explains why Jesus was born in a stable – Caesar Augustus wanted a census of the entire Roman world, and Joseph had to return to his home village to be counted.

From simple records of elites, **relative chronologies** became possible, such as the Egyptian King Lists. These not only showed who was who, but also who lived before and after who, and what happened at that time. The *Palermo Stone,* records the rulers of Egypt from the first to fifth dynasty when it was carved (c.2500BC). It is presented as a table, and includes historical events such as wars and floods.[55] Buildings became vehicles for symbols of legitimation, such as the *Chamber of Ancestors* in the *Festival Hall of Thutmose III* in Luxor, and the *King List of Abydos* (Figure 1.7). Chronologies permitted a historical analysis of causation, concerning ideological influence or land ownership, and most importantly they could be used to affirm the power of dynasties, and encourage tributes, as David Paton's transcription of an extract from *The Annals of Thutmosis III* in Karnak suggests (Figure 1.5).[56]

With the advent of reliable calendars, such as those of the Persians around 650–330BC, these lists could evolve into **absolute chronologies** – events and people were referenced objectively to dates – which provided the basis for more accurate genealogies and lineage charts. These permitted the writing of more reliable history books, such as *The Histories* of Herodotus (c.450–420BC), which record culture, politics and war in the Mediterranean (Athenian) and West Asian (Persian) regions, and established the discipline of historical method in the West. The Egyptian/Greek historian Manetho used the early King Lists for his *Aegyptiaca* – History of Egypt (c.300BC). He introduced the concept of 'dynasties' (*dynasteia* – 'governmental power'). These were organized chronologically, which gave Manetho a framework to identify probable errors and gaps in existing records. This represents an early form of 'reconstructive' research (C5.2).

```
              Behold the Princes of this Country coming
              on their bellies to kiss the earth because of the
              Fame of His Majesty and to beg the breath for
              their nostrils, because of the greatness of His
              might and of the magnitude of the Fame of [A]mon,
              who hasteneth their (?)
              [.....][all Countries
              .......] Country. Behold, all the Princes
              come because of the Fame of His Majesty, bearing
      1-2     their Tribute, consisting of (1) Silver, (2) Gold,
      3-4     (3) Lapis-Lazuli, (4) Turquoise, and laden with
      5-8     (5) Grain, (6) Wine, (7) Cattle, and (8) Flocks for
              the army of His Majesty.
              Every gang of prisoners of war
              among them
              was laden with tribute for
              the journeying South
```

FIGURE 1.5   The Annals of Thutmosis III in Karnak (c.1570–1320BC)

Source: David Paton (1918) *Early Egyptian Records of Travel*. London: Princeton University Press. p. 36.

Reliable calendars also permitted the 'triangulation' of data – the comparison of evidence from different sources (C6.3). In China, Sima Qian produced the *Records of the Grand Historian*, or *Shiji* (109–191BC). From existing annals he created genealogies from around 2600BC. He provided 12 volumes of 'Imperial Biographies' (*Benji*), and 30 volumes of 'Biographies of the Feudal Houses and Eminent Persons' (*Shijia*). Sima came from a family of historians to the Han emperor, which gave him access to the Han archives and other records. But he also travelled widely to triangulate data by comparing records from official sources, interviews with local elites and local literature. He often gave citations (references) for his sources, prefacing his analysis with 'I have read … '.[57] Calendars could also help to identify the manipulation of myths for political purposes. The stories about the existence of a female Pope, Joan, were resolved by establishing that there was no gap between the regimes of Leo IV and Benedict III, from 853–855AD, where Pope Joan is said to have existed. This was supported by images on coins which show both Benedict III and Emperor Lothair I, and therefore Benedict must have been recognized as Pope before the death of Lothair in September 855.[58]

In India, *The Harivamsa* explains the Krishna dynasty,[59] and the Indian ruler Ashoka (c.304–232BC) traced his **lineage** back to Buddha, although he only became a Buddhist after seeing the carnage of his war in Kalinga. Present-day Japanese Zen masters also trace the source of their knowledge (*dharma*) through a bloodline (*Kechimyaku*) of teachers, back to Buddha. Similarly, *Ijazah* is the certificate of 'permission' given to Muslim religious leaders, which shows that their status is legitimized by learning 'at the feet' of scholars who can trace their lineage back to the prophet.[60] Charts are often faked, either to gain prestige corruptly, or for benign reasons such as giving servants or their children an elite identity. Lineage charts use symbols to show relationships or missing data (Figure 1.7), and they must accommodate children of uncertain parentage. In the future these charts will need to reflect recent dynamics such as the international adoption of Chinese babies by same-sex couples in America. Similarly, **provenance** research assesses the lineage of objects. Where do objects come from, and who has owned them? East Asian art often demonstrates provenance in a unique way, because of the Eastern tradition of new owners stamping the work with their own name and sometimes writing comments. This not only traces the provenance of the object across centuries, but provides insights into the elites who owned such artefacts.

Pedigree charts – lineage charts for elites – are used by ancient legitimizing bodies such as the *College of Arms* which regulates the use of coats of arms in Britain, and they are the basis of elite lists such as *Burkes Peerage*.[61] DNA methods are providing new dynamics. In 2008, testing proved that remains that were thought to be the children of Tsar Nicholas II of Russia were almost certainly Alexei and Maria, murdered in 1918. Had DNA methods been available at the start of the twentieth century, the possibility that the mother of Mussolini's first child was not his wife could have been tested, and that might have changed the course of Italian history. Pedigree methodologies have financial implications for inheritance, and mating prospects – a significance that extends to elite cattle, dogs, and horses.[62] Animal records are often more reliable than those for humans. Cloned animals, and perhaps humans, will present new aspects.

Early leadership **ideologies** are preserved in texts such as the *Code of Ur-Nammu* (c.2050BC), the *Laws of Eshnunna* (c.1930BC) and the *Codex of Lipit-Ishtar of Isin* (c.1870 BC). China had a tradition of 'annals' recording elite histories. The lives of Emperors were documented in the *Huangming Shilu*, the Annals of the Ming Dynasty, and the *Daqing Lzhao Shilu*, the Annals of the Great Qing Dynasty. The tradition was copied by Vietnam, concerning the Nguyen Dynasty, and Japan in the *Sandai Jitsurokut*. Ancient Hebrew Deuteronomic Law institutes a hierarchy of the offices of elites, from Judges downwards (Figure 1.9). The supremacy of judges seems to reflect the tribal role of elders in dispute resolution, but Israeli judges were also the senior military leaders. The compiler of the Biblical *Book of Kings* evaluates the deeds of Kings in relation to the set of objective criteria embodied in Deuteronomic Law, which include the stoning of women (Deut. 22: 13–21), and the giving of captive beautiful girls to victorious soldiers as reward for winning wars (Deut. 21: 10–14).

The Art of War is now one of the best known ancient texts within contemporary business leadership studies.[63] It is attributed to Sun Tzu (or Sun Wu), who probably lived in China between 722-481BC. The ideology is about **strategy** and methodical planning. It seems to distinguish between leadership and management – the 'enlightened ruler', who makes plans well in advance, and the 'good general', who builds and nurtures his resources. It advocates creative responsiveness to unpredictable circumstances, and is presented as a methodology for winning wars: 'By method and discipline are to be understood the marshaling of the army in its proper subdivisions, the graduations of rank among the officers...' The author also provides a set of basic comparative *research questions* for military elites to assess adversaries:

1   Which of the two sovereigns is imbued with the Moral law?
2   Which of the two generals has most ability?
3   With whom lie the advantages derived from Heaven [night and day, cold and heat, times and seasons] and Earth [distances, danger, terrain, risk of death]?
4   On which side is discipline most rigorously enforced?
5   Which army is stronger?
6   On which side are officers and men more highly trained?
7   In which army is there the greater constancy both in reward and punishment?[64]

Perhaps the most interesting aspect of the book is that it has become so well-known in modern business leadership studies. It does not mention business, the existence of Sun Tzu is in doubt, and if he existed it is not certain that he is the author of the book.

To explain leadership ideologies, forms of **mass communication** were developed, which provide other insights. The Indian ruler Ashoka (c.304–232BC) communicated with his subjects through inscriptions on rocks and pillars, displayed in public places rather than in elite palaces and temples. The messages reflected seven **edicts** about right behaviour and Buddhist beliefs, which were originally in the official language Sanskrit, but local languages were used later. In modern terms, following the carnage of the Kalinga war, Ashoka was trying to legitimize his transition from war criminal to pacifist.

His pillars were the forerunners of modern political posters, which provide a wealth of data about contemporaneous values.

The Rosetta Stone (196BC), which records a seemingly tedious agreement between the weak young orphan King Ptolemy V and the priests at Memphis, is a fascinating example of political communication. At the time he became King, in 205BC, Ptolemy was aged six, and he was formally crowned when 12. The reason for the agreement provides another example of the importance of constructing legitimacy. In return for tax concessions, at his coronation the priests affirmed Ptolemy's lineage and credentials and made him an eternal god king.[65] The desire of the priests to publicize their successful agreement also provides an insight into the values of religious leaders of this era. It seems that they would say anything, and even sell their gods, for a tax break.

From understanding the political context – that Ptolemy V had to devise a method of communication that satisfied the Greek ruling classes, the priests, and also be intelligible to the populace – the archaeologists suspected that the text was probably the same inscription in these three languages. That may now seem very obvious, but different languages are often used to say different things to different communities – to explain different laws, dietary codes or religious rituals. By concluding that the three texts were translations, the European scholars realized that Ptolemy had unwittingly provided them with the means to decipher the hieroglyphics.[66]

Recent interpretations of ancient ideologies can provide further insights beyond the basic text, but these are often contested. The well-known *Code of Hammurabi* (c.1790BC) is now considered not only to reveal how Babylonian elites ruled, but also the limits of power, and the extent of cultural transfer across the whole region at that time. The Cyrus Cylinder from Persia (539BC) has been described as 'the world's first declaration of human rights'. It is kept by the British Museum and there is a copy in the UN HQ in New York. In the 1970s Iranian Shah Mohammed Reza Pahlavi even linked his regime with Cyrus to enhance its legitimacy.[67] The Code appears to bestow religious freedoms and outlaw slavery, which could be interpreted to mean that the Iranians abolished slavery 2293 years before the Americans discovered it. Unsurprisingly, some western scholars argue that the cylinder is not 'Iranian', but represents a broad regional history, including Jewish.[68] But in turn, Jewish ethics themselves reflect the first text-based religion, Zoroastrianism, which is Persian.

Sometimes historical texts are shaped by revisionist argument, not just fact. Modern Israeli leaders derive legitimacy from the Biblical *Book of Kings* which seems to describe the deeds of regional Kings from the tenth to sixth centuries BC. Present-day biblical archaeologists argue about the credibility of this 'United Monarchy', because of a lack of archaeological corroboration.[69] 'Biblical minimalists' point out that the genre of these texts is storytelling and religious, not historical method.[70] Some conclude that the texts are not historically accurate but are 'creative expressions of a powerful religious reform movement'.[71] Present-day archaeology itself can appear as a means of exerting power. Excavations at the 'City of David' in Siwan, Jerusalem, attract many Jewish tourists, but local Palestinians complain that the dig is causing roads, houses and a school to collapse. There is no scientific evidence of the existence of Kings David or Solomon, but that does not deter the guides from telling stories such as that of 'Jeremiah's Pit'.[72] Popular ideas of legitimacy often arise from misunderstandings. How many people realize that in the phrases – 'children of Israel' and 'tribes of Israel' – 'Israel' is a person (originally called Jacob)? The founders of the recent 'State of Israel' used the name in 1948, which links the land of the Southern Levant with the historical Jewish elites.

Despite the gendered impression given by many traditional textbooks, legendary "great women" are also recorded, although often this is in terms of their use to, and influence on powerful men, as in Rome.[73] A fascinating insight into female elites is provided by a Chinese scroll, *The Admonitions of the Instructress to the Court Ladies* (400), which provides guidance to courtly ladies about how to behave. The deeds of the English warrior queen Boudica (Boadicea) (d. 60/1) were described by the contemporary historian Tacitus (56–117). In Egypt, Khentykaues (4th Dynasty) was probably the first female ruler, but her legitimacy came from assuming male status. On her tomb in Giza (Cairo) she is called the "King and Mother of a King". Her image has been modified to give her a kinglike bearing, which includes a false beard.

Myth and mystery surround the records of female elites, and their existence was sometimes hidden – "airbrushing" powerful women has a long history. The King List of Abydos omitted two Queens including the powerful Hatshepsut (Figure 1.7). Arguments continue about the existence of the Queen of Sheba, and whether Sheba was in Ethiopia, Eritrea or Yemen. The rule of the so-called 'little Queen of Sheba' in Yemen, Arwa al-Sulayhi (1067–1113), seems more certain. But her existence is not well known, perhaps because her successful 50-year reign does not fit the male-dominated construction of subsequent Arabian and Islamic history. Did the Jewish god have a wife, Ashera, is she the 'queen of heaven' in the Book of Jeremiah, and why has she become lost in later discussions?[74] Why do British history books rarely mention Yaa Asantewaa (1840–1921), an Ashanti Queen Mother who led the courageous 'War of the Golden Stool' against British colonial forces in Ghana in 1900? Her adversary, Queen Victoria, is well documented.[75] Jiang Qing, the fourth wife of Mao Zedong, greatly influenced China's Cultural Revolution and was a member of the Gang of Four.[76] She is airbrushed out of photos at the Mao Museum.

The marriage of princesses to princes in other lands has been a form of affirming diplomatic relations and legitimacy throughout history and across the world. Recent innovations in forensic methods are confirming these legends. When a tomb in Magdeburg Cathedral was opened in 2008, an inscription stated that the internee was Eadgyth, an English princess and daughter of Alfred the Great, said to have married a German king around 936. Isotopes from the enamel from her teeth show what she was eating and when, which affirmed that the bones were of a woman who had lived and died at the right time, in England. Mike Pitts explains, 'Match teeth with landscape, and you can chart early residence and movements'.[77] It is being realized that migration at that time involved the free movement of elites around Europe, not just violent invasions.

Whether fact or fiction, elite women are used to shape the meaning of history and fuel controversy.[78] The exact identity of the Japanese Queen of Wa, Himiko (3rd century), is unclear,[79] but she is a basis for asking why there have apparently been no female heads of state in Japan since her time. The Japanese Empress Jingu (c.169–269) was said to have conquered the Korean kingdoms, and this was taught in school textbooks in Japan during the first half of the twentieth century, as a justification for the Japanese occupation of

Korea. But after World War II, other historians argued the opposite, that Japan had been conquered by nomads from Korea.[80] The "Korean Joan of Arc", Kwan Sun Yu, who was tortured to death in 1920 aged 16, for leading protests against the Japanese occupiers, still does not feature in Japanese history books.

Plutarch's *Lives of the Noble Greeks and Romans* (or *Parallel Lives*) is a seminal set of biographical studies of powerful people (all men), written towards the end of the first century. Twenty-three pairs of Greek and Roman biographies are compared to analyse moral standards. Plutarch evolves the methodology of historical text writing towards a psychological investigation of personalities. He explains: 'It is not histories I am writing, but lives; and in the most glorious deeds there is not always an indication of virtue or vice, indeed a small thing like a phrase or a jest often makes a greater revelation of a character than battles where thousands die.'[81] *Parallel Lives* is structured chronologically and developed comparative ('parallel') methodology.

The idea of objective historical methodology also evolved in the Arab world. In 1377, Ibn Khaldun (1332–1406) noted what is now termed the 'halo effect' (C3.2), 'Students often happen to accept and transmit absurd information that, in turn, is believed on their authority.' Khaldun was a historian and president of Cairo University, and at the start of his *Muqaddimah: An Introduction to History* (1377) he considers epistemology (C2), and concludes that, 'Untruth naturally afflicts historical information.' He explains research bias, 'various reasons that make this unavoidable':

1 Partisanship for opinions and schools … Prejudice and partisanship obscure the critical faculty and preclude critical investigation.
2 Reliance upon transmitters.
3 Unawareness of the purpose of an event. Many a transmitter does not know the real significance of his observations or of the things he has learned about orally.
4 Unfounded assumption as to the truth of a thing. It results mostly from reliance upon transmitters.
5 Ignorance of how conditions conform to reality. Conditions are affected by ambiguities and artificial distortions. The informant reports the conditions as he saw them but on account of artificial distortions he himself has no true picture of them.
6 People as a rule approach great and high-ranking persons with praise and encomiums [tribute]. They embellish conditions and spread the fame [of great men].
7 Ignorance of the nature of the various conditions arising in civilization … If the student knows the nature of events and the circumstances and requirements in the world of existence, it will help him to distinguish truth from untruth in investigating the historical information critically.[82]

Khaldun was prescient of subsequent situational and contingency theories of leadership (C2.3). Arguing that leaders are "made not born", he proposed:

No human being exists who possesses an unbroken pedigree of nobility from Adam down to himself. … Nobility originates in the state of being outside. That is, being outside of leadership and nobility, and being in a base, humble station, devoid of prestige, as is the case with every created thing.[83]

Much of Khaldun's work was based on the observation of nomadic tribes. His theorization of legitimacy developed the concept of *asabiyah* – a sense of 'solidarity', which might now be termed 'social cohesion'. Bali considers Khaldun's ideas about 'the qualities of rulership', concluding that for Khaldun:

> Leadership exists only through superiority, and superiority only through a*sabiyah*. ... Strong asabiyah also indicates good character and high qualifications of relationship ... A basic qualification of a good ruler is that he will be well informed about, and well acquainted with, the holders of *asabiyah* and willing to respect their positions; hence, the mutual respect between, and adjustment of, leaders and followers.[84]

Khaldun also explained the rise and fall of societies[85] and his insights were followed by works such as Gibbon's *The Decline and Fall of the Roman Empire* (1776), and discussion of the Ottoman Empire.[86] Khaldun's five 'stages' seem applicable to many dynastic eras, throughout history (Figure 1.6). In the present-day, the theory seems exemplified by the life of the nomadic leader of Libya, Muammar Gaddafi, and of president Hosni Mubarak in the country where Khaldun formulated his analysis, Egypt (Figure 0.2). Elsewhere, the rule of North Korea's Kim dynasty seems to fit the pattern. There was an 'overthrow of all opposition' by Kim Il-sung, who became 'a model to his people'. Then followed, Kim Jong-il's period of 'leisure and tranquility in which the fruits of royal authority are enjoyed ...' while he 'adopt[ed] the tradition of his predecessors and follow[ed] closely in their footsteps.' His son, Kim Jong-nam, who was arrested at Tokyo airport while travelling on forged documents on his way to visit Disneyland, was seemingly wasting 'on pleasures and amusements (the treasures) accumulated by his ancestors'. If the president is engaging in 'excessive generosity to his inner circle', will 'The dynasty [be] seized by senility ... and eventually ... destroyed'?

Centuries earlier, Korea demonstrated that historians could provide objective evaluations of powerful people, even of their own kings. The Choson dynasty (1392–1897) created a unique system of historical record keeping that aimed to be directly critical of its Kings. The 1893 volumes of the *Annals of the Choson Dynasty* cover 472 years of Korean rulers, and were compiled by official court diarists (*hallim*). These court historians collected and compared evidence about the conduct of the King, from different sources – data 'triangulation' (C6.3). They had their independence protected by law, and were to record with 'a straight brush' the King's deeds to create a 'Draft History' (*Sacho*), which even the King could not read. After the death of the King, the Office for Annals Compilation (*Sillokcheong*) would write the finite 'Veritable record' (*Sillok*).[87] These records were based on a format from the Chinese *Comprehensive Mirror for Aid in Governance* by Ssu-ma Kuang (1018–1086CE), a history of China from 403BC to 959. This was intended to help subsequent rulers reflect (in the 'mirror' it provided) on the mistakes and success of their predecessors, a process that would now be called 'reflexive methodology'.[88]

The distinct feature of the Korean process was that its primary purpose was to ensure the legitimacy of the whole system of governance, irrespective of the reputations of individual kings. The resultant *History of Korea* (1451) is based on one of the earliest

مقدمة ابن خلدون

The stages of the dynasties.

١ Success, the overthrow of all opposition, and the appropriation of royal authority from the preceding dynasty. In this stage, the ruler serves as a model to his people...

٢ The ruler gains complete control over his people, claims royal authority all for himself, excluding them...

٣ Leisure and tranquility in which the fruits of royal authority are enjoyed...

٤ Contentment and peacefulness ... He adopts the tradition of his predecessors and follows closely in their footsteps.

٥ Waste and squandering. The ruler wastes on pleasures and amusements (the treasures) accumulated by his ancestors, through (excessive) generosity to his inner circle and at their parties. Also he acquires bad, low-class followers to whom he entrusts the most important matters (of state) which they are not qualified to handle by themselves, not knowing which of them they should tackle and which they should leave alone ... The dynasty is seized by senility and the chronic disease from which it can hardly ever rid itself, and eventually, it is destroyed.

FIGURE 1.6 The rise and fall of elites (Ibn Khaldun, 1377)

Source: Ibn Khaldun, Rosenthal, F. (trans.), Dawood, N.J. (ed.), Lawrence. B. (ed.), (1958) *The Muqaddimah: An Introduction to History*. New Jersey: Princeton University Press. p. 353.

consistently used methodologies for elite and leadership studies. Chonng Inji explains in his introduction:

> We recorded the loyal and the deceitful officials as well as the evil and the upright individuals under separate categories ... We also clarified those parts of the annals of reigns that were confusing and established verifiable chronologies. We traced historical events as fully and clearly as possible and made sure that those aspects that lacked sufficient information were supplemented with additional data.

Only by probing into the past can we be sure of achieving the impartiality of historical writings: only by exhibiting the illustrious mirror of history can we ensure that the consequences of good and evil acts shall not be forgotten by posterity.[89]

The use of categories and the centrality of validity are significant.

The use of research for the accountability of powerful people, this time religious despots, was also evident in Europe. *Foxe's Book of Martyrs* (1563) is a remarkable example of using testimony evidence to document wrongdoing by political and religious leaders, and is a precursor of the work of present-day human rights organizations such as *Human Rights Watch*. It records the suffering of Christian martyrs from early Christianity to the sixteenth century. In particular it records the persecution of Protestants by Catholics, and so it also represents political advocacy. It was the biggest publishing project of that era. By 1563 it was 1800 pages long, three times bigger than the first edition. In the 1570 version, Foxe claimed he had removed unreliable material, and strengthened the evidence about accurate accounts that had been challenged. Foxe achieved this by using a research strategy that is now called 'crowdsourcing' (C5.2).

Despite examples such as these, the methodology of historical research was often not made explicit. In 1894, a German, Ernst Bernheim, tried to formalize approaches in his *Lehrbuch der Historischen Methode,* but the book is more philosophical than methodological.[90] Gilbert Garigan's *A Guide to Historical Methods* is closer to what would now be considered a systematic approach.[91] He bases critical analysis of historical texts on six 'inquiries': When was the text created? Where was it created? Who created it? What evidence is it based on? How was this evidence originally created? What is the plausibility of the content? This checklist approach is reflected in many subsequent documentary methodologies (C6.1).

Archaeological methods have been more systematic and better documented,[92] although early archaeologists were sometimes also guilty of altering the evidence to fit their conclusions. This included moving objects to different locations, or even chiselling stone artefacts to fit with mathematical theories. There is also a problem of reverse attribution. Archaeologists often name their findings in relation to modern concepts that are familiar to them. The Maltese prehistoric sites – *Ggantija, Hagar Qim, Mnajdra* and *Tarxien* – are described as 'temples', where 'priests' and 'community leaders' interacted.[93] But there is little evidence to support these terms. They reflected the nineteenth century worldview of the early archaeologists, not the probable world of the people who created these structures in 4000–2500BC. The buildings could equally well have been the prehistoric equivalent of supermarkets.

There is much to be learned from archaeologists about recording data. Techniques like the grid system are often used to ensure that the location of objects is recorded precisely, but grids also encourage meticulous observation, and can be applied to modern data such as the photos of the offices of powerful people (Figure 6.7). Perhaps the most significant methodological contribution from archaeology is the development of 'reconstructive' research frameworks for using and analysing incomplete data

(C5.2). In 1789, naturalist George Cuvier provided a 'principle of correlation of parts' arguing that

> after inspecting a single bone, one can often determine the class, and sometimes even the genus of the animal to which it belonged, above all if that bone belonged to the head or the limbs ... This is because the number, direction, and shape of the bones that compose each part of an animal's body are always in a necessary relation to all the other parts, in such a way that – up to a point – one can infer the whole from any one of them and vice versa.[94]

Now, even understanding the structure of the DNA of a fossil bone can provide a basis for understanding the whole creature.[95,96]

Archaeology has evolved from being purely a historical method, to playing a broader role in modern research. Considerations within forensic archaeology include the possibility of satellite images,[97] toxic chemicals, highly perishable artefacts, and evidence that is not just on the ground but scattered up buildings and trees because of bombs. Archaeologists a century ago would probably not have believed that the methods they were developing, to understand the deaths of powerful people of former eras,[98] would evolve to help with understanding the deaths caused by powerful people in the present day. Archaeological methods now embrace theories of power and ideology – 'archaeological records should be understood as actively manipulating their own material world to represent and misrepresent their own and other's interests'.[99]

How are historical approaches relevant to contemporary methodology? Arguably all research about powerful people is based on, will become, or already is, a historical text, and should be written and read with appropriate caution. The distinct characteristic of up-system history is that it is often not only created by, but also revised by, powerful people. History books can reconstruct the events of the past to fulfil the political needs of the present. The misuse and abuse of the history of elites and leaders still underpins many of the world's most intractable conflicts, not least in the Middle East. That is why UNESCO has an initiative to 'disarm history'.[100] The lesson from history is that all history is, as historian A.J.P. Taylor comments, just 'a version of events'.[101] Or more realistically, as Noam Chomsky points out, 'For the powerful, history is bunk'.[102]

1.3 PHILOSOPHY

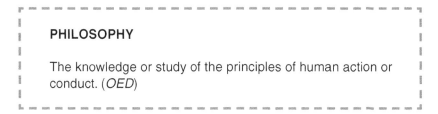

PHILOSOPHY

The knowledge or study of the principles of human action or conduct. (*OED*)

> **ETHICS**
>
> The science of morals. The rules of conduct recognized in certain limited departments. (*OED*)

> **SCEPTIC**
>
> One who maintains a doubting attitude with reference to some particular question or statement. (*OED*)

Whatever their failings, historical records have provided a basis for philosophers to analyse what was good and bad about powerful people, and to apply the resultant understandings to their own visions of how the moral authority of rulers should evolve. The significant difference between the historians who simply recorded evidence, and the philosophers who thought about it, was that the latter adopted a more critical, or in Greek tradition 'sceptical',[103] approach. It became important to question everything, and suspend judgment until all evidence and argument had been considered. The careful presentation of the arguments was often seen as more important than the conclusions. Pure sceptics argued that no knowledge could be fully justified and proved. Logical sceptics argued that this problem only applied in certain spheres such as ethics. The persistence of the approach is evident in Lisa Jardine's phrase, 'Science trades in organised doubt', and, 'Science is organised scepticism' from Martin Rees.[104] The elements of philosophical method therefore include: doubt and suspicion about existing understandings, problematizing and questioning, hypothesizing, and critical reflection. A range of intellectual tools have been devised to address these elements.[105]

Historically, China has contributed significantly to discussions of ethics. In *Tao Te Ching* of Lao Tzu (c.570–490BC), a well known passage sets out a hierarchy of ethical leadership, which is often cited as a precursor of theories of 'servant leadership' (C2.3).[106]

> The highest type of ruler is one of whose existence the people are barely aware. Next comes one whom they love and praise. Next comes one whom they fear. Next comes one whom they despise and defy … When his task is accomplished and things have been completed, all the people say, "We ourselves have achieved it".

Around the same time, in his *Analects,* Confucius (Master K'ong – *K'ung-fu-tzu* – 551–479 BC) envisaged a unified Chinese state where the legitimacy of rulers would be achieved through ethical behaviour, not through inheritance as in the past.[107] Benign leaders would lead by example, teach virtue and not impose their will through law and coercion. A powerful Emperor was necessary, but power should be limited, and truth and honesty were the most important characteristics of a supreme leader: 'To govern (*cheng*) is to correct (*cheng*). If you set an example by being correct, who would dare to remain incorrect?'[108] Confucian tradition argued that rulers should induce and persuade the masses to follow the right path, rather than using harsh laws and punishments. This philosophy of *li*, ruling by influence and persuasion, as opposed to legalistic and forceful *fa*, reflects the "carrot-and-stick" view of modern governance and diplomacy (C2.1).[109]

Subsequently, Confucian traditions underpinned the education at the world's earliest leadership education institutions for training public administrators, the Chinese Imperial Colleges (*Guozijian*, School of the Sons of State), which trace their roots back to the *Taixue* of the 3rd century.[110] The Imperial examinations, dating from 605, are the earliest civil service exams, and aimed to make selection for senior positions **meritocratic** and based less on heredity and nepotism. Candidates were locked in their exam cells for many days. The exam question was sometimes along the lines of "write everything you know". This was subsequently the methodology of confession for political prisoners during Mao's regime. Like the political prisoners, many candidates went mad, and some died. The stone records of successful candidates can be seen in Beijing today, looking like tombstones. Whether or not they identified the best candidates, the exams unified the values of the administrative elites across the country.[111] Elite ethics became elite practice.

In contrast to Confucian soft power (*Li*), an aristocrat, Han Fei (Han Fei Zi/Tzu) (c.280BC–233BC) argued a **legalistic** (*Fa*) view, which assumed that people are intrinsically evil and motivated by personal gain, which can only be controlled by punishment. The ruler was to maintain order in three ways: position and power, techniques and strategies, and laws that punish and reward. Despite his harsh views, Han Fei was prescient of aspects of present-day leadership theory. He considered 'reputation' based on 'the hearts of the people', 'technical ability' and 'influential status'. He provided a precursor of modern crowd psychology, 'the mentality of the people: a psychological analysis'. And he considered the way elites decline in 'The portents of ruin':[112]

4 If the ruler is fond of palatial decorations, raised kiosks, and embanked pools, is immersed in pleasures of having chariots, clothes, and curios, and thereby tires out the hundred surnames and exhausts public wealth, then ruin is possible.

6 If the ruler takes advice only from ministers of high **rank**, refrains from comparing different opinions and testifying to the truth, and uses only one man as a channel of information, then ruin is possible.

9 If the ruler is greedy, insatiable, attracted to profit, and fond of gain, then ruin is possible.

12 If the ruler is stubborn-minded, uncompromising, and apt to dispute every remonstrance and fond of surpassing everybody else … but sticks to self-confidence without due consideration, then ruin is possible.

27 If the ruler is fond of twisting laws by virtue of his wisdom, mixes public with private affairs from time to time, alters laws and prohibitions at random, and issues commands and orders frequently, then ruin is possible.

These insights about how power can decline remain relevant.

During the same era, Plato's *Republic* (380BC) envisaged legitimacy through philosopher kings, or 'Guardians' – 'philosophers [should] become kings ... or those now called kings [should] genuinely and adequately philosophize',[113] because, it was argued, those who were educated were less likely to be corrupt. This required a long discussion of how powerful men *and* women were to be educated, in modern terms a concern about the **reproduction of elites** (C2.2). These leaders were to be the elite of three cadres – military, producers and rulers. Plato argued that justice would arise from what these rulers would consider to be best for themselves, 'what is good for the stronger'. Reflecting Confucius, the possibility of bad decisions was obviated by the circular argument that if rulers made bad decisions they could not be considered legitimate rulers.

In his *The Laws*, Plato applies an historical international comparative methodology to understanding the decline of the power of Persian rulers after King Cyrus. Like Confucius, Plato recognized the use of hard and soft power, explaining that Cyrus ruled 'by a judicious blend of liberty and subjection'.[114] But he went on to criticize Cyrus because he 'never considered ... the problem of the correct education' of the next generation – the reproduction of elites. Plato concluded that as Cyrus was away fighting, his children were brought up by the women who 'reared them ... as though they were already Heaven's special favorites and darlings ... They wouldn't allow anyone to thwart "their Beatitudes" in anything, and they forced everybody to rhapsodize about what the children said or did.' The result of this 'womanish education', in Plato's view, was a generation of foolish spoilt brats.[115]

Plato's methodology relied on reasoning based on history, but his student Aristotle (384–322 BC) was more systematic. He proposed an approach to scholarship which provided a basis for modern scientific method and entailed: a study of what others have written [literature review]; identification of the general consensus about the topic [theoretical review]; a systematic study of everything related to the topic [empirical research]. The Greek historian philosophers would have been aware of systematic methods in medicine, probably from Egypt. The Edwin Smith papyrus (c.1600BC) is a medical textbook that explains examination, diagnosis, treatment and prognosis, and the Ebers papyrus (c.1550BC) is similar. For his book *Politics*, Aristotle used what would now be called documentary analysis (C6.1), to study and compare the constitutions of a sample of 158 real and theoretical city-states. He classified them in relation to objective criteria, determining 'true' constitutions which uphold the public interest, in contrast to the 'perverted' ones that only serve the needs of some citizens. He also created a typology based on the number of people who take part in the magistracies – one (royalty–tyranny), few (aristocracy–oligarchy), many (constitutional government–democracy).[116]

From a contrasting Hindu tradition, Chanakya (c.350–283BC), a professor at Takshashila University and Prime Minister of the Mauri Empire, India, is attributed with compiling the *Arthashastra* – 'The science of politics'. This argues a completely different moral stance. It represents a *real politick* manual for **autocrats**, which has an interesting contemporary resonance. It advises the Rajarshi – the wise and virtuous king – about assassination (including family members), spies (including women and children), bribery, breaking treaties, arrest on suspicion alone and justifying torture. As if aware of the modern media, it is suggested that the king should keep away from other men's wives, avoid drink and gambling, and look people in the eye and not frown.[117]

The *Histories* of Polybius (c.200–117BC) provide a Roman view.[118] A **plural** constitution is favoured – 'benign' rule based on government, monarchy, aristocracy and democracy – as opposed to 'malignant' rule – tyranny, oligarchy and **ochlocracy**. The model of the Roman Republic is consuls (monarchy and military), senate and public. Polybius discusses the role of fate (*tyche*), which seems prescient of contingency theory (C2.3), but *tyche* also seems to represent a goddess of leadership accountability, who can punish wayward leaders. The notion that powerful leaders could be punished by anyone seems a brave proposition at that time. He proposes a cycle of political decline, *anacyclosis*, and arrives at his conclusions about 'What makes a Constitution good' in part through comparative analysis of 'Sparta and with Rome' and 'The Cretan Constitution compared to the Spartan', in which he criticizes writers such as Plato for concluding that the two were similar.[119]

This form of political theorizing waned in Europe, but becomes evident again in works such as those of Sir Thomas Elyiot who proposed the type of education that was necessary for those likely to hold high office. His *The Boke Named the Governour* (1531) was the first English academic book to be written in the commoner's language of English, not Latin. Like the Greeks, he saw governance in terms of monarchy, aristocracy and democracy which he viewed as undesirable. Later, Sir John Eliot challenged the rule of Charles I, and was imprisoned in the Tower of London, which gave him time to write political treatises such as *De jure maiestatis* – 'Political treatise of government' (1628–1630).[120] In his *A Short Treatise on Political Power, and of the True Obedience Which Subjects Owe to Kings and Other Civil Governors* (1556), John Ponet, Bishop of Rochester, assessed 'from where political power grows', and concluded that Kings had no mandate from God. Unlike their forefathers, these theorists had an impact, culminating in the Civil War, Oliver Cromwell and his plans for a commonwealth, the execution of King Charles I who claimed that he was chosen to rule by God under the **doctrine** of the "Divine Right of Kings", and the establishment of a modern democratic system in Britain.

Meanwhile, the Italian Niccolò Machiavelli (1469–1527) had seemingly provided a harsh and brutal view of ruling, which was in stark contrast to the classical discussion. His ideas are linked with the autocratic ethics of Chanakya, by Max Weber.[121] He was a diplomat and senior civil servant for the Florentine **Republic**, and is often considered to be a founder of modern political science. His treatise, *The Prince* (1532), gave rise to the term **Machiavellian**, implying deceitful and underhand political behaviour. From a theoretical perspective Machiavelli affirmed a distinction between political realism and political idealism, which Plato had argued in *The Republic* (Part 7). Machiavelli described the skills needed by a 'new prince' who does not have the advantages of a **hereditary** ruler, and needs to gain and maintain control. The Prince must appear overtly honest, while covertly achieving 'ends' through deceitful 'means'. 'Acceptable cruel action' must be decisive, swift and effective. Machiavelli recognizes the familiar 'soft' and 'hard' duality – 'it would be best to be both loved and feared. But since the two rarely come together, anyone compelled to choose will find greater security in being feared than being loved.'[122]

But was Machiavelli really advocating the system he described? There is now discussion about whether *The Prince* was a treatise or a satire. Why would the techniques of tyranny need to be made public, when the elites already understood them well? Why, like Elyot's treatise published one year earlier, was *The Prince* written in the common language, Italian, and not the language of the elites, Latin? Is the real Machiavellian deceit that he was trying to educate ordinary people about the abuse of power by the elites, while fooling the powerful into believing that he was legitimizing their conduct? If so, Machiavelli's approach was prescient of recent evolutionary psychology which shows that humans are acutely attuned to cheating, and populations may respond more strongly to being told that they have been deceived by powerful people, than to the actions underlying that deceit.[123] Any man playing this Machiavellian trick would be wise to publish such a book after his death, as Machiavelli did.

1.4 UP-SYSTEM RESEARCH

As the Scottish joke at the start of this chapter suggests, understanding the legitimization of power has probably been a longer and more pressing motivating force for systematic study than other social or scientific problems. Had the Greeks determined a discipline called "legitimology", it would probably be evident that this predated astronomy, chemistry and enlightenment sociology. And had our Scottish tramp studied this discipline, and understood the need for a critical approach, he might have won his argument with the landowner by asking simply, "And how do we know that's correct?"

Even this brief history of up-system research challenges the familiar claim that 'the scientific method … emerged in the seventeenth century', and that subsequently 'the social sciences have adopted versions of the methods and assumptions of the natural sciences when constructing scientific explanations of social relations and processes.'[124] Emmanuel-Joseph Sieyès coined the term 'sociology' in 1780, and Auguste Comte (1798–1857) affirmed its meaning, but it would be more accurate to claim that this European tradition established ways to research and understand social problems among large down-system populations, and that is perhaps why social science has usually focused down-system.[125] Elites systemized eclectic ways to study, their ancestors, their enemies and their subjects, long ago.[126] The motives might have been to affirm their royal lineage, as for the Pharaohs, or to make spying more effective, as for Sun Tzu and Chanakya. But whatever the motive, this field of social inquiry certainly predates the European sociologists of the nineteenth century. This is not surprising. Powerful people control human resources, and when they first used scholars to do research, it would have been to serve their own interests.

But the origins of up-system study embody many questionable practices. The use of research to construct legitimacy to enhance power and wealth is central, for example claims to land. This has often been done through conflating empirical human data, and religious arguments that are not evidence-based. Research about power is itself a form of power, and this is sometimes an abuse of power as within colonial regimes. Interpretations of historical evidence sometimes wrongly conjecture that the past was like the present, for example assuming the worship of gods and the existence of religious leaders, which leads to calling constructions that appear to be tables "altars", or mysterious artefacts "votive objects". Historians who lived in male-dominated societies often assumed that female leaders were also non-existent in former times. Understanding these problems provides a basis for improving the integrity and ethics of present-day research (C4.6).

Whatever its failings, up-system research contributed to the foundations of social science by developing ways to systemize and classify evidence. The original meaning of 'methodology' was simply 'systematic classification' (*OED*), which then provided the basis for critical (sceptical) analysis of evidence, such as identifying gaps and inconstancies in records. Simple chronological elite **lists** provided basic data (Figure 0.1 and 1.7), and these evolved into **genealogies** and **lineage** charts using specific symbols and abbreviations to indicate gaps in knowledge (Figure 1.8). These charts sometimes encapsulate groundbreaking findings from meticulous large-scale research, perhaps establishing the existence of unknown dynasties such as those of ancient Armenia.[127] Simplified, they became the now familiar organizational and line-management charts, and elite network charts (C5.3). **Typologies** categorized and conceptualized forms of power and powerful people according to their characteristics, and **hierarchies** ranked elites and others from high to low status (Figure 1.9). In addition to systemization, there are many other examples of early contributions to methodology that seem prescient of later developments (Figure 1.10). These early methodologies may seem self-evident to present-day scholars, but someone had to invent and develop them. They reflected the basic questions and concepts of up-system research of their time, which remain relevant (Figure 1.11).

Until now, the origins of elite and leadership studies have not been conceptualized together and as extending back 4000 years, and it is rarely admitted that they have roots in non-Western traditions of scholarship. When trying to understand the foundations of researching powerful people, it is helpful to consider that:

- *elites, leaders and social hierarchies seem intrinsic to human groups*, except in extreme circumstances. If these structures are not obvious in texts and objects, they may be expressed through the 'performance' of power – decision-making forums or rituals (perhaps transient) that are accepted as framing the direction and values of a community. Understanding powerful people is therefore a basis for understanding societies and civilizations.
- up-system research is arguably the *oldest form of social research*, and researchers should be aware of the questions and methods that have underpinned relevant work throughout history. The roots of seemingly recent ideas are often missed because terminology is not the same – Khaldun's 'solidarity' amounts to 'social cohesion', Plutarch's *Parallel Lives* is a comparative methodology, and *Foxe's Martyrs* was compiled through 'crowdsourcing'.

- the significant contributions from this long tradition of research methods is the *systemization of data* – lists, lineage charts, typologies, hierarchies – and that *comparison* became a recognized basis for analysis. Although these ideas may seem simple and obvious, they still provide quick and efficient ways to start to understand how power is gained and maintained for any present-day study.
- research has often been used to enhance **legitimacy**. This has sometimes been an abuse of power, by justifying authoritarian or colonial rule, dubious claims to land and wealth, and questionable religious practices. The conflation of fact and belief has often underpinned religious abuse of power.
- the idea of ethics and the **accountability** of powerful people runs throughout history, but is not always expressed overtly, because it is sometimes dangerous to do so.
- one of the oldest approaches to up-system research is *spying* – intelligence gathering to gain a strategic advantage. This continues in military, commercial and many other fields. If used ethically, this approach can be relevant to other forms of up-system research, especially the use of observational methods and the mapping of power elites.
- the leadership of *women and people from minority groups* is often obscured – "airbrushed" from history. Art, objects, oral histories and poetry may provide better evidence than official records.
- up-system research often requires the *reconstruction* of events from minimal data, and extrapolation based on understanding underlying structures rather than conspicuous evidence. Archaeological methods can provide ideas.
- while the focus of up-system research is usually in how people use their power, history shows that eventually powerful entities **decline** or **collapse**, and this is an equally valid area of study.

Understanding the origins of up-system research helps present-day researchers to avoid "reinventing the wheel", and from taking a narrow western-centric viewpoint.

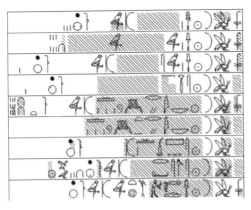

Order	Name in list	Familiar name
1	Sekhem..re	Sekhem..re
2	Sekhem..re	Sekhem..re
3	Sekhemre S..	Sekhemre S..
4	Sewadjenre..	Sewadjenre..
5	Nebiriaure	Nebiriaure
6	Nebiretaure	Nebiretaure
7	Semenre	Semenre
8	Seuserre..	Seuserre..
9	Shedwaset	Sekhemre

(16th dynasty)

FIGURE 1.7   Lists

From the 'Turin King List' created in the era of Ramses II (1303–1213BC). Accuracy is disputed. The interest is the systematic presentation.

Western lineage charts, or genealogies, may be in the form of a tree, the "roots" showing the oldest ancestor, or go from top to bottom. Specific symbols show the relationships.

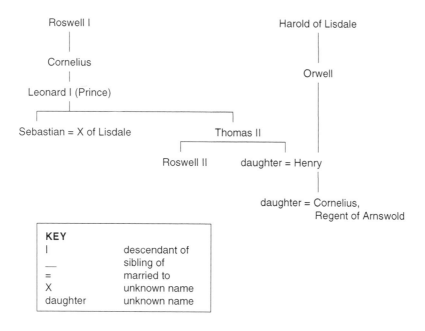

A recent Japanese family line diagram (Kakeizu). It goes from right to left, usually on a scroll, and additions are made as families grow.

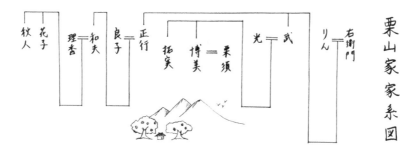

FIGURE 1.8 Lineage charts

Plato. *Republic/Laws*	Rule by
Aristocracy	the best
Timocracy	the honourable
Oligarchy	the few
Democracy	the people
Tyranny	the tyrant/despot

Polybius	Cycles of political decline through anacyclosis
Monarchy	A primitive state ruled by a wise King
Kingship	A system of hereditary rule by Kings
Tyranny	Hereditary Kings abuse their power
Aristocracy	Powerful oppositional leaders overthrow the tyrants
Oligarchy	Hereditary aristocrats become corrupt
Democracy	The people overthrow corrupt oligarchs
Ochlocracy	Democracy declines into chaotic mob rule
Demagogues	Chaos is controlled by absolute rulers, who become monarchs, and the cycle repeats

Jewish	Hierarchical status
Judges	Military leaders
Kings	Monarchs
Kohen	Temple priests (teachers)
Prophets	Planners

Korea, Choson era Sinbun class system	Hierarchical status
Yang-ban	Intellectuals (See Figure 6.6)
Jung-in	Professional and military
Nong-sang-min	Farmers and commercial
Chun-min	Untouchable
Nobi (slaves) were not ranked.	

FIGURE 1.9   Typologies and hierarchies

Akan chieftaincy (Ghana)	Hierarchical status
Omanhene	Paramount chief
Gyasehene	Personal Secretary
Obaatan	Counsellor
Tofuhene	Warrior, head of companies
Adontehen Nkyidom Nyimfahene Benhumhene	Military, forward Military, rear Military, right flank Military, left flank
Akyampimhene	Resource sharing
Mankrando	Purification, hygiene
Guantuahene	Sanctuary for people
Nsumankwahene	Oracle, foresight planning
Nkosuohene	Regional development
Entourage Okomfo 'Stool wife' Okyeami 'Queen mother'	 Priest(ess) Young girl Linguist, speech-maker Social organizer

FIGURE 1.9   *Continued*

Era	Source	Contributions
3000–300BC	King Lists. Census. Egypt	Chronology. Demography. Translation
1000– 6000BC	Book of Kings (Old testament, Bible)	Evaluation of Kings against objective ethical criteria (Deuteronomic law)
722–481BC	Sun Tzu. China	Observation (spies). Research questions
450–420BC	Herodotus. Greece	Historical method
300BC	Manetho. Egypt	Dynasties. Genealogy. Lineage. 'Reconstructive' frameworks
570–490BC	Lao-Tzu. China	Typology of ethical leadership
551–479BC	Confucius. China	Reasoned ethical standards
280–233BC	Han Fei. China	Reputation. Crowd psychology. Decline
380BC	Plato. Greece	Historical international comparison

FIGURE 1.10   Methodological contributions from early up-system research

(Continued)

Era	Source	Contributions
384–322 BC	Aristotle. Greece	Systematic study – literature, theory, empirical. Comparative documentary analysis of political leadership. Sampling. Categorization. Typology
350–283BC	Chanakya. India	Observation (spies). Prescriptive theory (autocracy)
304–232BC	Ashoka. India	Mass communication (pillars and stone carvings)
200–117BC	Polybius	Observation. Organization/system analysis
109–191BC	Sima Qian. China	Citation of written sources. Triangulation of data
1st Century	Plutarch. Greece/Rome	Biographical comparison. Comparison of elite ethics. Trait theory
973–1048	Abū Rayhān Bīrūnī. Persia	Ethnography of elites. Stated/demonstrated behaviour/values
1332–1406	Khaldun. Egypt	Critical documentary/historical method. Research bias. Decline
1451	*History of Korea*. Choson, Korea	Critical analysis. Observation. Diaries. Categories. Evaluation. Validity. Triangulation
1563	*Foxe's Book of Martyrs*. England	Testimony evidence. 'Crowdsourcing'
1789	*Cuvier*. France	'Correlation of parts'. Reconstructive research (forensic methods)
1835	Lane. *Manners and Customs of Modern Egyptians*	Ethnography. Access. Subterfuge. Appropriate research assistants

FIGURE 1.10 *Continued*

Questions	Concepts
Are elites intrinsic to human societies?	*Anarchical* and *acephalous* (leaderless) systems
How is power gained, maintained and lost?	Gerontocracy. Aristocracy. Lineage. Ascribed/achieved. Legitimacy. Democracy. Reputation. *Tyche* (fate-contingency). *Anacyclosis* – cycles of decline. *Asabiyah* (solidarity, social cohesion). 'Portents of ruin'
How do rulers create their image, and communicate their right to rule?	Legitimacy. Mass communication. Public languages. Symbolism – coins, statues, portraits, lineage charts, maps
How are elites reproduced?	Elite education, meritocracy
Who were the female and minority group leaders and elites?	Gender discrimination. Minority rights. "Airbrushing"
How is power structured?	Rank, classes, castes. Political systems
How is power exercised?	Soft–hard (legalism). Realism–idealism. Democracy. *Ochlocracy* (mob rule). Transactional relationships
What is 'good' and 'bad' leadership?	Leadership ethics. Abuse of power. Deceit. Accountability. Benign and malignant governance. Criteria-based evaluation

FIGURE 1.11 Questions and concepts

KEY READING

Bagini, J. and Fosl, P.S. (2010) *The Philosopher's Toolkit: A Compendium of Philosophical Concepts and Methods*. London: Wiley.

Cheater, A. (1999) *The Anthropology of Power*. London: Routledge.

Routledge, B. (2011) *Archaeology and State Theory: Subjects and Objects of Power*. Bristol: Duckworth.

2

THEORY

2.1 POWER
2.2 ELITES
2.3 LEADERSHIP
2.4 POPULACE
2.5 CRITIQUE

> **THEORY**
>
> A scheme or system of ideas or statements held as an explanation or account of a group of facts or phenomena. A hypothesis that has been confirmed or established by observation or experiment, and is propounded or accepted as accounting for the known facts. A statement of what are held to be the general laws, principles, or causes of something known or observed. (*OED*)

Understanding the origins of up-system research, outlined in Chapter 1, provides evidence of a long history of ideas that we would now term 'theory'. Ibn Khaldun's theory about the rise and fall of elites, in 1377, was clearly based on the systematic observation of nomadic tribes, and reasoned argument (Figure 1.6). Observation and reasoning are bases of all modern theory. The distinction between theory and practice is often explained in the context of medicine. Theoreticians might try to understand the nature and perception of pain, while practitioners try to cure it. Theory can inform practice. Mao Zedong built his political ideas for Chinese Communism on the theories of Karl Marx. He then explained how his policies must be developed through practical experience in his essay

'On Practice' (1937).[1] And he implemented them with the help of his military leaders, apparently concluding that, 'Political power grows from the barrel of a gun'.[2]

A theory may help to explain similar observations in the past or present, and to predict what could happen in similar circumstances in the future. But theories are not fixed or absolute. They are just the best possible explanation at a particular point in time, implying the probability of being correct (Figure 2.2). Unfortunately, in relation to power, theories sometimes mutate into political certainties, or become delusional about the supremacy of a particular (often western) perspective (Figure 2.1). Philosophers argue whether theories ever represent truth,[3] and the degree to which theory emerges from, or helps to form, evidence.[4] A *general theory* is a very broad abstract claim, for instance Pareto and Mosca's theory that elites are an inevitable aspect of large societies. A *specific theory* relates to a particular context, such as Mills's application of elite theory to American institutions (below). *Meta-theory* is an overview of theories – theories of theories – and can include an assessment of the methods used to support those theories. Theoretical research is based on reason, logic, calculation, modelling and argument, and may address themes such as network structures, bargaining and conflict, status characteristics and status organizing processes, justice and equity, social interaction and legitimation processes.[5]

Theory is constructed in relation to **ontology** – the study of how we know that something exists.[6] Discussions of ontology can be tedious, but the implications are intriguing. Unsurprisingly, past philosophers spent much time considering the existence of gods and the mind. Do things only exist because human minds are here to be aware of their existence, and if so would the gods still exist if humans did not? The existence of gods is important for up-system research – they have been central to legitimizing claims to power (C1.1). Twenty-first century philosophers such as Nick Bostrom ask, how do we know that humans exist as real entities, or are we just part of a computer simulation – avatars in a virtual reality game played by higher beings?[7] Ontological questions can be posed in the form of a null (C7.2) ontological hypothesis (C4.3) – a default assumption that something does not exist until it is shown that it does (Figure 2.2).

John Searle relates ontology to power,[8] and makes a useful distinction: some features are 'observer independent' – 'brute facts' that 'exist independently of us' (mass, gravitational attraction, the solar system); others are 'observer-relative' – 'institutional facts' that 'depend on us for their existence' (citizenship, rules, national boundaries).[9] Searle asks: 'Prior to answering such questions as "What is a just society?" and "What is the proper

---

We cannot foretell the future; but we can be sure it will be full of hybrid regimes – booming tyrannies and declining imperial republics, resource-rich theocracies and faltering knowledge economies, floundering democracies and makeshifts that have yet to appear. Any grand theory in which our own regime is set to crowd out all the rest is a delusion.

John Gray

FIGURE 2.1   The delusion of grand theories, John Gray

Source: Gray, J. (2010) 'The invisible idealist', *The Independent* (Review), 20 August: 26.

The *Atheist Campaign* slogan reflects a null ontological hypothesis, and that conclusions should be based on probabilities not certainties. The null hypothesis would need to be disproved in order to show the existence of God.

FIGURE 2.2   A null ontological hypothesis

Source: British Humanist Association. Atheistcampaign.org

exercise of political power?" it seems to me we should answer the more fundamental questions: "What is a society in the first place?" and "What sort of power is political power anyhow?"[10] A despotic leader, who gives a speech promoting genocide against people she does not like, would seem to be exerting political power. But if, at the time of making the speech, she was alone and unobserved in a secure cell in a psychiatric hospital, would the same act still represent the use of power? What is political skill, and what is the basis for believing that some politicians have more of it than others? Political skill is never assessed and accredited as are the professional skills of doctors or architects. Are parliamentarians therefore just amateurs?

Ontological questions can be case-specific. If, as in Bhutan, a government aims to improve 'gross national happiness', how can we show that mass happiness exists?[11] How do we operationalize research to measure it and the success of happiness policies? If we claim that despotic leaders are responsible for their wrongdoing, in what way does responsibility exist? Neuroscientists argue whether indicators for responsibility can be found in the brain, and American defence lawyers are using this evidence to claim that some criminals are not responsible for their actions.[12] What is the "spirituality" that legitimizes "spiritual leadership", who are spiritual leaders responsible to, and is that responsibility different in some way? A neat test for existence is proposed by Philip Dick, 'Reality is that which, when you stop believing in it, doesn't go away.'[13]

Having considered if and why certain elements of a theory exist, the next question is, how do we come to know about them? **Epistemology** – the study of theories of knowledge[14] – asks:

1   What is the *origin* of the knowledge?
2   How did the *empirical research* (and other experience) and *reasoned arguments* contribute to creating the knowledge?
3   How *certain* (valid and error free) is the knowledge?
4   Was the knowledge created *critically* (sceptically)?

5 How has, or might, the knowledge *change* as other knowledge and understandings change?

6 To what degree would the knowledge be seen as *generally true* (as 'a theory').[15]

An epistemology of power would add the question, whose knowledge counts most and why? Figure 2.3 applies these questions to American and British claims that Iraq had Weapons of Mass Destruction (WMD) in 2003. By coincidence, distinctions attributed to former US Secretary of State, Donald Rumsfeld provide an informal but useful epistemological typology: 'There are things we know that we know. There are known unknowns. That is to say there are things that we now know we don't know. But there are also unknown unknowns. There are things we don't know we don't know.'[16] To assess the bases of any theoretical argument we might ask: what are the 'known knowns', the 'known unknowns' and the 'unknown unknowns'?

Ontology and epistemology are often confused. Roy Bhaskar calls this the 'epistemic fallacy'.[17] But although they are not the same, they are linked. If the basis of a study is that despots have caused fear in a population, or a theory holds that oppressive regimes rule by fear, how do we know epistemologically that mass fear exists, and in what form does it exist? There can be 'observer independent' biological indications of fear in individuals, but how can we claim that fear exists in whole populations? The concept of mass fear seems 'dependent' on the arguments of people like terrorists and political leaders, not on objective knowledge.

But there is also an epistemology about mass fear based on observation. Famously, when George Orwell's *War of the Worlds* was broadcast as a radio play in the US in 1938, it started in the form of seemingly serious news announcements, and there was evidence of mass panic among the population.[18] People evacuated certain locations. Clinically, this phenomenon has been theorized within the concept of 'mass sociogenic illness'. Clinical

---

Before the US invasion of Iraq in 2003, US President George Bush and British Prime Minister Tony Blair claimed to know that Iraq had weapons of mass destruction, but:

1 This knowledge *originated* mainly from the testimony of one Iraqi refugee, Rafid al-Janabi ("Curveball") who wanted to claim asylum in Germany.

2 This testimony was a small piece of hearsay evidence, and the claim about Iraq's WMD depended mainly on the *arguments* of Bush and Blair.

3 The knowledge was *uncertain*, and turned out to be wrong. A German psychologist had warned the US that the informant was psychologically unsound.

4 The *critical* appraisal by US and British intelligence analysts was that the knowledge was very unreliable, but this was ignored.

5 It was known that it was possible that the knowledge might have *changed* had UN weapons inspectors finished their inspection.

6 The knowledge was not *generally* accepted by all countries.

In 2011 al-Janabi admitted that he had lied to get rid of Saddam Hussein's regime.

FIGURE 2.3 The epistemology of "Iraq's Weapons of Mass Destruction"

Source: Chulov, M. (2011) 'Defector who triggered war on Iraq admits: "I lied about WMD"', *The Guardian*, 16 February: 1–5.

symptoms, such as nausea and headaches, can result from information alone – true or false – even if there is no physical cause.[19] Groups may also behave in certain ways when faced with information about a threat, for example by vacating a particular location because of a belief that it is contaminated. Arguments about the ontology of mass fear (does it exist?) can there-fore be based on the epistemology (knowledge from observation) of clinical symptoms, or social behaviour, which coincides with acts that are hypothesized as likely to induce mass fear (a perceived threat). But without an ontological understanding of mass fear, those clini-cal symptoms would be no more than visible biological conditions, which would simply be described in terms such as 'nausea' or 'headache'. In countries with oppressive regimes, such as Iran, mental health problems seem so common that people joke that "If you don't have a mental health problem here, you must have a mental health problem."

Ontology and epistemology should be considered throughout a whole study, particu-larly when data is being tested (C6.3) and 'analysed' (C7). They provide a reminder that any research should be critical (C2.5), and this starts with an explanation of the assump-tions underpinning the study (C4.1). Why is the existence of certain things, or certain "facts", taken for granted? There should be objective definitions explaining how key concepts and terms are used, and why. If it is assumed that presidents have the greatest political power in a country, how are presidential powers defined in the constitution? What did the (then) British Prime Minister, Margaret Thatcher, mean when she made the seemingly ontological assumption that 'There is no such thing as society'?[20] How did she, on the basis of epistemology, know? And what methods could have been used as a basis for gaining the evidence to support the claim?

Four theoretical approaches have explained and informed up-system research, and structure this chapter. The central approach considers the use of **power**, from the perspective of sociology and political science,[21] and an aspect of this specifically concerns **elites**. The third perspective aims to understand **leadership,** which often contributes to leadership training. The concept of 'up-system' must exist in relation to a 'down-system', and the fourth area of theory therefore covers **populace**. The idea of critical theory is then introduced, and key questions are identified which provide a starting point for planning new studies.

2.1 POWER

> **POWER**
>
> Ability to act upon or affect something strongly. Possession of control or command of others; dominion; government, sway; authority over. Personal or social ascendancy, influ-ence. Legal ability, capacity, or authority to act; delegated authority. (*OED*)

John Scott defines social power as 'an agent's intentional use of causal powers to affect the conduct of other participants in the social relations that connect them'.[22] The 'agent' can be an individual, group, organization or social institution such as government, military or justice system. Causation is central to the concept of power, and therefore to up-system research and analysis (C7.2). Michael Mann provides a sophisticated typology of power (Figure 2.4).[23] This framework is particularly relevant to global conceptualizations, and Mann discusses changes in the twenty-first century.[24] **Domination** has a similar meaning, although Weber distinguished between domination (*Herrschaft*) 'the likelihood that a command within a given organization or society will be obeyed' and power (*Macht*), 'the capacity of a social actor to impose his or her will on others despite resistance from them'.[25] Dobratz explores power from the perspective of western sociology and politics,[26] as do Draper and Kesselman.[27]

Throughout the histories of powerful people, there has often been a distinction between the exercise of power through **influence** or **coercion** – "carrot and stick". This dichotomy is found in the Chinese tradition of *li* and *fa*, ruling by influence and persuasion, as opposed to law and force.[28] Ibn Khaldun distinguished between legitimate 'leadership' and 'domination',[29] Plato talked of a 'blend of liberty and subjection',[30] and Machiavelli mentioned leaders being 'loved and feared'.[31] Elite theorist Pareto (below) distinguishes between 'lions', the governing elites who rule through decisive action and force, and 'foxes', non-governing elites who use more subtle persuasion and manipulation.[32] Gramsci mentions 'consent' and 'coercion'.[33] More recently, Joseph Nye reconceptualized the idea in terms of 'soft power' and 'hard power'.[34] In real life the dichotomy is less polarized, and better viewed as a continuum – from softer to harder – or as a balance of the two extremes – carrot *and* stick.

When power is exercised through influence rather than coercion, those exercising that power are likely to have greater legitimacy – their claim to power is generally accepted and/or successful. Max Weber (1864–1920)[35] determined that **legitimate authority** is

---

Power has two forms:

- *Distributional power*, used by individuals to control others.
- *Collective power*, used by groups, for example between companies or states.

It is exercised in two ways:

- *Extensive power*, through organising people across large regions, as through religion or a TNC.
- *Intensive power*, through a high commitment from a select group, such as terrorists.

And it is of two types:

- *Authoritative*, an order from a senior to a subordinate, as in an army.
- *Diffused*, networked power which seems natural, such as nationalistic feelings during war.

Michael Mann (1986)

FIGURE 2.4   The sources of power, Michael Mann

Source: Mann, M. (1986 and1993) *The Sources of Social Power* (2 vols). Cambridge: Cambridge University Press.

in three forms: traditional (custom, habit), charismatic (strength of personality) and legal rational-bureaucratic (agreed rules, regulations, policies, laws).[36] Weber seems to ignore another legitimizing force – success. Pye provides an Asian perspective, where successful economic development has been a legitimizing quality.[37] Wittfogel's historical study of legitimated authoritarianism, *Oriental Despotism*, proposes that the management of water was relevant.[38] In leadership studies, 'authenticity' describes personal legitimacy.[39] At a state level, legitimacy is discussed in relation to 'social contract', reflecting the ideas of Thomas Hobbes (1588–1679) about authoritarian monarchy, John Locke (1632–1704) on liberal monarchy and Jean-Jacques Rousseau (1712–1778) advocating liberal republicanism. Bruce Gilley developed an interesting methodology for a comparative assessment of legitimacy across 72 countries.[40] Subsequently the concept has been applied at a global level,[41] and legitimacy theory is increasingly relevant in relation to institutions and organizations.[42]

Weber believed that the amount of power within a specific population is limited. This 'constant sum' argument claims that if certain people hold power, and use it in their own interests, this is at the expense of the power of others.[43] Weber also analysed **bureaucracy** – stable, rule-based, hierarchical organizations within which individuals communicate and cooperate in order to implement the policies of leaders or elites.[44] This raises the question, does power exist within an organization or institution independently of the people in that entity, as suggested by terms such as "institutional racism"? Education systems are a major form of bureaucratic social control, particularly in authoritarian, socialist and religious contexts.[45] Education controls through shaping elite culture,[46] ideas and language, and by deploying violence against those who do not comply.[47] Weber also made significant contributions to methodology – 'interpretative sociology', 'antipositivism' and 'humanistic sociology' – which contribute to the qualitative approach to research. He argues that social research requires conceptual models – 'ideal types' – which generalize the essential characteristics of an aspect of human behaviour but are not a perfect description in any one case. An ideal typical view of "government" can be sufficient for using the term in a comparative analysis of state power across different nations, yet it embraces systems that may be very different in detail. Ferdinand Tönnies (1855–1936) evolved the idea in terms of a distinctive 'Normal Type'.[48]

Marxian analysis elaborates the 'constant sum' perspective. Building on the ideas of Karl Marx (1818–1883) and Friedrich Engels (1820–1885), power, in the form of the economic 'means of production', is seen to be appropriated by the elite 'bourgeoisie' for their own interests, to the detriment of the 'proletariat' or masses who are controlled and coerced through the economic infrastructure.[49] Marx proposed 'the materialist conception of history' ('historical materialism') as a methodological approach to the study of history, economics and society. This provides a framework for explaining specific causes of social change – based on classes, political systems and ideologies – in terms of how societies create and control the resources that are essential to sustain life.[50]

In contrast to the 'constant sum' perspective, Talcott Parsons (1902–1979) sees power as a 'variable sum' – that for some people to have power does *not* reduce the power of others. Power is dispersed and in the control of a whole population, which is then mobilized to achieve certain shared objectives.[51] He used the analogy of western political leaderships as a bank, into which the electorate 'deposits' power that can be withdrawn if it is not used properly. Michel Foucault (1926–1984) also sees power as dispersed and impersonal, and apparent through regulation, discipline and **surveillance**, which adapt populations to social structures.[52] Other theorists saw dispersed power in terms of a **pluralism** of strong organizations in Western democracies as a 'constant sum'.[53] These included Karl Mannheim, Robert A. Dahl and Arnold M. Rose who argues a 'multi-influence hypothesis'. From this perspective, power is located among many interest groups in society, not just within governments and other conspicuous institutions. This plurality includes religions, media, trades unions and civil society organizations. The 'constant sum' and 'variable sum' theories can both seem plausible in certain contexts, and might be possible to demonstrate in small-scale closed societies. But these assumptions are very hard to prove, especially in large complex globalizing populations.

Dahl asked a crucial question, how is power measured? [54] Analysis can be based on examining how powerful people control decision-making,[55] and decision-making styles.[56] *Rational choice theory* is used to investigate if decisions, both by leaders and the public, are rational, and if so can we predict how decisions will be made?[57] Critics from evolutionary psychology argue there is considerable "interference" with rational behaviour from instinctive drivers such as sex, status and altruism, and understanding these underlying influences may be more important. The broader difficulty, as John Urry pointed out, is that powerful people can prevent issues even reaching the point of a transparent decision or policy-making process.[58] Powerful people can 'agenda set' through information management, and make sure a process only culminates in "safe" decisions.[59] Government officials might ensure that decisions are based only on research that a government or company has commissioned in line with its own agenda.[60] Elite international organizations, such as the OECD, may function by apparently finding solutions to policy problems that they have previously constructed through a discourse that arises by using data that is easily available to them.[61]

Gramsci developed Marxian ideas in relation to the ideological apparatuses of the capitalist state. His vision of 'cultural ideological hegemony' implies that the ruling classes control and manipulate the **ideologies** and **consciousness** of the masses.[62] He tried to explain why revolution had not happened in European countries such as Italy, concluding that capitalism had created a palliative form of consensual power within which the masses assumed that their interests were met within a capitalist structure, and so remained passive. Lukes proposes a 'radical view' of power, which has three 'faces' – public, hidden, insidious – and 'dimensions' – decision-making, non-decision-making (power exerted through preventing decisions being taken) and shaping desires (the manipulation of group values through misinformation, social engineering and propaganda).[63] People are often unaware that their seemingly free views are the result of social engineering. Carroll Quigley's historical analyses of power and secret societies,[64] and ongoing arguments about **conspiracy theories**,[65] are related.

Power can be assessed by its **outcomes**. Westergaard and Resler claim that 'power is visible only through its consequences',[66] but causation can be contested, as with the use of the *Iraq Body Count* data to attribute blame for war crimes to US and British politicians.[67] Public administration may be assessed in terms of the 'public value' it creates.[68] Broader social change can be analysed using before-and-after methodologies to explain why a particular outcome occurred instead of possible alternatives.[69] Historian David Kynaston proposes a simple indicator, 'The supreme test of a democratic politician is whether he or she leaves our democracy in a better or worse state.'[70]

Many of the early **social change** theorists – Comte, Spencer, Hobhouse – saw change as synonymous with the general evolutionary progress of western society, an "onward and upward" grand narrative of European enlightenment. Other theorists have focused on less general explanations such as technology, economic power, industrialization or globalization. Gaventa provides a global model to embrace the 'spaces' – closed, invited, claimed/created – where change can happen.[71] The role of powerful people is sometimes not explicit in explanations of social change, and the *Global Social Change Research Project* provides a comprehensive discussion.[72]

Traditional theories of power usually assume that nation states provide natural boundaries ('research sites') for analysis.[73] **Cosmopolitanism** argues for an undivided view of humanity and power.[74] This can embrace a non-nationalistic view of power within nations, and also trans-national entities such as Trans-National Companies (TNCs) and International Non-Government Organizations (INGOs), and regional analysis for example within the EU, AU or CIS.[75] But as nation states are a recent invention, cosmopolitanism could be seen as a return to earlier conceptualizations of power based on large Empires – Ottoman, Persian and Roman – or within preindustrial groups such as nomads and maritime peoples, or global movements such as Islam or Buddhism.[76]

Technology is changing the nature of power relations and governance.[77] Vikas Nath discusses **digital governance** and sees power expressed through 'wider domain models' which make information more accessible, 'critical flow models' which expose malpractice, and more sophisticated 'interactive service' models which allow the public to track administrative procedures or contribute to decision-making.[78] There are also digital power groups, such as *Luiz Security*, which challenge state and other digital power elites through hacking and disrupting entities such as the CIA.[79] Nye explores the role of technology in the use of power in the future.[80]

Academic theories generally assume that power will always be anthropocentric – that human beings will be the locus of control. What of smart machines – **technocentric** power?[81] Will technology eventually be seen as embodying forms of power independently of human beings, like institutions, bureaucracies and organizations? If decision-making is the measure (above), machines already have significant power. Decisions about High Frequency Trading ('algorithmic trading') on stock markets are made by computers in seconds without human intervention. During the '2010 Flash Crash', the Dow Jones Industrial Average fell around 1000 points (9%), and recovered, within a few minutes, because of computer dynamics that are not fully understood.[82]

Comparing 'rules for robots' proposed in 1942 and 2011 is interesting, not least that the prohibition on harming humans has been diluted (Figure 2.5). Is that because weapons with decision-making robotic components are now in-production? Drones that

'Three laws of robotics', Isaac Asimov, *Runaround* (1942)	'Ethical principles for robot design', Engineering and Physical Sciences Research Council (UK) (2011)
1 A robot may not injure a human being or, through inaction, allow a human being to come to harm. 2 A robot must obey the orders given to it by human beings, except where such orders would conflict with the First Law. 3 A robot must protect its own existence as long as such protection does not conflict with the First or Second Laws.	1 Robots should not be designed solely or primarily to kill or harm humans. 2 Humans, not robots, are responsible agents. Robots are tools designed to achieve human goals. 3 Robots should be designed in ways that assure their safety and security. 4 Robots are artefacts; they should not be designed to exploit vulnerable users by evoking an emotional response or dependency. It should always be possible to tell a robot from a human. 5 It should always be possible to find out who is legally responsible for a robot.

FIGURE 2.5 Rules for robots

can 'track and recognize non-cooperative targets (people of interest) in urban or rural environments',[83] and 'Future Attribute Screening Technology' that could detect 'mal-intent' such as terrorist activities,[84] are seemingly being developed by the US military. Potentially, these could be attached to weapons that fire without human intervention. But the existence of these technologies could merely reflect a much older and less complicated source of political power – lies and propaganda. Whatever the truth, perhaps the most significant aspect of technocentric power is about technological vulnerability. The immediate problem is probably less what machines might do, and more what would happen if they stopped doing it. Like all sources of power, eventually technocentric power would collapse. The unknowns are why, how, when, and would humans still be around to witness it.

2.2 ELITES

> **ELITE**
>
> Select; the choice part of society. (*OED*)

Elites seem intrinsic to human society (C1.1). *Classical elite theory* is rooted in the work of Italian sociologists Vilfredo Pareto (1848–1923) and Gaetano Mosca (1858–1941), who argue that personal characteristics, such as organizational skill, create an inevitable distinction between select groups of powerful people and others. Mosca claimed that governing elites are morally and intellectually superior, as subsequently did Bottomore.[85]

In parallel, during this era arguments about social Darwinism[86] reflected a belief in the "survival of the fittest". These were formulated within Francis Galton's[87] view of **eugenics**,[88] and culminated in Nazi Germany.

The initial methodology for elite studies was not sophisticated. Mills' *Qualitative Methods and the Empirical Study of Elites* started to systemize research from the 1950s.[89] In 1971, Parry provided a chapter on 'Empirical tests of elitist theories' in *Political Elites,* which provides a simple typology of types of elite research:[90]

- institutional positions
- social background and recruitment of elites
- the 'reputational' approach
- decision-making processes

The 1974 *British Sociology Yearbook: Elites in Western Democracy*, contained a methodological note in the introduction.[91] The early strategies relied on texts – speeches, articles, diaries, letters and autobiographies. These often provided very biased sources about elite ideology, with the result that this 'social background data' accentuated certain aspects of elite theory and ignored others.[92] In 1968, Menges defined 'three important schools of elite analyses' and their methodological approaches – Marxist (historical–deductive), **stratification** theories (influence–reputation), pluralists (decision-making process and participants).[93] The early studies rarely considered influence on policy,[94] and more robust methodologies appeared during the 1980s. Domhoff edited a book on *Power Structure Research*, which included explanations of methodology.[95] Moysner and Wagstaffe's *Research Methods for Elite Studies* in 1987[96] was more substantial. Hertz and Imber provided a fieldwork perspective,[97] and an edited collection, *Studying Elites Using Qualitative Methods*,[98] and Walford applied the debates in relation to education.[99]

One little-known study from 1952, *The Comparative Study of Elites*, provided an international dimension, and the methods are explained clearly. The RADIR project set out to 'reveal the significance of the vast revolution that is reshaping our contemporary world', on the assumption that, 'by learning the nature of the elite, we learn much about the nature of society', and therefore, 'by determining what is happening to the elites of societies around the globe … we can test the underlying hypothesis … that a world revolution is under way during our epoch'. The studies addressed familiar themes: 'the manner in which "leadership" is chosen; the breadth of the social base from which it is recruited; the way it exercises decision-making power; the extent and nature of its accountability'.[100] The studies could provide useful baseline data for future research. Future developments may include updates of national elite studies including South America,[101] Russia,[102] Europe[103] and East Asia.[104]

'Elite pluralism' provides a critique of the perspectives of the early pluralist theorists (above) by arguing that the groups within a plurality are often themselves elite.[105] Dahl uses the term **polyarchy**.[106] Keller talks of 'strategic elites',[107] and Schumpeter of 'democratic elitism', and the debate is ongoing.[108] In *Political Elites*, Parry makes distinctions between political[109] and non-political elites, and elite domains which include military, business, bureaucratic and 'the establishment'. 'Genius' provides another dimension.[110] Parry explains the basic epistemological and ontological critiques of elite theory. How are we sure about:

- the scope and reality of influence
- the process of decision-making
- the 'boundaries' of elite power
- the 'costs' of influence?[111]

Although honed in relation to America and similar western societies, writers such as Bottomore suggest that the political elite theories seemed more applicable to the (then) communist regimes than to the western countries that they were meant to explain.[112] In modern democracies, political elites are changing[113] and conceptualizations such as **corporatism**[114] are becoming more central.

Robert Michels (1876–1936) claims that organizations inevitably develop **oligarchical** leadership and conservative goals, because the elites eventually expend more effort maintaining their positions than running the organization.[115] C. Wright Mills analysed American society in the 1950s and argues that certain institutions – corporations, military and government – have 'pivotal positions' in society.[116] Within these, elites hold the 'command posts' and together form a **power elite** which has common, perhaps 'conspiratorial', interests, and is often unaccountable. But the assumption is that these groups are cohesive and fixed, which may not be true. During the same era, Canadian John Porter challenged the view that Canada was non-elitist.[117] He contrasted his methods – a biographical and social origins approach – with Mills's interviewing and observation.[118] The concern to hold powerful companies to account in a practical way appeared in the form of consumer movements,[119] such as the *Consumer Activism Project*.[120] *Corporate Watch* has developed its own practical methodologies for up-system research.[121]

Floyd Hunter distinguished between a **power structure** – a network of organizations and roles within a population – and the 'power elites' who fill certain roles within power structures.[122] His **reputational** approach was based on a hypothesis that power stems from the reputation of individuals in a community. Power structure research evolved to address questions such as:

- What is the meaning of fragmentation and conflict within the dominant class?
- How do a few people maintain control, coordination and loyalty from the many?
- How can one explain the "successful" opposition by **subordinate** classes?
- How does the control of upper-class members in one organization relate to the control of other organizations and to the rest of society?[123]

Subsequent conceptualizations related to elite networks include 'elite interlocking' (networks of individuals with more than one elite position),[124] 'elite unity' (cohesiveness), **'inner circles'** (elites within elites),[125] female elites,[126] the 'trans-national capitalist class' (TNC elites),[127] and 'upper **echelon**' theory (how managers influence companies).[128]

Reputational research is also applied to organizations, elite networks,[129] and states,[130] and is evolving to embrace digital reputation. The concept of 'action branding' is based on the claim that 'brands are the sum of their actions'. Through the internet, reputation in many forms can be assessed through 'activity streams'.[131]

Bourdieu distinguished different forms of personal 'capital' – social, cultural, economic and symbolic assets that can facilitate social status and mobility.[132] Talking of the 'field of power' rather than 'elite', he assesses how power stems from relationships not just status. Bourdieu[133] and Passeron[134] and Bowles and Gintis[135] analysed the hierarchical nature of social institutions and the **reproduction of elites**, principally through education systems. They argued that schools themselves were based on the structures and values of capitalist workplaces, reinforcing ideas of unquestioning obedience and systematic thinking. Cookson provides a similar American perspective.[136] While reproduction theory may explain how elites emerge as a group, individual stories often entail circumstance and luck – an opportunity to gain power may arise because senior people suddenly resign, become ill or die.

Haas assesses the **epistemic communities** of elites – those who believe a particular narrative of events. What are the expert groups, such as university departments, which define and create the knowledge that elite decision-makers use?[137] A **community of practice** describes a group who share a profession or trade,[138] linked by 'social presence', 'motivation' and 'collaboration'. They may have no formal base, and perhaps only interact through discussion boards or newsgroups. Scientific communities have been described as 'Invisible colleges',[139] a concept that goes back to the network that created the British *Royal Society*. 'Trans-epistemic communities' have relationships that go beyond the obvious boundaries.[140]

Geographical perspectives consider **elite spaces**,[141] particularly in local contexts.[142] Interests include new and emerging places, dispersed places, regenerating places, maintaining/maturing places, the politics of time and hybrid elites.[143] Contrasts might be made with 'placeless' leaders and elites, who represent migrant, nomadic and stateless communities, such as the Roma. Leadership training encompasses 'global nomadic leaders',[144] who move between trans-national companies and have little affiliation to a particular place, which may be reflected in a reduced sense of responsibility for locality. The approach appears recent, but studies of animals have related leadership to territory since the 1940s.[145]

While the early elite theorists described what they saw as an inevitable social phenomenon, arguments about **meritocracy** seemingly explain change and social mobility. Michael Young first coined the term for his book *The Rise of the Meritocracy*, in which he contrasted aristocracies and gerontocracies with a more equitable system based on merit.[146] The seventh century Chinese Imperial College is usually seen as the first example of a meritocratic education system (C1), but this was only meritocratic within an elite and literate upper class. Even modern, universal meritocratic education systems have biases that favour certain people, for example those who can pass a particular type of exam. Lee talks of South Korean leaders as 'memory elites', within a 'distorted meritocracy', because they gain their positions through having a cognitive style that suits rote learning and a memory-based exam system.[147]

The role of elites in **transition** was a significant interest within colonial regimes, but principally to maintain control (C1.1). Transitions and the fall of despots towards the end of the Cold War,[148] global dynamics,[149] and the concepts of 'humanitarian intervention' and 'regime change' have presented further perspectives about supporting favoured elites. Questions include: Who are the (actual/potential) new elites, how do they relate to traditional elites, what are their motives, how do they respond to global dynamics, what are their goals and how do they achieve them, and what is their media credibility? The role of business elites has received less attention than political.[150]

Notions of **global elites** focus on the global misuse of power. Rothkopf's assessment of the 'superclass' shows the concentrations of power, and the role of elite networks such as universities.[151] Dorling conceptualizes recent elites in relation to injustice and inequality. He talks of five beliefs that are used to legitimize modern elitism – 'elitism is efficient, exclusion is necessary, prejudice is natural, greed is good, and despair is inevitable'. Elites seemingly assume that around 20% of a modern labour force needs to be excluded from mainstream life, and that a dislike of immigrants, poor people and refugees is justifiable. He perceives these attitudes as explaining the 'new injustices' and inequality.[152] John Pilger considers new ruling classes, with his usual acute insight.[153]

Recently it has been argued that **evolutionary theories** of dominance and status are central to understanding power groups. Steven Pinker explains an obvious example: 'in all societies people recognize a kind of dominance hierarchy, particularly among men. High-ranking men are deferred to, have greater voice in group decisions, usually have a greater share of the group's resources, and always have more wives, more lovers, and more affairs with other men's wives.'[154] Evolutionary perspectives contribute to understanding why certain people do not trust decision-makers,[155] whether political orientations are genetically transmitted,[156] and relationships between political attitudes and physiological traits.[157]

Pareto describes the **decline** of elites, due to complacency and laziness, as the 'circulation of elites', which reflects Polybius's *anacyclosis* (C1.2). Khaldun distinguished between leadership and domination, and claimed that domination led to decline – 'as soon as domination begins to replace leadership in a dynasty, the *asabiyah* [solidarity] gradually loses its vigor and its binding force and eventually dies out' (Figure 1.6). Marx argues, on the basis of 'dialectical materialism', that the bourgeois capitalist class embodied the seeds of its own destruction.[158] Toynbee provides a more recent historical perspective: 'First the Dominant Minority attempts to hold by force – against all right and reason – a position of inherited privilege which it has ceased to merit; and then the Proletariat repays injustice with resentment, fear with hate, and violence with violence … '[159] He identifies stages of social evolution – genesis, growth, time of troubles, universal state and disintegration. Anthropology provides studies of the fall of specific elites.[160] Mosca argued that elites achieved and maintained power because they could mobilize and act more quickly than the uncoordinated masses.[161] But this is now in question, as e-networked populations are changing the relationship through extensive exchange information about the use and abuse of power.[162] Often now, these e-masses can mobilize faster than the elites.[163] The "leaderless revolutions" since 2000, which are facilitated by ICT, seem to be creating new elite dynamics and power shifts.[164] In intellectual domains, what will be the future role of the cyber elites – the '**digerati**'?[165]

Systems science provides an analytical approach to assess the **collapse** of whole societies. Joseph Tainter argues that overdependence on energy appears to be a reason for collapse, but that diminishing returns on an investment in social complexity is more significant. As leaders become better at solving past problems, they become less adept at solving new ones.[166] Carrol Quigley links decline of civilizations with power groups,[167] Joseph Tainter explores energy theory and collapse,[168] Jared Diamond discusses the role of leadership in determining the collapse of societies,[169] and McAnany and Yoffee develop their discussion covering resilience and ecological vulnerability.[170] Proposals that global 'survival research' should become a core discipline, aim to mitigate the large scale collapse of modern societies and the decline of humanity as an elite species.[171]

In 1377, Khaldun concluded that: 'Prestige is an accident that affects human beings. It comes into being and decays inevitably.'[172] From the study of elites throughout history, the only thing we know for sure is that, at some point, they (and the gods and myths they invent) all come to an end. Might the next phase of theorization embrace a more transient view of elites, and Andy Warhol's prediction that, 'In the future, everyone will be world-famous for 15 minutes'?[173]

2.3 LEADERSHIP

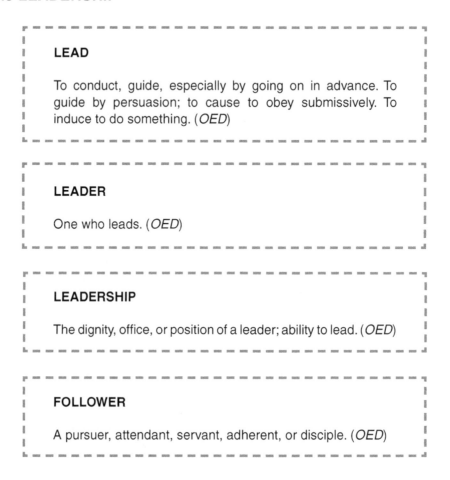

LEAD

To conduct, guide, especially by going on in advance. To guide by persuasion; to cause to obey submissively. To induce to do something. (*OED*)

LEADER

One who leads. (*OED*)

LEADERSHIP

The dignity, office, or position of a leader; ability to lead. (*OED*)

FOLLOWER

A pursuer, attendant, servant, adherent, or disciple. (*OED*)

In parallel with the generalized theories of power and elites, are studies of the relationships between specific leaders and specific followers. Although there are Egyptian hieroglyphics for 'leadership', leader' and 'follower',[174] in the *Oxford English Dictionary* the English word 'leadership' is only traced back to the nineteenth century. But by 1993, Rost was able to analyse 221 definitions, concluding that, 'neither the scholars nor the practitioners have been able to define leadership with precision, accuracy, and conciseness so that people are able to label it correctly when they see it happening or when they engage in it.'[175] A central difficulty is distinguishing between leadership and management. *Bass & Stogdill's Handbook of Leadership*[176] and the later *Bass Handbook of Leadership* have provided seminal discussions of twentieth century perspectives.[177] Stogdill identified the methods in use by 1948:

- observation of behaviour in group situations
- choice of associates (voting)
- nomination or rating by qualified observers
- selection (and rating or testing) of persons occupying positions of leadership
- analysis of biographical and case history data[178]

Northouse provides a concise survey,[179] contemporary perspectives are covered in the *Sage Handbook of Leadership,*[180] and Chemers neatly explains the changing 'fashions' of leadership theory.[181] Many texts apply theories in the form of self-improvement manuals, some e-based, to create better personal leadership skills.[182]

Traditional leadership studies usually addressed the age-old question – are leaders born or made – are they the result of nature or nurture – are their qualities 'ascribed' or 'achieved'? The trait theories argued leaders are born; the situational and contingency perspectives that they are made. Only later was the relationship with followers considered.

The **trait** theories[183] tried to identify distinctive personal characteristics of those born to be "great men", defined by Hegel in 1820: 'The great man of the age is the one who can put into words the will of his age, tell his age what its will is, and accomplish it.'[184] Plutarch's *Parallel Lives*, is one of the earliest examples (C1). Thomas Carlyle's *Heroes and Hero Worship* (1841) considered a range of physical and intellectual qualities displayed by powerful men. Francis Galton's *Hereditary Genius* (1869) attributed leadership qualities to heredity and family influence. Subsequent studies tried to find the distinguishing characteristics of leaders[185] including physical, social background and economic status. They assessed mental aspects (intellectual and social ability, emotional stability) and personality traits (conscientiousness, confidence, obsession, narcissism, pragmatism, integrity, charisma and ideology). Harold Lasswell identified the self-destructive attributes of political and business leaders in *Psychopathology and Politics* (1930),[186] and provided a general theory of political personality, which made the link with power in *Power and Personality* (1948).[187] The discussion of the "characteristic" of being female was usually overlooked in general texts on leadership until the 1970s, and then conclusions were often negative.[188] But subsequently ideas such as the 'glass ceiling'[189] became widely discussed in feminist literature.[190] 'Role congruity theory' explains the problem in terms of female leadership not matching social expectations.[191]

In contrast, the **situational** theories, such as those of Herbert Spencer (1884)[192] claimed that history created powerful people – less often did the powerful create history. Fiedler developed a **contingency** model which contrasts style and situation.[193] Among the difficulties of these approaches are the questions, how do we define the causal effects of 'situation', and what is 'contingent' on what? The concept of '**situated** leadership'[194] (rather than 'situational') embraces the idea that situation creates leadership and leadership creates situation, and that unpredictable crises also give rise to leadership opportunities.[195] Case studies, such as that of Nelson Mandela, show that actual leaders do not fit the theories so neatly when we look at the broader picture (Figure 2.6). Western perspectives ignore the role of chance, or fate, in creating leaders. Arguably, often it is just a random selection process.

Non-western traditions for creating leaders have rarely been considered in the general leadership literature, for example those concerning the Tibetan Dalai Lama.[196] The 'mindstream' of a deceased Dalai Lama is thought to have been transferred to the intended body of the next, and the Nechung Oracle searches for the young child who is the Lama's reincarnation. High Lamas may visit a holy lake and watch for a sign, wait for a vision, or follow the direction of the smoke of a cremated Dalai Lama. Having found the child, they apply tests such as showing various objects to see if the boy will identify

Nelson Mandela was president of South Africa from 1994 to 1999, and was awarded the Nobel peace prize in 1993.

His great-grandfather was the King (*Inkosi Enkhulu*) of the Thembu people, his father was chief of the town of Mvezo and a member of the Privy Council of the *Inkosi* clan, and his mother was from the royal family of the *Mpemvu Xhosa* clan. When his father died, Mandela was informally adopted by Jongintaba Dalindyebo, a Thembu King. Inheriting his father's Privy Council position, he moved to Healdtown in 1937, and attended a Wesleyan college in Fort Beaufort where most of the Thembu royal family were educated.

Mandela inherited an elite status and, it seems, the **traits** of a leader, which were reinforced by an **elite education**. His family tradition helped him to gain power within the ANC, becoming leader of the armed wing, Umkhonto we Sizwe.

Yet had the **situation** of the Apartheid system not existed, there would probably not have been an oppositional elite in the form of the ANC. His legitimacy would not have been enhanced by spending 27 years in prison, and his knowledge of law would not have been so good because in prison he studied law by correspondence at London University. Had President F.W. de Klerk not initiated the end of Apartheid, Mandela may have died as an almost unknown 'terrorist' in prison. His eventual international status was **contingent** upon de Klerk's decision.

FIGURE 2.6   Are leaders born or made? Nelson Mandela

Source: Photo by permission of the Department of Government Communication and Information System, Republic of South Africa, Pretoria.

those that belonged to the previous Dalai Lama. If there is more than one possible candidate, names cards are put in an urn and one is drawn out, in public, like a lottery. The present Dalai Lama promises to leave written instructions about whether or not he is to be reincarnated, based on an assessment of the attitudes of the Chinese government. The overall process can be taken at face value, but if analysed from a functionalist perspective, it is also an effective system for creating a new leader randomly. It ensures absolute legitimacy, and avoids any claims to power from descendants and influence from ancestors. It provides for selective tests that will to some extent measure intelligence, embraces the need for intensive leadership education, and the *real politick* of changing political contexts. Is a Dalai Lama therefore "born or made"?

By the 1950s, it was being argued that people who are leaders in one context may not be leaders in another, and so the causal link between traits and leadership depended more on the situation in which an individual operated. In the 1980s that argument was again challenged, as different methodologies seemed to find that certain individuals did, as trait theory had proposed, assume leadership roles in a variety of contexts, and that the link with distinctive traits seemed strong.[197] This still did not accommodate the likelihood that successful leaders need to be adaptable and flexible, and therefore static personal qualities cannot explain leadership in a fast changing world. Theories such as the 'leader attribute pattern approach' emerged, which consider integrated combinations of personal qualities,[198] including 'sensemaking'.[199] But the earlier criticisms continued, along with the obvious question, do the relevant traits change over time?[200]

The practical dilemma posed by both the trait and situational theories was that, if they demonstrated that leaders are born or are a product of circumstance, this implies that leadership training may be futile. Behavioural theorists provided a seemingly more positive alternative, because behaviour can be taught and modified. Theorists examined the degree to which 'styles' such as 'authoritarian', 'democratic' and 'laissez-faire' achieve desired results[201] and the efficacy of humour.[202] One approach culminated in a 'managerial grid model' based on five leadership styles.[203]

Exploring the relationship between leaders and followers, functionalist theories consider how leaders achieve results by enhancing group effectiveness and cohesion,[204] including 'mood' and 'emotions'.[205] The **transactional** theories focused on the negotiated relationship between leaders and followers – the use of rewards and reprimands, salaries and sanctions – to encourage followers to achieve the goals of the leaders and organization.[206] A **transformational** approach takes broader perspectives about changing situations – how leaders motivate followers to be effective and efficient to achieve social and organizational change.[207] The application of 'social identity' theory links the perception of leaders and the social cohesion of followers,[208] and the notion of 'authentic leadership' considers aspects such as the 'true self'.[209] Interestingly, discussion of the relevance of the self-perception of leaders seems rare.[210] Gardener usefully distinguishes different forms of relationships, those of 'direct' leaders – like Churchill, Florence Nightingale, Ban Ki-moon – and 'indirect' – such as Albert Einstein, Michael Jackson, Tracey Emin or John Lennon.[211] Grint discusses a 'constitutive' approach, within which leaders 'actively shape our interpretation of the environment' and 'try and persuade us that their interpretation is … correct.' He concludes that leadership is an 'art' – based on identity, persuasive communication, strategic vision and organizational tactics – not a science.[212] Peck considers 'performance' within leadership – the significance of enactment, narrative and audience,[213] and Ladkin exemplifies this in relation to musicians.[214] Other perspectives include 'strategic',[215] 'charismatic', 'virtual' and 'critical' leadership.[216]

Ideas of 'shared',[217] 'collaborative',[218] 'collective', or 'distributed' leadership[219] seem to question the assumption that leadership should stem from individuals. In practice, the concepts often reflect delegation of responsibility, or **decentralization** or **subsidiarity** which aims for decisions to be taken at the lowest possible level in an organization, region or country. The result is not a leaderless system (C1.1), simply an efficient distribution of power and responsibility. An idealistic vision of non-hierarchical leadership stems from Greenleaf's 1970s vision of 'servant leadership'[220] within which modest leaders lead with the aim of serving others better and putting others first, not of increasing their own power, as is implied by the term 'civil servant'. They should exhibit qualities such as collaboration, trust, empathy, foresight and ethical use of power. But leadership will always embody a power relationship of some sort. At the very least, it means that one person has the power to give away their power to others.

A pragmatic aspect of leadership theory focuses on assessing and predicting *leadership effectiveness*, reflecting the idea that it is less important how and why leaders gain and maintain their power, and more important to assess how effectively they do, or might, use it.[221] Understanding the causal links between what leaders do, and the results, is the most significant factor.[222] Since the 1950s, understandings of effectiveness have translated into personality[223] selection tests for job interviews for senior executives,[224] such as 'leaderless group discussions'.[225]

As leadership theories burgeoned they became unwieldy to apply in leadership training. So writers often provided synopses in the form of paradigms and models. Adair's 'three circles approach' derived from the need to explain his ideas clearly while teaching military history at the British Royal Military Academy at Sandhurst during the 1970s. Viewed from the perspective of motivating followers, he encapsulated leadership in terms of *task*, *team* and *individual* members of the team.[226] Combining situation and personality, Tannenbaum and Schmidt's 'leadership continuum' describes seven 'styles' from highly boss-centred to highly subordinate-centred. They claim that personality dictates the degree of authority a leader permits subordinates to exercise. But the theory was not based on research.[227] House and Podsakoff systemized group theories of charismatic, transformational and visionary leadership in their 'outstanding leadership theory'.[228]

Behavioural and situational theories were combined and provided optimism that skills could be taught and learned effectively, while accepting the reality that circumstances could thwart even the best trained leader. Stout's IDEAL model is based on teachable Leadership Capital 'capacities' (vision, values, wisdom, courage, trust and voice), in relation to the 'leadership conditions' necessary for these capacities to operate (place, period, position and amenable people).[229] Carmazzi's 'environmental theory' of leadership considers how group dynamics change the 'situation' and create rewarding environments which fulfil the emotional needs of followers, to optimize efficiency. Carmazzi's website claims, in similar style to many others, 'Understand the Psychology of Your Environment and You have the POWER to CHANGE YOUR WORLD!'[230]

It was concluded that during the twentieth century there was surprisingly little theorization of **political** leadership,[231] and of leadership within democratic theory.[232] The importance of leadership was often acknowledged, but not explored. In 1977 Paige provided a whole chapter on 'the surprising lack of disciplinary focus',[233] although an excellent account of leadership in South Korea had appeared a year earlier.[234] Paige argued that the topic was relevant, and provided a comprehensive methodological discussion. Yet, at the start of this century, Elcock's conclusion was similar.[235] Korosenyi has examined the lack of systematic analysis and the reasons for this.[236] Since the 1980s the literature has increased,[237] models of political leadership emerged,[238] and psychological approaches developed.[239] Leadership in local government and public services has received attention,[240] where trends are identified towards more executive and less committee-based decision-making.[241]

As in elite studies, a geographical perspective considers leadership and place.[242] Many forms of leadership emerge in response to local circumstances. Barker provides a distinctive perspective in terms of the leadership of **social movements**, which he frames in relation to 'personal resources', 'structural resources' and 'context'.[243] 'Personal' and 'context' reflect the familiar 'traits' and 'situation'. But the 'structural' aspect is distinct, as social movements cannot take these resources for granted. Fundraising and maintaining this operational base is difficult and central to their work because 'followers' are not tied into a relationship as they are in a company. This 'resource' could quickly disappear if public mood and perceptions of an organization change.

Commercial concerns dominated much of the twentieth century leadership literature, and there has been relatively little questioning of immoral behaviour. At the end of the twentieth century, a small literature on bad leadership started to emerge. Marcia Whicker talks of **toxic leaders** who abuse their power and make relationships and circumstances progressively worse.[244] Lipman-Blumen developed this idea in terms of followers being attracted to authoritative or dominating corporate and political leaders, which fulfils a psychological need in many people. She sees toxic leaders as more than inefficient and as having 'dysfunctional personal characteristics' and 'destructive behaviors' which 'inflict reasonably serious and enduring harm' in many spheres.[245] Barbara Kellerman created a useful typology of the behaviour of bad leaders.[246] They can be:

- *incompetent* – do not sustain positive action and create positive change.
- *rigid* – are inflexible, and do not accommodate new ideas, information and social change.
- *intemperate* – lack self-control, and followers do not question this.
- *callous* – are uncaring or unkind, especially towards junior colleagues.
- *corrupt* – ignore ethical norms, and put themselves first.
- *insular* – have little concern for the wellbeing of those outside their group or organization.
- *evil* – use pain and fear as instruments of power.

Turknett's 'Leadership character model' provides a framework for assessing character more generally in terms of 'respect' (empathy, no-blame, humility, emotional control) and 'responsibility' (accountability, self-confidence, courage, holistic focus).[247]

Price provides an ethical development of the toxic leader theories, arguing that bad leaders know what is morally wrong, but that the 'justificatory force of leadership' engenders a self-deceit that they are exceptions and that the standards may not apply to them, or to others, in particular circumstances.[248] Janis identifies the problem of '**group-think**' – that leadership groups often make mistakes because they exclude information that challenges their view.[249] Dominic Johnson takes an evolutionary view of how leaders arise, also seeing self-deceit as central. His 'positive illusions' theory holds that leaders come to power through a key adaptive psychological trait – overconfidence. The result is a decision-making style reflecting overestimation of the strength of one's personal following, underestimation of the opposition and neglect of inconvenient information.[250] The relationship between power and hypocrisy was investigated by Lammers who found that 'power makes people stricter in moral judgment of others – while being less strict of their own behaviour', but not if the power base was illegitimate.[251] Other studies show that powerful people are more confident about risk-taking.[252]

Bad leadership can arise from a chain of events. 'Sunk-cost fallacy' ('Concord fallacy')[253] provides further explanations. Within endeavours that require front-loaded investment, economic or personal status, there can come a point at which leaders will not stop a project, even if all rational evidence proposes that continuing will entail greater tangible costs than benefits. Leaders and decision-makers enter a state of denial, and "throw good money after bad" because "now there's no turning back". The building of Concord was a seminal example. At the extreme end, the bad leadership debate considers why people become **tyrants**.[254] Do leaders carry out violence and genocide because of a lack of empathy with others,[255] or because power increases dehumanization – powerful people more readily perceive humans as objects or animals?[256] A latent question is whether it is defensible to remove a very bad leader by force. Is 'tyrannicide' morally acceptable – the killing of a tyrant such as England's Charles I, Nazi Germany's Hitler, or Iraq's Saddam Hussein?[257] Banks argues that 'dissent' is important to prevent leadership failure and abuse of power.[258] Combining these ideas, an explanatory theory of 'cumulative lock-in' proposes that if, when solving a problem in an uncertain context, leaders make 'belief-based decisions', rather than 'evidence-based decisions', these precipitate 'a string of interrelated factors, which create a situation whereby turning back becomes increasingly more difficult'. Eventual deceit precipitates 'significant challenges' from others, because human beings have an evolutionary instinct to respond strongly against cheating (Figure 2.7).[259]

Leadership ethics were central to early European and Chinese theories of leadership (C1.3), yet there is remarkably little work on contemporary leadership ethics. Ciulla's *Ethics at the Heart of Leadership* is a useful exception.[260] Lammers and Stapel have assessed whether power influences moral thinking.[261] In professions such as medicine and dentistry, codes of conduct create personal responsibility for correct behaviour. Most of the business-oriented leadership literature focuses on the characteristics and capabilities of

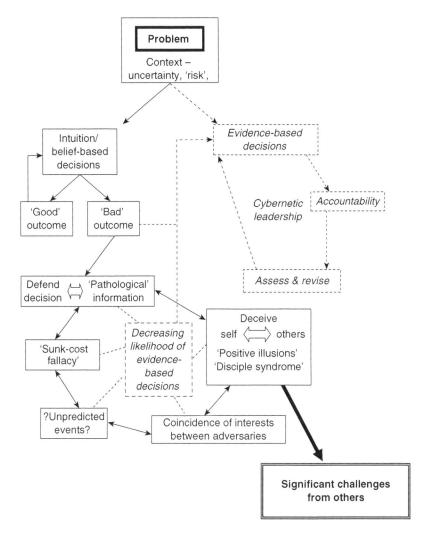

FIGURE 2.7 How leaders fail – cumulative lock-in

Source: Williams, C. (2006) *Leadership Accountability in a Globalizing World*. London: Palgrave Macmillan. p 110–19.

the individual leader, yet ethics become generalized under the heading 'corporate social responsibility'[262] which suggests that ethics may not entail personal responsibility. In contrast, the idea of leadership **accountability** discusses the practical implementation of ethics and takes a personal perspective.[263] A central outcome of leadership research and theorization concerns leadership 'qualities', but these qualities do not intrinsically describe morally good behaviour. A significant example of 'qualities and values which constitute … the personality of the individual' fitted to become a good leader comes from Europe: 'honour', 'loyalty', 'ready for service and sacrifice', 'courage', 'bravery', 'straightforwardness', 'truthfulness' and 'honesty'. These were the qualities for the ruling elite of Hitler's Germany – the *Fuhrerprizip*.[264]

Understandings of **global leadership**[265] often aim to increase the skills of business leaders in a multi-cultural[266] or international context.[267] The GLOBE research project is adapting methodologies to serve this interest.[268] Global perspectives also explain leadership in contemporary contexts of global risk[269] and uncertainty, and considers issues such as how national, commercial and religious leaders exercise their power globally. International ('between nations') leadership, is a distinct aspect, which includes the role of international organizations such as the United Nations (UN) and the law of the international civil service.[270] These and other relevant international norms can inform theoretical codes of international and global leadership standards.[271] 'Global ethics'[272] are increasingly reflected in the work of civil society organizations such as *Amnesty International* and *Human Rights Watch*.

Early studies of leadership, which include the perspective of **followers**, asked questions such as:

- Why are the individuals in this group?
- Why do they accept direction of their activities?
- Why does a leader arise?
- How is the leader to be characterized?
- How does the leader arise?
- Why does the leader lead?
- What is the function of the leader?
- Can all leaders be conceptualized in the same way?[273]

Understanding leader–follower 'cognitions' subsequently become relevant.[274] There is an assumption that down-system populations have static roles and a single "for or against" persona, which does not change, and that leaders and elites never become followers and masses. But as Hughes points out, 'The question *What is leadership?* cannot be separated from the question *What is followship?* There is no single line dividing them, they merge.'[275] The same is true of 'cultural commercial elites' – 'they cannot be effectively studied apart from their relationship to their key audiences.'[276] Theories such as those describing 'transactional' and 'transformational' leadership describe roles, not identifiable individuals who intrinsically fulfil those roles.[277] A useful distinction is made by Lee, who distinguishes between 'accepting followers' and 'questioning followers', and reminds us that they can all create and control human and other 'resources' to exert power. This 'does not describe particular individuals, simply behaviour in relation to particular issues' and it is necessary to know whether or not the accepting–questioning role results from coercion.[278]

Although most leadership theory is oriented towards **leadership training**, there has been little analysis of the teaching, assessment and accreditation of leadership. An interest within the psychological literature stems from the 1950s.[279] Leadership education is evident in four forms: elite-creating national systems of education, specialist university courses and institutions, in-house pre- and in-service training, and mid-career tuition at specialist institutions.[280] The US has run an International Visitor Leader Programme (IVLP) since 1940, which seems to have been very successful at identifying young people from outside the US, who end up in senior political positions.[281] But is it possible to identify future leaders for specialist training, or is an impression of success created by noticing a few high profile successes, and ignoring the countless numbers that simply disappear? Howard Prince, the founding dean of the *Jepson School of Leadership Studies* concludes, 'nowhere can we find a complete theory of how to develop leaders.'[282] Is leadership like a profession, and if so how should we distinguish between professional leaders and non-professional leaders? Does leadership training actually create better leaders?

The business-oriented leadership literature of the last 50 years is vast, and hard to assess. It is often hard to distinguish between significant theoretical discussions, and simple paradigms intended to create the bases of leadership training. Do leadership theories embody increasingly subtle understandings of very complex human phenomena, or do they represent cycles of pendulum swings and recombination reflecting the simple traditional question – born or made – presented under novel terminology? What have the advances been since books such as Browne and Cohn's comprehensive and research-based *The Study of Leadership* in 1958?[283] Grint concludes that, 'most leadership research has tended to be either a review of successful leaders or grounded in survey approaches. Either way, the results are often informative but not definitive.'[284]

2.4 POPULACE

POPULACE

The mass of people of a community, as distinct from the titled, wealthy, or educated classes, a mob, the rabble. (*OED*)

CROWD

A number of persons gathered so closely together as to press upon each other. (*OED*)

MASS

An aggregate in which individuality is lost. (*OED*)

Conceptualizations of power, elites and leaders are intrinsically in relation to a down-system population that has less power – the populace, proletariat, masses, constituents, workers, crowds, poor and powerless, or identifiable followers (C2.4). For up-system studies, it is often relevant to understand how powerful people perceive amorphous down-system groups. Usually it is in terms of control.[285] There are also theories about oppositional power groups, a related perspective concerning **victims** of abuse of power and poverty, and discussion of the relationships between up-system and down-system groups based around mass communication.

The need for powerful people to understand the power of the populace in order to **control** them – because the masses are perceived as a threat – pervades history. The fear of **ochlocracy** – 'mob rule', 'majoritarianism' – can be traced back to ancient Greek philosophy such as the *Histories* of Polybius, the Talmud, and concerning Rome in Gibbon's *Decline and Fall of the Roman Empire*. In Rome, at one time the word *demokratia* – 'rule of the people' – carried the negative connotation of mob rule, as did J.S. Mill's 'tyranny of the majority'.[286]

This perspective emerged strongly in the nineteenth century, prompted by the experience of the French Revolution (1789–1799). Hegel argued the necessary role for 'great men', in *Philosophy of Right* (1820): 'Public opinion contains all kinds of falsity and truth, but it takes a great man to find the truth in it. The man who lacks sense enough to despise public opinion expressed in gossip will never do anything great.'[287] The perception that elites should fear the power of the masses was fuelled by works such as Charles Mackay's *Extraordinary Popular Delusions and the Madness of Crowds* (1841),[288] and Gustav Le Bon's, *The Crowd: A Study of the Popular Mind* (1896). His explanations included 'contagion' and 'ancestral savagery'.[289] World War I inspired books taking a more scientific approach such as Totter's *Instincts of the Herd in Peace and War*,[290] and McDougall's *The Group Mind* (1920).[291] Sigmund Freud's *Group Psychology and the Analysis of the Ego* (1922) asked: Do crowds have a psychological stance that, as individuals, those people might not have? The concern about crowds continued throughout Europe, for example the Spanish perspective in Ortega y Gasset's *The Revolt of the Masses* (1929),[292] and the German one in Erik von Kuehnelt-Leddihn's (pseudonym, Francis Stuart Campbell) *The Menace of the Herd* (1943).[293] Studies of the characteristics of leadership and groups were often carried out on children, evaluating aspects such as 'behavioural contagion',[294] and determining characteristics such as 'the tyrant', 'the seducer', 'the hero' and 'the bad influence'.[295]

The 1850s brought another perspective, **degeneracy**, which implied that, for biological reasons, the "weakest" of the populace were likely to threaten the whole of society. A French doctor, Bénédict Morel, based his arguments on the proto-evolutionary theories of Jean-Baptiste Lamarck, who claimed that criminality and other degenerate behaviour was inherited. In 1890, Max Nordau's popular book *Degeneration* linked the argument to the arts. These views about social decline[296] underpinned the concept of eugenics, in USA and Europe, which culminated in the holocaust and Nazi death camps, and reflect a continued desire to create **utopian** society.[297]

Hitler's manipulation of the military and the masses before and during World War II[298] produced further perspectives about crowd control and following orders. One of the most controversial studies was Milgram's research in 1963 into whether people would follow the orders of an authority figure, even if that seemed to cause intense pain to an innocent person.[299] Milgram was well known for designing experiments based on events he observed in the world. Having seen Nazi Adolf Eichmann defend his war crimes on the basis that he was "only following orders", Milgram used actors feigning the pain of electrocution, as the research subjects, called 'teachers', were ordered to administer apparently lethal electric shocks when they gave 'wrong' answers. He found that most – 65% – of the 'teachers' would comply.

Other mass movements inspired renewed interest in crowd behaviour, for example the French student protests of the 1970s.[300] These discussions merged into the fields of group psychology,[301] crowd psychology[302] and social psychology, often emphasizing polarized perspectives of "bad crowds"[303] and "good crowds".[304] A self-evident methodological critique of traditional approaches comes from convergence theory which argues that crowds are not a random sample of a population. They behave in specific ways because those with specific outlooks converge into specific crowds,[305] and communication is central.[306] Recent perspectives acknowledge rational, moral and organized behaviour even within violent protest groups.[307]

The discussions of **oppositional** power embrace studies of protest movements and activists. This form of power is usually fuelled by a perception of wrongdoing by governments or large commercial organizations, and a shared perception of moral purpose, particularly among students.[308] Movements have a long history, the English suffragettes for example. But academic discussions were, like the movements themselves, often marginalized. The student protests from the 1960s – in South Korea, France and later America – created a renewed interest under the heading 'new social movements',[309] and more recently 'civil society organizations'. 'Movements' may, or may not, be organized, are often small and situational, and are sometimes poorly coordinated.[310] The usual aim of such groups is accountability.[311] Noam Chomsky encourages a broad critical perspective, and advocates that people should not be complacent or fatalistic about their position.[312] Journalists such as John Pilger provide the evidence.[313] Social networking sites provide increasing amounts of front-line data from within street protest groups.[314] Explanations for the **decline** of oppositional groups embrace factors such as success (no need to continue), internal weakness or conflict, leaders being co-opted into the mainstream, repression and being absorbed by the mainstream.[315]

The industrial revolution gave rise to assessments of mass **poverty** and the impact of industrialization on the populace in Europe. Engel's *The Condition of the Working Class in England* (1844) concluded that poor people had not benefited. Henry Mayhew's *London Labour and the London Poor* (1851) provided an exceptional ethnographic picture of the lives of poor people.[316] He not only described daily life – such as people eating snails, rat-catchers and street-working children – but he also used general government statistics to estimate, for example, how many traders existed per mile. In parallel, Charles Dickens was depicting a similar impression of the poor through his novels, such as *Oliver Twist*. Although Marx conceptualized the bourgeoisie in relation to the proletariat, unlike Dickens and Mayhew he did not study those masses in depth or as individuals. He provides little analysis of the thousands of working children, or the role of women, who were clearly victims of the economic system and made a contribution to the wealth of the elites. Remembering that these writers lived in the same place during the same era, the difference in their perception of the situation is striking.

The idea of **powerlessness** was introduced into the theories of poverty and international development by Robert Chambers, who saw a lack of power, together with 'physical weakness', 'isolation' and 'vulnerability' as key factors explaining poverty.[317] The concepts of **empowerment** and advocacy, especially in relation to human rights, have subsequently been applied to minority groups such as women, ethnic groups and people with disabilities, and in management studies.[318] On a global scale, relevant theories about international aid – dependency, conditionality, governance – embody significant power relationships.[319] Amartya Sen reconceptualizes these debates in terms of the 'capabilities' of people in disadvantaged regions to convert natural resources (oil, minerals, crops) into valued resources (education, health care, energy).[320] Innovative international research on wellbeing, reported in *The Spirit Level*, proposes that the crucial factor is the gap between rich and poor in any nation, rather than simple GDP.[321] This explains why countries such as UK and US do badly. In organizations such as professional armies, where morale is essential for effectiveness, the pay differential is often comparatively small.

There is a related literature within victimology. In 1985 The UN General Assembly produced a *Declaration of Basic Principles of Justice for Victims of Crime and Abuse of Power*,[322] which demonstrated that the concept of **abuse of power** was internationally accepted (Introduction, p. 3). Methodologies evolved for the achievement of justice for specific forms of victimization including environmental victims,[323] 'invisible victims' such as people with disabilities,[324] victims of human rights abuses,[325] and children abused by powerful people such as Catholic priests[326] and the police (Figure 8.2). Testimony literature from victims, for example from refugees from North Korea,[327] is interesting but is difficult methodologically because refugees are likely to give emotional and biased accounts in order to affirm their status.[328]

The main discussions linking up-system and down-system come within **mass communication** theory,[329] which Harold Lasswell summed-up as 'Who says What to Whom through What Channel with What Effect'.[330] Lasswell also contributed to the systematic study of wartime **propaganda**.[331] A year later Edward Bernays, a nephew of Sigmund Freud, considered the same topic, defining it as 'a consistent, enduring effort to create or shape events to influence the relations of the public to an enterprise, idea or group.'[332] Deceit and hypocrisy seem symbiotic with political power.[333] *The Propaganda Project* provides methodologies for analysing misleading discourse, including techniques such as 'appeal to feel', 'red herring', 'quote out of context' and 'virtue words'.[334] In modern form, propaganda is 'spin'[335] – cherry picking information, denial, false assumptions, euphemistic language, obfuscating inconvenient truths, and pre-emptive deceit which entails getting in first with a misleading message. The NGO *Spinwatch* organizes anti-spin initiatives.[336]

Theories of **massification** argued that modern communications gave elites increasing means to control and manipulate, politically and commercially. In *The Power Elite*, C. Wright Mills distinguished between a democratic 'public' and a controlled 'masses'.[337] But, information communication technology (ICT) is increasing the power of oppositional and powerless groups, as in Egypt in 2011. Powerful people need to cheat in order to do malevolent harm, and ICT makes cheating more visible, and accountability more feasible, through improved 'surveillance', 'information management', 'time–space compression', 'activist self-perception', 'activist perceptions of immunity' and perceptions of 'effective sanctions'.[338] Power relationships are therefore likely to change.

2.5 CRITIQUE

> **CRITICAL**
>
> Involving or exercising careful judgement. (*OED*)

Whatever the theoretical approach, theory should be used critically, and if necessary developed and adapted in relation to new data or circumstances. 'Critical' can simply involve a reasoned questioning in relation to other research and objective criteria. More politically, it can involve an approach, based on Marxian values and honed by philosophers such as Jürgen Habermas at the *Frankfort School*, termed 'critical theory'.[339] This argues that the purpose of scholarship is to understand and change the social structures that provide the means to dominate and oppress, and that science and knowledge have been used as instruments of oppression. It goes further than describing "what is" to reveal "what could be".

Critical theory is an influential approach within history, law, literature and the social sciences, and is especially concerned with 'the interests of knowledge' – an epistemology (C1) that asks why are certain types of knowledge sought and valued more than others?[340] The approach has been adopted within specific methodologies, such as 'critical ethnography':

> a type of reflection that examines culture, knowledge, and action ... Critical ethnographers describe, analyze, and open to scrutiny otherwise hidden agendas, power centers, and assumptions that inhibit, repress, and constrain ... Conventional ethnographers study culture for the purposes of describing it; critical ethnographers do so to change it.[341]

Although now much evolved, critical theory still has relevance to the study of powerful people.

At a more functional level of critique, Thomas Kuhn argues that knowledge and research do not proceed in a neutral manner following their own internal logic and laws, but instead reflect 'scientific paradigms' – widely accepted sets of ideas 'that for a time provide model problems and solutions to a community of practitioners'.[342] (See 'epistemic communities' C2.2.) 'Paradigms' are often shaped by socio-economic demands and intellectual fashion. Most medical research has focused on western lifestyle problems – such as cancer, obesity and ageing – for which there are likely to be lucrative cures. Poor-nation diseases such as hookworm have been sidelined.

To what degree might up-system research and theory represent a paradigm? Across the three areas of study (power, elites, leadership), a difference seems evident in terms of their 'utility' function – their economic value as 'goods' and 'services'.[343] The theories of power and elites are relatively uninfluenced by utility considerations – they are not shaped by financial rewards, but they sometimes reflect a 'critical theory' ethos. Leadership studies seem to provide greater utility rewards, because they provide material for the commercialized endeavour of leadership training, and they rarely reflect critical theory.

One result of a leadership literature that exists by selling itself to those it concerns seems to be that it is conspicuously optimistic and up-beat. Airport bookshops do not sell books about bad leadership, accountability and how managers can cope with failure. Prevailing conceptualizations present leadership as a wholly positive achievement, yet when academics are not writing textbooks to be bought by leaders, their style is more realistic. Goodall provides an example,

> leaders are apt to be found at the top of organisations (or states or armies); they graft for long hours in jobs that most of us do not want to do. For that work they are paid more than the rest of us, have more power, and when the writs hit the fan they get canned.[344]

The 'Peter Principle' – 'In a hierarchy every employee tends to rise to his level of incompetence' – is an inconvenient truth about senior management in many organizations,[345] but it is rarely mentioned in leadership texts. Why are there relatively few theories explaining why numerous intelligent, charismatic and capable people avoid leadership positions, especially women? Why do theories about 'e-leadership' only concern how leaders can use ICT more effectively?[346] Unlike discussions of power (C2.1), they do not consider the degree to which technology may exert power in a questionable way without human intervention.

Research that claims to understand and promote the strategies of "successful" people is, statistically, also studying and promoting ways to fail. For every one person who attains a senior position, there are hundreds with the same capacities and characteristics who do not. The achievement of a position is often a matter of chance, a random outcome, or in East Asian terms, fate. As Dominic Johnson's 'positive illusions' theory suggests (above), the trait of over-confidence that drives people to achieve power is the same reason why countless others, and eventually many senior people themselves, fail.[347]

There are many plausible arguments about whether the leadership literature is biased because of its utility function, but these hardly ever appear in the leadership texts. Critical views, like those expressed by Peck and Dickinson are a rare exception.[348]

> Leadership theory has been particularly prone to gurus who wish to exploit the income generation potential … Clearly, the way in which the phenomenon of leadership is conceptualized and popularized can have significant implications for the attractiveness of the interventions which are then put in place to develop leadership in line with that conception. Furthermore, the creation or adaptation of organizations to design and deliver those interventions gives considerable momentum to their thriving and surviving.

From the perspective of critical theory we might ask: if recent leadership theories often satisfy a paradigm of leadership training, are they circular and self-fulfilling, and therefore do they represent a form of power that itself needs to be questioned?

More broadly, what is the future of these areas of theory? The former distinctions between the literatures on 'power', 'elites' and 'leadership' often overlap and are evolving. The reasons why some studies appear under a particular heading sometimes seem more related to fashion and circumstance than objective criteria. The RADIR project (C2.2) talked of 'the nature of the elite' and 'the elites of societies around the globe' but specifically considered 'the manner in which "leadership" is chosen'.[349] Similarly, Hunter's concept of 'power structures' (above) spans theories of power and elites, and his 'reputational' approach relates closely to Weber's 'legitimacy', but his methodology for researching his 'city leaders' could well be from leadership studies.[350] The former distinctions between leaders and elites may not remain viable in the future, and there is sufficient common ground to identify key research questions and considerations for up-system research in general, and likely sources of information (Figure 2.8).

Theory about powerful people draws on studies of elites and leadership, and the unifying factor is the use of power. When developing a theoretical framework for a new study, it is useful to consider:

- **ontology** – how to argue that something exists – and its relationship to **epistemology** – what knowledge is relevant and how should it be assessed?
- that power is usually exercised through a mix of **influence** and **coercion** – "carrot and stick".
- **legitimacy** – why is the use of power accepted and/or successful in some way?
- assessment of **outcomes**, such as decisions, but that this can be subverted by preventing certain issues reaching the outcome or decision-making stage.
- whether **technology** is evolving from being a way to implement power to becoming a source of power.
- that **elites** can be identified through institutional positions, backgrounds and reputation. But they may decline because they expend more energy maintaining their power than using it effectively or, as systems get highly complex, solving existing problems rather than addressing new ones.
- the degree to which **leaders** are "born or made", and whether their power is 'situational' or 'contingent' on events. Individual leaders usually embody a mix of all aspects.
- why leadership studies less often consider the reasons for **bad leadership** and the need for accountability.
- assessment of **populace** and **followers**, which ranges from fear of 'mob rule' to valuing the 'wisdom of crowds'. 'Powerlessness' often arises from 'abuse of power' which is now recognized by the UN.
- **mass communication**, which is central to the relationship between up-system and down-system, but is often deceitful and manipulative.
- that leadership studies are influenced by the **utility function** of providing a basis for leadership training. Studies of power and elites are more "pure", and are more readily related to critical theory.

Questions	Considerations	Sources
How have they been studied previously?	Academic, empirical, historical, theoretical. Commercial assessments. Internal reviews. Job interviews. Investigations, inquiries. Media interest. Private agencies. Spies, intelligence agencies.	Academic publications. Company reports. Self-assessments. Personality/selection tests. Professional/public inquiry reports. Public records, police/court records. Media reports. Intelligence reports.
Who are they?	'Nominal fallacy', names and networks, persona changes. Elite groups, power elites. Group/individual power. Personal histories – who they *were*. Family history, social/professional background.	Auto/biographies. CVs. Correspondence (letters, email). Public records, birth and deaths. Job titles/descriptions, secondary occupations/income. Disclosure of interest records. Organization websites and reports. Professional/voluntary/club membership lists. Elite lists. *Who's Who?* Speeches, media reports, pictures. Family, colleagues, friends, rivals.
What are they like?	Traits, qualities, attributes. Stated/demonstrated behaviour/ values. Public perceptions. Education. Self-presentation. Self-perception. Ideologies, propaganda, policies.	Personality/assessment tests. Personal publications. Unpublished dissertations, theses. Auto/biographies. Correspondence. Medical and school records. Tax and property records, expenses claims. Personal/official libraries. Organization websites and reports. Speeches, media reports, pictures. Opinion polls. Family, colleagues, friends, rivals.
What is their legitimacy?	Group/personal. Charismatic, tradition, legal rational, successes. Ascribed/achieved status. Reputation, recognition. Education, qualifications, meritocratic. Titles, honours, memberships. Political/non-political status. Perception, intended/interpreted status. Ethics, moral authority. Accountability, personal/social responsibility.	Auto/biographies. CVs. Constitutions. Professional bodies. Military records. Professional codes of conduct. Rules of inheriting status. Genealogies, pedigree lists. Criminal and misconduct records. School records. Religious affiliation lists. Family, colleagues, friends, rivals. Opinion polls. Election/ballot results.

FIGURE 2.8 Questions, considerations and information sources

Questions	Considerations	Sources
Who, and what, do they have power over?	Place. Domain. Resources. 'Ideal type'. Scope, boundaries, 'costs'. Distributional – collective. Situational, contingent. Constant/variable sum. Crowds, masses, workers, powerless people. Corporate/collective responsibility. Global reach. Nation/cosmopolitan.	CVs. Auto/biographies. Correspondence. Constitutions. Professional bodies. Job descriptions. Property records. Organizational/line management charts.
What is their power/organizational structure?	Hierarchies. Plural. Intra/inter-organizational networks. Fragmentation, conflict, opposition. Elite networks. Comparisons with peers.	Constitutions. Organization websites and reports. Company records. Colleagues/followers/subordinates.
How do they exercise their power?	Soft/hard. Domination. Control. Extensive/intensive – authoritative/diffused. Communication. Deceit, propaganda, spin. Oligarchical, authoritarian, despotic. Toxic/bad, groupthink, belief-based. Transformational, transactional. Shared, collaborative, collective, distributed. Oppositional, activist, protest. Covert, conspiratorial. Asymmetric. Techno-centric. Digital.	Policies, speeches, media reports. Correspondence. Followers and subordinates. Members/decision-making bodies. Personality/assessment tests. Auto/biographies. Speeches, media reports. Family, colleagues, friends, rivals. Opinion polls.
What are their aims?	Control, competitive. Financial, social, personal. Oppositional, advocacy, empowerment. Accountability, social change, regime change. Excellence.	Organization websites and reports. Mission statements. Policies, speeches, media reports. Correspondence.

FIGURE 2.8   *Continued*

(Continued)

Questions	Considerations	Sources
How do they make decisions?	Control of process/information, agenda setting. Overt/covert, conspiracy. Policy/systems analysis.	Organization protocols and rules. Members/decision-making bodies. Colleagues/followers/subordinates. Minutes and formal records. Correspondence.
What are the outcomes?	Causation, evidence, indicators. Direct/indirect. Improved/reduced capabilities, empowerment, advocacy. Effect on organization/system. Bad/'toxic', lock-in. Before-and-after. Social/organizational change, trends-impetus. Gaps between elites and populace. Victimization, poverty. Accountability. Control.	Auto/biographies. CVs. Organization websites and reports. Speeches, media reports. Court, criminal and misconduct records. Colleagues/followers/subordinates. Public/organization records. Testimony. Opinion polls.
How did, or might, their power decline and end?	Cyclical change, democratic process. Misunderstanding of populace/followers, opposition. Overthrow, revolution, crowds. Decadence, laziness. Bad/toxic leadership. Cumulative lock-in, overconfidence, corruption, deceit, inconsistency. Age/health. Internal conflict, mutiny, fracture, fault lines. Resource shortage – human, economic, physical. Situation, contingency, social change, trends. Co-opted/absorbed, bought. Success (no need to continue). Collapse, complexity, risk, uncertainty.	History. Constitutions, rules. Medical records, genetic history. Family/colleagues/followers/subordinates/rivals. Public/organization records. Opinion polls. Conflict monitors. Policies, speeches, media reports. Company records. Criminal and misconduct records. Risk assessments. Resignation letters/speeches. Personal view.

FIGURE 2.8 *Continued*

The distinctions between leadership and elite studies, which have been developed over the past century, are not always clear. It seems likely that theories of elites and leadership will become more unified, creating a more objective approach to understanding powerful people. Talking of 'elite roles' and 'leadership roles', rather than 'elites' or 'leaders', may help to clarify discussions. Analysis of the *interplay* between these roles, especially when studying individuals who use multiple personas to enhance their power, such as those who head revolutionary-religious movements (Appendix 1) and royal figures who engage in commercial activities, could provide useful developments of theory.

KEY READING

Audi, R. (1997) *Epistemology: A Contemporary Introduction to the Theory of Knowledge.* London: Routledge.

Bottomore, T.B. (1993) *Elites and Society.* London: Routledge.

Bronner, S.E. (2011) *Critical Theory: A Very Short Introduction.* Oxford: Oxford University Press.

Bryman, A. et al. (2011) *The Sage Handbook of Leadership.* London: Sage.

Griffin, E. (1997) *A First Look at Communication Theory.* New York: McGraw-Hill. pp. 34–42.

Jacquette, D. (2003) *Ontology.* Montreal: McGill-Queen's University Press.

Mann, M. (2011) *Power in the 21st Century.* Cambridge: Polity.

McPhail, C.(1991) *The Myth of the Madding Crowd.* New York: Aldine de Gruyter.

Searle, J. (2007) *Freedom and Neurobiology: Reflections on Free Will, Language and Political Power.* New York: Columbia University Press. ('Social ontology and political power'.)

PART TWO

DOING

Chapter 3 – Doing research usually starts with finding and reviewing relevant literature. But literature by and about powerful people is often very unreliable and needs to be used critically. Although there has been a lot of up-system research, there are many exciting new areas for study, which have been marginalized and overlooked so far.

Chapter 4 – Any study starts with a plan – a research design or "map" of how the project will work. The main problem is to achieve 'access' to powerful people and data about them. Research ethics and the law also need careful thought, because action against researchers who make mistakes can be severe.

Chapter 5 – Up-system research can be based on research frameworks that are used in both academic and professional research. These depend on whether face-to-face interaction is possible, at what distance research can be carried out, or whether organizations and systems can be analysed.

Chapter 6 – Collecting data entails thinking about diverse sources including texts, people, objects and buildings. Data needs to selected to match the purpose of the study, tested to ensure it is sound, and presented as findings in an appropriate and effective way.

3

LITERATURE

3.1   SEARCHING
3.2   REVIEWING
3.3   TOPICS
        3.3.1   Issues
        3.3.2   People
        3.3.3   Conceptualizations

> **LITERATURE**
>
> The body of books etc. that treat of a subject (*OED*).

Theoretical perspectives, discussed in Chapter 2, arise from assessment of a range of empirical studies and reasoned arguments, over a significant time period, and are usually created by academics. 'Literature' is more likely to be in the form of reports of single studies, statistics, books about specific topics, and front-line accounts of events. These may be by academics, but also by journalists and practitioners such as NGO staff and public officials, and people who have lived remarkable lives. Getting to know the literature about a topic is the starting point of any research, but it must be read critically. As Chapter 1 shows, the literature about powerful people can be particularly misleading. Even seemingly respectable sources can be unreliable. From her study of Guatemalan military elites, Jenifer Schirmer concludes of the CIA, 'They get promotion by listing assets, not for getting information right'.[1]

Academic research often provides freedom to choose a topic. Other professional research seems more limited, but there is always room for originality. Journalists may spend much of their time investigating issues set by an editor, but the big stories come from those who notice something new. Professional investigators may spend most of their job investigating public complaints or political demands, but sometimes the most significant issues arise because someone finds something unexpected. To be meaningful, research needs to be original in some way, and that requires questioning previous endeavours in the same field. How can a study not "reinvent the wheel", but be "cutting edge" and "state of the art", or make "an original contribution to knowledge"?

This chapter helps with finding and reviewing relevant literature critically, and then with identifying an original topic. The starting point is to find and understand the general and specific literature, and from this to identify the gaps and potential new approaches. Figure 2.8 suggests key sources in relation to types of research question. This helps to formulate questions or hypotheses that can direct the research to address those gaps (C4.3).

3.1 SEARCHING

Initial searches may start through internet search engines such as *Google*, or sites like *Colossus*[2] which lists 1000 search engines by country.[3] This is likely to produce an overload of sources, and many will be irrelevant or unreliable. But they could help to identify keywords, significant writers and relevant organizations. Similarly, *Wikipedia*, and other information-bases, are likely to have numerous entries. The content may be biased, flawed or incomplete, but it can help to "map" the main concepts of a topic and indicate further reading. More reliable academic databases – such as *ISI Web of Knowledge*, and *WorldCat* from the *Online Computer Library Centre* (OCLC) – and sites specific to up-system research can then be searched. The list of 'internet sources', at the end of the book, provides examples, but not a comprehensive list, of the type of sites that can assist up-system research, or that could be a result of research. Retrospective searches entail searching backwards through the literature, as in a traditional library. Prospective searches use software that facilitates setting up an ongoing search on specific keywords, and as new sources appear they are reported to the user. Some databases permit tracking the citing of a particular study from the date of publication, which creates a network of related literature. For investigative or biographical research, numerous personal data search engines are available.[4] For high profile people, media sites such as the *China Daily*, *al Jazeera* and *BBC* are worth searching directly. But, exciting ICT can lead to overlooking another simple and long-standing way of finding important literature – reading the 'references' and 'sources' lists in previous relevant studies, and looking along library shelves for books *next* to the one you thought you wanted. Not everything is stored on a digital database.

Archives often hold unresearched material, or previously secret material collected by organizations such as the CIA,[5] which at some point becomes available. When the Chinese *Public Security Bureau* archives were opened in 2006, they revealed meticulous records of the brutality of Mao Zedong's regime.[6] Specialist libraries make declassified documents easy to search.[7] Problems with government archives include

- Incomplete records which give a misleading impression.
- A focus on administrative process rather than cause and effect.
- Reports that are deliberately misleading.
- A 'self-justificatory element'.[8]

Open access sites such as *Wikileaks* are subverting state secrecy by presenting leaked material in searchable formats.[9] Online discussions of secret material appear, such as that about 'Operation Northwoods', a plan by US Department of Defense leaders, to stage acts of terrorism on US soil and blame Cuba, to provide an excuse for invading (Figure 3.1).[10]

TOP SECRET SPECIAL HANDLING

MEMORANDUM FOR THE SECRETARY OF DEFENSE

13 March 1962

UNCLASSIFIED

Subject: Justification for US Military Intervention in Cuba (TS)

a. Incidents to establish a credible attack (not in chronological order):

  (1) Start rumors (many). Use clandestine radio.
  (2) Land friendly Cubans in uniform "over-the-fence" to stage attack on base.
  (3) Capture Cuban (friendly) saboteurs inside the base.
  (4) Start riots near the base main gate (friendly Cubans).
  (5) Blow up ammunition inside the base; start fires.
  (6) Burn aircraft on air base (sabotage).
  (7) Lob mortar shells from outside of base into base. Some damage to installations.
  (8) Capture assault teams approaching from the sea or vicinity of Guantanamo City.
  (9) Capture militia group which storms the base.
  (10) Sabotage ship in harbor; large fires -- naphthalene.
  (11) Sink ship near harbor entrance. Conduct funerals for mock-victims (may be lieu of (10)).

b. United States would respond by executing offensive operations to secure water and power supplies, destroying artillery and mortar emplacements which threaten the base.
c. Commence large scale United States military operations.

3. A "Remember the Maine" incident could be arranged in several forms:

  a. We could blow up a US ship in Guantanamo Bay and blame Cuba.
  b. We could blow up a drone (unmanned) vessel anywhere in the Cuban waters. We could arrange to cause such incident in the vicinity of Havana or Santiago as a spectacular result of Cuban attack from the air or sea, or both. The presence of Cuban planes or ships merely investigating the intent of the vessel could be fairly compelling evidence that the ship was taken under attack. The nearness to Havana or Santiago would add credibility especially to those people that might have heard the blast or have seen the fire. The US could follow up with an air/sea rescue operation covered by US fighters to "evacuate" remaining members of the non-existent crew. Casualty lists in US newspapers would cause a helpful wave of national indignation.

4. We could develop a Communist Cuban terror campaign in the Miami area, in other Florida cities and even in Washington.

The Joint Chiefs of Staff (1962) Washington DC.

FIGURE 3.1 Operation Northwoods

Source: www.smeggys.co.uk/operation_northwoods.php?image=01#tt

Freedom of information (FOI) systems[11] provide a "right to know" in relation to information held by a government. Many countries have helpful legislation – but the efficacy varies. The Canadian government provides a useful international comparative review,[12] and *Open Government: A Journal on Freedom of Information*[13] presents ongoing discussions. Details of how to access FOI systems are country specific, and usually available on websites or from any governmental organization.[14] Officers working in FOI departments can sometimes be obstructive, and may be attached to national intelligence services. Inquiries should appear low-key and harmless. If a first attempt fails, try again using a different persona and approach. Asking for a large number of seemingly related documents can provide "cover" for getting the one that is crucial. Information relating to central government can often be accessed in more than one way through local government departments and organizations. Sensitive central government information is sometimes repeated in secondary documents such as local policy and planning reports. A process chart can help to map possible secondary sources (see Critical Process Analysis C7.6).

3.2 REVIEWING

> **REVIEW**
>
> An inspection, examination, general survey or reconsideration.
> A general account or criticism of a literary work. (*OED*)

Most research reports include some form of literature review, which comes from an awareness of a general literature – politics, management, popular culture – and then identifies, describes and assesses the nature of specific literature – Icelandic leaders, women CEOs, African rock stars. From initial searches (C3.1), it should be possible to determine the structure of the review. This will help to systemize further specific searches, and eventually the report. There are many ways to structure a review, but however it is structured, the reasons should be explained – why were those particular headings chosen? For studies based on other similar research, the structure might simply copy the structure of previous reports. Alternatively, the structure might relate to sources of literature – government reports, human rights organizations, academic research, internet video and audio material, press cartoons. Alternatively, it could be thematic – perceptions of political leaders, elite networks, ethical standards, cultural perspectives. It might be arranged in terms of related issues, for example, child trafficking in Laos, political corruption in Asia, gang leadership. Sections may be chronological, or for small-scale narrowly focused research the whole review might be chronological to show the development of a specific area of literature, for example, US policy on international corruption. Large reviews may combine a number of these approaches.

A review demonstrates that a study is based on, does not repeat, but develops existing knowledge. A literature review is distinct from 'documentary research', which treats a text as a form of data (C5.2), although some of the approaches to assessment may be the same. Similarly, biographical research (5.2) goes much further than a literature review, although a review may provide some background by, for example, studying biographies of contemporaries, or contextual factors. All sources must be considered critically, especially internet material. The questionable value of 'pheets' – phony tweets – is just one example.[15] The nature of a literature review is fully discussed in Hart's *Doing a Literature Review*.[16] The introduction to any review should explain succinctly:

- its *purpose*. Developments in ICT have made the traditional "comprehensive" literature review almost pointless, and so clear aims or questions at the start of a review are necessary to focus the content, and should be addressed in the conclusion to the review.
- the *parameters*. What's in and what's out, and why? What period does the review cover? Which fields/disciplines are included? What types of literature are assessed? What countries and languages are considered?
- the *searches*. Which databases were used? What keywords are relevant? Are there any unique problems, such as confusing terminology? How were searches for non-text based material (photos, videos, films, You Tube) carried out? How was non-digital historical and "grey" literature accessed?
- the *critical* approach. How were sources tested and assessed? How were the principles of epistemology (C2) applied?

A concluding assessment of literature should summarize and provide insights into the nature of specific aspects of the literature as a whole (Figure 3.2).[17] This might identify key writers, schools of thought, trends and influences, which might be presented as tables, flow charts or spider grams. Care should be taken not to repeat terminology uncritically. Oppositional groups that may be termed 'terrorists', 'rebels', or 'insurgents' by some writers are, from the perspective of others, 'freedom fighters', 'patriots', or 'resistance movements', which may well become the next legitimate government.

A 'systematic review' is a more specific assessment of selected research studies, not of contextual literature, and is common in health research where ethical considerations and access to research participants is problematic.[18] This aims to critically consolidate comparable research reports,[19] and is usually designed in terms of: problem-oriented questions, a framework for focusing the literature search, systematically identifying and collecting papers, evaluation and conclusions. In up-system research, this form of review may be useful to assess specific empirical research such as the psychological literature on leadership training or crowd psychology. 'Secondary analysis' goes further and re-uses the data from other studies, and 'meta-analysis' combines and then analyses data from studies that have similar purpose and methods (C5.2).[20]

Section	Summary	Gaps in the literature	Possible further research
5. Women and Leadership	– Historically, women leaders have been significant in both regions, and this is well documented. – In both regions women are now not well represented within political and other leadership. – The problems for women leaders are seen as rooted in so-called "tradition", family power relationships, and social attitudes.	– Almost no texts about women and leadership. – The few texts that exist are biographies of the leaders themselves ('Great women'). They do not conceptualize women and leadership.	– The *history* of women leaders in both regions needs to be explored and presented in relation to the *contemporary* belief that "tradition" does not accept women leaders. – There is significant potential for studies about the common problems for women leaders in both regions.

FIGURE 3.2   Extract from the summary of a literature review

Source: Lee, Yun-joo (2004) *Leadership and International Understanding: Linking Korea and the Middle East. A Historical and Literature Review.* Amman: United Nations University: International Leadership Institute. p. 83.

Assessing literature created by powerful people or organizations presents a distinct problem – the **halo effect**.[21] Poor judgement can arise because the perception of one particular above-average trait – wealth, fame, tradition, position – can generate a perception that other qualities are above average – honesty, accuracy, intelligence or diligence. The Arab historian Ibn Khaldun (C1.2) was aware of this in his discussion of historical methods in 1377: 'People as a rule approach great and high-ranking persons with praise and encomiums [tribute]. They embellish conditions and spread the fame [of great men].'[22] Company reports and government propaganda usually deploy high quality presentation to generate an impression that the content is high quality and can be trusted, which can deflect critical questioning. Even if we are aware that up-system evidence might be selective or biased, we usually assume that there were viable processes and methods for creating that information. But that is not always the case. If judging a political statement, we should go beyond the obvious question – Is it true? – and ask the deeper questions of epistemology (2.1) – How was that information created? From ontology we might go further and ask: If there seem to be no feasible methods to create that information, does the circumstance it purports to describe exist? How did they measure 'offense', 'legitimate', 'sacred' or 'terrorized'? Critical Process Analysis (CPA) provides a strategy for analysing whether the process of information is creation (C7.6).

The internet has significantly increased the availability of information but also opportunities for manipulation, and cyberspace 'halo' effect, and these problems might be mentioned in a review. 'Shills' – people or organizations that pose as independent experts and create fake sites or news stories – are common.[23] But 'fake news'[24] can itself represent data for analysis. Information is sometimes presented within disguised websites, which can only be identified properly by checking domain names. Right wing groups such as *American Majority* train members to manipulate ratings for books on Amazon, and films, giving liberal texts low ratings and negative comments, and conservative texts high ratings so that these appear first on keyword searches. PR companies such as the *Bivings Group* specialize in internet lobbying and attack scientific articles that challenge the companies they work for. Comments critical of the Chinese government will be attacked by thousands of individuals paid by the Chinese government.[25]

Questionable statistics are often repeated uncritically. Hazel Smith provides an example that is often used to create a negative view of North Korean leaders:

> Foreign observers have regularly cited the figure of three million dead from famine, or 10 per cent of North Korea's population. Those who use these figures also frequently argue that the government left the people in the northeastern provinces of North Hamgyong, South Hamgyong and Ryanggang to starve to death …

> The figure of three million was extrapolated from a 1998 survey of North Korean migrants and refugees in China, and was published in the reputable British medical journal *The Lancet*. These North Koreans in the main came from North Hamgyong province, and the scientific work in question specifically stated that their findings could not be extrapolated to the whole country. Firstly, the North Koreans interviewed in China were not a representative sample of their home province; secondly North Hamgyong, which has an urbanised, non-agricultural population, was not representative of the country as a whole. There is no doubt there was a terrible humanitarian disaster in the 1990s. … However, the truth is that nobody – including the government – probably knows the real figure.[26]

Uncritical repetition can be exacerbated by the internet, and dubious "facts" can gain authority because of an elite source *and* an "e-halo effect". Figure 3.3 provides an example. In 2009, an Israeli Ministry of Foreign Affairs report stated, 'Israel was bombarded by some 12,000 rockets and mortar shells between 2000 and 2008...'[27] This figure was repeated by Israeli Embassies as, 'an 8-year-long barrage of 12,000 rockets'.[28] The word 'some' has been omitted, and the page was soon removed, but the figure was repeated on hundreds of other sites. Applying the CPA framework (C7.6), this neat figure raises a 'doubt' – is it likely that the number of rockets fired was precisely a tidy number of 12,000, or is it a guess? How 'should' that data about the number of rockets have been collected, and even 'could' it be collected accurately? 'Further information' came from a *Google* search on '12,000 rockets', which shows that this figure appears in various forms around 12,400 times, and that the figure had seemingly originated from Hezbollah in May 2005.[29]

'Halo' sources – Israeli government sites	
Israel was bombarded by some 12,000 rockets and mortar shells between 2000 and 2008... (The Israeli Ministry of Foreign Affairs, website, 2009)[i] **On December 27, 2008, after enduring an 8-year-long barrage of 12,000 rockets and having exhausted all other options, Israel launched a military operation against Hamas in Gaza.** (Israeli Embassy, London, website, 2010)[ii]	
Related statements from other sources	**Questions – how could/should that evidence be collected?**
Hamas indiscriminately fired over 12,000 rockets. (YNet News[iii])	Counting the 'indiscriminate' firing, of a 'barrage' of rockets over 8 years is not an easy task. How was it done accurately? The word 'over' suggests an estimate.
Hizbullah has some 12,000 rockets facing our northern border. (Sound the Shofar[iv])	If rockets 'facing' a border were sufficiently visible to be counted, why did the Israeli army not destroy them? 'Some' suggests an estimate.
Iran and Syria have also armed the Hezbollah with about 12,000 rockets of various ranges. (*Zionism and Israel* – Encyclopaedic Dictionary[v])	If the supply of rockets from Syria and Iran was sufficiently visible to count them, why were they not intercepted? 'About' suggests an estimate.
The head of Lebanon's Hizbullah movement said his fighters have more than 12,000 rockets they could use to attack northern Israel. (Al-Bawaba[vi])	Did the Israeli Ministry rely on statistics from Hizbullah? The 12,000 figure appeared on the al-Bawaba website in May 2005. The official Israeli version is dated 27 December 2008 – 3 years later.
As international pressure increased for Hezbollah's disarmament, the group's spiritual leader, Sheikh Hassan Nasrallah, announced, "They say [we have] 12,000 rockets ... I say more than 12,000 rockets."[vii] (*Middle East Quarterly*, 2006/Associated Press, May 2005)	*Associated Press* reports that the figure had originated from Hezbollah, before the Israel government used it.

FIGURE 3.3   Questioning the 'halo effect' of elite sources

i   MoFA (2009) The Operation in Gaza - Factual and Legal Aspects, 29 July. Israeli Ministry of Foreign Affairs. Available at: www.mfa.gov.il/MFA/Terrorism-+Obstacle+to+Peace/Terrorism+and+Islamic+Fundamentalism-/Operation_in_Gaza-Factual_and_Legal_Aspects.htm

ii   Israeli Embassy (2010) Gaza Facts – the Israeli Perspective [18 June]. Available at: www.mfa.gov.il/GazaFacts/ [Later became unavailable].

iii YNet News. Available at: www.ynetnews.com/articles/0,7340,L-3791096,00.html

iv   Sound the Shofar – prayer alert. Available at: www.shofar1.org/letter/index.shtml

v   *Zionism and Israel*, Encyclopaedic Dictionary. Available at: www.zionism-israel.com/dic/Hezbollah.htm)

vi   Al bawaba. Available at: www1.albawaba.com/en/news/nasrallah-over-12000-rockets-can-be-used-against-israeli-targets (or find with *Google* search: 'nasrallah 12000 rockets'.)

vii Devenny, P. (2006) 'Hezbollah's strategic threat to Israel', *Middle East Quarterly*, Winter: 31–38. Available at: www.meforum.org/806/hezbollahs-strategic-threat-to-israel#_ftnref2 (reporting: Associated Press, 25 May 2005).

A specific approach to an up-system literature review is to discover the possible influence of writings among elites and leaders. This entails not just asking – What did they write? – but also – What did they read? The reference lists in books by powerful people provide a good starting point. Scottish philosopher David Hume influenced Darwin and Einstein. Gustav Le Bon's book, *The Crowd: A Study of the Popular Mind* (1896),[30] was so influential that Hitler used Le Bon's ideas about propaganda in *Mein Kampf*, and it is said that Mussolini kept a copy of *The Crowd* by his bedside. In East Asian countries, books, paintings and other artefacts owned by powerful people were often endorsed by all those who owned them, sometimes with comments. The methodologies of provenance research (C1.2) are relevant to a literature review that assesses literary influence.[31]

Up-system literature is notoriously unreliable. This may arise from deliberate deceit, a tendency for powerful people to inflate their importance, or a desire by others to discredit. Seemingly reliable documents may have been created by spies or counter-espionage agents to entrap or deceive power elites, as did Francis Walsingham acting on behalf of English Queen Elizabeth I.[32] In general, the difficulties of accessing and researching elites and leaders mean that even genuine studies can be flawed or incomplete. Two edicts, old and new, should be above the desk of a researcher when dealing with this area of literature:

> *Accept nothing on authority.* (Motto of the Royal Society, 1660)

> *Trust nothing, debate everything.* (Jason Calacanis, internet entrepreneur, 2010[33])

3.3 TOPICS

Literature reviews create awareness of the strengths, weaknesses and gaps in the literature, and of longstanding topics that might be revisited. But detecting areas of research that are unique and underexplored also comes from a broader awareness of world events and trends. Assessing 'directions for leadership research' in 1993, Chemers and Ayman provided a conservative view of future areas of work – contingency, process, subjectivity, culture, ethics, emotions and coconscious processes'.[34] Since then, a broadening view of researching powerful people has started to draw on more diverse issues and areas of conceptualization. Below, examples of marginalized issues, different types of powerful people for study, and potentially innovative conceptualizations and methodological approaches are identified, together with sources for reading. This does not provide a comprehensive list, but helps to develop an awareness of how to find original topics and frame relevant questions.

3.3.1 Issues

- *Accountability* of powerful people, including politicians,[35] is changing through the use of new technologies and civil society movements.[36] New conceptualizations are emerging, such as '**state crime**'[37] (Figure 3.4). How is this happening and what is the effect on elites and leaders?

- *Asymmetrical power* and unbalanced conflict, is altering the realities of power at many levels – between nations and oppositional groups,[38] governments and civil society, individual victims and repressive regimes, and retired experts and the organizations they understand well.[39] How can the benefits and threats of this change be assessed?
- *Exceptionalism* is an extreme form of elitism. Throughout history, certain communities and countries have viewed themselves as having a divine or unique right to be better than others, and therefore to protect and extend their power. Nazi Germany and Meiji Japan provide historical instances, and recent discussions consider America,[40] China,[41] Iran,[42] North Korea,[43] the Middle East,[44] Islam[45] and Israel.[46] In *Guns, Germs and Steel,* Diamond argues that the seeming supremacy of elite Eurasian (including North African) societies is not genetic, but arises from environment,[47] yet western leaders sometimes present

---

The most serious crimes in the modern world are acts that are largely committed, instigated or condoned by governments and their officials. However, state crime is under-acknowledged by popular and academic authors. Calling these activities 'crimes' should be largely uncontroversial as in the majority of cases they violate international and/or national criminal law. A purely legalistic definition of state crime, however, is unsatisfactory for at least three reasons:

- It would exclude some of the greatest mass violations of human rights of the past century, such as the Chinese famine of 1959–61 in which an estimated 30 million people died ... But international criminal law does not appear to prohibit starving your own population in peacetime, unless the intention is to destroy a particular ethnic group.

- When two or more armed factions are committing atrocities in a territory they seek to control, it seems arbitrary to denote one side's activities as 'state crime' and the other as something else.

- Criminal law is concerned mainly with individual liability. The study of state crime is more concerned with the role of organizations in committing, perpetrating or condoning crime.

ISCI takes the term 'crime' to include all violations of human rights that are 'deviant' in the sense that they infringe some socially recognized norm ... We take 'states' to include all bodies that seek to achieve a monopoly of the legitimate use of force in some substantial territory, whether or not they are internationally recognized as states. 'State crimes' are crimes committed or condoned by the personnel of such organizations in pursuit of organizational goals.

International State Crime Initiative (ISCI), King's College, London.
http://statecrime.org

FIGURE 3.4   Reconceptualizing the abuse of power – 'state crime'

an impression of innate superiority. Whatever the explanation, exceptionalism usually culminates in harmful outcomes for exceptionalist elites and others. How can harmful exceptionalism be addressed, while respecting diversity and different group identities?

- *Hypermobility*[48] – the exponential increase in human movement around the world – creates the possibility that democracy may change because the links between political leaders and their constituants will weaken. Migrant labour is increasing. The large numbers of international students, who currently migrate to study abroad, are creating new global elite networks. How can theorizations of elites and place (C2.2) accommodate hypermobility?

- *Medical conditions* of elites and leaders in the present-day[49] (perhaps as part of international intelligence analysis) and the 'retrospective diagnosis' of historical elites,[50] are ongoing interests. Can this help to engender more sympathetic public attitudes towards powerful people with disabilities and health problems?

- *Memorials and museums*[51] about abuses of power are common but not widely studied. In Seoul, the former *Seodaemun* prison is now a museum showing the horrors of Japanese occupation, and the adjacent *Monument to Patriotic Martyrs* shows the fate of the 'Righteous Army soldiers' to Japanese soldiers (Figure 3.5). Do these forms of public education have any significant effect on the public and specifically children? (See Figure 7.5, beheading by Japanese soldiers.) Do they redress or worsen past conflicts?

- *Small states* are often ignored in discussions of international relations. But historically, they have sometimes made significant contributions to the evolution of governance. New Zealand often leads with innovatory legislation including the nuclear-free zone, and ban on traditional slaughter of animals.[52] Iceland had a parliament in 930, and provided Europe's first female president, who was the world's first democratically, and longest serving, elected female head of state, Vigdís Finnbogadóttir. The Isle of Man has the oldest continuous governing body, the Tynwald, since 979, and was the first country to introduce votes for women in 1881. The UNDESA Division of Sustainable Development runs a 'Small Island Developing States' (SIDS) programme.[53] What is the role of small states, in a globalizing world, and how can leaders of small states work effectively? *States without status* – 'non-nation states', 'non-self governing territories', 'stateless nations'[54] – are trying to shift perceptions of power. The *International Romani Union* represents 12 million people, and in 2000 talked of becoming a 'non-territorial nation' with its own government and court. How could these states and their leaders be accommodated within a UN-focused world order.

- *Traditional abuses of power* – habits, customs and religious beliefs, often rationalize harm.[55,56] The tradition of *Bacha bazi* (Persian, 'playing with children') permits warlords and local elites in Afghanistan to use young dancing boys as sex slaves and prostitutes.[57] Female genital mutilation (FGM) raises questions of power abuse between and within gender groups, compounded by traditional and religious leaders. Who has the moral and practical authority to challenge these problems?

- *Powerless groups* have their own power structures,[58] hierarchies[59] and vulnerabilities.[60] Research is not straightforward. For example, leaders may want to affirm their fragile status by refusing to use 'backward' local language in interviews, or the dynamics between local and national elites may confuse issues, as Hinton explains:[61]

(Photos: Christopher Williams)

FIGURE 3.5   Memorials to abuse of power

The *Monument to Patriotic Martyrs*, Seoul, Korea
The Christianized images and discourse are curious. In the 1940s, few Koreans would have related to a crucifixion scene. It indicates the power, and subsequent influence, of the American Christian missionaries who arrived after World War II.

A group of camp leaders gathered in the privacy of the camp committee room for discussions on caste… During discussions other 'important' refugees wandered in, as was the norm…The topic of caste was raised and immediately an onlooker who had joined the group objected. His status meant that no one spoke out… Only later did I see why the question of caste was perceived as a threat. Bilateral government talks had concluded with a decision to reclassify the refugees into distinct groups, only some of whom would be eligible for repatriation.

How can positive leadership be developed within powerless groups?

- *U-turns* by political leaders are perceived as weakness, but may be astute re-evaluations of evidence or circumstance.[62] Ashoka (c.304–232BC) provides a historical example, becoming a peace-promoting Buddhist after seeing the carnage of his war in Kalinga. In 1993, F. W. de Klerk was awarded the Nobel Peace prize, with Nelson Mandela, for his reversal of views about the Apartheid system, which led to its demise. Similarly, Mikhail Gorbachev became a Nobel laureate in 1990 for helping to bring an end to the USSR while serving as its final head of state. How can the public become more aware of the difference between heroic and expedient U-turns?

3.3.2 People

- *Celebrities* represent role models and power elites.[63] How can we understand celebrity charisma, narcissism and commoditization, using methodological approaches such as semiotics and cultural materialism?[64,65,66,67] What happens when celebrities become political leaders, such as body builder, model, actor and then Governor of California Arnold Schwarzenegger, and Haiti's President Michel Martelly formerly the musician "Sweet Micky"? Might musicians, such as Burma's rap group *Generation Wave*,[68] contribute to political change?
- *Children* have been studied as leaders[69,70] and heroes,[71] in relation to leadership training[72] and giftedness.[73,74] How do we assess leadership among child soldiers, and young resistance leaders such Korea's Yu Kwan-sun who was tortured to death in 1920 aged 16? How do we discover young people's perceptions of adult leaders (Figure 3.6) and elites of the future (Figure 3.7)? How can longitudinal studies track outcomes?[75] Examples of 'educational bypass' question the reproduction theories (C2.2).[76] What can be learned from elites such as Leonardo da Vinci, who had little formal education, industrialist Li Ka-Shing who stopped education before he was 15 and became the world's 11th richest man, and former Brazilian President Lula da Silva who only learned to read and write at the age of ten? Can bypass be predicted in certain children? Is it a characteristic of certain elites?
- *Despots and/or political prisoners* need to be understood in relation to extremism,[77,78] terrorism,[79,80] religions and cults,[81] 'ideological' and 'non-ideological leaders',[82] and state crime (Figure 3.7).[83] How does **despotism** arise, and how can despots be rehabilitated?[84,85] Is exile, in places such as Calabar in Nigeria, an appropriate course of action? What is the role of military tribunals,[86] interviewing,[87,88] and prisoners' letters?[89] How can the research of advocacy and human rights organizations be made more effective?[90]
- *Latent leaders* – secret societies can be analysed in terms of recruitment, history, famous members, rituals, symbols, founders, ties, size and events,[91] but access is problematic.[92]

Left: The good president of S.Korea, Kim Dae-Jung, says, "I hope you can score" (football).
Right: The bad president, of Japan, says, "If you don't score, I will kill you". He has a gun with him and he smokes and drinks alcohol.

The President of North Korea, Kim Il-Sung orders his assistant to torture innocent people. [The assistant appears as Japanese.]

FIGURE 3.6 Perceptions of political leaders by South Korean children, age 9–10. Draw and tell method – "Good and bad Presidents"; reproduced by permission, Yun-joo Lee

President Chun Doo-Hwan imprisoned innocent people. [The President is wearing military uniform.]

The son of President Kim Dae-Jung says, "Wow! Father! I am rich! Look I am so rich now!"
The child wrote, "Kim Dae-Jung ordered his son to steal money again, but he got caught by policemen".

[Kim Dae-jung's son, Kim Hong-up, was imprisoned for corruption in 2002]

FIGURE 3.6   *Continued*

On an international level, how can 'closed society research',[93] in former[94] and present[95] 'closed regimes', develop more innovative methods?

- *Military leadership* has been studied widely by historians,[96] enthusiasts[97] and those offering military style training.[98] But there is little objective critical analysis of their broader roles in society.[99] How can the legitimacy of military elites be conceptualized in the context of changing civil society and democratic movements? Although much is written about military leadership in war, there is little about the roles of military and political leaders in instigating war, yet war is impossible without leadership in some form.[100]

- *New elites* are emerging from changing contexts and power relationships,[101] for example in relation to energy[102] and oil within the Middle East,[103] Africa[104] and Russia.[105] International legal elites are forming around the international criminal and commercial courts.[106] Media elites[107] are evolving, and so is the elite use of new media.[108] How do we understand the use of power by hackers, and distinguish between 'black hat activists', 'script kiddies' or 'fame whores'.[109] How are elite mindsets changing as a result of immersion in modern ICT.[110] How do historical accounts of former 'new elites', such as those of the Mamluks,[111] help us to understand present-day shifts?

- *Religious leaders* and *elites who are religious*[112] are creating concerns about abuse,[113] harmful cults and sects,[114] and evangelical political influence.[115,116] Should their religious personas protect these elites from scrutiny and accountability? Are the actions and rhetoric of religious elites consistent (C7.3) with the values of their religion?

- *Sub-elites and leadership* – such as advisers, intelligence officers, acolytes and industrialists – all shape the decisions of the conspicuous leaders.[117] How do their unseen 'epistemic communities'[118] influence major decisions?

- *Wealthy elites*[119] – how should we monitor land owners,[120] bankers and financiers,[121] and related corruption?[122] The gaps between rich and poor may be more significant than GDP for national wellbeing,[123] and than high senior staff salaries for organizational effectiveness. The military, which depends on cohesive cooperative working between ranks, has much smaller pay differentials than in companies. How can wealth gaps be reduced positively?

3.3.3 Conceptualizations

In addition to identifying interesting issues and people to study, up-system research is also being reconceptualized through work in diverse fields. Again, this is not a comprehensive review, but an indication of how to think about investigating new conceptualizations.

- *Animal leadership* can contribute to understanding the bases of human leadership, and has been related to territory ('space' and 'place' – C2.2) since the 1940s.[124] A study of stickleback fish found that 'leader' fish take risks, and will leave their safe weedy cover to find food. If successful, follower fish will follow.[125] Similar studies assess birds,[126] cows,[127] pigeons[128] and chimpanzees.[129] But laboratory experiments seem not to assess another probability, that animal "leaders" are more likely to get eaten or killed, and most fail. These studies may reveal more about leadership studies than about leadership. One lesson is probably that the few potential leaders who succeed become the data, and the majority who don't just disappear. And that is probably true of the human leadership literature. Eventually animal studies could generate a new but unpopular conceptualization of leaders past and present. Instead of being the brave entrepreneurs, perhaps they are just the foolhardy risk takers.[130] The idea is emerging in human leadership literature. Goodall provides an example, 'leaders ... graft for long hours in jobs that most of us do not want to do. ... and when the writs hit the fan they get canned.' [131]

Many animal studies suggest that the familiar "born or made" question (C2.3) should have another element, "survived", and how that was achieved – through skill, luck or supportive 'followers'? Chimpanzees, who organized themselves into teams to protect and extend territory, often attacked mothers with babies. Having a tough mum was a key to staying alive.[132] Robin Dunbar's studies of group-size among primates have been adapted for leadership training.[133] Understanding that it is intrinsically hard to function in a network with more than 150 others is a useful understanding for managers. Leadership theory is also being applied to animals – the degree of 'distributed leadership' has been assessed in monkeys; females succeed best.[134] It is helpful to recognize that some aspects of human power are biologically fundamental, but the human brain can build on basic animal abilities by being able to give orders and devise systems to make others comply, as within armies.[135] Animal studies of the nature of groups could contribute to understanding populations, crowds and followers. Knowing that ravens eventually pair bond because they find youthful 'gang life' biologically stressful[136] might indicate how to manage young gangs and their leaders.

- *Evolutionary psychology* provides interesting arguments about how power – and related aspects such as human cooperation, altruism and group size – are based on (but not determined by) evolutionary traits.[137] In their critique of twentieth century sociology, Tooby and Cosmedes dubbed the prevailing approach the 'Standard Social Science Model' (SSSM). This, they argued, assumed wrongly on the basis of little evidence, that culture was far more significant than human biology.[138] The realization is that many of the problems that human beings face arise, in part, because they have "stone age bodies" which include "stone age brains". Peter Singer questions why the political left does not embrace evolutionary perspectives that explain human cooperation and altruism.[139] There is a growing literature assessing whether political orientations are generically transmitted[140] and have a biological basis,[141] and the trust of powerful people.[142] Brain scans provide new evidence.[143] Our 'stone age brain' and resultant 'brain lag'[144] can explain why leaders and followers do not readily perceive contemporary global problems. Evolutionary perspectives are sometimes seen as contradicting Marxian claims that power relationships are socially constructed, yet the evolutionary view simply suggests that there are biological fundamentals that underpin social behaviour, not that they dictate it.

- *"Leaderless" groups*, which self-organize through social networking sites and other new ICT, create the need to reconceptualize the leadership of social movements. There are a few precedents – Israeli Kibbutz dwellers, the Quakers and the anarchists in Catalonia[145] – but it is not clear if the more recent manifestations share common factors with these groups. The so-called 'leaderless revolutions' that ousted Egyptian President Mubarak and other Middle Eastern depots in 2011[146] need explaining.[147] In parallel there are more violent 'leaderless movements' that are viewed as harmful by the international community.[148] How do these groups relate theoretically to those described by anthropologists in the past (C1.1)?

- *Risk and uncertainty* pervade the contemporary world, as Ulrich Beck's view of the 'risk society' explains.[149] Technological vulnerabilities, natural disasters, creeping emergencies such as climate change, and complexity[150] now seem to make leadership increasingly difficult. The evidence-base upon which leaders act seems uncertain,[151] for example in economics,[152] and the future is hard to predict.[153] In terms of leadership, it is not clear what is entirely new about the contemporary 'risk society' or whether the circumstance has always existed but in different guises. Do standard conceptualizations of leadership accommodate risk adequately, or do they need to change? When are leadership problems genuinely about 'risk' – "global economic trends," "new technologies" – and when is this rhetoric just an excuse?

- *Robot leadership* seems to be trapped in the realms of science fiction. But before dismissing the idea that machines can give orders, consider why drivers stop at red traffic lights. Before arguing that the traffic light is not conscious, think about the sensor on it. Consider why drivers reduce speed when an automatic speed camera recognizes that they are speeding and a sign illuminates saying 'SLOW DOWN', and they obey because that machine also has the power to impose a speeding fine without human assistance? (In South Africa, traffic lights have always been called 'robots'.) The capacity of artificial intelligence is increasing exponentially. Japan's *Machine Industry Memorial Foundation* predicts that by 2025, robots could be doing the jobs of 3.5 million people.[154] In 2010, *Playstation3* was reckoned to have 1% of the power of the human brain. *Playstation5* exceeds the power of the human brain. In 2003, a Japanese robot, Asimo, attended a state dinner in the Czech Republic, shaking hands with leaders and talking.[155] The Facebook page 'The Earth will be taken over by robots' is worth a look, as are discussions about robot ethics.[156]

- *Global elites* may arise as global problems create "survival of the fittest" cadres, who will aim to move around, or leave, the planet to continue human life elsewhere and "save the species". From the story of Noah and his ark, the idea has appeared on a local scale in many science fiction visions including John Christopher's 1950s version in *The Death of Grass*, and the religious elites implied within the 2010 film *The Road*. Intra-planetary elite migration is already happening through acquiring passports, families and property in safe regions. Elites are forcing non-elites out of cities such as Geneva, London and Mumbai, through their economic power to purchase property at a high price. Cosmologist Stephen Hawking predicts inter-planetary elites, and argues that sending a spaceship 'ark' to another planet will be the only way to perpetuate the species – 'Once we spread out into space and establish colonies, our future should be safe.'[157] Plato's view of society was based on the import of 'goods' and export of 'bads' to and from the 'colonies', material and human.[158] But he did not envisage the elites abandoning his model Republic for better habitats. Theorizations of elites and place

(C2.2) assume elites are generally static, and so far no political vision of society has been based on the idea that certain elites may simply run away if things get bad at home. Without knowing of Hawking or Plato, young people in China seem to think this could happen (Figure 3.7).

Understanding the relevant literature provides the basis for ensuring that a new project is building on, and does not repeat, previous research. It finds a "gap in knowledge" that a study will fill, based on existing knowledge. This is true from large-scale academic projects, to research for novels or films, and small-scale pieces of investigative journalism. But before embarking on a literature review, it is helpful to identify a topic area that may deserve more attention. Improved search engines, render the old-style "comprehensive review" a waste of time. There will always be something new on *Google* tomorrow morning. It is therefore important to decide clear, well-focused aims for a review, which are not too wide. Having done that, it is relevant to consider:

- that information may be *unreliable*, especially from official sources. It may be incomplete, misleading, focus on process rather than outcomes, and be self-justificatory.
- the likelihood of *fake news* and other manipulation of web-based and other media sources.
- the problem of **halo effect** – that literature by or about powerful people can create an impression of being accurate simply because of the charisma or exceptional abilities of that person.
- whether to use *freedom of information* (FOI) processes to access hidden documents. But it is important to have a clear idea what should be available, and where it might be found. Former employees of relevant organizations, or other documents released under FOI, can often help.
- that a *review report* will first explain its purpose, parameters (where, when, what, who), how searches were made, and how the sources were tested for reliability.

Owing to manner of destroying the environment, catastrophic disaster will come one after another – tsunami, earthquake, volcanic eruption, sand storm (Yu & Liu)

China will use up the last renewable resources, lots of people will die from water scarcity. World war III will break out for plundering natural resources (Yan & Xiong).

In order to protect soil, the city will be moved in the air, leaving fertile soil to plant trees. Traffic will be moved in pipeline (Peng & Jin).

Due to population explosion and limited land surface, people will move to another planet by Shezhou ['divine vessel'].

Because of environmental worsening and rapid development of space technology, humans will move to outer space. At that time Chinese will spread all over the universe, and peaceful communications will be built between each planet (Han).

Source: Yan Ni (2010) 'Evaluation of patriotism education in secondary schools in China in the context of globalization', unpublished MA dissertation, Centre for International Education and Research, University of Birmingham (UK)

FIGURE 3.7 Elites abandoning the planet – perceptions by Chinese children

- that a literature review is not the same as *documentary* or *biographical research*, which uses texts as sources of data and systematically "interrogates" them much as interviewees would be interviewed.
- whether the review amounts to a *systematic review* which consolidates a specific set of studies, uses problem-oriented questions and a framework for systematic collection, and culminates in a formal evaluation and conclusion.
- what powerful people have *read*, not only what they write – what may have influenced them and provided their knowledge-base.
- that under-researched *topics* are likely to reflect new, marginalized or sensitive issues, new forms of elite or leadership roles, and new conceptualizations or methodologies.

Traditional elite and leadership studies have covered specific populations – a region, company or 'domain'. What of the future? Technology is giving rise to 'global' elites and leadership which functions above, and can potentially exercise power over, the whole world population. This is likely to require innovative global methodologies and conceptualizations, and an ability to search and comprehend vast and diverse literatures. This will demand collaboration and 'crowdsourcing' on a global scale (C5.2).

KEY READING

Cooper, H., Hedges, L.V. and Valentine, J.C. (eds) (2009) *The Handbook of Research Synthesis and Meta-analysis.* New York: Russell Sage Foundation.

Ford, N. (2011) *The Essential Guide to Using the Web for Research.* London: Sage.

Fouchard, G. and Young, R. (2001) *A Simple Guide to Searching the Internet.* New Jersey: Prentice Hall.

Hart, C. (1998) *Doing a Literature Review: Releasing the Social Science Research Imagination.* London: Sage.

4

PLANNING

4.1   DESIGN
4.2   FOCUS
4.3   PROBLEMATIZATION
4.4   DEFINITIONS
4.5   ACCESS
4.6   INTEGRITY

> **PLAN**
>
> To devise or design something to be done, or something to be carried out; to arrange beforehand. (*OED*)

Planners often joke that, "*The plan worked very well, but it was the wrong plan.*" Planning is relatively easy, but designing the right type of plan requires careful preparation. Reviewing theory (C2) and literature (C3) creates an understanding of what has already been achieved in a particular field, which provides the basis for a study. Planning entails creating a strategy for going further than previous endeavours – how to find out something significant that is *not* known already. A research design, usually explains the "how" of research, based on decisions about what, who, when and where. But the starting point for any plan should be the "why", the strategic aims, the endpoints – what type of data, findings, results and evidence are eventually required? A plan and research design must be made on the basis of deciding which frameworks and methods are likely to be feasible, efficient and cost-effective.

But the planning stage does *not* happen only before consideration of research frameworks (C4) and data collection methods (C5). These aspects should all be considered at the same time, and are ongoing throughout a study.

Plans often seem linear and inflexible, but in reality they should just provide a provisional "map" which may evolve and 'emerge' as methods are thoroughly explored and implemented.[1] Like any plan, the purpose is just to transform ideas into action – to operationalize the study through using appropriate planning tools. It is just a means to an end. Logically, it seems necessary to first consider the basic elements of a design – the focus, access and integrity – and then research frameworks (C5), data collection methods (C6), and likely forms of analysis (C7) – before completing a design. In reality, the process is circular, fluid and continually changing, and it is helpful to think about all aspects in parallel. A central consideration is to make sure that things that cannot be changed can be accommodated – availability of elites, public meetings, end points – and things that seem flexible really can be changed if necessary – archive use, interview questions, interview timetables.

4.1 DESIGN

> **DESIGN**
>
> The preliminary conception of an idea that is to be carried into effect by action. (*OED*)

Many methods books explain planning in terms of 'research design',[2] some take design as the central aspect of methodology,[3] and there are online resources.[4] A research design can be presented as a diagram showing how specific aspects of the research link or evolve from other aspects (Appendix 3), and how they lead to potential outcomes. This can provide the basis for using specific planning tools, such as Gantt charts to decide the "who" and "when" (Appendix 4),[5] which are useful for managing a project team.[6] It is usually better to start collecting data at the lowest level in an organization, and hone the design and methods as the research proceeds upwards towards research among busy senior personnel. That avoids wasting time asking senior staff questions that can be answered (probably better) by subordinates, and senior staff may be very interested in an initial analysis of down-system findings which provides them with some 'payback' (below) for giving their time. Initial research questions might provide the basis for a focus group of junior staff, the results from this might generate the questions for a questionnaire survey of middle managers, and this might lead to purposive in-depth interviews with selected CEOs.

Up-system research has distinct characteristics, which a good design should address:

- '*Nominal fallacy*' should be assessed. It is easy to make false assumptions about who really has power in relation to a particular issue. Design needs to account for establishing where power lies,[7] and defining 'elite' and 'leadership'[8] (Appendices 1 and 7) before finalizing who to research. Senior people often work in a "black box" of expertise, and are unaware of what others do and of the whole picture. Large companies may deliberately isolate middle managers from knowing too much, as did Hitler. It is also wrong to assume that all those within a particular leadership or elite group agree with one another and work together for the same ends. The Guatemalan civil war dictatorship embodied a split between right wing elites and the army.[9] A flawed assumption about who has power can construct false findings – hospital surgeons might be blamed for poor hygiene when the hospital managers control that factor. The significance is greater in political research. In 2010, a 'senior Taliban leader', Mullah Mansour, gained access to high level governmental meetings in Afghanistan, but he was just a Pakistani shopkeeper.[10]

- *False assumptions* can arise from believing that we know who powerful people are by what they do. Schirmer advises, 'We need to find out why *they* think they do what they do. What are their beliefs and motivations, and justifications? What provides the agency? And interviewers must be aware of their own baggage. It is wrong to assume that all military personnel tell lies, and all civilians tell the truth.'[11]

- *Self-selecting data* means that up-system research tends to study those who are conspicuous because they succeed – the few MPs who are elected not the many who fail, successful business leaders not the countless bad ones, foolhardy heroes who take risks and are lucky not the majority who do the same thing but get killed, leaders who failed at school but still became rich not the majority of school failures who become poor. Analysis always needs to be aware of this intrinsic bias and not propose simplistic conclusions such as, "A good education is not needed to become a millionaire."

- *Set-backs* are inevitable, and risks should be assessed and alternative strategies identified – different interviewees, interviewers with a different persona (below), other data sources. Doing up-system research can be disappointing and frustrating, and a good plan helps researchers to move forward, pursuing alternatives.

- A *"surgical"* plan is often necessary to achieve desired outcomes quickly and efficiently. Data collection often requires a large time investment to get very little data, and there are sometimes no second chances.

- *Upsetting* powerful people, and those who protect them, unnecessarily should be avoided. This can cause a study to collapse. Necessary permissions need to be arranged early, and intentions explained clearly. Controversial or persistent techniques should be deployed later rather than earlier in a study, so if they fail most of the study is "in the bag".

- *Outcome-oriented*, purposive research may need to maintain a focus on advocacy or campaigning (C8). A design may aim to obtain specific data relevant to a media report or fundraising campaign, or it might closely reflect the type of evidence and arguments used in courts and create an evidence bank for lawyers and witnesses. But academic neutrality and professional advocacy need to be distinct, perhaps by using different personnel for the two roles.

In general, up-system research design is not categorically different from other social research plans but, if not addressed, the familiar problems may have more significant consequences.

A pilot study may be used to test the whole, or an aspect of, a research design before large-scale data collection. Research instruments – questionnaires, interview schedules, observation charts – may have been designed and tested previously by other researchers, such as Stodgill's 'Leader behaviour description questionnaire' (LBDQ),[12] and the originator credited. Instruments sometimes use proxy measurements which measure something that is easy to measure to assess something that is hard to measure, or data may be used to create indicators and aggregate indexes (C7.1). These should be tested at the design stage, to ensure the data can be used to produce the form of finding or analysis that is required. Questionnaires may be created or adapted for a specific study, in which case they will first be piloted on a small scale to identify ambiguous or misleading aspects. Confident interviewees sometimes enjoy giving very literal but unhelpful replies to unclear questions (Figure 4.1).

"Do you feel 90 years old?"
   "That's a difficult question to answer. You see, I've never been 90 before."
(P.D. James, writer, interview on the BBC on her 90th birthday)

"Have you lived in this town all your life Mr Thostlethwaite?"
   "No ... not yet."
(Yorkshire town mayor to BBC interviewer)

FIGURE 4.1   Literal responses to unclear questions

4.2 FOCUS

FOCUS

That point or position at which an object must be situated, in order that the image produced by the lens may be clear and well-defined. (*OED*)

PURPOSE

The object for which anything is done; end, aim. (*OED*)

RATIONALE

A statement of reasons. The fundamental reason, the logical or rational basis of anything. (*OED*)

Research normally stems from interest or concern about a topic (C3), but the wording of this is important to provide a clear workable research *focus*. Topics expressed in terms such as "Refugee leadership" or "Corporate crime" might provide a good title for a book, but do not describe a practical piece of research. The notions of a 'perspective',[13] 'frame of reference' or 'lens'[14] are often used, which helps to decide the boundaries and parameters – "what's in and what's out".

The *purpose* of a research study provides focus and affirms the value of the topic. Put bluntly, does the proposed research "pass the 'so what?' test"? Who is the study for – what client, reader or interest group – and will they be interested? Thinking about this may engender a change of direction or radical change of a topic. That may be a difficult decision, but it is best made earlier rather than later. In the past, research was often curiosity driven, and the aim was simply to create new understandings in a particular field – a "contribution to knowledge" was a good enough justification. Now that can be done easily in a few hours with the help of *Google*, and so there are increasing demands that research must be useful. It is more often 'problem-solving'[15] or 'solution-oriented'[16] in relation to practical or intellectual problems. But a research problem should not be narrowly constructed simply to suit the narrow strategic interests of a powerful entity, for example, "How can we increase the reputation of OILDIS?" It will be more effective if it reflected an objective stance because that will get better answers – "How do oil companies enhance their reputation?" The implications for a specific entity can be explained later. Research for campaigning organizations is often action-oriented. If data is to be used for specific purposes – court cases, documentary films, political advocacy – the design must produce appropriate data and findings in relevant action-oriented forms (Figure 4.2).

The familiar 'central purposes', which set the parameters of research studies include:[17]

- *Descriptive*. The components of an up-system structure, and how they are related – "The management structure of the Serbian Ministry of Defence".
- *Analytical*. Description of relationships and identification of causal factors to explain why certain things happen – "The management and operational rationale of the Serbian Ministry of Defence".
- *Interpretive* and *explanatory*. Similar to analytical, but with less description, and can provide understandings that statistics alone cannot provide – "The influence of EU policy on the Serbian Ministry of Defence".
- *Evaluative*.[18] What is the value of a particular activity – "The effectiveness of collaboration between the Department for International Military Cooperation (Serbian Ministry of Defence) and the EU".
- *Predictive*. Description and analysis of causal factors, and assessment of past trends to propose what might happen in the future – "The threat of terrorism in Serbia over the next ten years".
- *Planning*. Practical application of predictive analysis – "Reforming the Department for Strategic Planning (Serbian Ministry of Defence) to respond to future terrorist threats".
- *Methodological development*. The testing of new or adapted frameworks or methods – "Effective interview strategies among Serbian elites".

Every piece of research should seek to gather empirical data that can be used to design, influence, or implement policies and practices that will contribute to the organization's vision. It should seek to influence those who are in a position to effect change.

"Researching in the traditional academic sense is only a part of what doing research at Amnesty International (AI) *is all about. Research is also about ensuring that the human rights agenda most suitable for a country and sub-region is put forward and followed. Research at AI is, first and foremost, about designing and targeting actions."*

"I am always aware of why I am doing the research. AI is a campaigning organization and I seek to provide high-quality research work, which can be used to take action. If the research does not help, then there is not much point to it."

"Research without action would be academic and fruitless. Action without solid research would be foolish and damaging".

Source: Amnesty International, Research Policy Manual (internal)

FIGURE 4.2 Action-oriented research

Any research study needs to be 'problematized' (C4.3), but some up-system research also has a distinct *problem-oriented purpose* which culminates in practical outcomes (Figure 4.3). Academic researchers often overlook work by professional researchers such as police and journalists, and vice versa, but it is helpful for all researchers to consider the spectrum of those who might have done research with a similar purpose. This provides a basis for effective literature searches, selecting theoretical stances and identifying relevant methods.

The reasons for the purpose of a study are usually elaborated under the headings *rationale* or *justification*, and derive from objective authorities, which may include:

- *Recommendations* – "This study found that there is little research about women leaders in Iceland."
- *Needs assessments* – "Before health centres are built in rural villages, local chiefs need to be identified."
- *Experts* or politicians – "The Ministry has concluded that Italian businesses need to understand Chinese companies better."
- *Policies* – "The agency will assess the relationship between good governance and successful multilateral aid."
- *Public* or *media* demands – "The leaders of these criminal gangs must be identified."
- *Reasoned arguments* – "If computers achieve consciousness, the law will need to decide the limits of their power, and discussion of ethical implications is essential before this happens."

Figure 4.4 provides examples of academic rationale, but such claims should be used critically – when was it said and is it still true, is it specific or general, is it supported by evidence? Sometimes, personal motivation is also acceptable – "My family were refugees from Armenia in 1915, and my grandmother tells me that her parents were landowners in Turkey". But personal academic studies must still be based on a systematic process of investigation.

Problem-oriented purpose	Likely researchers	Possible rationale (reason)
Accountability. Preventing abuse of power	Investigative, civil society organizations, police, journalists, moral philosophers, lawyers	Evidence is needed for judicial inquiries, media stories, ethical debate or law reform
Artistic integrity	Novelists, playwrights, film makers, art historians, satirists	Accurate context is essential for credibility
Commercial intelligence	Investigation agencies, diplomats, company staff	Information about commercial rivals is needed to gain competitive advantage
Documentary integrity	Historians, diarists, documentary film makers, museum curators, journalists, information officers	Records should be accurate and consistent
Gaining and maintaining power	Politicians, CEOs, party workers, diplomats, religious leaders	The power of our leaders must be maintained by assessing peers, rivals and allies
Leadership training	Psychologists, trainers, course managers, writers, publishers	Training should be evidence-based
Legitimacy	Genealogists, diplomats, international negotiators	Claims to inheritance and power must be verified
Public relations	Press officers, PR staff, spin consultants, advertising agencies	The image of elites must be presented favourably/ unfavourably
Religious	Theologians, religious leaders, secularists	Religious power must be upheld, or challenged, credibly
Reproduction of elites	Elite dating agencies, marriage brokers, 'head hunters', elite educational institutions	Elites must self-select carefully to maintain their abilities, status and power
Security, public order	Spies, diplomats, UN, military, police	Intelligence must be good to achieve strategic advantage
Development of systems	Constitutional experts, organizational/systems planners, educationists	Better governance structures and selection processes need to be developed
Voyeurism, curiosity, cash reward	Journalists, 'paparazzi'	The public wants to know about the lives of celebrities

FIGURE 4.3 Problem-oriented purposes and rationale

The presentation of purpose and rationale can affect *access* (below). Powerful people are more likely to cooperate with a research study if they understand and appreciate its purpose, see it as unthreatening, and believe that they might benefit in some way. Studies that might give away commercial secrets, or reveal weaknesses, need careful presentation. Military leaders are more likely to permit a study of "Unrecognized acts of heroism", than of "Foolhardy decisions". Research on corporate ethics might avoid the word 'ethics', and use phrases such as 'difficult situations' and 'value conflicts'.[19]

'*We know too little about leadership. We fail to grasp the essence of leadership that is relevant to the modern age and hence we cannot agree even on the standards by which to measure, recruit, and reject it. Is leadership merely innovation – cultural or political? Mobilization of followers? Goal setting? Goal fulfillment? Is the leader the definer of values? Satisfier of needs? If leaders require followers, who leads whom from where to where, and why? How do leaders lead followers without being wholly led by followers? Leadership is one of the most observed and least understood phenomena on earth.*' (Burns, J.M. (1978) *Leadership*. New York: Harper and Row)

In social psychology, '*Leadership is a topic that has had a central position in the field of group dynamics for several decades but has not, in my view, been successfully conceptualized nor empirically investigated.*' (Rywick, T. (1998) quoted in Elcock, H. (2001) *Political Leadership*. Cheltenham: Edward Elgar. p. 16)

'*It is somewhat surprising… that the study of politics as a social science has not focused attention more sharply upon the concept of "political leadership"*' (Paige, G.D. (1977) *The Scientific Study of Political Leadership*. London: The Free Press. p. 11)

'*Another problem as we seek to identify the attributes and support needed by political leaders at the end of the 20th century is that …the tools available to do this are strangely lacking. Studies of political leadership … are less satisfying and illuminating than they should be because of the absence of analytical frameworks sufficiently robust to make sense of the common issues and problems such leaders face or to permit effective comparisons among them …*' (Elcock, H. (2001) *Political Leadership*. Cheltenham: Edward Elgar. p. 16)

In 1977, Paige talked of '*…a unique reference to "followship" by McCloskey, the only mention for half a century*'. (Paige, G.D. (1977) *The Scientific Study of Political Leadership*. London: The Free Press. p. 13)

FIGURE 4.4   Academic support for research 'rationale'

Sometimes purpose can be presented more appropriately by re-framing a large-scale study in terms of one specific area of data collection. Data collection for a book about, "The religious affiliations of CEOs" might be better presented as "The sources of moral values among CEOs".

Another aspect of focus is the scale of what is to be investigated. This is likely to mean one or more *levels* of inquiry. If the topic is war criminals, a biographical approach may focus on one interesting person, such as Nazi war criminal Albert Speer,[20] or the way in which countries made their war criminals accountable could be compared.[21] The two may be linked. International comparisons could generate questions for an in-depth biographical study, or vice versa. Alternatively, a *cross sectional analysis/study* might study a 'slice' across levels.[22] A significant aspect, such as communication between policy-makers, could be examined across a number of levels – hospital directors, regional authorities, ministries and the WHO. Scale requires decisions about depth versus breadth, and this entails consideration of potential frameworks (C5) and methods (C6), which can be mapped against relevant levels. Appendix 5 provides a template for doing this.

4.3 PROBLEMATIZATION

> **PROBLEM**
>
> A difficult question proposed for solution. A question proposed for academic discussion or scholastic disputation. (*OED*)

> **PROBLEMATIC/PROBLEMATIQUE**
>
> Of the nature of a problem. (*OED*)

> **HYPOTHESIS**
>
> A provisional supposition which accounts for known facts, and serves as a starting point for further investigation by which it may be proved or disproved. (*OED*)

A topic does not intrinsically describe a research problem. Problematization involves asking questions to identify relevant practical or theoretical unknowns within a topic – "How was accountability improved?" or "What is the evolutionary explanation for leadership?" It is also a way for the researcher to gain more objectivity, and not jump to hasty conclusions about a topic.[23] The problematization reflects the purpose, and supports the rationale, of a study.

A research problem is an unknown that demands a solution or resolution. The Club of Rome report *The First Global Revolution* was structured in terms of a world '*problematique*' and '*resolutique*'.[24] Holmes talks of a 'problem (solving) approach',[25] and the brackets indicate that etymologically the word 'problem' embodies the idea, 'for resolution'. But not every issue is amenable to a solution, as Gwyn Prins argues in relation to climate change:

> there was a fundamental framing error, and climate change was represented as a conventional environmental 'problem' that is capable of being 'solved'. It is neither of these ... climate change is better understood as a persistent condition that must be coped with and can only be partially managed more – or less – well.[26]

'Tame' problems may be complex but have 'defined achievable end states'; 'wicked problems' are 'issues that are often formulated as if they are susceptible to solutions when in fact they are not'. It may be possible to solve the problem of "a crime", or maybe of a specific "type of crime", or even of "a high crime rate", but probably not to "solve the problem of crime". However, an issue that cannot be solved may still be problematized, for example in terms of public information, deceit and resultant abuses of power. The obvious problem about problematization, as French Marxist Louis Althusser warned, is that a 'problematic' may contain presuppositions, structures and boundaries that lead to a prejudged resolution.[27] His argument may have had personal resonance. He ended his life in a psychiatric hospital because he murdered his sociologist wife.

Having justified and problematized a study, this can be expressed as initial *hypotheses* and/or *research questions* which have emerged from the literature review (C3). A hypothesis is an informed guess which can be tested to create a generalizable conclusion. Often, hypotheses test causal relationships – that if A happens B will follow (C7.2). It might test a predictive theory, be a guess about a causal relationship arising from relevant literature or observation, or be a "Eureka" insight – "that political parties are not necessary for modern democracies". Formal hypotheses need to be proved or disproved on the basis of statistical probabilities, which is very difficult outside experimental research.[28] A guiding or soft hypothesis can also be used, which is "addressed" but not proved or disproved in the conclusions of the study. Research questions similarly guide a study. Questions are usually "addressed" rather than "answered", unless the study is investigative or evaluatory and demands finite answers, and need to be framed in relation to the data collection and analysis methods.[29] *Initial* research questions/hypotheses may be elaborated as a result of an ongoing literature/theoretical review, or other data collection, to create sets of *specific* hypotheses/questions, which can be investigated through interviews and surveys, observation or interrogation schedule.

The cause-and-effect aspects of hypotheses and questions are often framed in terms of *variables*. *Independent* variables are either fixed – age, gender, birthplace – or assumed to be fixed – income, property ownership, education. Independent variables are hypothesized as causing an effect on less fixed *dependent* variables – political choice, favoured film stars, abuse of power. The plausibility of causal relationships proposed by hypotheses can be tested initially through reverse logic – age might affect political choice, but could political choice also affect age? No, so this is potentially a strong hypothesis. Education may affect family power, but could family power also affect education? Yes, so this is not a strong hypothesis. Analysis entails comparing the results for different variables – men compared with women in relation to who they vote for, younger CEOs compared with older CEOs in relation to involvement in corruption. An easily measured *proxy* variable may be used to represent an *inferred value* that is hard to measure directly – "income" might be a proxy for "social status", "GDP" for "standard of living". Similarly *indicators* (number of doctors, access to clean water) may assess a *concept* (health) (C7.1). But proxies and indicators are often flawed. If "percent of population voting" were used to assess "level of democracy", Iran or North Korea would score better than America or Britain.

Although pure research aims to discover something new, researchers have often made a good guess about what they will discover, and hypotheses/questions are constructed so that they can "wrap the data around their conclusions". This is common in funded research, where everyone wants to ensure that there will be a value-for-money outcome. It avoids wasting time on irrelevant endeavour, but can lead to research that is set up as a foregone conclusion. It is necessary to distinguish clearly between what is being researched, and the *assumptions* of a study. These form the "taken for granted" bases for the hypotheses or questions, and are accepted as correct and are therefore not questioned further – that "democracy is better than fascism", "women are disadvantaged when seeking leadership positions", "stamina is a prerequisite of being a successful politician". But assumptions must be referenced to theory, strong evidence, or ontological and epistemological arguments, which support their general acceptance (C2).

To operationalize the hypotheses/questions, a study can be further focused by determining a hierarchy of *aims* – aim, sub-aims, sub-sub-aims – but terms relating to this are very muddled. For example, one study might be framed in terms of – PURPOSE > AIMS > OBJECTIVES – but another study might use the terms – GOAL > OBJECTIVES > AIMS – to imply the same hierarchy. Terms are less important than the need to frame hierarchical relationships appropriately, which can then be mapped onto specific research questions and specific sub-hypotheses relating to those main questions/hypotheses, and perhaps then linked to questions in a questionnaire or interview/observation schedule. Whatever the problems with terminology, the key consideration is the unknowns: what does the researcher aim to find out that is not known already? Appendix 6 suggests how a table or spidergram can show how the aspects of focus might relate to one another, and also possible overlap in terms of practicalities such as fieldwork planning. In any study, it should be possible to trace the chain of systematic inquiry from any conclusion – back through analysis, findings, methods – to aims, questions, rationale and purpose. The evidence of a systematic process is what makes research different from a casual conversation in an airport lounge.

4.4 DEFINITIONS

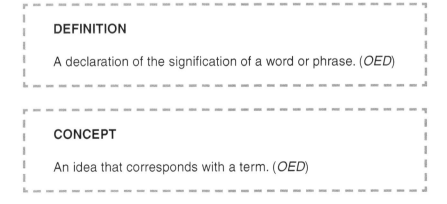

DEFINITION

A declaration of the signification of a word or phrase. (*OED*)

CONCEPT

An idea that corresponds with a term. (*OED*)

Definitions and *concepts* are useful to further focus and clarify a topic, but also in order to identify *keywords* for data searches, which should be listed in the literature review of an academic research report (C3.1). These come from noting keywords in similar studies, and by authors thinking about how they would search for their own study. *Wordle* provides an interesting visual way to test if the frequency of words in a text reflects the key concepts of that text, by creating 'word clouds' which may prompt amendments to titles and headings, or to the whole text. [30] It is crucial that the title of a study, and section headings for digital versions, include the relevant keywords. A good title is best constructed by identifying the main keywords, and then assembling them into a title. This can then be tested on search engines for its effectiveness. Literary titles, used in the past, are now best avoided. It is not self-evident that Frantz Fanon's *The Wretched of the Earth* is a seminal work in anti-colonial Marxist liberation studies, which links colonial war to mental health problems.

Dictionaries are a useful starting point for defining terms (as throughout this book). General dictionaries remind researchers that some words have many meanings – 'development' can refer to nations or children. Specialist dictionaries – politics, sociology, philosophy, social psychology – help to ensure that the terminology in a study reflects current usage in relevant disciplines. A thesaurus helps to find the best keywords and related concepts. Etymological dictionaries not only explain the roots and linguistic derivations of words, but show linkages that can inspire interesting lines of thought. How many people involved in leadership training know that 'education' is derived from the Latin *educere*, which derives from *ducere* meaning 'lead', and that the Greek roots of 'pedagogue' – *agogos* – also mean 'leading' because pedagogues were the slaves who took the children to school. Education is, of course, a significant form of leadership and vice versa.

A central decision for any up-system study is to decide whether those concerned will be conceptualized in terms of their elite roles or leadership roles, or both (Introduction, Appendix 1). The important consideration is that any study is framed in a way that is appropriate to the aims of that study (above). To decide which approach is appropriate, it is useful to ask, in relation to the research subjects and Figure 0.9, basic questions such as:

1   What is their up-system role, and is it best framed as a *group* or as an *individual*?
2   Is the down-system *population* over whom they have power best described as anonymous *populace* or specific *followers*?
3   What is the *legitimacy* of their relationship with the down-system group?
4   Is their status *ascribed* or *achieved*?
5   What is the form of their power – *influence* or *coercion*?
6   What is the *place* or *domain* of this power and influence?

The deciding factor is how the research is conceptualized, not who it concerns. Appendix 7 shows how the same person, King Hussein of Jordan, could be conceptualized in relation to his roles as a military leader or royal elite. Many other conceptual distinctions can be made, not least is the study about leadership or management – what is the difference between the two, and is there any agreement about what those words mean? Similarly, how is the power of the person assessed, beyond a formal or job title that may be misleading. The important point is to provide adequate definitions, perhaps in a glossary, and to be able to justify them either through reference to another authority, or by logical, perhaps linguistic, argument.

Up-system concepts and terms are culturally shaped, and need to be considered in relation to locally relevant languages, particularly in cross-cultural comparative studies. A meticulous approach helps with basic understandings of different cultures, which can be useful when writing questionnaires and clarifying analysis (Figure 4.5). Original terminology should be maintained when translating or mentioning specific sources. A cross-cultural study is likely to be read by people who understand those languages, and they can be confused by an arbitrary use of terms. A Ghanaian would be confused if Omanhene, Gyasehene, Obaatan and Tofuhene (Figure 1.9) were conflated under the heading "village chief", as an English reader would be if Queen, President, Prime Minister and Head of State were muddled. Cultural understandings within groups that have their own slang or professional jargon need similar consideration, such as "commission" in mafia studies, "juiced" in gang research, or the hundreds of terms used for the police, from "pigs" and "poulets" to "smurfs" and "soggies".

There are many ways to present the focus of a study, including the type of diagrams explained in this chapter. An academic thesis will usually provide a detailed account, but a professional report may only include a few sentences. Appendix 8 suggests in outline how focus might be explained in a text. The important point is that all elements of focus are logically connected to one another and to other relevant parts of the report. Whatever the style, the outcome should be that the researcher could explain what the research is about in a few words, to anyone at a party, without ending up as the bore who no one else wants to talk to.

The Korean word for leader – *ji-do-ja* – means 'instructing person', but another – *dae-tong-ryong* – means 'big controller of territory' and is used only to refer to the head of state. In Arabic, *zaa-a-ma*, means 'to command people', but another word – *qya-da* – literally means, 'to walk in front of the animal in order to give it direction'. A separate term – *al-rais* – only describes the head of state, as in Korea. Concerning 'elite', the Korean *sag-ryu-in-sa* means a 'higher type/system/tendency of people', and this is distinct from *bu-ja* which is reserved for wealthy people. In Arabic, the general term for elites is *aaliyatul-qaum*, meaning 'high profile people', but *al-kheirou fi al-qaoum* is also used, meaning 'the best of men'. Like Korean, there is a separate term for wealthy elites, *aghniya*.

FIGURE 4.5   Conceptualizing a cross-cultural study of leadership

Source: Lee, Yun-joo (2011) 'Leadership and development in South Korea and Egypt: The significance of "cultural shifts"', unpublished PhD thesis. SOAS, University of London.

4.5 ACCESS

> **ACCESS**
>
> A way or means of approach. (*OED*)

Access to powerful people is a distinct problem of up-system research, which needs consideration early in any research planning.[31] Access includes gaining entry to the research site,[32] arranging for interviews, and other interpersonal data collection methods such as survey questionnaires, emails and participant observation.[33] In a highly controlled country, it may be difficult to travel beyond a "safe" area, to assess what is happening throughout a country.[34] It may be helpful to identify places and things of interest – historical sites, dams, volcanoes – because permission may be more readily granted to visit things that a regime wants to show off. Powerful people are often 'reluctant respondents',[35] and either actively evade being researched, are busy and do not have time,[36] or do not wish to engage with a researcher who does not clearly support their point of view.[37] Researchers find that 'cold calling' to arrange interviews is often unproductive and demoralizing, for instance being told to call again when they 'have better questions'.[38]

Any approach should explain the nature of the research, why the researcher needs to interview that person, the ethical protocol (see below), and what the questions are likely to be.[39] Assure the interviewee that all relevant publically available information has already been collected and considered, but that there are a few specific questions that only that particular person can answer – "What did you learn about leadership from being a fighter pilot in Vietnam?" An interview could end by asking – "Who else would you suggest I talk to?" – which might help to gain access to others through 'snowballing' (C6.2).[40] Investigative journalists and investigators often have much more experience of up-system interviewing than academics. It is useful to consider different access and optimization techniques (Appendix 11).

Identifying potentially cooperative research subjects can be useful. Retired or retiring leaders may be more willing to cooperate than those in mid-career. They are probably bored and want to remain relevant, and may be less reticent to talk. Even if their knowledge of issues is not current, their knowledge of how a system works and the people within it may be invaluable. People in hospital, under house arrest or in prison may be pleased to pass the time with an interviewer.[41] Bernard Madoff was happy to disclose the complicity of other bankers in financial irregularity to a *New York Times* reporter, after he had started his prison sentence of 150 years.[42] An assessment of the likely motives of powerful people to take part in research is useful and may become a research finding in its own right. They may range from 'media' – wanting publicity – to 'therapy' – wanting to talk to a good listener about aspects of their life that are difficult.[43]

The first access problem is often to get past gatekeepers and spokespeople.[44] There may be a series of different gatekeepers to negotiate in different ways.[45] Celebrities often employ PR staff who assess the publicity cost-benefit of an interview, and make up any perceived deficit by charging a fee for brief access.[46] Recommendation can help – "The chairman's brother suggested I should talk to Mr Ahmed" – as are mutual elite forums – "I am also a member of the *Royal Society of Arts*." In non-western contexts, mentioning family connections or status is often essential, and it might be considered bad manners not to do this because it warns that the researcher might have prior knowledge. But in a western setting this approach could be counterproductive, and viewed as improper use of connections. If access cannot be gained to workplace or home, a journalist would try to meet by chance elsewhere – bars, clubs, gyms, airport lounges. Letters of recommendation and business cards are helpful, essential in countries such as Japan. Status symbols such as university crests, company logos and titles reassure nervous gatekeepers because they can then justify their decisions. Papers will usually be retained, so multiple copies are vital. Gatekeepers can themselves become informants and data, revealing aspects of elite culture, within a 'from below' approach.[47] If civil servants are told to say nothing about a particular issue, that may be interesting data about their line managers and politicians.

Postal, phone and email *inquiry systems* are also set up to gate keep. Company, and other official, websites usually try to deflect correspondence and callers, through obtuse or limited 'contact' details. 'Customer services' and 'customer relations' are similar. Companies often use overseas customer service agents that deter inquiries structurally. These centres are often run by low-skilled frontline operators, who provide muddled replies. Often, each communication is handled by a different person who does not read the previous correspondence, details are lost and requests to refer an issue to a line manager are ignored.[48] Staff may have little incentive to investigate properly to provide helpful replies, feel little sense of responsibility, but simply need to get through a large volume of calls or emails. Inquirers who give up in frustration may be logged as 'resolved'. Customer Service staff may reply to complaints by asking for 'additional information' and closing files before there is time to reply.[49] But these systems themselves can provide a good source of data for research about gatekeeping (bad practice is often good data) and pointing out that replies may be published often inspiring better service.

'Systematic correspondence' (C5.2) may help to overcome e-barriers. A number of people can be accessed through different routes, and the data triangulated (C6.3). Working out the pattern of email addresses can help to get around frontline systems. If the address for MP Lynne Jones is – L.jones@parliament.az – it is likely that others are similar. Using the webpage link for 'investors', 'sales' or 'press' may provide an effective route in, especially if the inquirer adopts an appropriate *persona* when making contact, for example that of another press officer. In low-tech countries where e-contact details are not easy to find, access may, paradoxically, be easier. In these settings, the offices of senior people are not surprised by unexpected visitors, and are used to accommodating them.

The *persona* of the researcher – the identity issue'[50] – is important. Might it be best to adopt a 'journalistic', 'therapeutic' or 'investigative' style?[51] This 'self-presentation dilemma' means that the benefits of appearing to be a knowledgeable 'insider' need to be balanced against being an amateur 'outsider' who is keen to learn.[52] How necessary is it to gain mastery in the field of the interviewee? 'Positionality'[53] entails a trade-off between appearing 'informed' or 'naïve', 'sympathetic' or 'unsympathetic'.[54] Should the researcher try to make those being researched 'complicit' in the project?[55] Does empathy help, for instance sympathizing that appearing in 'rich lists' may be annoying for an elite, even though that list provided the sample frame?[56] Elites may even value the fact that a researcher will take 'a longer view' of their achievements.[57] Women experience advantages and disadvantages when interviewing powerful people, who are usually men,[58] and interviewing powerful women has its own problems.[59] Elites and leaders may respond best to being researched, or interviewed, by particular people in particular circumstances, but what works well with one may be inappropriate with another.[60] Few elites are likely to turn down an interview requested by researchers from organizations such as NHK, BBC or *China Daily*. Mention of an elite university or NGO might be helpful.[61] Promises of some form of resultant benefit for the interviewee might be appreciated, even if it is just feedback on the research.[62] And not least is the problem, what should you wear?[63] (Figure 4.6).

A Korean researcher, Yun-joo Lee, wearing Muslim dress to interview an Islamic leader, Professor Muhammad S. Tantawy, Grand Sheik of *Al-Azhar*

FIGURE 4.6   The persona of the interviewer

Similarly, *organizational persona* brings benefits and problems. UNESCO, *Amnesty International* and ICRC have long histories of working through governments, and of researching political prisoners, some of whom later become powerful politicians and presidents. But this persona needs to be presented very carefully to government officials when negotiating access. Other organizations such as UNICEF and *Human Rights Watch*, try to work directly with the public, and their credibility comes from that persona. An appropriate persona might also stem from building mutual respect between elites of very different backgrounds. The Christian persona of British members of the House of Lords, Lord Alton and Baroness Cox, did not prevent constructive discussion with leaders in North Korea.[64] The persona of *Harvard University* helped researchers investigating the role of military leaders in rape, in the Democratic Republic of the Congo. They even managed to get the Congolese national military to create a 48-hour ceasefire while researchers interviewed militia leaders.[65]

But the effectiveness of *persona* is very circumstantial, and could include seemingly contradictory approaches involving:

- the use of other *elites* – 'borrowing power from the powerful'[66]
- an *attractive* woman, or man
- *powerless people* – children, people with disabilities, representatives of a grass roots organization or minority ethnic group
- a *foreigner* – someone who has no obvious links or knowledge
- someone with *special empathy* – same religion, race, birthplace, club, profession
- a high profile *TV/radio interviewer,* even if the interview is not recorded
- someone who will *film or record* the interview and produce a high quality output which will be distributed or could be useful for the interviewee (Figure 6.4)
- someone from a *prestigious organization*, which the interviewee might want to impress or influence
- someone who can provide "*payback*" – enhance the status of the research subject
- someone who the research subject can clearly *help,* without payback.

There is usually only one chance to present the persona of the interviewer appropriately. Thoughtful planning – including finding out who has gained access previously, and what type of people the interviewee likes – is worthwhile.

Although interpersonal data collection lends credibility to any research, particularly journalistic accounts, meeting and interviewing powerful people is not always the best way to answer relevant questions and discover the truth. Not least, people at the top of large organizations do not understand every detail of how their own organizations work,[67] and assessing publically available web information, or insider accounts such as trades union reports, might be better. Powerful people are very skilled at information and impression management, and an interview may be little more than a theatrical performance. 'Indirect' research frameworks (C5.2) and 'remote observation' (C6.1.2) may provide better findings than can be achieved through direct access, which may be personally exciting but also empirically disappointing.

4.6 INTEGRITY

> **INTEGRITY**
>
> Unimpaired or uncorrupted state. Soundness of moral principle. (*OED*)

> **ETHICS**
>
> The rules of conduct recognized in certain limited departments of human life. (*OED*)

Ensuring the integrity of a research project entails thinking about objectivity, impartiality, bias and research ethics.[68] These are closely linked because subjective or unethical research practice often leads to biased data collection and analysis, and vice versa.[69] The ethics of up-system studies require balancing the desire to do sound objective research which avoids unnecessary harm, with the need to investigate and engage with people who may use their power in unethical and harmful ways.[70] Within organizations such as the *International Committee of the Red Cross* (ICRC) and *Amnesty International*, the need to ensure integrity in the form of neutrality or impartiality goes beyond the normal requirements of ethical research. It encompasses duties to an organization, and its goals and principles (Figure 4.7).

Impartiality means that the organization conducts research on human rights abuses regardless of the nature of the governments or armed political groups, the nature of the conflicts, the identity of the perpetrators or the victims.

'Our work is based on the fact that it cannot be attributed to partisan propaganda of one kind or another. Being able to demonstrate impartiality is an important source of credibility. We are rendered completely open to attack on all fronts if one bit of biased info goes out and is discovered.'

'We are here to promote human rights but not political systems, ideas or individuals. Fortunately, you don't have to like the people to protect them. It's nice when you can, but it's not important. Treat everyone alike and it becomes easy to uphold an impartial stance.'

Source: Research Support Unit, International Secretariat, *Amnesty International*

FIGURE 4.7 Impartiality

Perhaps the greatest ethical mistake in up-system research is an assumption that powerful people do not need, or deserve, the same ethical considerations as others. Power does not intrinsically protect people from an abuse of power in the form of unethical research, and people in conspicuous public positions are, in some circumstances, more vulnerable than others, as are their families, friends and subordinates. Powerful people who are political prisoners and refugees may have unique problems.[71] Research ethics codes often omit a simple standard that is sometimes ignored in up-system research – do not misrepresent data. Findings must be 'morally plausible',[72] and not be calculated or presented in a way that primarily suits political convenience.

Up-system research also needs to be framed within an awareness of the genuine dilemmas facing many elites and leaders in a complex globalizing world. While adopting a critical stance, researchers need to appreciate problems such as risk and uncertainty,[73] novel diseases and other security threats, responsibility to the public or employees, and violent challenges to legitimate power. Research should always assess reasons for success in difficult contexts, not just failure. It is unethical to exploit an apparent weakness which arises simply because someone is doing a very difficult job.

The starting point for considering research ethics is the numerous *ethical codes* and regulations available from research bodies, professional organizations, universities, public services, government departments and the civil service. Any description of the ethical approach for a particular study should take account of these, and then identify and discuss aspects that are not fully covered or seem unique to a particular study. Consulting previous, similar studies is also useful, and quoting ethical standards used previously can be a strong basis for the "ethical considerations" of any proposed study. Many books explain the basics of research ethics,[74] but the principles may need to be developed for up-system work.

- *Voluntary participation* – the research participants should be acting freely and not pressured or coerced into taking part in a study. But if a leader instructs a spokesperson to answer questions as part of their job, is this voluntary participation in an interview?
- *Causing harm* – research should not create a risk of adverse outcomes for research subjects, researchers and those related to them. But do these considerations extend to the organization or country that the researchers, or research subjects, represent? How does investigative research about abuse of power fit within this principle? For a war criminal to end up in jail as the result of research could certainly be perceived, by some, as "harm" to the research subject.
- *Informed consent* – those concerned should understand the research and its implications, and agree to take part. But might the fact that a powerful person answers a question intrinsically imply informed consent simply because they have power? Distance research through ICT (C5.2) raises new questions. If despots are appearing at a trial that is being broadcast in real time, they would probably not give informed consent for their body language to be analysed by a researcher in another country. If the purpose was to assess their mental health, that might seem unethical and intrusive. But what if intelligence experts were doing the same thing in order to assess the likely truth of the statements?

- *Privacy* – international human rights law protects privacy. But what is the distinction between the public and private life of public figures? To what extent is it acceptable to investigate the private lives of public figures?
- *Payment* – it is often considered ethically correct to pay vulnerable people for inter-views, to compensate for lost earnings or work time. If there is no financial loss, pay-ment is seen as unethical. But is payment appropriate for powerful people, for example if the agent of a celebrity requests this "to cover costs"?
- *Confidentiality, secrecy,*[75] *anonymity* and *disclosure* – should data and participants be pro-tected and disguised?[76] For human rights organizations this has distinct implications (Figure 4.8). In up-system research, careless practice can endanger people in significant ways, especially if the findings are publicized widely. But is anonymity always possible in relation to public figures holding specific posts that will inevitably identify them? Any information that is already in the *public domain* can usually be used freely without further permission, even if it is incorrect, although some countries still act against those who repeat unfavourable information.
- *Approval* – interviewees may demand to see and approve the write-up of the interview or draft report. If so, is there a distinction between factual, and analytical correction such as the juxtaposition of data in a way that suggests that the interviewee was lying? How does *academic freedom* apply?[77]
- *Opportunistic data* should be used ethically in terms of protecting innocent third parties, but there is little agreement about what that entails. Is a document found in a public rubbish bin "ethics-free", or is there a difference if a person put it there intentionally, or unintentionally, and how does the finder know? If a politician makes an unguarded private comment wrongly believing that a microphone is not on, should that com-ment be broadcast? The outcome could contribute to the fall of a politician.[78]
- *"Off the record"* usually means that a comment must not be repeated.[79] Under the tradi-tion of "Chatham House rules", it can be repeated but not attributed. From an NGO perspective, *Corporate Watch* argues that off the record comments should be respected, in part this is because such organizations need to maintain ongoing diplomatic rela-tions with their adversaries, and preserving helpful informants is important.[80] In gen-eral the value of "off the record" insights, in terms of understanding the context of data, often outweighs any instant reward for revealing a specific secret. Alternatively, an interview may be more straightforward if it is agreed from the start that everything is "on the record".[81] But what if an interviewee reveals a criminal act?
- *"No comment"* – no-go and taboo topics are often made clear by interviewees or gate-keepers. But should these be seen as secrets that must be discovered by other means or as data about avoidance to be reported? An important part of any study might be assessing what these off-limits topics are, who does not want to talk about them, and why? There are no ethical constraints about analysing what was not said, provided the data is true and the reasoning is overt.

Ethics discussions often muddle harm and deceit. The aim should be to avoid or mini-mize harm, but it is virtually impossible to do face-to-face, or distance, research without deceit in some form. If research subjects were fully aware of the nature of the research, that would inevitably bias the way they responded or behaved. Deceit may be acceptable

Confidentiality can provide a safeguard for contacts whose contribution to Amnesty International's (AI) research may put them at risk of human rights abuses. In some circumstances confidentiality can protect an individual from being ostracized by the family or community. A victim may have strong personal reasons for information provided to be treated confidentially. It is important to note that AI cannot provide absolute guarantees for the safety of people who come into contact with the organization. Respecting confidentiality builds up a relationship of trust with contacts – something which itself can contribute to the quality of research. The trust should never be jeopardized by false promises that the organization cannot keep.

'If confidentiality is breached, it could endanger the very same people we are trying to help. It could also endanger contacts and even Amnesty International members in that or other countries. In the end it could be disastrous for the movement as a whole. Confidentiality is a life-saver.'

Source: Research Support Unit, International Secretariat, *Amnesty International*

FIGURE 4.8   Confidentiality

to facilitate observation and evidence gathering, but it is less acceptable to use deceit to entrap people into doing wrong – "setups" and "stings". There are few absolutes in up-system studies. Research conduct that is essential in some settings may, in other contexts, simply be desirable and the "least worst" option. Alternatively, a standard "ethical" approach may be very dangerous. Even reporting accurate data can be problematic – repeating accounts of torture or surveillance by despots can help to increase their power through fear. The idea of getting informed consent in the form of a signed letter may be a generally accepted approach within research ethics. But if the research were being carried out among illiterate village elders in a war zone, other considerations may be more important. Those concerned may not have the background knowledge to be, or become, 'informed', and signing anything may be a meaningless or very risky act. University researchers who have worked in dangerous contexts often say that they only described the safe part of their work to their research ethics committees. Journalists are sometimes ahead of academics in evolving ethical codes,[82] because journalists have direct contact with those their work affects and, when a readership numbers millions, getting something wrong can mean significant repercussions and even the downfall of a newspaper.

A distinct ethical dilemma in up-system research is deciding the degree to which research norms might be adjusted because powerful people might be abusing their power to avoid the truth being known about their own unethical behaviour. Achieving access (above) can raise the question – is covert research acceptable? Is it ethical to adopt a false persona, or gain access by joining an organization or providing a service, as Dalton did for his book *Men who Manage*.[83] While it is sensible to avoid obvious "no-go" questions when trying to gain access to the interviewee, and at the start of the interview, is it acceptable to drop them in at the end? Dress can create a conundrum – should it reflect the persona of the interviewee or the interviewer? If a non-Muslim woman wears a hejab to interview a Muslim leader, is that respectful or deceitful (Figure 4.6)?

If those being researched cannot, or will not, understand and consent to the research, there are ways to argue that a *non-consensual approach* is ethical. Internet research provides interesting new arguments.[84] If public officials are in a public place, it seems reasonable to assume that anything they say or do will happen with them understanding that they are acting publically in an *official capacity* and can therefore be quoted freely. But could the answer to a question asked in a taxi on the way to a venue, or in a bar later, be seen in the same way? We all exercise a degree of common sense caution when talking to unfamiliar people in public places – we would not tell a stranger about a partner's intimate health problems or reveal a bank pin number. It seems reasonable to assume that a powerful person is sufficiently informed about the world to exercise similar caution. But what if the encounter were at a private family party?

If a politician answers a question while giving a political speech in a shopping mall, there is arguably no need to inform them that your question is part of a research project, because the comment is automatically in the *public domain*. The same could apply to university lecturers while giving a lecture in a university, sports celebrities talking while pursuing their sport, and rock musicians while playing at a gig. Although *Wikileaks* were seen by many people as unethical and even unlawful, once public they were widely used, even by a Lloyd's Insurance syndicate for a court case.[85] Although the court certainly would not condone or encourage such leaks, once such information is public, a court will use it.

The concept of *best interests* is often applied when research subjects cannot give informed consent, for example arguments concerning children's rights.[86] Is reporting the findings of research likely to be better for all those concerned, than any potential harm? This type of dilemma is familiar to doctors who must balance the edict to "do no harm" with the reality that any medical intervention embodies an element of harm. Like medics, military and police ethics address the same concern in terms of *proportionality* – is the risk of harm less than the benefit arising from taking that risk. Interviewing environmental activist leaders at an airport, which causes them to miss a flight, may be disproportionate, but not if they were talking about threatening others with poisonous chemicals. A broad *public interest* is often argued in relation to powerful people, by journalists and by whistle blowing organizations, such as *Public Concern at Work*, and the differences in international law on this are significant.[87]

Similarly, in clinical settings, *substituted judgement* may be applied in non-consenting circumstances.[88] It asks a counterfactual question: if those concerned could fully understand the research, and its risks and benefits, what might they decide? This concept can be applied to up-system research. If village elders do not understand the threat to traditional shrines posed by drilling for oil, it is arguably acceptable to reveal the secret sacred sites that they have identified to provide evidence for international human rights NGOs. If the elders could understand what a human rights NGO is, they would probably take the same decision.

Reciprocal ethics – behave to others as you would like them to behave to you – provides a broad guiding principle, but in practice it raises challenging questions. If it is acceptable for factory workers to secretly film abusive managers, is it acceptable for managers to film their lazy workers? If companies record phone calls for quality control, is it reasonable for the customer (or researcher) to record calls to create a record of any misleading claims or promises? Is it unethical to use data from a casual chat with a supermarket manager, who is unaware that it amounts to research, when that manager does not tell customers that every item they buy provides data about them for the supermarket, and that their progress around the store may be monitored by researchers analysing store use on CCTV? It might seem ethically defensible for a journalist to use undercover methods to expose abuse and child trafficking by mafia gang leaders,[89] but is it acceptable for students and children to use the same approach for informal up-system data collection about teachers and lecturers, especially when it may also reveal the weaknesses of classmates? YouTube provides examples under 'angry teacher'.

Legal issues are closely related to research ethics,[90] not least because powerful people often have the means to seek and achieve redress, if wronged. This chapter cannot give comprehensive advice for all contexts, but there are key aspects that should be considered. The *Index on Censorship*[91] provides updated information about changing laws and actions against journalists and other researchers, internationally. Professional investigators often join organizations that can advise on legal issues and produce ethical codes.[92] The law may sometimes conflict with research ethics. Some researchers may have a professional *duty of care* which overrides other considerations. If, in an interview, a doctor admits abusing a patient, a social or health worker would have a duty to report this.[93] In some countries, France for example, there is a legal requirement to report suspected crime.

Is a *research permit or visa* necessary? Any request will certainly take time to process, and in many countries research about political elites is likely to be refused. What are the risks associated with undercover research?[94] Covert techniques, particularly entrapment, are often illegal. Shadowing might lead to criminal action for harassment or stalking. It is unlikely that government officials will agree to an interview without the correct permission, and in some countries even teachers and university staff are civil servants. One compromise is to apply for a visa for an aspect of a research study which is harmless. If a study is about "Political leadership and national development", interviews about the "Management of AID for health and education programmes" might appear less problematic than "Corruption among donors and recipient ministries".

What are the *data protection* issues, in the relevant country? How far is 'blagging' acceptable – getting data by posing as someone else? If digital data were seized, could it form the basis for a prosecution? Names and identifiers may need to be used with care in transcripts and recordings, and also file names and other computer meta-data. If there is a requirement by a funder that data is deposited in data archives, will this be the raw or anonymous data? Investigatory powers are regulated in many countries,[95] including surveillance, intercepting communications and privacy. Creating extensive files about high-profile figures could be construed as terrorist activity.

Are photos and drawings acceptable? In many countries, photography in public places is lawful, but in others not.[96] Pictures of security personnel, government buildings, bridges, airports, royalty and religious sites may be illegal in any country, even America and Britain. Images of factory operations and politically sensitive activities, including teaching in schools, may be problematic. Even if not illegal, photos of children or people in vulnerable situations can be considered unethical. In private spaces – museums, art galleries, shops, private houses – photography may not be directly illegal but can lawfully be prevented, by force if necessary.

Defamation includes slander (harmful speech) and libel (harmful text). Laws vary internationally. Misusing a picture of a political leader could lead to imprisonment in countries like North Korea. Laws can also be combined to prosecute those who offend local norms. A factual report, or even a novel, could be interpreted as 'propaganda against the system' in countries such as Iran, and might constitute an act of terrorism or treason. In Islamic states, statements contrary to religion can lead to the death penalty, and in monarchies such as Thailand statements that defame royalty may be harshly punished.

Laws can seem an irrelevant irritation to researchers. But before simply ignoring them, it is worth considering the penalties for being found doing up-system research illegally. The police are likely to take any reports very seriously, and charges may amount to terrorism or spying.[97] Being caught without the right papers in a foreign country can cause a very sudden shortening, or lengthening, of a stay.

Planning can seem tedious and time-wasting, especially if a team of researchers are keen to embark on an exciting project. But up-system research is particularly accident-prone and mistakes are often hard to rectify. Powerful people are busy and often quickly irritated, and may not give researchers a second chance when things go wrong. So it is worth considering:

- potential *problems* that are more significant for up-system research – 'nominal fallacy' (who exactly has the power?), false assumptions from poor media reports or gossip, focusing only on those who have succeeded and become well-known, what alternatives can be tried when there are set-backs, how to approach research in a "surgical" way, how to avoid upsetting powerful people, and how to separate objective research from advocacy.
- the specific *focus* – is the study problem-solving or solution-oriented, and does it need to create data in a specific format?
- how to *problematize* a research topic, and being aware that there are 'tame' problems that can be solved, and 'wicked' problems that cannot. Hypothesis and research questions should be discussed with others who do not know about the project to test if they are clear and comprehensible.
- how the *assumptions* underpinning a study are justified. If it is assumed that a population lives in fear of a despotic regime, how do we know that 'fear' exists?
- what needs to be *defined*, and whether the study is conceptualized in terms of elites or leadership. Do terms and concepts have the same meaning in different languages?
- how *access* can be achieved. How can gatekeepers be circumvented or used? What is the "safe" way to present the project? What 'persona' should researchers and organizations adopt?
- how to ensure the *integrity* of the project, methodologically and ethically. Are there aspects of the research that do not fit standard understandings of research ethics, and can ethics be evolved in terms of best interests, public interest, substituted judgement, or reciprocal ethics?
- *legal* aspects, especially if working in another country, or using a team of researchers.

While it is important to ensure that planning is thorough and plans are clear and well-understood by all researchers, excessive planning can also kill the energy of a project. A balance needs to be achieved. Planning documents should perhaps be headed with John Lennon's reminder, *"Life is what happens while you are making plans."*

KEY READING

Cresswell, J.W. (2009) *Research Design: Qualitative, Quantitative, and Mixed Methods Approaches.* London: Sage.

Dawson, J. and Peart, N.S. (2003) *The Law of Research: A Guide.* Dunedin: University of Otago Press.

Denscombe, M. (2002) *Ground Rules for Social Research.* Milton Keynes: Open University Press.

Dexter, L.A. (1970) *Elite and Specialized Interviewing.* Evanston, IL: Northwestern University Press.

Hertz, R. and Imber, J.B. (1995) *Studying Elites Using Qualitative Methods.* London: Sage. p. 42.

Israel, M. and Hay, I. (2006) *Research Ethics for Social Scientists.* London: Sage.

Morris, P.W.G. (1994) *The Management of Projects.* London: Thomas Telford.

Ward, S.J.A. (2010) *Global Journalism Ethics.* Quebec: McGill-Queen's University Press.

5

FRAMEWORKS

5.1   DIRECT
5.2   INDIRECT
5.3   NETWORKS AND SYSTEMS

> **FRAMEWORK**
>
> To give shape, expression or direction. The combination and fitting together of parts and adaption to a design. (*OED*)

> **STRATEGY**
>
> The art of projecting and directing the larger operations of a campaign. (*OED*)

The planning phase, explained in Chapter 4, sorts out strategy and logistics, and happens *at the same time* as deciding on research frameworks (this chapter) and data collection methods (the next chapter). The format of a methods book can give the misleading impression that these activities are sequential – that deciding on the framework and methods come after the planning stage. Researchers often approach a proposed study from the perspective of a favoured discipline, data collection method or even desired findings. But the most effective research is approached from the questions, what don't we know, how do we best find it out and how do we need to present those findings? Relevant data collection methods are then fitted within a framework to investigate those unknowns in a systematic but pragmatic way, and to achieve outputs in appropriate formats.

In recent social science methods books there is usually a distinction between research 'frameworks'[1] (also called 'strategies',[2] 'approaches',[3] or 'designs'[4]), discussed here, and 'data collection methods', discussed in Chapter 6. But these distinctions have not been used consistently. Research frameworks generally provide the bases for *empirical* research, and assume the use of primary or secondary data. *Theoretical* research is usually based on reason, logic, calculation, modelling and argument (C2),[5] and may, or may not, be based on frameworks. A research design may be based on more than one framework, frameworks may overlap and are not mutually exclusive, and a framework can involve a combination of different qualitative and quantitative data collection methods and analysis. Unless a particular framework or method is being tested as an aim of the research, the focus of the study (C4.1) should dictate the selection of frameworks and methods, not vice versa.

Many methodology books provide comprehensive discussions about the standard frameworks,[6] and sites such as *SAGE Research Methods Online* make the sources easily searchable.[7] Therefore those general frameworks are not repeated in this book, but outlined in Appendix 9. Some of these may be difficult to apply to up-system research because of the problem of access (C4.5). Frameworks that are directly relevant, but less familiar in the standard books, are discussed in more depth here. They are divided into frameworks entailing *direct* or *indirect* access to individual elites or leaders, and *network* and *system* frameworks which aim to understand those individuals through understanding the context and outcomes of their power. A matrix relating frameworks to the basic questions of up-system research, and likely sources of information, is a useful initial planning tool (Appendix 10).

5.1 DIRECT

Direct frameworks assume the possibility of some form of access and interpersonal interaction with individual elites or leaders, but this is often difficult to achieve (C4.5).

Investigative research[8] is often seen as distinct from academic research, with very specific aims, sometimes simply to establish a single fact about a powerful person – he gave money to him, she met him, she slept with her – often to understand wrongdoing.[9] Police investigations into crime[10] often have case-specific methods – murder,[11] drugs dealing,[12] fraud[13] – and traditionally revolve around looking for means, opportunity and motive. For fraud investigators a suspicion or doubt might come from an informant or arise from computer-assisted profiling of a particular population, which creates a purposive sample (C6.2) of likely suspects to be investigated in more detail.[14] Legal investigations by lawyers are also based on specific methodologies to organize and analyse data in a way that is appropriate for courtroom arguments,[15] and specific software is available.[16] For an investigative journalist,[17] establishing and nurturing relevant contacts (a form of 'purposive sample') is important. For UNESCO, Lee Hunter has devised a 'story-based inquiry' methodology, and advises journalists not to search for secrets, but to use publically available evidence to test hypotheses.[18] Self-study guides[19] exist for private investigators, but in general investigative researchers are usually not keen to disclose their methods, and training is closely guarded through organizations such as the *Association of Crime and Intelligence Analysts.* An investigative approach can be an element of a broader academic study, to establish a pivotal fact that strongly supports a hypothesis or definitively answers a specific question.[20]

Undercover research is usually associated with journalists, investigators and spies, and has a long history,[21] but has also been used in academic studies.[22] The associated technology also has a long history. Cameras designed to be hidden beneath a shirt appeared in 1886 and have been hidden in objects such as watches since 1905. Two-way mirrors have permitted hidden surveillance for a century. Cameras and voice recorders hidden in pens and sunglasses, and wireless devices that can be hidden in objects such as clocks, are now easily available through internet sites.[23] Spyware ('privacy invasive software') appeared around 1995 and tracks surfing habits and keyboard use – keylogging.[24] It can be used by anyone who has access to a shared network to spy on others. There are many technical manuals for professional and amateur spies.[25] Video and audio evidence from undercover research is usually heavily edited, but it is important to keep all data because the context of an event may turn out to be more important than a brief, exciting clip, and may be needed later to defend challenges about misinterpretation. Conclusions about a doctor forcefully restraining a mental health patient would be different if earlier that patient had been running around with a knife. 'Stings' and 'set-ups' – investigators adopting a false persona to trap corrupt elites – often achieve dramatic results. In 2001, journalists from Tehelka.com posed as arms dealers and managed to get government officials to accept bribes. The result of this 'Operation West End' was to expose Indian government corruption, and a defence minister and others resigned.[26] The technology is now simple, but the ethical and legal questions are complex (C4.6).

Leadership assessment evolved in the twentieth century, and usually helps to select those with leadership potential for promotion or senior positions, or to assess training needs. It uses a range of techniques including observation of behaviour in group situations, choice of associates (voting), nomination or rating by qualified observers, selection (and rating or testing) of persons occupying positions of leadership, and analysis of biographical and case history data. These approaches are usually based on objective criteria for the qualities that are essential for good leadership.[27] Standard psychological, intelligence and personality tests have been adapted, and specific skills measured, such as decision-making skills.[28] In the past, personal characteristics such as age, height, health and fluency of speech have been assessed, and studies have been carried out on groups of young children, which would probably be seen as unethical now.[29]

Natural experiments entail opportunistic observation and comparison of circumstances created by "nature" not experimenters, and can be based on present or past events.[30] The collapse of a government, or death of a CEO, could provide an opportunity to research how civil servants or middle managers cope in a crisis. Press letters pages, and online comment to media sites such as the BBC,[31] can provide a wealth of data for analysing public perceptions or the understanding of significant events. Public investigations – courts, inquiries, press campaigns – might represent a natural experiment. Sometimes data that is irrelevant to public investigators can be relevant to the researcher – attending inquests can ascertain elite social networks. Peer research can be a form of natural experiment. Powerful people often investigate one another to increase their power, as during the election of trade union or political party leaders, which can provide a very interesting data flow for other researchers.

Psychological studies can be based on observing actual leaders and elites,[32] but there is also a long history of *experimental* studies[33] and sophisticated methods[34] which could also be applied to *natural experiments* (above). The focus is often on *behaviour* such as aggression,[35] hypocrisy,[36] emotion[37] or risk taking.[38] As powerful people are unlikely to cooperate with experiments, other research subjects are often used. Experiments have included studies on children that would probably now be precluded for ethical reasons.[39] Research is often carried out in university psychology departments, and use students to role play situations relating to the use of power. A role play intervention of a board meeting, with two *cohorts* (groups that share an experience), could entail one group experiencing a surprise event, such as the resignation of the CEO, and comparisons are made with another similar *control* group that did not experience that event. The degree to which this form of role play – for example subjects 'primed with a high-power mindset'[40] – reflects the behaviour of real leaders and elites in real-life situations should always be considered carefully.

5.2 INDIRECT

Indirect frameworks are mainly desk-based and assume that there is little or no chance to interact with individual research subject(s). As direct access to powerful people is often not possible, indirect approaches are a significant aspect of up-system research.

Biography is one of the oldest frameworks for researching powerful people (C1.2). It entails an in-depth account of the life of an individual, and often relies heavily on secondary data, which is often biased.[41] The aim of collected biographies is often to inspire and educate young leaders.[42] Elite oral history can provide a more reliable approach[43] and psychological approaches can contribute further.[44] The release of classified political documents or letters can form the basis of biographical accounts that challenge traditional perceptions of individuals and history, and graphologists might help to test the validity of handwritten documents.[45] The methods of *autobiography* are hard to formalize, but often rely on many years of methodical diary-keeping and personal *diaries* themselves can provide detailed data.[46] Celebrities may be documented by ghost writers, who may work with film or similar agents to reconstruct a particular vision of the life of a famous individual. The autobiography of *Wikileaks* director Julian Assange was written in this way and, on seeing the drafts, he wanted to withdraw it, but it was still published. Autobiographies by powerful people usually explain little that is new or interesting about the author, but may reveal a lot about their peers and process. A selection of autobiographies might be studied systematically:

1   Autobiography of Mr A analysed in relation to a specific period of time.
2   Friends, colleagues and others are identified.
3   Autobiographies of those people are analysed during the relevant time period.
4   Further data for that time period is sought through web and other searches.
5   A 'reconstructive' analysis (below) of events during that time period compares 1, 2 and 3.

Fiction by power elites may also reveal insights into themselves and others.[47] *Memoires* tend to be more personal, focusing on feelings and emotions about significant events. *Biographical analysis* might compare biographies, which are categorized under relevant headings (violent, non-violent), looking for factors (negative self-image, victimization, corruption), and rating the degree of these factors on a scale, to identify predictors of a characteristic (violent leadership).[48]

Crowdsourcing entails outsourcing tasks to large groups. Volunteers and others are organized to contribute to research in three areas – large-scale *data collection, analysis* and *dissemination*. Experts may contribute by systemizing and presenting complex data in easily searchable formats, and following-up on particularly interesting shared findings and analysis. This may be organized by civil society organizations, companies or governments. The Kenya-based *Ushahidi Project* provides online crowdsourcing tools which permit mass research about the use of power, including election monitoring via mobile phones.[49] Advocacy organizations such as *Amnesty International* see the empowerment of people to contribute to its research as an important aspect of their role in up-system accountability (Figure 5.1).

Examples of *data collection* are diverse. Archaeologists now recognize the value of responsible amateurs who discover new sites and objects through metal detectors or diving, and record them through central organizations such as the *Portable Antiquities Scheme*.[50] The UK *Royal Society for the Protection of Birds* (RSPB) organizes thousands of enthusiasts to collect data through the 'Big garden Birdwatch'.[51] Crowd *analysis* may include 'crowds' searching a large number of online documents for significant items to create a 'human search engine'.[52] When in 2009 the UK newspaper, *The Guardian*, investigated MP expenses, it deployed 25,000 people to search 500,000 documents for dubious expenses claims.[53] Sites such as *Iraq Body Count*[54] and *Wikileaks*[55] provide a mass of data which professional, students and amateur researchers can freely use.

On a professional level, crowdsourcing includes *open notebook research* which started in the natural sciences. In 1986, the *Wellcome Trust* realized that there was duplication of medical research because scientists kept their data and initial findings secret. They decided to only fund projects that made data available immediately. The idea that all aspects of a project are made public as the research progresses can be applied to social science. This has significant potential, particularly for civil society organizations. ICT tools such as blogs and wikis can be used,[56] and sites such as *Scribd* and *Social Science Research Network/leadership* provide platforms for sharing working papers (C8).

Both the act of carrying out research and the way in which the finished product is designed and used form part of a process of empowerment.

Developing an effective set of contacts can involve assisting them in learning new skills or developing existing ones. Sharing techniques for information gathering and for accessing national and international forums is something that can form part of the process of carrying out research. Developing an effective set of contacts may often require listening to and responding to needs and requests. Amnesty International's research contributes to and benefits from this broad-based development and consciousness-raising, aimed at all AI members and the wider public.

Researchers have at their disposal impressive mechanisms and a large number of dedicated staff to carry out campaigning actions. The entire research process needs to be guided by a solid understanding of the movement, in terms of its potential for action.

Source: Research Support Unit, International Secretariat, *Amnesty International*

FIGURE 5.1   Collaborative research

Distance research has been developed by anthropologists[57] and, in relation to leaders, by psychologists using nonverbal, paralinguistic and content analysis.[58] This has the advantage of avoiding reactivity (the "Hawthorn Effect") – the presence of the researcher changing what is being researched. It can use non-participant 'remote observation' (C6.1.2). This is becoming increasingly easy through improved ICT and media, for example the online archives of formal Tribunals and Inquiries (Figure 5.2). Powerful people can also be observed remotely through assistants in other countries who are instructed to observe systematically at public meetings or from public galleries. Tweets with, or about, elites provide a wealth of data about the personal and public perceptions of those people. *Remote shadowing* may entail remote observation and the use of archive material. Political and other leaders often maintain public diaries of their activities. The traditional diary of the British Monarch – the Court Circular – is now on *Facebook*. These records provide the means to track activities through checking for media reports, press releases or activist blogs. Constructing timelines of activities might indicate causal links, and gaps in activities – regular or erratic – can be worth exploring further. These can build up a profile of activities to assess whether the leader sets or responds to agendas, is strategically successful, or only opts to attend media-oriented events. Even powerful people in open and closed countries, such as Iran and North Korea, can be shadowed to some degree through websites (see 'Internet sources', p. 256).

Documentary research is a significant aspect of up-system research as it avoids the need for direct access. It treats any form of text – written word, images, internet resources, transcripts of conversation and rhetoric[59] – as primary data which can be interrogated much as an interviewee would be questioned. Documentary research is often confused with a literature review (C3.1), which examines the nature of relevant literatures but does not treat the content as data. At a basic level, documentary analysis addresses a series of obvious questions, such as the what, where, when, how, why checklists of Ganigan (C1.2).

Many international courts and tribunals have websites, which permit the 'remote observation' of proceedings. Videos and transcripts permit analysis of what was said, and of nonverbal body language. Sam Hinga Norman was one of the first defendants to appear at the Special Court for Sierra Leone, but he refused to attend further and the trial continued without him.

Photo by permission of the Sierra Leone Special Court, press room. Available at: www.sc-sl.org/filephotos.html

FIGURE 5.2   Sam Hinga Norman at the Special Court for Sierra Leone

Many books provide elaborations.[60] Documents and other mass media that are targeted at specific elites – elite magazines, professional journals, websites – can provide insights into the nature of those elites.[61] Less public texts, such as PhD theses, may be more revealing. *Discourse analysis* (C6.1.1) specifically assesses how power is exercised through texts, but this does not necessarily entail long and complex research. The coincidence of interests between royal and religious power are very evident in the text of the nineteenth century children's hymn 'All things bright and beautiful'. Having declaimed '*All things wise and wonderful, the Lord God made them all*', Verse three legitimizes the established order: '*The rich man in his castle. The poor man at his gate. God made them high and lowly, and ordered their estate*'.

Ethics (moral philosophy) studies compare the behaviour of powerful people against ethical norms – laws, human rights agreements, traditions, codes, professional standards.[62]

- *Theoretical* studies assess and provide the bases for ethical claims[63] – Why is it wrong to kill civilians in war? If unethical, how can that behaviour be precluded through codification?
- *Normative* studies consider the "normal" pragmatic bases of moral behaviour – Is it acceptable to kill civilians who are being used to shield a military base?
- *Applied* studies identify how ethical standards should be used in particular circumstances – Are a few civilian deaths acceptable when there is a clear, significant and immediate threat from a military base?

- *Descriptive* research discovers how moral standards are actually applied – Did military leaders try to avoid civilian targets?
- *Psychological* studies assess moral capacity and agency – Are child soldiers, or senile politicians, cognitively responsible for war crimes?

Consistency is often assessed (C7.3) through a combination of interviews and observation.[64] 'Stated values' – claims about what is right and wrong – may be compared with 'demonstrated values' – how people behave in relation to their stated values. Does a CEO who claims to be environmentally responsible use recycled paper?

Legitimacy research aims to establish the truth about claims to power (C2.1) and is arguably the oldest form of up-system research (C1). Family history and life story methods provide a basis,[65] and there are many online resources. The methods for creating and interpreting *lineage charts* are usually very specific. Symbols and systems envision a lot of information in a small space. Patrilineal or (more reliably) matrilineal relationships may be shown by single lines, and double lines link husband and wife. Abbreviations save space – BC for 'brother's children', and Z for sister, because S means son (Figure 1.8).[66] *Pedigree charts* form the elite lists of legitimizing bodies such as *Burkes Peerage*.[67] These methodologies support claims to inheritance, and influence marriage opportunities, and animal methodologies are relevant.[68] *Provenance studies* of objects can help to affirm the legitimacy of their owners, and when applied to books can indicate who has owned certain books since they were created, and that therefore certain books may have influenced certain powerful people.[69]

Public investigation agencies provide a distinct aspect of up-system research, and are often ignored by academics. There are many official public organizations that will investigate an issue and collect data for free, provided a request fits their mandate. There is little point in trying, initially, to do research that these entities can potentially do better. Company customer-services departments will often investigate genuine complaints about senior staff. Their response may be guarded, but much can be learned from what they do and do not want to discuss. Politicians are often subject to investigation by regulators, and usually reasonable public complaints will be investigated. Many professions – dentists, doctors, health workers – have self-regulatory bodies that have a duty to investigate genuine complaints. Financial services usually have independent regulators. If misconduct is suspected, making a complaint to a regulator might trigger research into professional conduct, including formal inquiries and public hearings, which would create a natural experiment (above) that would be beyond the capacity of individual researchers to implement. Power networks are relevant – trades unions or local political parties can often put pressure on MPs to ask formal questions in parliament or committees, which will be researched by parliamentary researchers. Pragmatically, a formal complaint can be a means to get an expert organization to do an aspect of a research project very thoroughly at no cost.

Reconstructive techniques rely on hypothesizing from knowns to unknowns, to fill gaps in an area of knowledge. This is common in forensic (law-related) research, and should be a significant aspect of up-system research, because often data is missing, incomplete or deliberately obscured. Much can be learned across diverse, seemingly unrelated, disciplines, particularly archaeology (C1.2).

At a basic level, reconstruction can be approached by looking for *patterns*. Techniques used by archaeologists to analyse broken or incomplete objects, can inspire the development of methods to reconstruct gaps in information about powerful people. If the fragments of a broken pot have a certain pattern, it is possible to surmise how that pattern would continue on the missing pieces. From the patterns of a heavily censored document, an intelligence analyst may be able to guess the nature of the missing parts, and assessing why certain information is missing may be more important than knowing exactly what the content was. Gaps in historical accounts can be identified and redressed.[70] For a historian, the pattern of how long Kings ruled can indicate how many kings might be missing from an ancient record. The Egyptian/Greek historian Manetho used the pattern of chronological 'dynasties' in the early King Lists to find the gaps in existing records (C1.2).

Discovering the *underlying structures* (patterns that are not immediately obvious) of an incomplete record of something, can also help with reconstruction, just as knowing only the rhythm or beat of a piece of music could disclose whether it is waltz, tango or heavy metal. Building on the work of Georges Cuvier (C1.2), modern archaeologists often claim that, if you can work out the function of any part of an animal fossil, you can work out the source of that part – what the whole animal is like. Archaeological methods can be adapted to other spheres. A policy analyst might "put the flesh on" a vague policy announcement made by a despotic leader in response to international sanctions, based on theories and methods about the "bones" of economic and political options available to a leader in that situation. The secretive world of oil elites might be better understood by looking at the underlying structure of their operations, revealed by maps of world oilfields and pipelines.[71] Habermas's approach to 'reconstructive science' is theoretical discussion from a linguistics perspective which might inspire innovative approaches. Notions such as 'surface structures' and 'deep structures', in relation to 'the rational reconstruction of concepts, criteria, rules, and schemata' might be applied in other ways.[72]

Backcasting, used within military futures analysis, is also relevant in reconstruction, and entails working back from a policy to identify enablers and barriers.[73] From evolutionary psychology, Steven Pinker's notion of 'reverse engineering' is similar. In forward-engineering a machine is designed to do something; 'in reverse engineering, one figures out what a machine was designed to do.'[74] A government policy, despotic event or company report might be reverse engineered to discover what it was really intended to achieve. Arguably the relevance of historical studies would be improved if they proceeded backwards from a present-day event or problem. Critical Process Analysis develops these techniques further (C7.6).

Secondary analysis is based on data that has already been collected and probably analysed, such as census data, transcripts, parliamentary voting records, court records or international indicators. It usually goes further than a *systematic review* (C3.2), and although the way in which the data was collected cannot be changed, that data can be manipulated to do different types of analysis (Figure 6.1). Simple but original analysis can arise from combining seemingly unconnected data sources, such as the age of despotic leaders compared with the average life expectancy of the people they control. In 2006, when the Zimbabwean President Robert Mugabe became 82, WHO data showed that the average life expectancy for women in his country was 34 years.

Secondary analysis can include a range of *meta* ('after' or 'about') techniques. *Meta-methods* are methods to study methods, perhaps in order to evaluate them.[75] Analysis of how a piece of paper was made may provide more reliable evidence about the source of a document than the text written on that paper – forgeries might be detected because the type of paper is later than the date on the document. The integrity of a statement about a company's environmental responsibility might be checked by finding out if it is printed on environmentally friendly paper. For investigative research, *meta-data* – data about data – in the form of the record of when and where a mobile phone was used, may reveal more about the sender than what is written in a text. In statistics, *meta-analysis* describes a process of combining and assessing data from a range of studies that had the same purpose and methods.[76] But any bias in the sources of the data cannot be controlled, as is the original analysis. Non-statistical approaches are also well-established.[77] A modified form of meta-analysis is *meta-synthesis* of qualitative studies, which entails an aggregation by looking for 'recurring themes', which relate to the aims of the synthesis.[78] In statistical studies, *post-hoc analysis* entails looking back at data after an experiment has been completed, to assess outcomes that were not envisaged a priori the start. Post-hoc findings can be flawed, and should always be presented separately from other data, but they might indicate new areas of research.

Systematic correspondence entails a planned series of letters, emails or other communications, which start with a simple inquiry and then delve deeper into an issue, perhaps sent from, and to, different people in an organization. Inquiries may reflect interview techniques, but also elicit information by complaining and pushing a system. Politicians and parliamentary bodies will often provide responses to questions, although answers are usually carefully presented. But even brief formal answers can build into interesting data over time, and bad practice may become wonderful data. The research may be in the form of a longitudinal study, and might assess something other than the direct content of the answers – the difference in the discourse between prepared replies about topical issues and one-off replies about obscure issues that have required thought and research by a respondent, or meta-data such as response rates. When respondents become defensive, while arguing about one thing they sometimes confirm interesting facts or give hints about something else – "We cannot answer your question because it has legal implications", "We do not condone the practice, but the government does not clearly permit us to regulate it."

5.3 NETWORKS AND SYSTEMS

Intelligence analysis[79] is used in settings such as embassies, but also in companies,[80] and it is rarely formalized as an academic methodology. For outsiders, the blogs of the 'independent diplomat', Carne Ross, provide fascinating insights,[81] as does his book discussing diplomats as elites.[82] A manual, *Discovering National Elites*, provided a comprehensive non-classified manual for diplomats and intelligence officers for 'discovering the leadership of a society and it vulnerabilities', which is still relevant despite being written in 1954.[83] Diplomats and intelligence officers often start by assessing "What are they not telling us, and how can we find it out?" They will not learn much that is significant from official documents from other governments, except by asking "what should be there, what's missing, and why?" In tightly controlled regimes, diplomats may not take much notice of the pre-packaged answers to their own questions, but may pay careful attention to the questions they are asked, or not asked. If an official asks about the outcome of a football match in another country, which took place yesterday, their international monitoring is obviously quite good. If they are unaware who was elected president three months ago, it will appear less impressive. Opportunistic observation, perhaps to analyse the outcomes of political and other decisions, is far more important. Noting the availability of food and other goods in local shops can indicate how well a government is managing the context of a famine, sanctions or other economic factors. Reading the local press is routine, but in countries where the media are constrained, the cartoons might be more revealing than the headlines. Satire (Figure 6.2) indicates how far intellectuals and artists think they can push against the system. In closed countries such as North Korea, workers in organizations providing humanitarian assistance may be the best sources of regional information.[84] Intelligence gathering can be long term. Providing education for future elites, for example language training, is a form of *cultural diplomacy* that can set-up a way to track and understand them for decades.

Protocol analysis is based on the unwritten rules about the courtesies of interpersonal international relations – who meets who, where and when, who sits next to whom, and which office or function room is used.[85] (There are other forms of 'protocol analysis', including behavioural psychology, international agreements and international telecommunications.) Specialist consultancy companies provide advice,[86] and manuals provide the chance to check what should have happened, with what actually happened at a particular public event.[87] Diplomats analyse elite gatherings – state banquets, weddings, funerals – to assess how the host nation views other countries. It is likely that since 2000, Chinese representatives have moved up the table at a rapid rate. They also note protocol. Ambassadors to North Korea should present their credentials to Kim Il-sung, because he is officially the 'eternal president', but he died in 1994.

Security intelligence analysis partly relies on robust 'on the ground' techniques, which are outlined on defence ministry websites.[88] Often, military analysts must rely initially on local journalists and NGO workers as sources of local intelligence. Methods have been developed to identify and assess the 'decisive groups' among an enemy or occupied population, based on questions about their 'political goals' and 'economic/political/military resources'. 'Centre of Gravity Analysis' determines the strengths and weaknesses of 'principal protagonists' ('the elite of the group') – friendly and hostile – in relation to critical 'capabilities', 'vulnerabilities' and 'requirements in order to act'. Conclusions relate different groups to frameworks – 'irreconcilable' (neutralize), 'hostile' (isolate), 'neutral' (engage), 'positive' (reassure) (Figure 7.3). But this is a western view of the stability of group allegiances, and works less well in settings such as Afghanistan where individuals move between groups depending upon potential rewards and resources. Human geospatial analysis can be used to assess power and populations in relation to space,[89] much as epidemiologists do in relation to disease. Software can assist 'political, military, economic, social, infrastructure and information' analysis and training in relation to factors such as demography, leadership types, alliances, decision-making style, policy preferences, support levels and legitimacy. The *GeoTime* programme can map people's movements from data such as cash transactions and mobile calls.[90] Military style approaches could be relevant when assessing power in marginalized groups such as street children, criminal gangs or hill tribes. But there are many insider critiques of the methods and integrity of intelligence agencies.[91]

Organizational analysis considers the use of power within an organization, and by organizations, by analysing factors such as context, situations, systems and change.[92] The purpose is often to gain a competitive advantage over rival companies.[93] Methods include ethnography, case study,[94] and organizational storytelling ('narrative knowledge').[95] How does the narrative of a CEO match the narrative of the company, is it perceived as authentic and do the narratives reflect reality?[96] What happens to the narrative when CEOs from another country take over a company?[97] Stories that may appear as myths or jokes about leaders and managers may represent a safe way to create solidarity for an eventual challenge to abuses of power, and can therefore provide indications for deeper research. *Organizational network analysis* specifically studies communication,[98] for example where communication is impeded or perverted to facilitate abuse of power, and can be linked with policy analysis and network analysis. *Context analysis* and *situation analysis*[99] assess social trends and the strengths and weaknesses of competitor organizations. Investigative research about organizations asks questions such as: who owns it, does it do any harm, how does it treat its employees and does it present itself honestly?[100] Corporate crime is a significant aspect.[101]

Outcomes analysis assesses the consequences of the use of power.[102] On a macro-level this can be analysed in terms of 'social change',[103] and more specific interventions through 'impact assessment' and 'evaluation' analysis[104] of the outcomes of actions such as policies or violence, to identify how a specific change was caused by a specific intervention.[105] Large-scale data sets, such as those from the *Political Instability Task Force*[106] are often used to provide the evidence. Inaction can also represent an act – laws usually recognize that crimes can be committed by 'act' or 'omission'. Indicators of how power is being used include budgets and the allocation of other resources. *Impact evaluation* may use *counterfactual* analysis, which asks "what if…" and compares what is happening with what might have happened if a particular intervention had not been made. This might be done through a *historical comparison* – five years ago, sales to China were 2%, but since a Mandarin-speaking manager was appointed, Chinese sales have risen to 50%. Would that have happened without that appointment? A *prospective* research design would collect baseline data when the appointment was made and track changes. This could be in the form of an experiment – certain company branches appoint Mandarin speakers, others do not. A *retrospective* design would seek data about changes during the period through documents or surveys – sales figures and Chinese customer feedback since the manager was appointed. But the increase might just reflect a general 'secular' (of the world) trend[107] in greater sales to China. Therefore a *contemporaneous comparison* should also be made with similar companies that do not have Mandarin-speaking managers.

Impact analysis can also be theoretical, a mapping of the causal links between inputs and outcomes within a process, to test underlying theoretical assumptions.[108]

Policy analysis[109] is likely to be based on secondary analysis, but may also include observation and interviews.[110] There are two distinct forms: analysis in order to make policy, and analysis to assess policy-making. Frameworks for the latter are often based on protocols, regulations and theories describing how a policy should be made. Analysis of the process arises from comparing what did happen, with what should have happened (see C7.6). *Game theory* is a mathematical approach to understanding how strategic decisions might be made, when the outcome for one person/entity depends on the decisions of other people/entities in the same context.[111] 'Games' are interactions of conflict and cooperation, and are familiar in terms of the 'prisoner's dilemma' and assessments of the likely behaviour of Cold War enemies. Forms of game theory have been used by military leaders throughout history,[112] and are often used by business strategists. The framework does not account so well for real world dynamics such as irrational behaviour and unexpected contextual factors. Game theorists did not manage to predict the end of the Cold War.

Process analysis assesses efficiency within industrial production or business offices, and the role of senior staff in those processes.[113] The standard process model assesses – input > process > output. *Process tracing* uses any data – documents, elite interview transcripts,[114] electronic records – to trace causal links and mechanisms, to assess how independent variables (new laws, new products) influence dependent variables (staff rules, training programmes), and how they relate to a theory or hypothesis.[115] Critical Process Analysis develops this approach for assessing the actions of powerful people (C7.6).

Power structures[116] can be analysed by working upwards through the hierarchies of a social network, to assess where, how and by whom power is exercised (Figure 5.3). Data collection often entails 'snowballing', 'referral' or 'inductive methods of discovery' – respondents are asked to recommend others who might cooperate (C6.3). For his *reputational* research, Domhoff asked elite women interviewees to suggest 'another

---

Hunter's 'Reputational approach'
Hypothesis: that power stems from the reputation of individuals in a community.

Methods:

(i) a list of 175 city leaders was compiled from standard public sources.
(ii) the top 40 leaders were selected from this list by a panel representative of the community (similar to a 'focus group')
(iii) 27 of these 40 were interviewed, asking them to name the top 10 from the 40
(iv) a "winner" was then elected from the 10.

Validity:

Agreement about 'reputation' was then assessed, in relation to objective indicators of status and power. The agreement was high, which affirmed the hypothesis.

FIGURE 5.3   Power structures

Source: Hunter, F. (1953) *Community Power Structure: A Study of Decision Makers*. Chapel Hill: University of North Carolina Press.

woman of your social group, with a background like yours, who might be willing to talk to me'. Likely interviewees were then checked against objective criteria for 'upper-class membership'.[117] The reputation of organizations, such as universities,[118] and nations can be analysed similarly.[119] The methods of **genealogical** research (C1.2) can contribute a historical dimension, often to describe systems of subjugation.[120] A range of traditional and ICT tools[121] are available to trace the antecedence of elites.[122]

Social network analysis[123] is usually desk-based but could also include observation, interviews and modelling. It identifies 'nodes' of individuals or organizations, who are 'tied' by interdependency arising from characteristics such as kinship, interests, beliefs, status, profession and ethnicity. Useful analytical software includes UCINet, ORA, Pajek and GIU for Linux,[124] which can handle small and large-scale studies. But simple pen-and-paper methods can work equally well – government records will list 'commercial affiliations' and online CVs may provide 'cultural affiliations' (Figure 5.4). Networks are analysed through network theory, and data is often presented in the form of spidergrams. Journalists use simple versions to suggest political influence.[125] Basic analysis simply maps 'interlocking',[126] which links affiliations such as charity committees, governing bodies, publishing interests, alumni networks or hybrid networks,[127] but an interlock is not itself proof that people know and influence one another. Understanding networks is an important aspect of intelligence research. In 2009, western intelligence agencies and the media were trying to find out more about the likely successor to North Korea's leader, Kim Jong-il. They assumed it would be his youngest son, Kim Jong-un, and they analysed photos of his school friends at an elite international school in Berne, Switzerland, to trace networks. They found that Jong-un was taught basketball by an Israeli, was involved in charity projects, and liked Japanese *manga* cartoons and Arnold Schwarzenegger.[128]

Deeper analysis might assess the nature and frequency of those relationships and the financial, cultural or social capital of the actors. What was their education (languages

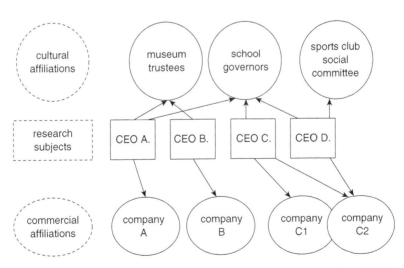

FIGURE 5.4 Basic network analysis – cultural and commercial interlocks of CEOs

learned, study abroad)? Which clubs or networks do they belong to (sports, hunting, professional)? Where do they live (elite districts, second homes)? What are their interests (antiques, fine art, classical music, international food)? Specific approaches are used to analyse closely cohesive elements of a network, the cliques or 'maximal complete sub-groups'.[129] Analysis may suggest possible influence among power elites, such as those within public quangos[130] or the global corporate elite.[131] Social network sites such as Twitter provide opportunities to see who follows who, and searching across groups can give indications as to who the hidden followers might be. Palestinian leaders seem to follow their Israeli counterparts, but not *vice versa*. The identification of 'epistemic communities' and 'communities of practice' helps to understand how networks based on knowledge and professional expertise are related to power in specific situations. A report, discussing radioactive pollution from a Japanese nuclear power station destroyed by a tsunami in 2011, shows a journalistic awareness of this:

> Japan's government has been accused of allowing an incestuous relationship to develop with power giant Tepco to the detriment of safety standards. Senior government figures have become accustomed to lucrative posts in the energy sector on retiring from public life and criticism of companies like Tepco has consequently been muted.
>
> Mitsuhiko Tanaka, a retired nuclear engineer who had worked on the Fukushima reactors said the 'nuclear village' in which public officials, academics and power company employees avoided criticising each other had created a dangerous consensus which had made the industry less accountable...
>
> Taro Kono went further, suggesting the power lobby's influence on the media, where it is among the country's leading advertisers, had insulated it from proper inspection. 'The power industry is one of the largest spenders so media can't criticise it.'[132]

The implications in relation to the dynamics of power between the industry, media and government are likely to be similar in many countries.

Social reproduction research examines how systems reproduce elites. Bowles and Gintis[133] analysed the hierarchical nature of social institutions and the reproduction of elites, principally through education systems. They started by identifying and theorizing the workforce needs of a capitalist system. They then analysed the relationship between exam grades and personality traits, among 237 high school students. They found that being given low grades was linked to traits such as 'creativity' and 'independence', which were not seen as helpful in a compliant labour force. Being awarded high grades was linked with 'subordinacy and discipline' traits such as 'perseverance', 'dependability' and 'punctuality'. They affirmed their findings through meta-analysis of related research, and they later argued that schools themselves were based on the structures and values of capitalist workplaces, reinforcing ideas of unquestioning obedience and systematic thinking.

Socio-legal[134] and *ethics*[135] research assesses the relationship between law and other norms, and society and politics. The former is usually empirically based, and the latter theoretical. The behaviour of powerful people can be analysed in relation to ethical codes, laws, professional standards, and human rights law and norms. A comparative approach might assess whether similar codes are consistent within and between countries. Socio-legal research also examines how power is used by courts, public officials, law enforcement agencies and administrative justice officials. The abuse of power is a significant aspect (C2.4). Throughout history powerful people have used justice systems to protect themselves and enhance their status, and this continues. Jails such as Lancaster Prison in England have held catholic priests, witches, children who were transported to the colonies, Quakers and more recently "terrorists" such as the 'Birmingham Six' who were eventually released. Globally, justice systems have criminalized and imprisoned people such as Nelson Mandela, Aung San Suu Kyi and Antonio Gramsci. Organizations such as *Amnesty International* specialize in research about political prisoners (Figure 6.8).

A starting point for social-legal research is to identify how power is implemented, what are the instruments of power, and what are the relative strengths of these instruments? These will vary in different countries, but might entail creating a framework reflecting the examples in Appendix 12. Understanding different instruments of power can be complicated by translation problems. Lee Jae-min complains that in Korean company law the Korean term '*si-haeng-ryeong,* meaning a governmental regulation to implement a statute, has been translated as either *enforcement **decree,** presidential decree,* or simply *decree.* The term *si-haeng-gyu-chik,* which is to implement *si-haeng-ryeong,* has in turn been translated as ether *enforcement regulations,* or *enforcement rules'.* [136]

Systems analysis was developed initially by the (then) American Secretary of Defence, Robert McNamara, during the Vietnam War,[137] and was adapted to organizational and social systems.[138] It tries to provide a holistic understanding of interconnections and interrelatedness, including interpersonal relationships with a closed system, such as a factory, but the framework can also be applied to open systems such as religions. A distinction is made between 'hard systems' – which are amenable to simple functional analysis much in the way that an engineer would analyse a mechanical system – and 'soft systems'[139] – which are complex, and definitions and structure are unclear, because of human dynamics. Systems analysis usually aims to improve the efficiency, or bring about change, within a particular system such as a hospital.[140] But the same techniques can be used in order to find out how elites and leaders use power in relation to a system (C7.6).

The planning stage will have included consideration of frameworks and data collection methods. The broad decision, when selecting which framework(s) to use, is whether access to the research subjects is best achieved through direct or indirect contact, or system and network analysis, or a combination of approaches. To decide this, the following questions need to be considered:

- if *direct* frameworks are to be used – what are the planned and opportunistic ways to achieve face-to-face contact, and what are the alternatives if these do not work?
- if *indirect* frameworks seem appropriate – how can they be used efficiently and will they provide reliable information in the right form? If remote researchers are used, how will they be trained and how can it be ensured that they do what they promise they will

do? Are all the 'distance' systems reliable and likely to remain available throughout the project? If not, what are the alternatives?

- for *network and systems* analysis – can the right balance of direct and indirect contact, and primary and secondary data, be achieved? What can be assumed about theoretical interaction? For example, does 'interlocking' happen in practice, do 'nodes' mean that people meet and interact in truly significant ways, how strong are 'tied' links, do 'affiliations' really mean that people influence one another?

Frameworks help to ensure that research is driven by the aims and focus of the research, not by favoured data collection methods, or prejudgements about findings. For a research team, they also help to build a shared understanding of how a project will work. But frameworks should not become like a corset that restricts a project to predetermined forms, even if these forms become unsustainable. Inevitably, things will go wrong and the shape of a project will need to change. Frameworks should not constrain by moulding a project by external pressure. They should support by providing an internal structure. Like skeletons, frameworks help to ensure that when things go wrong on the outside, a project does not collapse completely.

KEY READING

Cresswell, J.W. (2009) *Research Design: Qualitative, Quantitative, and Mixed Methods Approaches.* London: Sage.

Ford, N. (2011) *The Essential Guide to Using the Web for Research.* London: Sage.

Jupp, V. (2006) *The Sage Dictionary of Social Science Research Methods.* London: Sage.

Moyser, M. and Wagstaffe, M. (eds) (1987) *Research Methods for Elite Studies.* London: Allen & Unwin.

6

DATA

6.1   SOURCES
        6.1.1 Texts
        6.1.2 People
        6.1.3 Objects
        6.1.4 Buildings
6.2   SELECTION
6.3   TESTING

> **DATA**
>
> Something known or assumed as fact, and made the basis
> of reasoning or calculation. (*OED*)

Nobel laureate Conrad Lorenz commented that the purpose of research is '*to see what has never been seen before*',[1] which implies seeing what other people see, and thinking what other people have *not* thought. Charles Darwin saw life forms that were seen by countless people, but he thought about what these observations meant in a new way – 'evolution' – which even contradicted his own religious beliefs. How can 'seeing' and 'thinking' be effective when researching powerful people? The start is to collect relevant and interesting data, and 'see' it clearly through testing and initial analysis. But the process is circular. The choices about what and how to 'see' can only be made if there is a clear idea about how the in-depth thinking will happen. The data collection methods discussed in this chapter need to reflect the proposed forms of further analysis explained in the next chapter.

There are many general methodology books,[2] useful typologies,[3] internet sites,[4] and texts on data collection,[5] and therefore these general and technical discussions are not repeated here. This chapter provides explanations and adaptations of methodologies that are directly relevant to up-system research, including the spheres of leadership,[6] elites,[7] politics,[8] political leadership[9] and investigative research.[10] Decisions about data collection and analysis should be closely linked to the focus of the study (C4.2). If data is to be used for specific purposes – court cases, documentary films, political advocacy – methods must produce appropriate data and findings in relevant solution-oriented or action-oriented forms (Figure 4.2).

The terminology within methodology texts is not consistent. But usually, *methodology* describes the general study and explanation of frameworks and methods by experienced researchers, in methodology books. *Methods* describe how particular researchers carried out their particular studies. An academic methods chapter should discuss both aspects fully, but a short report may only mention the latter. The need for data collection implies that data is not immediately available, as it might be in an academic textbook or government report (C3), and so a systematic approach is required to get data in an efficient, accurate and appropriate way.

Getting *primary data* entails data collection that is controlled by the researcher. This often involves *fieldwork* in one or many[11] research sites, which may also provide other contextual data – art collections, libraries, unplanned interactions. For up-system research, fieldwork has specific problems,[12] not least the ongoing negotiation of access (C4.5). *Secondary data* has already been collected by someone else, collection methods cannot be controlled, but this data can be analysed in different ways.[13] The annual scores from the *Transparency International* 'Corruptions Perceptions Index' can be reanalysed in the form of a trends graph across a number of years, to show the upward and downward trajectories of each country, which may indicate trends in corruption levels among political and commercial elites (Figure 6.1). *Meta-data* is data about data, such as records about computer or mobile phone use. The *UN Special Tribunal for Lebanon* has GPS/mobile phone data of who seemed to be following Rafik Hariri's movements before he was assassinated. *Raw data* describes the basic material – printouts, transcripts, numbers, images – which is then presented in a more comprehensible way as *findings* (C6.3).

Academic studies often used to start with a decision to use either a *quantitative*[14] (positivist – numbers, measurement, statistics) or *qualitative*[15] (interpretive[16] – words, images, meanings) approach. But the distinction is not clear-cut, and it is more helpful to consider the 'degree' to which a study needs to be quantified,[17] and to move beyond the traditional distinction.[18] Qualitative research often uses quantitative terms – "most", "less", "more", "many", "few". All quantitative research starts with qualitative judgements about what to study, why and how. These studies often use qualitative coding criteria, proxies and indicators, and usually end with a qualitative selection of data and interpretation of its importance. Small-scale and in-depth studies tend to use qualitative methods, because statistical methods are usually not considered robust with fewer than 50 people. But even single transcripts can be analysed quantitatively, for example by counting the number of times certain types of words are used. For up-system research there are two specific considerations to balance: it is often hard to get data from sufficient numbers of powerful people to create statistically meaningful findings, yet qualitative research is often perceived by decision-makers as inferior.

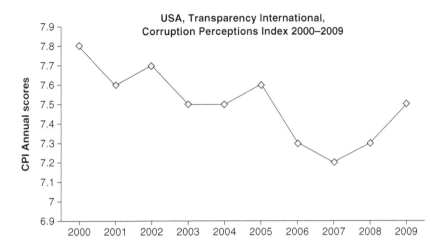

FIGURE 6.1   Secondary analysis – a trend from annual data

Unless the intent of the research is to test and develop a specific method, a study is very likely to entail *mixed methods*.[19] Different types of data are collected in different ways, which may or may not be compared, and may involve a multidisciplinary approach combining social and other sciences.[20] The focus of a study (C4.2), such as corporate crime,[21] needs to be linked carefully to the choice of methods.[22] 'Nested analysis' can be applied to mixed method comparative analysis.[23] Mixed methods approaches have been more common in relation to large aggregate units of analysis such as nations,[24] but can be applied to individuals. The research design (C4.1) for mixed methods should account for both sequence and convenience. Sometimes one method may need to be used before another can be used – documentary analysis to identify questions for focus groups, focus groups to identify key issues for interviews. But fieldwork often needs to be done pragmatically by collecting data where and when it is feasible and cost-effective.

Research *instruments* operationalize research questions or hypotheses, and each element of an instrument should relate to a research question/hypothesis, even if the elements are not organized under the same headings, for example because it is best to put confrontational questions last. Instruments include:

- *Survey questionnaires* – distributed by post, delivery systems, email, or inclusion in magazines or newspapers. Software is available (sometimes free) for online surveys.[25]
- *Interview schedules* for face-to-face questioning.
- *Observation charts* to note verbal/nonverbal behaviour and contextual factors.
- *Analytical frameworks* to organize and assess data from images, objects, buildings and texts such as websites.

Surveys generally use *closed* questions, which require a yes or no answer, or an indication of the strength of agreement on a scale,[26] because this data can be quantified easily. Longer in-depth interviews use *open* questions which elicit longer verbal replies, which will be noted or recorded, and the records may then be typed-up as *transcriptions*, and data is usually analysed qualitatively.

Although there might seem to be a clear distinction between data collection and data analysis, in practice data collection usually entails forms of initial analysis, which provide the basis for further analysis. This chapter outlines the basics of data management linked to examples that are relevant to up-system research. It first discusses the four common sources of data, and the potential and problems of using those data sources. The next section considers how units of study are selected, and how qualitative data is selected and organized for analysis. Ways to test data and carry out initial analysis are outlined, which makes data ready for presentation as findings for further analysis (C7).

6.1 SOURCES

Reviewing relevant historical background (C1), theories (C.2) and academic literature (C3) will help to identify likely research *sites* or *domains* (Figure 0.9) and sources of information (Figure 2.8), which will then need to be *accessed* (C4.5). The likely sources of data are in the form of texts, people, objects and buildings, but there is often overlap. A Queen's tomb could be analysed in terms of political inscriptions, biography, wall paintings and artefacts, and/or mausoleums.

6.1.1 Texts

Texts are a set of symbols that communicate a message – words and images[27] – in forms such as documents, posters, memorial plaques and internet sites. Texts provide primary data because texts are created independently of the researcher and the researcher can control how that data is collected. When documents are used as a data source,[28] rather than literature (C3), they can be selected on the bases of a sample (C6.2). The researcher's records – observation notes, transcripts, voice or video recordings – cannot be analysed as texts by that researcher because the researcher helped to create these. However, another researcher might analyse research records as texts.

The alteration of images by, or about, powerful people can sometimes be more revealing than the original image. The airbrushing of people who had gone out of favour, from formal photos, was common in Communist China and the Soviet Union. In the former Yugoslavia, Milosevic's photographers added extra people to make crowds look bigger at his political rallies – the same group appeared many times across one picture.[29] *Photoshop* makes such techniques simple, but also simple to detect. Egypt's *Al-Ahram* newspaper changed a photo, which originally showed (then) US President Obama walking in front of a group of world leaders, to show Egypt's (then) President Mubarak at the front with Obama behind.[30] When political leaders visit dangerous places, they can be presented in front of an appropriate but fake backdrop. As with documentary analysis, what is missing can be revealing. When then British Prime Minister Tony Blair visited Iraq during the 2002 occupation, he was pictured in front of rows of British troops. The image-maker did not notice that the sun on Blair's face was clearly coming from the left of the picture, but there were no shadows to the right of the soldiers in the background as there should have been.

Texts are often easy to access through databases, library catalogues and the web.[31] Organization texts can be found online under headings such as 'company profile', 'about the company', 'staff profiles', 'management structure', 'organizational charts', 'financial report', 'chair's report'. Texts that organizations inadvertently leave online might be found by using keywords and adding 'pdf' or 'ppt'. Training or promotional presentations can provide interesting insights into how a company works. Using brand names instead of company names can provide alternative perspectives on companies. Headers and footers might show that a document's title had been changed at the last minute, leading researchers to seek out earlier versions, as with the UK government's *Iraq Dossier*.[32] *Wikileaks* proposes a simple methodology for accessing and 'crowdsourcing' analysis (C5.2) of its online data.[33]

- Search for events you remember that happened for example in your country
- Browse by date or search for an origin near you
- Pick out interesting events and tell others about them
- Use twitter, reddit, mail whatever suits your audience best

But not all online texts are what they seem and the sources need to be verified through checking the web address and contact details against other information (C3.2).

Coins, banknotes, stamps and *posters* are a readily accessible source of up-system data, which does not even necessitate collecting the actual objects (Figure 0.8). They can be viewed in museums, or on dealer sites such as eBay. The appearance of royal heads on coins was a way of affirming authority, as Neil MacGregor, Director of the British Museum, puts it, 'The message is on the money – The coin is the billboard of the boss.'[34] Recent methods such as carbon dating help to reconstruct and confirm chronologies of kings and queens, such as the lineage of the early Parthian rulers of Persia.[35] Coins provide a wealth of information about rulers, regimes and their priorities. The youthful head of Caesar Augustus stayed the same on coins and statues until his death, aged 76. When the head of Alexander the Great appeared on coins, around 300BC, he had horns which symbolized the gods of the Greeks and Egyptians, Zeus and Ammon. This legitimized his power through the deities of both regions. His head remained on coins after his death to affirm the power of subsequent rulers. In much the same way, the heads of Mao Zedong, George Washington, Kim Il Sung and Ayatollah Khomeini continue to appear on Chinese, American, North Korean and Iranian banknotes (Figure 7.7).

Stamps are similar, and sometimes also mark perceived abuses of power, such as the 'Martyrs of the Struggle for Israel's Independence' (1982), and a similar series about China in 1940. Political posters can be used to compare public and official attitudes to significant events such as war.[36] They may also show the changing nature of propaganda over time. Mao Zedong was originally depicted as a worker among the Chinese people. His body then rose above the people, gaining a halo-like glow, and eventually his face was in a circle, godlike, in the sky.

Documents and documentary analysis[37] are central to up-system research, and start from collecting the physical documents (books, reports, magazines), and then selecting and extracting the relevant texts from those documents. In general, most documents used in up-system research are scarce and texts will be selected purposively or opportunistically. But if there is a large "population" of documents – elite magazines, American autobiographies, political speeches – they could be selected by sampling (C6.2). A specific difficulty, when analysing texts by powerful people, is to ascertain exactly who wrote them. Were they drafted by speech writers or assistants, and the named authors simply approved and put their names to the script, as with most company or government reports?

Documents can also be analysed as objects (below), which may happen as part of police or museum work. Analyses might entail discovering how and when the paper was made, what printing process was used, watermarks, changes, damage and incidental marks such as food stains. Infrared photography can identify different types of ink or reveal what was written underneath obliterations.[38] Diaries, purportedly by Mussolini and Hitler, were found to be fakes because the straw fibres and optical brighteners found in the paper were introduced after the stated dates of writing.[39]

Content analysis uses specific tools for analysis of any type of communication, and is often applied to transcripts.[40] Analysis can be based on simple questions to discover the unwritten aspects of a document as in historical research (C1.2),[41] or can take a more theoretical approach such as analysing rhetoric.[42] Questioning the terminology promoted by powerful people is an obvious aspect. Why do politicians often talk of 'rehabilitation' in contexts such as Afghanistan – what do they mean, 'rehabilitation' to what – the Taliban, the Soviet Era, the **feudal** warlords, or a westernized system that has never existed in that country?[43] *Discourse analysis* treats any text as primary data.[44] Analysis can be at a detailed level, using methods and theories of linguistics to assess aspects such as the frequency of certain phrases. Software is available to help.[45] *Critical discourse analysis* (CDA) considers how language is used to increase domination and power,[46] and assumes that texts mediate power.[47] Fairclough's CDA framework combines:[48]

- *micro-analysis* of syntax, metaphoric structure and metrical devises – Does this speech reflect a particular linguistic style?
- *meso-analysis* of the production and consumption of the text, and related power relations – How many copies were circulated free, to whom, and why?
- *macro-analysis* of the general societal trends affecting the text – How has Chinese soft power influenced African political speeches?

An *epistemic* approach to CDA links discourse and sources of knowledge.[49] It is often relevant to notice what is missing or hidden in a text, but that needs objective criteria indicating what should be included and conspicuous. Texts might also be analysed in terms of *mass communications*.[50]

Maps, private and public, are a significant means of legitimization, and are therefore also a means to understand elites. They have been displayed to demonstrate dominion or erudition in galleries, political meeting rooms and audience chambers such as the Terza Logia of the Vatican Palace. The primary purpose is to demonstrate power, and in the past many of these public maps were even too inaccessible to be used or updated. The Roman *Forma Urbis Romae* (200) was 13 by 18 metres in size and carved on 150 marble slabs. A similar map adorned a Roman colonial tax office in Provence, France.[51] Such maps not only demonstrated the extent of dominion, but also that the rulers understood and controlled the methods of mapping and plan making. To see that the Emperor knew how many steps led up to your front door sent a clear message about who was in control.

Maps commonly exaggerate property, colonial lands and the centrality of power elites.[52] The English *Hereford Mappa Mundi* (c.1300) shows Jerusalem at the centre of the world, symbolizing the importance of Christianity. Chinese maps put China central, and the Chinese character for 'China' means 'centre of the world'. Some modern Australian maps have South, and therefore Australia, at the top. Maps were often ornamented with royal crests and pictures. Like others, *John Speed's Map of England and Wales* (1603) included a genealogical chart. It showed King James II and Queen Anne at the top, traced back to William the Conqueror.[53] At that time the legitimacy of James was in question, because he had combined the thrones of England and Scotland for the first time, under a new name 'The United Kingdom'. A significant use of politicized maps has been in school classrooms, and that continues. Jewish sources complain that Palestinian school textbooks omit details of modern Israel.[54] The Kuwaiti *Not to Forget Museum* displays Iraqi school textbooks from Saddam Hussein's era, in which maps show an Iraqi empire spanning North Africa, and Kuwait as part of Iraq (Figure 0.3).

Satire, in the form of words and images concerning powerful people, caricatures and exaggerates the less desirable features of the subject. What did the artist want to communicate with artistic devices such as the exaggerated sexuality of a prince? Satire not only highlights key issues within a society, but also abuses of power that are dangerous to challenge through mainstream channels, such as the English corrupt trading 'monopolists' (Figure 6.2).[55] More recently, in similar style, the cartoons of Iranian, Ardeshir Mohassess, appear surreal with their headless and limbless bodies, but they serve as an ongoing critique of oppression and torture under the regimes of both the Shah and Khomeini's Islamic Republic.[56] Methods for analysing political cartoons are developing.[57] Songs may provide relevant texts in the form of propaganda for and against war,[58] and protest songs provide contrasting views about public attitudes towards their political leaders.[59] The style of satire can give a false impression that it is mainly based on gossip and guesswork, but satirical magazines such as the 50-year-old *Private Eye* are very thoroughly researched and are exemplars of investigative journalism. If they were not, they would quickly be made bankrupt through defamation cases.

Published by W. Holland, London, 1795

The English 'Monopolists' were commercial elites who corruptly inflated the price of food, and were eventually brought to account by the public at the end of the eighteenth century. Traditionally, the devil played the violin or 'fiddle' which is also English slang for cheating. 'Dance' refers to the involuntary movements of hanged men. Villages had a central 'green' where people met, public punishments were carried out, and the 'fête' (pronounced like 'fate') happened.

FIGURE 6.2   Satire – The Fate of the Monopolists and Dance at Fidler's Green

Titles provide fascinating questions about textual claims to legitimacy. What is a 'gentleman' and how is his gentility measured? Titles can change subtly for political reasons. When Britain's Princess Diana divorced Prince Charles, 'the' was dropped from her title, 'The Princess of Wales', which left room for 'the' successor to her. What is the value of a title? In Britain it is illegal to buy a peerage, yet titles from the feudal system – Lord of the manor – are marketable. Titles from The Principality of Sealand can be purchased from its website shop. The Malaysian King is styled, *Yang di-Petuan Agong*, ('He who is made the supreme lord'), but 'made' by whom and 'supreme' on what criteria? What is the basis for being a Dutch *Jonkheer* – an invented title for supposedly prestigious families who have no claim to a formal title? Why do British male school teachers wish to be styled 'sir', as do prison officers? (And is there a connection?)

Why should titles impose respect? Why should we all address an unknown Marquis as '*My* Lord' or a Viscount as 'Dear Lord'? What amount of honour is required to be a 'Much Honoured' Scottish feudal Baron? Others titles appear ambiguous. When a British Duke is called the 'Most High, Potent and Noble Prince', are we to assume something about his ability to father children? Does German nomenclature reflect eugenics in the term *Hochwohlgeboren* ('High Well Born')? Often, there seems a mismatch between elite status and behaviour. Why are clerics addressed as 'reverend', and why should they expect to be revered by people who do not recognize their gods? The Catholic 'Reverend Father' or 'venerable', or 'Most holy father' for a pope, might seem a questionable sign of respect for a cadre that includes and protects paedophiles.[60] Why are British and American parliamentarians addressed as 'honourable' when there have been so many instances of dishonourable practice? Presidents of the Philippines are styled 'His Illustrious Excellency' which includes Joseph Estrada who was impeached and convicted for corruption. Do ambassadors always display their 'excellence'? The Canadian ambassador in Guatemala, His Excellency Kenneth Cook, appeared less than excellent when he was found guilty of defamation over a film that discussed a Canadian company's human rights abuses in that country, in 2010.

6.1.2 People

People can be questioned or observed and, unless a specific method is being tested, research designs usually combine these methods in a pragmatic way.

Interviews with powerful people are often seen as having distinct problems,[61] because of access and a reluctance by respondents to answer questions in a straightforward way.[62] Experienced researchers provide a wealth of strategies,[63] and specific advice for less experienced researchers.[64] Specific considerations include access (C4.2), openness of respondents, feedback,[65] and power imbalance[66] such as gender relations.[67] Interviewees may try to take control of the interview process, but this may provide insights into how they use their power.[68] Researchers who have interviewed despots warn that antipathy towards those who have seemingly abused their power may lead to biased understanding of what is said. It is important to suspend judgement, and accept responses on the terms of the interviewee even if that is uncomfortable. After interviews, objective criteria can be used for analysis. Schirmer explains that during ten years of interviewing Guatemalan despots she needed to remain 'open to their realities'.[69] But up-system interviewing is not always categorically different from other forms of interviewing. The difficulty is that the usual problems are exacerbated.[70]

Before interviewing busy people, every effort must be made to get background information from other sources. Experienced interviewers conclude, 'It is virtually impossible to over prepare for an interview!'[71] – 'Preparation is ultra-important'.[72] Busy people can become irritated if they are asked to repeat information that they know is readily available elsewhere. Good background research can be used to assist access (C4.5) – "I have read your book, studied your website, and talked to many of your staff. But there are three questions that I need to ask you directly, because this will help to correct misinformation/clarify exactly what you mean/make people more aware of the difficulties you faced." The effectiveness of giving advance notice of questions is hard to predict, and this will often be requested.[73] Notice might help the interviewee to think about the questions and prepare detailed answers, or it could lead to sanitized answers prepared by lawyers, or to a short email reply and no interview. A compromise is to outline the areas of questioning – "Your time in India", "What you learned from your music teacher at the Academy" – but not the exact questions.

Discussions about interviewing in different contexts include: international organizations,[74] large companies,[75] political elites[76] in national contexts[77] and leaders,[78] elite white collar criminals,[79] city elites,[80] high tech elites,[81] spies[82] and intelligence officers.[83] Different disciplines discuss specific approaches, such as those of economic geography,[84] international relations[85] and development studies.[86] Email, Skype and phone interviews require very careful preparation,[87] because upsets are hard to put right at a distance. If an interviewer represents an organization such as *Amnesty International*, there are broader considerations beyond simple data collection (Figure 6.3).

Interviews are likely to be *semi-structured*, to permit flexibility yet maintain focus, and will usually appear to avoid contentious issues.[88] Research interviews with elites are often closer to extracting specific 'memoires' (C5.2) than information.[89] An interview *schedule*[90] might move from 'non-threatening' to 'threatening' questions,[91] or be graduated from unstructured to highly structured, with diverse responses related to a 'shopping list' of areas to be covered.[92] The structure may be staged, in terms of 'the opening, the grand tour, and the follow-up', reflecting different styles – 'journalistic', 'therapeutic' (building trust and rapport), or 'investigative'.[93] In general interviewing, contentious but important topics are usually left until the end of an interview, in order to avoid the possibility that they may cause an interviewee to curtail the discussion before answering most of the questions. But this might be reversed if there is a chance that a very busy interviewee may cut short an interview before the end. There might be 'tandem' interviewers – one asking questions and one noting answers, body-language and context – switching roles strategically.[94] Will translators or interpreters be used, how will they be briefed, and will their transcripts be double checked by back-translation?[95] Assistants are likely to do a better job if they have a good understanding of the aims of the whole project.

A decision needs to be made about how to record interviews – notes, voice recorders, videos – and the interviewee needs to be made aware of this before the interview.[96] Powerful people may take an interview more seriously if it appears very professional and for a broader audience. Leaders may respond well to being filmed, and perhaps interviewed by a known TV interviewer, even if it is not for a TV programme (Figure 6.4). As with other forms of interview, a few friendly *warm-up questions* can be helpful.[97] But friendly questions could invite long answers and the whole interview time might be consumed. In general, "surgical" questioning is essential – 'purposive interactions'[98] that

---

An effective interview with a contact not only requires information gathering skills, it frequently requires being a sympathetic listener and a good ambassador for Amnesty International (AI).

'Research is about investigation and quick decision-making, but also about being diplomats, spokespersons, counsellors and sympathetic listeners. Researchers are often the first and sometimes the only point of contact between victims and AI, NGOs and AI, media and AI.'

Source: *Amnesty International*, Research Policy Manual (internal)

FIGURE 6.3   The wider role of interviews

optimize, and perhaps extend, the access time. Sometimes powerful people try to *control* the whole interview,[99] or researchers are in awe of a powerful person and believe everything that is said – the 'halo effect'.[100] Interviewers can usefully study the tactics of TV presenters,[101] such as the *Big Think* interviews,[102] comedians such as Ali G,[103] or the BBC series *Five minutes with …* in which the presence of a large alarm clock keeps both interviewer and interviewee concise and focused, up to the "killer question" at the end.[104]

Figure 6.4 shows part of a transcript of an interview, by the author, with Abdusalam Majali (b.1925), twice Prime Minister of Jordan. The interview was part of a series of interviews with UN leaders.[105] It was filmed using two cameras, one on the interviewee and one on the interviewer The location was the home of the interviewee, which provided a fascinating 'back drop' of memorabilia for other shots, including a book about Majali signing the peace treaty with Israel in 1994, with US President Bill Clinton, which provided a conversation point for extending the interview. The facts about Majali's life were researched from written sources and his colleagues, and the questions did not repeat this but explored his personal feelings about events in his life. A semi-structured interview schedule was used, but the discussion appeared to build on comments made by the interviewee, as in a conversation, rather than representing a list of fixed questions that could seem like an interrogation. The main aim was to elicit views about global problems and leadership education. The interview started with a friendly warm-up question, which itself provided interesting data about leadership training. It was not known if Majali would talk about signing the peace treaty, because this had become politically sensitive, but an open question elicited an answer, which was extended by asking what advice he would give young leaders, based on that experience.

It is usually assumed that powerful people are in powerful positions, but that is not always so at the time of a research inquiry. They may be victims of aggression or severely traumatized, as political prisoners, refugees or hospital patients. They may be interviewed because they are suspected of wrongdoing. *Investigative interviews* often use psychological methods, and in forensic settings interviewers need a good knowledge of process and relevant jargon.[106] *Cognitive interviews*[107] use techniques to enhance memory and increase recall by people who appear unconfident when replying to questions. Techniques include reconstructing context, insisting on complete unedited descriptions, recalling events in forward and backward timescales, changing the perspective of the recall – seeing from a different angle or as another person. A central principle is that each interview needs to be planned in a way that is compatible with each interviewee.[108]

Experienced interviewers may use techniques for *extending* interviews. Having asked a few key questions they might

- comment on an object in the interviewee's room – a picture, vase, carpet – which may lead to a discussion about where it came from, which provides data about social and family networks.
- build on what the interviewee has just been doing – if they have just come from a meeting or field visit, ask about it.
- ask for advice[109] – "If I (my son/daughter/friend/students) wanted to get a job like yours, what would you suggest?", "What would you put in a curriculum for leadership training?"

CW… *Among your many educational achievements, you were responsible for founding the United Nations International Leadership Academy. How did that come about?*

Abdusalem Majali (AM)… Well, I was the President of the University of Jordan. And it always struck me that there was a gap between present leaders, in every walk of life, and future leaders. So I started a small programme called, 'Potential Leadership'.

We used to pick the top three students from every department. And I made a committee of three deans to meet with these people and try to discover who has the potentiality to become a leader.

Those selected would meet with a decision maker in Jordan once a week for three hours: His Majesty the King, the Crown Prince, the Prime Minister, Foreign Minister and then Commander of the Army, the British Ambassador, the American Ambassador, Japanese Ambassador. They would sit with such a person and he would talk about anything he likes and they respond. Then I used to send them to an Arab state in winter so they met with the leadership of that state for two weeks. Then I would send them to Europe in summer to meet with the leadership of that country for one or two weeks.

So when I was a member of the United Nations University Council, I suggested to them to establish an academy whereby young leaders come together in one place and interact with each other. And then to invite a number of leaders in the world, present or retired, and let them interact with them.

They go and meet leaders all over the world, and when they all finish they come back to base, and each group will do a briefing – what they have heard, what they have seen. And it will be their own analysis, their own ideas about what they have seen.

And the philosophy is: 'EXPOSE DON'T IMPOSE'. In other words, it's not a curricula. It is to look into problems of the world, and to try to find a solution. Nowadays, the world is getting smaller, so you need leaders with a global attitude.

CW… *What a fascinating vision. You mentioned the problems of the world. What are those problems? How does that relate to training young leaders? What are the tasks for leadership in future?*

AM… One of the big problems in the world is poverty. So these leaders of rich countries if they have been visiting the poor countries of the world and saw with their own eyes the problems, now once they become in the chair they are going to treat things differently than somebody who never felt who never saw with his own eyes the poverty in the poor countries…

CW… *You have enjoyed many many successes in your life. Do some stand out and how did they come about?*

AM… Well, I am very thankful to God, and to His Majesty King Hussein, who give me the opportunity to serve my country. To be able to secure their rights in the peace negotiation, which I carried out, I hope successfully. And I got my country safe on that because it would have been really a disaster. Our situation would have been absolutely desperate. Luckily we have done what we have done in the right time.

CW… *Indeed. You must have experienced many frustrations and problems during that course of events. What advice would you give to your young leaders about overcoming problems and frustrations?*

AM… Well, let me tell you one thing. At the very beginning of negotiations with Israel, with the man on the opposite. He was an ambassador of that time. He was a younger man, he was an experienced person and I was older and not experienced in politics of negotiation. So when I met him the very first time, I said to him, 'Look, you are very experienced, I am not. I am a scientific man. My approach is a scientific way I hate to be fooled. Don't try to fool me. Tell me whatever you want to tell me, however bitter it is. But do not put any grain of sugar on it because you will not find me here the second day if you do.'

And we dealt with each other in the best manners you ever could imagine. Because right from the beginning, I was absolutely open and he was very open with me, so we could succeed. And that is I think very important.

So to any young person, he has always to put himself in the shoes of others and say how would like that other to treat him. He has to treat that other in the same way. I think if he does this, he will be very successful. This has been always my motto: 'Trouble the trouble before the trouble troubles you. Do not ever wait for the trouble to trouble you.'

FIGURE 6.4   An interview with Abdul Salam Majali, former Prime Minister of Jordan

The interviews were filmed with two cameras, at the home of Dr Majali, which provided excellent background. Similar interviews were filmed with one camera, first recording the whole interview from angle 1, then moving the camera to take a few shots from angle 2, and then repeating the questions and adding 'noddies' (shots of the interviewer apparently listening and nodding to the interviewee) without the interviewee being there. Additional shots of the room were used to cover any editing problems, and illustrate certain topics. The famous BBC series 'Face to Face' – which included interviews with Gandhi, Martin Luther King and Carl Jung – used just one camera over the shoulder of, but never showing, the interviewer John Freeman.

Angle 1	Angle 2	
1a	2a	Long-shots showing interviewee and interviewer together. (2a could be shot by moving a single camera.)
1b	2b	Close-ups from the same angle. (2b could be a 'noddie' without the interviewee present.)
1c	2c	The final 'thank you' from both angles. (2c could be shot while shooting 2a.)
1d	2d	Background shots. After Dr Majali signed the 1994 Jordanian-Israeli peace treaty, a dove landed on his head.

Photos: Hiromi Yamashita

FIGURE 6.4 *Continued*

Source: Unpublished transcript of an interview (2003) by the author (edited).

- use flattery[110] – "Your staff all seem so cheerful. Why is that?", "I don't think there is anyone else who could explain this properly", "I think you understand this better than anyone else."
- mention mutual, or impressive, friends or colleagues – "I also studied English at that college, did you know … ?"

Using false statements to extend a response can be methodologically and ethically questionable, not least because the interviewee may know the truth. A vague statement such as "The director of BVZ seems to think that …" may be acceptable, but direct comments such as "Your brother told me that …" can bring an interview to an abrupt end. Interviews may be optimized if the interviewee believes s/he will be compared with others. Other interviews can be mentioned to prompt or provoke more discussion – "I believe that the Imam does not completely agree with you …". In other circumstances it might be more effective if the person believes s/he is the only interviewee. In his research among Taliban leaders, Matt Waldman used a 'divide and rule' strategy – 'all interviewees were contacted and interviewed separately … none is based in the same district as another, and none disclosed to comrades that they were being interviewed'.[111] It is always worth asking, "Who else would you suggest I talk to?" because this reveals networks and provides the basis for negotiating access ('Chain referral', C6.2). Providing feedback of initial analysis to elites may be an effective means to gain more data and improve accuracy,[112] because at that point they have invested time in the work and have an interest in ensuring its accuracy. But attempts to manipulate findings and conclusions should be recognized.

Perhaps the most distinct aspect of interviewing powerful people is the unexpected diversity. The settings for interviews can range from formal government offices to a sofa in the kitchen. Interviewees are often pre-occupied with other things – they might have had a good day, or a very bad day. Their perception of their own power, and self-esteem, may vary greatly, and is not easy to predict. The lesson is, be ready for anything (Figure 6.5).

Opinion poll surveys assess public perceptions of powerful people. Polls are based on perception theory which recognizes a likely difference between fact and opinion – what is, and what appears. Opinions about who should be a leader can become the fact of who is, and perceptions might be changed by external influences such as political propaganda. Contemporary polls trace their history back to a straw poll carried out by *The Harrisburg Pennsylvanian* in 1824, concerning a presidential election. Similar polls followed, and in 1916 the *Literary Digest* carried out a national survey, which predicted Woodrow Wilson's victory. The editors simply sent out millions of postcards and counted those that were returned. In 1936, a similar endeavour failed because there was no accounting for bias in those who received and returned the cards. In the same year George Gallup carried out a smaller but more methodologically sound survey, which correctly predicted the success of Franklin D. Roosevelt. Gallup believed that the populace was always ahead of their leaders in judging issues. It is usually more cost-effective for general researchers to commission polling companies to carry out their research, because this saves the time and cost of setting up a complicated system for a single study. The 'Corruption Perceptions Index', and other tools from *Transparency*

Formal

President of the Busan Municipal Assembly, South Korea.

'This was more formal than any other interview. But I felt he was excited to be interviewed, because his assistant came to take photos during the interview.'

Informal

Director of Queen Zein Al-Sharaf Institute for Development, Jordan.

'I felt sorry to interrupt her as she was very busy. At first she was not comfortable, as she was not used to being interviewed. But then she made things more relaxed as we sat on the sofa over drinks. I figured that she was younger than me, and she was very enthusiastic about her job.'

Extending interviews and snowballing

Member of the National Assembly, Chairman of Health and Welfare Committee, Chief Spokesman of former President Kim Young-sa, South Korea.

'I was a bit nervous as this was my first interview with a Korean politician. I was given three minutes, during a break in a parliamentary session. But the interview became twenty minutes. Then he introduced me to other relevant leaders. The journalist who introduced me to this guy was impressed, so he introduced me to many other politicians.'

FIGURE 6.5 Yun-joo Lee interviewing Arab and Korean leaders

(Continued)

Gender questions

President, Su-young District, Busan, South Korea.

'She seemed more nervous than me, I think because she felt she was being judged like a man. She had just come from a meeting. The first thing she said was it was not easy to have meetings with an all-male team who are subordinate to her. So my nervousness quickly went, and I used what she said, and linked to one of my questions about being a women leader.'

A seating mistake

President of the Student Union, American University in Cairo, Egypt.

'He was very eloquent. I felt this was because he was still young, pure (in a political sense), not scared of anything, and had the strength to do what he believes. I was sitting in a lower chair than him, which was a mistake because that made him seem more powerful while interviewing.'

Opportunism

Mayor of Busan, South Korea.

'I was working as a volunteer at the Asian games. At a reception, I noticed that the Mayor was alone. I quickly approached him and asked a few prepared questions. I always had three questions in my head for unexpected opportunities. He was very happy to talk with me, as he preferred to be with someone who was not a threat. He was politically isolated at that time, and not popular at the reception. Two years later, following a minor corruption scandal, he committed suicide.'

FIGURE 6.5 *Continued*

Negotiating access

Baba Shinuda, Coptic pope, Cairo, Egypt.

'At first, the security staff would not let me in. I asked for a glass of water, and started talking to them in Arabic, which they liked, and they started asking me about Korea. I then asked to use the toilet, and so they let me enter the building. I came back and they seemed relaxed, perhaps because I had been in and not made a problem. They told me to go where the pope walked back after the mass. If I saw him then, that was apparently not their responsibility! I could only ask him one question, but it was a very interesting answer which showed that the pope had insight into local circumstances, and was aware of a hidden gender problem that affected men.'

Source: Lee, Yun-joo (2010) 'Leadership and development in South Korea and Egypt: The significance of cultural shifts', unpublished PhD thesis, School of Oriental and Asian Studies, University of London.

International (TI), is a notable example of a non-commercial opinion survey, which builds-in an element of advocacy because those who contribute gain an interest in promoting the findings (C8.3).

Focus groups[113] provide a compromise between one-to-one interviewing and a full survey, and can be done online.[114] They are rarely used for collecting data from elites and leaders, but are useful for gathering the perceptions and opinions that specific populations or followers have of up-system individuals. Politicians often commission focus group research because it is a quick way of assessing perceptions of current issues, including an understanding of which terms and slogans are effective. A facilitator will ask basic questions, and perhaps use prompts to elicit further views.[115] The significant difference with interviews is that group dynamics can also be noted – how members of the group influence one another.

Observation – listening to what powerful people say and watching how they behave[116] – provides the chance to formally analyse language[117] and body language.[118] Observation can overcome the problem of achieving direct access,[119] but may also involve interviews, group discussions, life histories, local documents and reflection on how the experience has affected the researcher.[120] Qualitative and quantitative methods can be used – speech patterns and aspects of body language might be described or counted. Ethnographic approaches, originally honed by anthropologists to study traditional leaders in the colonies (C1.1), are being applied more broadly.[121] Traditional 'participant observation'[122] is difficult to achieve among present-day power elites, although it has sometimes been achieved in very difficult contexts such as gangs[123] and Hollywood.[124] The approach may be seen as a method, 'interpretive methodology' or 'constructivist modern empiricism', which uses ethnographic approaches in conjunction with other methods to understand policy-making processes and outcomes.[125] Innovative 'visual research' may consider clothes, documents being carried, who people talk to and for how long.[126] Observing a population can give indications about what leaders and elites are thinking. Noting that the hair styles of North Korean athletes at the 2002 Asian Games had suddenly changed from 1960s communist cuts to modern international coiffure indicated something about how the minds of political elites in North Korea were evolving.[127]

ICT is creating many new opportunities for *remote observation* as part of distance research (C5.2), and the principles of traditional forms of observation can still be applied. Parliaments, War Crimes Tribunals, shareholders meetings, and many similar events are webcast in real time, and have archives, podcasts and transcripts of proceedings. These provide the chance to observe powerful people responding to challenging questions in great detail, which creates opportunities for analysis of aspects such as question–response styles, the use of prepared versus spontaneous responses, media skills and obfuscation.

Opportunistic interaction is often an aspect of investigative frameworks (C5.1), but can contribute to other forms of research. This may involve attending public appearances by powerful people, where it might be possible to ask questions. Journalists might try to frequent places where elites are likely to appear – office lobbies, clubs, gyms, operas, gigs – and engage them in casual conversation. Companies might organize seminars and invite department heads and experts from rival companies, and note and analyse how they react to certain information, or question them about budgets and R&D plans. Remote shadowing (C5.2) can increase the likelihood of productive encounters. Three things distinguish opportunistic research from everyday encounters – it is intentional, planned and systematic. If there is the likelihood of being in taxis with government officials because you are working as a PA at the Asian Games, an opportunistic interview might not use notebooks or voice recorders, but could entail casually asking the three key questions of a study. It must be more systematic than a casual chat.

6.1.3 Objects

Objects – sculptures, art collections, prizes – can provide primary and secondary data. Museums and galleries present a wealth of objects to study, often through superb online sites. Relevant historical,[128] archaeological[129] and provenance[130] methods are now well-developed and 'visual' methodologies are being developed.[131]

Art has a long tradition of depicting, legitimizing and challenging powerful people, and art historians have a wealth of methodologies.[132] Goya's *The Third of May 1808* depicts Napoleon's troops executing civilians. This inspired a similar painting by Picasso, *Massacre in Korea* (1951), which is a critique of American intervention on the peninsular, which probably explains why it is not well known. The more famous *Guernica* (1937) protests about the bombing of innocent people of that town, but before this, *The Dream and Lie of Franco* (1937), and accompanying poem 'Evil-omened polyps', satirized the dictator's claim to be defending Spanish interests, showing him eating his own horse. Miro's 'Barcelona Series' (1944) caricatured devils and dictators that plagued Spain for many years. Other abstract depictions of women and birds showed vulnerability to the bombing of German war planes. The tradition continues through organizations such as *Antiwarartsists.com*.

Portraits provide a wealth of accessible data, but can be misleading because of the desire of elites, and those creating the portraits, to enhance or distort reality. Before the twentieth century, external visits to Korea, the so-called "Hermit Kingdom", were rare and descriptions were unreliable. The English picture of Korean 'mandarins' (1890) depicts accurate dress, and the men appear as calm and meditative intellectuals of the upper class (Figure 6.6). The artefacts surrounding them symbolize their status – culture (vase), literacy (text) and elite (tea ceremony). 'Mandarins' is a Chinese term not usually applied to Korean leaders, but the images accurately represent the intellectual *Yang-ban* class. In the French depiction of *Chef Coreen et sa suite* (1830), the hats on the attendants are not Korean, nor are the pointed shoes. The 'chef' seems to carry a sword, which is improbable as his dress mimics that of the highest class which comprised the non-military intellectuals. The belts around the waists appear wrong as Korean belts are high, just below the chest, as with the 'mandarins'.[133] The picture seems to be an artist's impression based on a collection of museum artefacts, which was not uncommon.

Portraits embody a range of information that the subjects wished to portray in the way they wanted, and could afford, to portray it. Simple understandings of artistic methods can provide fascinating insights. In the past, English painters charged more to paint arms, legs and hands which are particularly hard to get right. Hence the saying about an expensive purchase, "It cost an arm and a leg". A quick trip around a portrait gallery shows the array of artistic devices to hide hands and avoid extra cost, and full-body pictures represent a deliberate display of wealth and therefore power. Other methods may rely on scientific analysis. Art historians analysing the portrait of a Queen might have suspicions that there are previous restorations or alterations. They would use meta-methods, such as stereomicroscopes and fluorescence illumination, to analyse paint pigments, which would create meta-data which helps to understand the original process used by the artist. Were the paints organic (plant or animal extracts), or inorganic (metallic oxides)? The resultant meta-data, along with other information about existing methods for restoration, could then form the basis for understanding and restoring that particular artwork. But there may be other interesting findings. Traditional Korean royal portraits used inorganic paints because these did not decay like the organic paints used in the west. These portraits were meant to impress future, not just contemporary, generations.

The historically focused methods for analysing objects, images and their contexts can be adapted to present-day up-system studies. The methods used by art historians can be applied to photographic data of present-day elites. The art historian might analyse why a

Korean Mandarins (c.1890)

Chef Coreen et sa suite (1830)
(Private collection of Yun-joo Lee, Geneva)

FIGURE 6.6   Images of Korean elites

Using a grid system to analyse backdrop.
Lee Sang-hee, former South Korean Minister of Science and Technology, displays a model satellite (A1) and a space shuttle (A2), and magazines with his picture on the cover (B3).

FIGURE 6.7 Backdrops as data

Source: Lee, Yun-joo (2010) 'Leadership and development in South Korea and Egypt: The significance of cultural shifts', unpublished PhD thesis, School of Oriental and Asian Studies, University of London.

portrait painter used certain *backdrops* and objects in a painting – Holbein's *The Ambassadors* depicts all the paraphernalia of international understanding, science and European culture to symbolize the status of the diplomats. Photographic records of senior people in their offices can be viewed similarly. Recording this data can come from simply asking to have a photo taken with the interviewee. Artistic quality is less important than what is in the frame, so getting a wide angle shot is useful. High resolution digital photos are valuable because they can easily be magnified. Politicians and other powerful people will usually have a photo backdrop carefully prepared, which reveals a lot about that person's self-image, and how they fit within other power hierarchies. In Turkey, allegiances can quickly be identified from noticing whether there is a picture of Ataturk or Islamic texts.[134] Figure 0.2 shows an Egyptian government official sitting beneath a picture of his (then) superior, President Hosni Mubarak, which the official complements with Islamic texts and a prize. A grid system, as used by archaeologists, can encourage careful analysis of photographic data and backdrops (Figure 6.7). A Korean technology minister displays space technology (A1, A2) and, on careful inspection, photos of himself on magazine covers (B3).[135]

6.1.4 Buildings

Buildings provide the opportunity to study how legitimacy is literally constructed through architecture, by conflating past and present symbols of power. The first mosques in Egypt were modelled on Coptic churches, which linked Islam to the strong Abrahamic tradition. This strategy is also manifest in the grand Greek columns and Roman decoration of many European company and government buildings, for two millennia. These often merge symbols of power such as religion, science, commerce and royalty. The *Church of Scientology* in London enhances its status through its new HQ in the regally named 'Queen Victoria Street', a building with a classical façade designed for the building's first occupants, the Christian *Foreign Bible Society*, and then used by *BP*.[136] The home of the *Christian Scientists* in Curzon Street is similarly grand. The façade reflects the grandiose architecture of religions and royals across two millennia, and a stone inscription reads, 'Third Church of Christ, Scientist'. It was built in 1910.

Inside grand buildings, murals and sculptures are an obvious area of study. Lobbies and board rooms are adorned with modern versions of King Lists in the form of portraits, sculptures and mission statements of chairmen and politicians. Elite attendants and sub-elites also feature. Lucy Worsley explains how 45 murals on the Kings Grand Staircase in Kensington Palace, London, depict courtiers, including 'Peter the wild boy', a possibly autistic child locked in an iron collar and kept as a pet, and 'Mohammad the Turk' who was the only servant allowed to treat the King's haemorrhoids, which gained him the reputation for having a sexual relationship with the King.[137]

The conflation and reciprocal legitimization among powerful groups is very evident in religious buildings. The thirteenth century façade of Notre Dame in Paris provides a clear example. The Rose window symbolizes the power of eternity, below which 28 "elites" – saints – look down on the masses. The doors are adorned with religious leaders and managers, and prophet-teachers with their symbols of vice and virtue. The statue of the head teacher–leader, Christ, blesses all who enter through the central door. Once inside, images of gods, prophets, kings and bishops mingle and merge, as do concepts, for example those equating heavenly hierarchies with earthly ranks such as 'King', 'Lord' and 'Prince'. Statues above the 'red door', linking the Cathedral with the close, depict an angel putting a royal crown on the head of Mary, symbolizing the tradition of mutual support between religion and royalty.

Royal architecture can also suggest how power and influence operated. The Gyeongbokgung Palace in Seoul was modelled on Chinese palaces, reflecting the prevailing superpower, but the curved roof design was uniquely Korean. The relative strength of certain Kings can be seen in the different number of claws on their symbolic dragons – more claws, more power. The King's office was placed between the reception building for political advisers, who usually had vested interests in the policies they proposed, and the academics' building where scholars who had no political affiliation might work and have regular sessions instructing the King. This reflects modern democratic theories about the value of plural power systems. When King Sejong was considering replacing the use of Chinese as the written language, with a simple phonetic alphabet, the political advisers were against this because their power would have been threatened had the public become literate. But young scholars argued that democratizing literacy would give men and women a better chance to contribute to building the country. The scholars won, and the result was the beautiful Korean alphabet in 1446, which made possible the first movable type printing press which pre-dated Guttenberg. The evidence is there for all to see in the buildings, related artefacts, and Chinese and modernized Hangul texts.

6.2 SELECTION

Having identified likely data sources, specific *units* of study then need to be selected which may reflect any form of *population*, human or non-human – warlords, bishops, wills, websites, tombs, film festivals. Small-scale research may involve the whole population of a particular research site – a *census* of all units. But more usually a smaller manageable *sample*[138] of units within that population will be selected. A sample of people could comprise a few individuals who will be interviewed in-depth,[139] or thousands who will need to be accessed by a *survey*. The same approach could be applied to other forms of 'population'. A *sampling frame* lists all the units in a population from which the sample will be selected. *Representative* samples are usually achieved by *probability* sampling – units are selected randomly, and each unit in a population has an equal likelihood of being chosen. *Sampling error* describes the chance difference between a population and its probability sample, such as a different percentage of children or women. *Non-sampling error* arises from factors such as bad questions or data processing, or poor response rate. Response rates are usually better with surveys of followers or populace than with leaders and elites. But the two populations can sometimes both be surveyed for the same study.[140] If a sample is representative, the findings of the study can be *generalized* to the whole population, and sometimes to similar populations.

Non-probability samples cannot be generalized, and the findings are only indicative of what may happen within a population. But these less rigid methods are common in up-system research because of the difficulty of accessing powerful people (C4.5). Even if access is achieved, elite groups are intrinsically small, and it is often hard to justify statistical analysis. The non-probability approaches to selecting up-system respondents are often very pragmatic:

- *Opportunistic* selection arises from chance or luck, and is sometimes not considered to create a true sample.[141] But any interview, however informal and brief, can still be systematic and reflect the purpose and main questions of the research. Opportunities may arise at public meetings addressed by elites. This requires preparation of a short question that (apparently) relates to the event, and the courage to ask the first question. Members of the audience are usually nervous and unprepared to speak first, but the first question will usually get a longer answer. Posing questions through radio or TV phone-ins or other questioning forums is similar, and analysing the style of previous programmes can help to formulate good questions.
- *Purposive* samples may focus on units that are chosen for a reason, which should be explained. Respondents may have relevant responsibilities or qualities – permanent secretaries, senior customs officers, orchestral conductors, prize winners – or comprise small homogeneous groups – news producers, surgeons, Armenian female elites. A relevant and accessible research site may be used – trade fairs, conferences, sports meetings. Journalists will use press conferences to question individuals purposefully, but they will also be aware of answers to questions posed by colleagues because seemingly unrelated answers can, when analysed together, provide new insights.

- *Chain-referral, network* or *snowball*[142] sampling is arguably more appropriate than probability sampling when studying hidden populations,[143] exploring reputation,[144] identifying policy-makers[145] and specific elites,[146] and understanding networks or processes[147] (C5.3). This method is central to investigative research. Investigators "follow up leads", but the aim is to identify specific causation not to provide generalizable findings. Social or professional networking or sites, such as *Facebook* or *LinkedIn*, can make tracing networks very quick (Appendix 2).
- *Convenience samples* are common in experimental studies. University students might be rewarded for participation by extra credits or small fees, and may role-play powerful people such as 'charismatic', 'ideological' and 'pragmatic' leaders to assess resultant decision-making.[148] But to what degree can student role-play provide indications of how actual elites and leaders behave in real-life situations?

Although it is wrong for a researcher to over-claim the generalizability of a study, a reader can generalize from indicative findings. The way a despot used torture in South America may indicate, to an African reader, how torture is used in an African country.

A further selection process is involved in qualitative studies, after data collection. This entails a method for selecting and organizing relevant data from notes, transcripts or observation records. This method should be systematic – the data must be *coded,*[149] and how this is done should be explained.[150] This is likely to entail a *coding frame*[151] which should be developed when the questionnaires or schedules are being devised. At a basic level, coding may just mean reading through a transcript and putting the research question number next to the data that it relates to. If interview or survey questions are well organized in relation to the research questions, this should be very simple, but respondents do not always give tidy answers.

At a more sophisticated level, each question might relate to a research hypothesis, and even to specific "mini-hypotheses" – detailed predictions about the expected response to each question, based on literature or theory. A research hypothesis might be, "That East Asian political leaders rely more on family networks than European leaders." A linked mini-hypothesis could be, "That MPs in Japan are likely to have relatives who are also in leadership positions", and this could be investigated through a question such as, "Are any of your family members also in leadership positions?" Conversely, inductive or open coding permits the categories to emerge from the data, as in grounded theory. The coding then structures the analysis of data in relation to literature and theory, and the reasons for agreement or disagreement between responses and hypotheses discussed. After expected types of data have been identified and coded, *saturated coding* can be used to assess the unexpected data that does not seem to fit anywhere. This data may either be the most important data in the study, because the researcher did not envisage it, or garbage.

6.3 TESTING

Data is simply a measure or account of something, which can be true or false, and so before it can be assumed to represent fact it needs to be tested. The starting point is to revisit the relevant aspects of ontology and epistemology (C2) considered when the study was initially conceptualized. This should then be applied to data from two perspectives. How are the core concepts of the study reflected and supported in the data – what is the evidence for the existence of "mass fear" and "terror"? And what are the sources of the knowledge that support the claims made in the data – how do respondents know who the "terrorist leaders" are?

Testing may then happen as data is being collected, or during analysis. Interview and documentary data can be tested by asking: who is speaking, who are they speaking to, for what purpose are they speaking, and under what circumstances?[152] Other factors include style, manner, experience and social position, comprehensibility, plausibility and consistency of the testimony.[153] Certain forms of evidence may be more trustworthy than others – first-hand accounts better than hearsay, data from senior level elites better than from subordinates (or vice versa), or responses from interviewees known to be reliable better than from unknown informants. Data from elite interviewees with little public accountability may need greater corroboration.[154]

Defector and asylum-seeker testimony is particularly problematic, as elites in these situations often need to present a specific view of why they have fled from their persecutors and are often 'countering' a prevailing view of recent history.[155] Hazel Smith explains in relation to North Korea:

> Defector interviews can be useful if they are taken as part of a wider intelligence picture and with the caveat that defectors may have an interest in exaggerating or distorting their claims. In the North Korean case, the problem was exacerbated because most of the defectors, even the most senior, had only a partial picture of their own society – as one would expect in a closed country.[156]

Once testimony data has been collected and analysed, respondents are rarely asked to check its accuracy.[157] The statements of Iraqi defector Rafid al-Janabi ("Curveball") fooled western intelligence officers, in 2002, into believing that Iraq had biological weapons programmes, which underpinned the invasion of Iraq. In 2011 he admitted that he had lied to get rid of Saddam Hussein's regime (Figure 2.3).[158] Analysing drawings of events can also be problematic, as material may stem from a graphic repertoire, such as Manga cartoons, rather than actual events. Corroboration against other factual evidence is therefore vital (Figure 6.8), particularly if researchers represent organizations such as *Amnesty International*. Demick deliberately chose North Korean refugees in South Korea, who came from the same town because she believed she 'could verify facts more easily if [she] spoke to numerous people about one place,'[159] and 'triangulate' her data.

Triangulation was originally a form of testing applied to navigation and map making.[160] Two or more fixed points were located (mosque towers, mountains, trees), the angles between them measured, and the results plotted on a map by drawing triangles to calculate their relative positions. The concept was then adapted by social researchers to redress the deficiencies and biases of survey data.[161] In social research, triangulation tests data by comparing it with other relevant data, as a police officer might test a witness

> Testimony from prisoners or others, about human rights abuses in oppressive regimes, is difficult to validate. Victims may have many personal reasons to embellish their stories, or may be very traumatized and not remember clearly. Testimony should, if possible, be corroborated by other testimonies from people who are not known to one another, and by physical facts. For example, a former prisoner might tell of how she was held blindfolded in a secret place of detention. She might explain that she heard certain sounds while in her cell – a clock striking, train noise, a market. When blindfolded and moved along corridors, she might tell that she was always told to duck her head at a certain point, and how metal doors being opened and closed made certain sounds. A visit to the suspected location could confirm the noises around the building, and a walk along the corridors might reveal that there are low arches and doors made of metal which make particular sounds. And the train line nearby may be another indicator.
>
> Ingrid Massage, Research Support Unit, International Secretariat, *Amnesty International*

FIGURE 6.8   Testimony evidence

statement against other statements, and against forensic evidence such as mobile phone records and DNA samples. But to triangulate data, the research design (C4) must ensure that data has been collected in an appropriate way. A triangulation research design might entail comparing:[162]

- *frameworks* – documentary analysis might be checked through remote observation, biographies through life history interviews.
- *methods*[163] – questionnaires to check press reports, observation (demonstrated behaviour) to check documentary accounts (stated behaviour), interviews to check survey data.
- *respondents*[164] – the perspectives of politicians, managers, planners, professionals, and public to assess, "Why did that policy fail?"
- *investigators* – young women and older men, English and other language speakers, insider and outsider researchers.
- *theories* – the policing of a riot understood through crowd psychology, leadership and political theory.

In up-system research, triangulation is often pragmatic and opportunistic. Diverse data that can be accessed easily may be used to detect if powerful people are giving accurate accounts,[165] to assess the consistency of processes (C7.3) and to ensure greater reliability and validity[166] of findings (below). Using testimony data, Demick created a novel form of triangulation of North Korean refugees in South Korea, when she selected people who all came from the same town and could therefore help to reconstruct and verify a fuller picture of one place, rather than the normal random picture of the whole country that refugee research normally provides.[167] Ensuring accuracy of research for organizations such as *Amnesty International* permeates all aspects of the process (Figure 6.9).

Validity describes the degree to which data and findings represent what they claim to represent. Ontology (C2) is the starting point – do the things that are being measured actually exist and if so why? If an elite magazine ranks Sir Frederick as "the most respected person", what does 'respect' mean, how do we know it exists, and is the claim

Accuracy is the cornerstone of the organization's work, allowing it to wield a strong and consistent influence throughout the world.

Research staff always seek to verify or corroborate information. This is a process that affects every step of the research process. Building networks of reliable contacts; gathering information from different sources; pursuing all sides of one story; collecting testimonies from different witnesses; distinguishing types of information – rumours, allegations and confirmed reports; analysing information; identifying patterns; and careful use of language in the presentation of information are all techniques that help ensure that the final product is accurate.

'Accuracy is Amnesty's ultimate weapon. Amnesty's ability to influence governments and public opinion is based on the accuracy of its research.'

Source: Amnesty International, Research Policy Manual (internal).

FIGURE 6.9   Accuracy

supported objectively, for example by reputational analysis? Validity is often assessed through mixed methods[168] and triangulation (above). Validity tests are often applied to interviews.[169] The *aggregation* of statistical data ('composite data') can increase validity because the likelihood of a misleading score from a single source is greater than from taking the average score of a range of sources. This can be tested further by a *split-half* check which randomly divides the indicators into two groups, and checks if the aggregate figure is similar for both.[170]

Significance tests contribute to validity by assessing how likely a result is due to chance (but not the degree of the causal relationship). Tests set up null hypothesis – that there is no difference between two variables, which the tests confirm or not. In statistical terms 'significance' implies that there is little likelihood that a result occurred by chance – usually less than 5%. But these 'significance levels' have arisen from tradition not objective statistical fact.[171] The word significance can also have political, social or statistical meaning, denoting importance. To learn that a prime minister believes that genetically modified (GM) foods are harmful is a politically significant finding; for supermarket CEOs to decide to stop selling GM foods is socially significant; to show that 66% of a population does not want GM foods may be statistically significant. Statistical tests also do not assess the validity of data. If the data was collected carelessly, that will probably not be detected or corrected by tests. All statistical analysis embodies the GIGO problem – "Garbage In, Garbage Out."

Objective tests of validity are hard to create, but critical planning and piloting, when designing research instruments, can minimize serious problems. If the indicators 'car', 'house' and 'art' ownership are used to measure the concept 'power', are there other factors that might influence these indicators, such as inheritance or winning the lottery? What is the 'face validity', the common sense view of the link between indicators and concepts – would proxies such as "liking classical music" or "having a PhD", intrinsically indicate power? If findings are not valid, no form of testing can correct the problem. If interview questions that aim to assess the popularity of a president turn out to be measuring the unpopularity of the leader of the opposition, the only option is to redo the research with better questions.

Reliability is the degree to which, if the study were repeated in exactly the same way, it would provide the same findings. If three researchers independently map the networks of the same CEO, would the findings be the same? Assessing reliability is often hypothetical in up-system research because the likelihood of repeating a study is low. But the reliability of previous studies can be assessed by, for example, identifying unclear or leading questions or concepts, particularly with translations – does "people who voted" include people who must vote, those who voted but deliberately spoiled their papers as a protest? Simple *test–retest* checks can assess reliability. In an interview a key question might be repeated throughout the interview, in different ways – "Were there any political prisoners?", "Did the police detain people from the opposition party?", "What happened when people criticized the president?", "Were extra prisons built during this period?"

Findings – short factual statements, graphs, charts, extracts from transcripts, comparative tables, images – are created from data that has undergone testing, and perhaps some brief initial analysis. Any possible problems with the findings – bias, omissions, ambiguity – should be explained. Findings are usually "pure", reliable and virtually free from opinion or further analysis. They can therefore be compared with other findings, or presented as formal evidence to courts and other forums. Findings are particularly helpful to journalists, research officers and expert decision-makers (C8). Clear findings also provide the bases for further analysis (C7).

Data collection should be driven by the aims and focus of the study and, unless the purpose of the study is to test a specific method, this is very likely to entail more than one approach. The conundrum with data collection is to avoid trying to collect too much unnecessary data, which can be overwhelming and a waste of time, while keeping in mind that there will probably only be one brief chance to interact with powerful people. Relevant considerations include:

- whether to collect *primary* data or use *secondary* data, or a combination.
- to what degree the data should be *quantitative*.
- the *sequence* of data collection. Is it better to arrange a focus group with general staff before interviewing senior managers? If a visit to a remote site, or reclusive interviewee, is necessary, how can data collection be optimized during that visit?
- what are the relevant and available *sources* – texts, people, objects – which may be accessed during a particular field visit? Would interviewees permit a visit to their private library or art collection at the time of an interview? What can be learned from observing the building where an interview happens, and how can this be recorded?
- if *mixed methods* are to be used, how will that diverse data be managed and used – triangulation, checks for validity and reliability, or comparative analysis?
- how will research *instruments* be developed and piloted?
- how will data be *tested* and initial analysis be carried out? Does this need to happen at the time of data collection, or later?
- the form that *findings* will take. Will they be in a format required by a funding or other agency? Do they need to be produced in a specific way for further analysis?

The divide between data collection (this chapter) and analysis (the next chapter) is often less clear than it appears in methodology books. And the distinctions between initial and further analysis, and between findings and conclusions, are sometimes hard to define. There is a Chinese saying, "You can make fish soup from a fish, but you cannot make a fish from fish soup." Initial analysis and findings are the fish, further analysis creates the soup, and the conclusions are whether or not it tastes good.

KEY READING

Atkinson, J.M. (1984) *Our Masters' Voices: The Language and Body Language of Politics*. London: Methuen.

Dexter, L.A. (1970) *Elite and Specialized Interviewing*. Evanston, IL: Northwestern University Press.

Gillham, B. (2008) *Observation Techniques: Structured and Unstructured Approaches*. London: Continuum.

Klenke, K. (2008) *Qualitative Research in the Study of Leadership*. London: Elsevier.

Kress, G. and van Leeuwen, T. (1996) *Reading Images: The Grammar of Visual Design*. London: Routledge.

Margolis, E. and Pauwels, L. (2011) *The Sage Handbook of Visual Research Methods*. London: Sage.

Olsen, W. (2011) *Data Collection*. London: Sage.

Saldana, J. (2009) *The Coding Manual for Qualitative Researchers*. London: Sage.

Scott, J. (2006) *Documentary Research*. London: Sage.

Welch, C. (2007) *Interviewing Elites in International Organisations*. Sydney: University of Western Sydney.

PART THREE

USING

Chapter 7 – Having tested and presented data as findings, these can then be used. Findings may be used directly by other researchers or decision-makers, or analysed further by the researcher. Analysis entails comparisons, which may be formal or implied. For up-system research establishing causation and outcomes of the use of power is often central, and accountability studies will access consistency. 'Critical Process Analysis' can provide the framework for assessing all forms of data to check the integrity of the actions of powerful people. Eventually conclusions may be conceptualized to contribute to broader understandings.

Chapter 8 – How will a study be useful? The outcomes of research include academic reports, evidence for formal inquiries and advocacy, and strategies for redressing abuses of power. This requires the effective presentation of evidence in appropriate ways, and understanding how social action can be achieved by finding 'spaces' for change.

7

ANALYSIS

7.1   COMPARISON
7.2   CAUSATION
7.3   CONSISTENCY
7.4   CONTRA-ARGUMENTS
7.5   COMMON SENSE
7.6   CRITICAL PROCESS ANALYSIS
7.7   CONCEPTUALIZATION

> **ANALYSIS**
>
> The resolution of anything into its simple elements. The discovery of principles underlying concrete phenomena. (*OED*)

'*The more important the subject and the closer it cuts to the bone of our hopes and needs, the more we are likely to err in establishing a framework for analyses*' warns Stephen Jay Gould.[1] Basic questions provide a good checklist to ensure that analysis is less influenced by personal preference and is comprehensive. Put simply, analysis within up-system research firstly assesses – who apparently did what, when, where and how, and why? And then secondly, who has the power to control perceptions of this and are the perceptions true – who, in relation to the official view of events, did what, when, where and how, and why? An evaluative study would also assess if the outcomes are good or bad, and an ethics study if they are morally right or wrong.

Hopefully, the choice of research frameworks (C5) and data collections methods (C6) will have provided findings that are in the right form, either for informing decision-makers directly (C8), or for further analysis by the researcher or others. As up-system research frameworks and data collection methods are very diverse, it is not possible to explain every probable form of analysis in detail. Instead, this chapter considers broad principles of analysis which provide the bases for constructing specific analytical frameworks.

Comparison is central to analysis as that is how new knowledge is created. The difficulties of establishing causation, the significance of assessing consistency, contra-arguments, and the conundrums of applying "common sense" are then outlined. The chapter explains a new framework for managing and assessing up-system data, Critical Process Analysis (CPA), and discusses how data can eventually contribute to broader conceptualizations and theory. The chapter focuses on the interpretation of qualitative data,[2] because quantitative analysis is not common in up-system studies, outside psychological research, opinion polls and using large secondary data sets from official sources. By definition, leaders and elites operate as individuals or in small groups, and so large-scale survey data collection and analysis is often not appropriate or feasible. But it is still useful to understand the basics and weaknesses of statistical method, so that psychological studies, opinion polls and public statistics can be understood critically.

7.1 COMPARISON

> **COMPARISON**
>
> Noting similarities and differences. (*OED*)

'Knowledge is the perception of the agreement or disagreement of two ideas', claimed John Locke in 1690.[3] But this explains more how knowledge is created, than what it 'is'. In David Deutsch's view, knowledge is information that exists in the human mind, as a basis for action – it has 'reach'.[4] Knowledge is not just an objective fact. Raw data – "570 prisoners are Muslim" – is not knowledge. It is a factual description and has no meaning. As Locke suggests, creating knowledge from that data requires comparison. To learn that "90% of prisoners were Muslim" has a meaning, implying by comparison that 10% are not. But the meaning is increased when we know whether the context was Omarska during the Bosnian War in 1992 or Iraq during the American occupation in 2003, and how those figures compare with the normal religious demography of those communities. If the statistics were collected at different intervals in time, a trend graph could show temporal comparisons, providing knowledge about increases or decreases in Muslim detentions, which might be explained further by comparing with events such as conflicts in particular towns.

Analysis creates knowledge through comparison, by identifying and explaining similarities and differences, and by merging qualitative and quantitative data.[5] This might entail comparing research data with data from the same or other studies. It might compare findings with other findings or literature (C3), with norms such as laws and professional codes, or with theory (C2). There must be a common basis for comparisons – anti-corruption law, personality traits, reputation. Comparisons may be overt – "Iran, Syria, Afghanistan and North Korea have ratified the UN Convention on the Rights of the Child, but America has not". But they may also be implied – "powerless" implies a comparison with a group that has more power, "talented" with others less talented.

Analysis requires comparative presentation, which requires *standardization* to ensure that comparisons are of "like with like". For quantitative data, standardization as percentages makes it possible to compare data even if the raw numbers are different. When standardized, "200 out of 400 agree" is greater than "1000 out of 3000" – 50% compared with 30%. But while this form of standardization helps comparisons, it loses information, and so it is often helpful to show percentages *and* numbers. Standardized, *aggregate* data can be used to create 'constitutive' or 'substitutive' *indicators*,[6] for example to compare the success of governments or other entities in relation to achieving 'latent' conceptual goals.[7] The *Human Development Index* aggregates a large number of statistical indicators to assess concepts such as 'poverty' or 'health'. The concept of 'state legitimacy' can be assessed through indicators such as 'political violence', 'political prisoners', 'mass emigration', 'anti-system movements'.[8] On the basis that political leaders have the responsibility to ratify international conventions and other codes, indicators based on how many international codes nations have ratified – about war, corruption and environment – can be aggregated to create an index and rankings about the concept 'global leadership responsibility' (Figure 7.1).

Computer-generated charts are helpful for showing statistical data, but their professional appearance can create a false idea of the validity of the data. Pie charts can give a quick impression of relative number and percentages in relation to a whole, but if the total number is only 17 people, do figures such as "15% accept" and "21% agree" have any sensible meaning, and what might "40% other" hide? Block graphs provide a quick way to envision quantities and compare them in relation to one another, but what is being compared and what is the meaning of those numbers? Would "55 murders" be more, or less, important than "555 rapes"? Line graphs compare quantities over time and suggest trends but we can only be certain about the data at the points it was collected. The line between those points is just a guess about what happened in the interims – there could have been wide fluctuations. Politicized trend graphs often choose points that hide the most interesting data, for example by starting or ending at points that show a politically favourable period. The trendline on a scattergram may give an impression of correlation that is easy to grasp, but the extremes on the chart may reflect the most interesting pieces of data.

For qualitative data, standardization may entail determining categories – 'coercion', 'influence', 'violence' – which can create typologies and other charts (Figure 1.9). Presentation may entail selecting and contrasting statements from transcripts, for example to show inconsistency (Figure 7.6). When analysing complex intangible data such as aphorisms (summaries to make an impact, as in political speeches) analytical frameworks

Global Leadership Responsibility Index

Rank		VIOLENCE				CORRUPTION			ENVIRONMENT			Score
		War	HRcodes	SECcodes	ICC/ICJ	CPI	BPI	CORcodes	Eco.Foot	ESI	ENVcodes	
1	Sweden	0	10	3	2	9.3	8.4	3	−5.9	7.2	5	42
2	Netherlands	0	9	3	2	8.7	7.8	3	−5.3	5.4	5	38.6
3	UK	−3	10	3	2	8.6	6.9	3	−6.2	7.5	5	36.8
4	Canada	0	9	3	2	8.5	8.1	3	−7.7	6.4	4	36.3
5	Belgium	0	10	2	2	7.5	7.8	3	−5	4.4	4	35.7
6	Germany	0	10	2	1	8.2	6.3	2	−5.3	5.7	5	34.9
7	France	−1	10	3	1	7.1	5.5	2	−4.1	5.5	5	34
8	Japan	0	8	3	1	6.9	5.3	3	−4.3	5.7	5	33.6
9	Spain	−1	9	3	2	7.1	5.8	1	−3.8	4.9	5	33
10	Italy	0	11	2	1	4.8	4.1	2	−4.2	5	4	29.7
11	S.Korea	0	9	1	1	4.5	3.9	3	−3.4	4.3	3	26.3
12	China	0	6	2	0	3.4	3.5	2	−1.2	3.9	4	23.6
13	Malaysia	0	2	2	0	5	4.3	2	−3.3	5.4	4	21.4
14	Russian F	−4	8	2	0	2.8	3.2	2	−6	5.6	2	15.6
15	USA	−3	5	2	0	7.5	5.3	3	−10	5.3	0	15.1
	AVERAGE	−0.8	8.4	2.4	1.1	6.7	5.8	2.5	−5.1	5.5	4	30.4
	MAX	0	13	3	2	10	10	3	0	10	5	56

FIGURE 7.1 Aggregate data based on ratification of international agreements

Source: Williams, C. (2006) *Leadership Accountability in a Globalizing World.* London: Palgrave MacMillan. pp. 207–209.

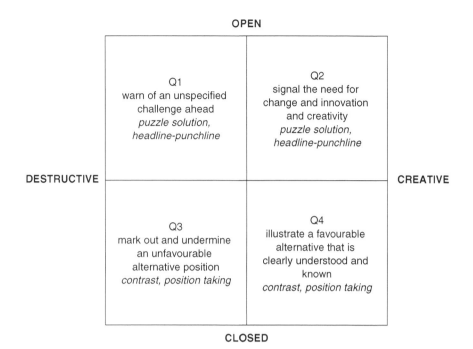

FIGURE 7.2   A framework for analysing aphorisms in political discourse

Source: Morrell, K. (2006) 'Aphorisms and leaders' rhetoric: A new analytical approach', *Leadership*, 2(3): 367–382.

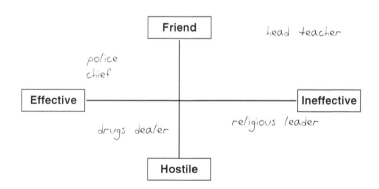

Based on: MoD (2009) *Security and Stabilisation: The Military Contribution*. Joint Doctrine Publications 3–40, Chapter 9, Political and social analysis. Available at: www.mod.uk/DefenceInternet/ microsite/dcdc.

FIGURE 7.3   Mapping local elites for military intelligence analysis

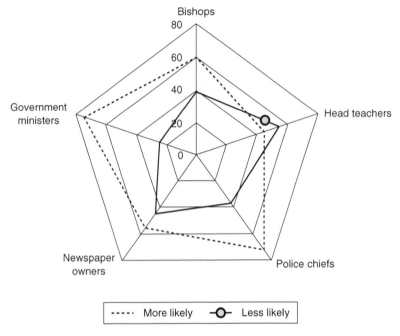

Who is more/less likely to lie? (Percentage of responses)

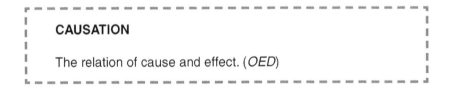

FIGURE 7.4 A radar chart

and plotting charts can help to compare and rate (less to more) data effectively (Figure 7.2).[9] Mixed method findings might also be presented visually on plotting charts, through plotting charts, which indicate priorities and necessary action, as with military intelligence (Figure 7.3).[10] Quantitative comparisons can be shown very effectively on simple radar charts (Figure 7.4).

7.2 CAUSATION

CAUSATION

The relation of cause and effect. (*OED*)

Causation is central to the definition of the concept of power, and much up-system research analysis aims to discover the causal relationships leading to specific 'outcomes' of the use of power (C2.1). Scottish philosopher David Hume argued the need to identify 'necessary connections' when assessing cause-and-affect.[11] When concluding that a powerful person "caused" something to happen, it is helpful also to consider 'agency' – the degree to which they could have acted freely and independently – in relation to 'structure' – the systems that limit the choices and opportunities available.[12] A hypothesis is often a guess that one thing causes another (C4.3) and is often based on causal theories. Therefore research that is focused by hypotheses must provide analysis and conclusions about causation.[13] Some research questions have similar causal implications – "Does a politician's dress influence public opinion?", "Does the perception of intelligence influence the perception of celebrity status?"

To argue a causal link, it is necessary to consider the ontological questions (C2). Do the causes and effects (independent and dependent variables), and the 'necessary connections', truly exist? If an act of "terror" is said to have caused "mass fear", it is necessary to explain the evidence of the existence of those two variables, and then how the former was connected to, and affected, the latter. If mass executions by a despot "caused" people to stop meeting in public, what were the 'connections' that informed them about those executions – TV footage, press photos, posters – and did people see these and say that they were consequently afraid? From the perspective of epistemological analysis (C2), there is a growing interest in analysing how knowledge may cause 'outcomes' amounting to abuse of power. War and conflict are a central concern, for example in Africa.[14] Fricker uses the term 'epistemic injustice' when a knower is wronged through knowledge,[15] which develops the tradition of analysis in terms of mass communications, information and propaganda. A distinction can be made between basic information (apparent facts, but which may be true or false) and knowledge (information that has 'reach', is critically understood and is a basis for action). This can relate to the absence as well as the presence of information, and to misleading information. If religious leaders withhold, or deter, information about HIV/AIDS, that absence of knowledge could be life-threatening. If, as in Thailand, girls are told falsely that fat westerners do not have AIDS, the outcome could be similar.

Arguing a causal link – that A caused B – implies a comparison that B was not caused by C, D, E etc. But eliminating the other likely causes is very difficult in social research. To assist analysis, causes can be classed as 'necessary' (if B happened, A must have happened), 'sufficient' (if A happened, B must also have happened) or 'contributory' (if A were altered, B would be altered). In real life, there are many examples of alternative causal explanations – *confounders*. A longitudinal study from Sweden concludes that children who are 'leaders' in school enjoy better health as adults.[16] The school status of children born in 1953 was categorized in terms of 'marginalized', 'peripheral', 'accepted', 'popular' or 'favourite'. This was matched with hospital admissions between 1974 and 2003. But analysis needs to consider whether the children who were already unhealthy at school, for example overweight, had less school status and also tend to become unhealthy adults, or whether a confounding factor such as poverty causes both low status and poor health. Arguing causation or influence requires stronger evidence than simply showing correlation or coincidence. Was the Korean child who drew a Japanese-style man decapitating a prisoner influenced by the war memorial in Seoul? Unless the child confirms a direct causal link, the pictures are just coincidence (Figure 7.5). Other 'confounders' might include the likelihood of a culture of similar images, for example in school or cartoon books.

Causation might be investigated through an experiment in which one group was exposed to intervention 'A', compared with another well-matched 'control group' that was not (C5.2).[17] Alternatively, actual and hypothetical data can be compared when assessing or evaluating[18] the impact of an intervention, such as a new policy – "If 'A' had *not* happened, would 'B' have happened"? This 'counterfactual' analysis compares what did happen with a "what if ..." scenario to test assumptions about interpretations of events – "What if Hitler had not been born? Would the Nazi regime still have happened?" Theoretical outcome evaluations trace causal links from inputs to outcomes by testing the theoretical assumptions that explain the links through comparison[19] – "Police corruption is likely to increase if police chief's pay is low; so is there a difference between low and well paid police chiefs in similar settings?"

Statistical analysis[20] assesses *if* a specific causal relationship is evident – *Does* an elite education influence the problem-solving skills of leaders? Qualitative analysis, which can also be assisted by software tools,[21] will argue causation in terms of the existence or absence of variables and the probable nature of cause and effect – *How* does an elite education influence the problem-solving skills of leaders? Statistical analysis assesses the degree of a relationship in various ways:

- How the *value* of variables may be relevant – do more educational qualifications from elite universities equate with greater income?

Japanese soldiers executing Koreans, from a Korean war memorial (see Figure 3.5)

A Japanese-style figure executing a Korean, from a Korean child's drawing (see Figure 3.6)

FIGURE 7.5   Causation or coincidence?

- The comparative *strength* of the causal relationship – how much does elite education affect income – very little or very much.
- The *completeness* of the causal relationship – what is the gap between the average elite graduates' income, and the lowest and highest elite graduates' income – big (less complete) or small (more complete).

But *correlation* (a coincidence of events) is not the same as *causation* (one event caused another). The finding that 'graduates earn £12,000 a year more than non-graduates' does not prove, as claimed, that 'the financial advantages gained by graduates through employment' amount to £12,000 a year.[22] Those who went to university are likely to be intrinsically more capable, and would therefore earn more irrespective of whether they have a degree. It is methodologically very difficult to show what is being claimed. Obviously a study cannot track the same people who simultaneously did and did not attend university. The alternative would require comparing a large "graduate group" with a carefully matched "non-graduate" cohort, and it would be virtually impossible to find a control group of similarly capable young people who could have attended university but did not.

Probability theory provides a way to express the belief that cause-and-effect has happened or could happen – the risk that a political disagreement will lead to war, or that the death of a president will affect the economy. But this is not 100% certainty. In a court, proof "beyond reasonable doubt" is required in criminal cases, and reflects a notional 95% certainty; "balance of probabilities", in civil cases, reflects 51% – it is more likely than not. But a court never claims a decision is 100% certain. Arguably cause-and-effect can never be proven conclusively, only 'inferred'.[23] Popper's view of scientific method is that research can only create a better 'corroborated' hypothesis, which might be disproved ('falsified') but can never be confirmed as absolute truth,[24] because however many times the research is repeated and gives the same result, the next time may provide a different outcome. He therefore argued for the use of 'null hypotheses', a default position, written in a negative form to be disproved – "That A does *not* cause B" (Figure 2.2). This default starting point is reflected in the court assumption that a person is "innocent until proven guilty". Popper's approach is a consideration in social science research, but rarely a strict method.

Statistical "proof" of causation is therefore often argued wrongly, particularly if the issue is political.[25] Confusions often concern:

- *correlation* – showing a coincidence between two or more variables – a change in an independent variable is simply followed by a change in a dependent variable.
- *causation* – demonstrating that the independent variable clearly influenced the effect in the independent variable.
- *confounders* – identifying other factors that may change two or more variables at the same time.
- *causal direction* – showing which variable was the cause and which was the effect.

A reduction in reports of sexual harassment may coincide with a CEO's new policy on harassment – a simple *correlation*. But arguing *causation* would require interviewing staff to discover if they knew about the policy, and if they thought it had influenced them. Perhaps a political speech about harassment may have caused both the policy and/or the reduction – a *confounder*. Then, what was the causal *direction*? Perhaps the CEO was aware of a general reduction in harassment, and introduced the policy to create an impression of her good leadership. Similarly, survey research that found that 'a firm that changed its chief executive in a two-year term was discovered to record better earnings' and 'firms that reseated chiefs more often than every two years showed poorer performance' does not prove that all companies will do best if they change their CEOs every two years.[26] It could just mean that successful companies can afford, and choose, to change their CEOs every two years, perhaps to gain regular media attention. This study also raises the problem of attributing population findings (an average of many CEOs) to individual situations. It may be that companies that rely on tradition for their reputation will do best by keeping their CEOs much longer, or that others in a consumer-sensitive market should fire bad CEOs quickly.

One of the few certainties in judging causation is that time cannot run backwards – if B happened after A, B could not have caused A. (Although a predictive *belief* that B would happen, could cause A.) But a time sequence does not intrinsically mean that A caused B, and other evidence must be used to argue causation. And the absence of the same evidence does not mean there is no causal link – those factors may have occurred but people are too scared to talk about them. In all quantitative analysis there will be unexplained factors, including data collection errors and the effects of other unknown or omitted independent variables. It is incorrect to assume that these unexplained factors are all known and can therefore be named, because they have not been measured and tested. Naming all the unknown factors in an attitude survey "fear" would not be correct unless fear had been measured.

Critically assessing causation and coincidence is particularly important for up-system research. Throughout history there are many examples of powerful people trying to increase their legitimacy through illusory coincidences. In Cairo, the ancient Egyptian 'nileometres' would show when the water level of the Nile started to rise, but they were kept locked. When the nileometre showed that the river was rising, this gave the kings and priests the opportunity to pray for the much needed inundation to come, knowing for sure that they could demonstrate to the public that their prayers would soon be answered and therefore that they could influence the gods. In 2011 US Republican Michele Bachmann claimed, 'it was an interesting coincidence' that swine flu only appeared when there were Democratic presidents.[27]

Evolution has programmed humans to notice patterns and coincidence. This instinct leads to valuable predictive understandings, and complete nonsense. Early humans who worked out that when certain seeds fell on certain soil, new plants appeared, would have an advantage in an agrarian society. But noticing that the movement of the stars correlated with the seasons led to the nonsense conclusion that star movement caused the seasons, rather than that the Earth's orbit caused both the stars and the seasons to change. For early humans, wrong understandings of coincidence usually cost very little, but correct guesses provided great rewards, so we tend to overestimate causation. This evolutionary instinct has become a major failing of analysis, and of the reporting and use of research. Laurence Sterne noted the problem in his novel *Tristram Shandy*:

> It is in the nature of a hypothesis when once a man has conceived it, that it assimilates everything to itself, as proper nourishment, and from the first moment of your begetting it, it generally grows stronger by everything you see, hear or understand.[28]

Sound causal analysis derives from simple evidence-based chains of reasoning and critical self-censorship, not from complex analysis that is only accepted because no one can understand it.

7.3 CONSISTENCY

CONSISTENCY

Agreement with something. (*OED*)

Within human beings there is a natural desire for consistency, but for powerful people this becomes an expectation relating to duties and responsibilities, which becomes a measure of legitimacy and credibility. The social expectation is that, if powerful people use their power in a rational and responsible way, their actions should be free from contradictions. That is often difficult for deceitful people to achieve, and identifying inconsistency is therefore a distinctive part of up-system analysis. Inconsistencies may indicate mistakes, badly formulated systems, or abuse of power. In 2002, Iranian president, Mahmoud Ahmadinejad, claimed 'In Iran we don't have homosexuals like in your country … In Iran we do not have this phenomenon.'[29] But Iranian law formally addresses homosexual acts by men (lavat – sodomy) and women (mosahegheh), and Iran executes people for breaking these laws.[30] If there were no homosexuals in Iran, why is there a need for laws and punishments to deal with homosexual behaviour?

Many norms and traditions hold rulers to consistent behaviour, for example in the form of "non-discrimination" or "equity". Formal administrative standards often require consistency, as in the formulation of law,[31] or drafting of public documents[32] or court judgments. Volokh found that ideologically motivated judges choose an interpretive method that 'comes as close as possible to their favored outcome', but that they must also appear plausible (consistent with) statute, which 'will make them deviate from their own ideal points in the direction of the "most plausible point" of that method.'[33] An honest accountant would be expected to ensure the consistency of financial records, and a fraud investigator would seek inconsistencies as indicators of wrongdoing. Public officials and professionals should not engage in activities that create a 'conflict of interest', because this would be inconsistent with their duties.[34] Standards are often formalized in Codes of Conduct, which provide a good basis for analysing conduct.[35] Many other aspects of up-system processes can be checked in a similar way – do outcomes match aims, were all those involved treated equitably, were rules followed, was all relevant information taken into account?

Psychological theories can also be relevant. 'Role congruity theory' claims that social groups are seen as more acceptable when their characteristics match that group's typical social roles. This helps to explain the problem that female leadership is sometimes difficult because it does not match social expectations.[36] People are very uncomfortable with personal inconsistencies – when their actions do not agree with their beliefs. 'Cognitive dissonance theory' arose from a study of how a group that predicted the end of the world coped when the prediction was proven false. The inconsistency between their actions, attitudes and beliefs had to be resolved.[37] Leaders often defend or enhance their power by appearing to resolve inconsistencies. If the existence of a god is questioned on the basis of a contradiction between claims that they are benevolent and peace-loving, and cruel events such as wars, the astute spiritual leader will have standard answers to reconcile the inconsistencies – "It is arrogant for mere humans to try to understand the reasoning of god" or, "God created humans with free will, and it is for us to choose how we use that freedom."

Time scales are an important approach to assessing consistency, but have often been ignored in academic research.[38] In contrast, initial police interviewing and cross examination in courts usually elicits a chronology of events from witnesses, which can then be compared with accounts from other witnesses, and with objective evidence such as mobile phone records. People cannot be in two places at once, and if that seems to have happened, why? At the same moment powerful people sometimes contradict one another, or at a later date contradict themselves (Figure 7.6).

Economic consistency is central to the proper use of commercial power. If a development company had built new hotels in a place where they could not possibly make a profit, or where they are likely to be destroyed by environmental impacts such as tsunamis, there are likely to be other reasons for that operation. Why would investors want to lose money? This would not be consistent with the usual goals of investors. Might the hidden motivation be to make insurance claims, engage in short selling, use the hotels for money laundering, or take development grants from a government scheme knowing that the businesses will fail?

Analysis of simple texts on objects such as banknotes might also reflect the principles of consistency (C6.1.1). Why are the heads of political leaders used on notes in Islamic states, including Iran and Saudi Arabia, when this seems inconsistent with Islamic theological objections about depicting the human form? In the 1980s, the

Comparing the consistency of statements and outcomes Heads of State at the UN General Assembly		
Head of State	Statement to the UN General Assembly	Outcome
Alberto Fujimori, President of the Republic of Peru	'The concepts of democracy and fairness must prevail ... the twentieth century has been deeply scarred by enduring human failures: by greed and lust for power, by hot blooded hatreds and stone-cold hearts ...' (1999)	In December 2000 Fujimori resigned and sought asylum in Japan, from where he could not be extradited. He was simultaneously sacked by Congress as 'morally unfit' for office. Three months later, charges of 'illicit enrichment' and inappropriate use of public funds were filed against him, and then in March 2001 legal proceedings were started in relation to the murder of 14 Marxist rebels in 1997. By August, the Peruvian Congress had removed Fujimori's immunity to permit his arrest for murder.
President Pasteur Bizimungu of Rwanda	'...stresses that mankind must never again witness horrors of genocide or ethnic cleansing.' (1995)	Bizimungu became president following the 1994 genocide. In 2000, he resigned, was put under house arrest, and his privileges as a former head of state were removed. In 2004, he was sentenced to 15 years in prison for embezzlement, inciting violence and associating with criminals.
Prime Minister Benazir Bhutto of Pakistan	'...says that the principles of equal rights and self-determination lie at the heart of the UN Charter.' (1995)	Bhutto was twice removed from office, accused of corruption. She then went into self-exile in Dubai.
President Jacques Chirac of France	'...says that the United Nations affirms a universal conscience through legal instruments and programmes of action.' (1995)	In March 2001, amid allegations of corruption, Chirac became the first head of state of the French Fifth Republic to receive a formal witness summons by an investigating judge. A petition for his impeachment was then started. Chirac's daughter, Claude, was questioned, and his wife, Bernadette Chirac, became the first French first lady to be required to give evidence. Chirac's immunity was contested in the courts, and could be removed after he leaves office.
President Jean-Bertrand Aristide of Haiti	'...says that the United Nations helped bring about a political miracle in restoring democracy to Haiti.' (1995)	Months after becoming President in 1990, Aristide was forced out by a military coup, and was helped by the US military to return in 1994. He was forced out into exile again in 2004, a day after Washington questioned 'his fitness to govern'.

Source of statements: UN General Assembly. Available at: www.un.org/UN50/UNHQ-Photos/

FIGURE 7.6 Political consistency

(Continued)

Consistency in press reports

'Our objectives are clear ..., because the Taliban have chosen to side with al-Qa'ida, to remove them.' (Tony Blair, UK Prime Minister 30 October 2001)

'The objectives are clear, and the one about the removal of the Taliban is not something we have as a clear objective.' (John Prescott, UK Deputy Prime Minister, 31 October, 2001)

Source: Morris, N. (2001) 'Allies demand new tactics to win propaganda war,' *The Independent*, 1 November: 1.

'The assessed intelligence has established that Saddam has continued to produce chemical and biological weapons.' (Tony Blair, 24 September 2002)

'I have to accept it seems increasingly clear that Saddam did not have stockpiles of chemical or biological weapons.' (Tony Blair, July 2004).

FIGURE 7.6 *Continued*

Source: Independent (2004) 'The Butler Report', *The Independent* (Insert), 15 July: 1.

Iranian revolutionary leader Khomeini's head directly replaced that of the secularist Shah he had deposed (Figure 7.7). That is not consistent with the ideology of a total regime change, from secular to Islamic. Other images were similar to those of communist countries, yet Islam and communism are antithetical. In contrast, Afghan bank notes during the Taliban era did not depict the head of state. It is logical that former and current monarchies, such as Spain and Saudi Arabia, might name their unit of currency the 'Real' and 'Riyal' (meaning 'royal'), to conflate the power of money with the power of regal rulers, in the way that Britain had the 'sovereign' and 'crown'. But why does an Islamic 'Republic', Iran, still use the 'Rial' (Spanish – 'royal'), which was the currency of the deposed **royalist** Shah? If nothing else, studying a nation's currency warns you who, when visiting that country, not to make unguarded jokes about.

Specific approaches to analysing consistency include comparing:

- *stated and demonstrated values.* Does what people say match what they do? How does the declared ethical stance of individuals match their behaviour? If a CEO claims moral authority for a company on the basis of disability rights, how does her Annual Report reflect the standards in the UN Disability Convention? Why would feminist parliamentarians work within a system that discriminates against women, without questioning it?
- *elements of a process.* Are there unexplained gaps or irregularities? Why did some topics suddenly appear/disappear within the minutes of a series of related meetings? Why did the members of a specific committee change unexpectedly? Why did sudden staff changes happen – what was the rationale for the erratic hiring and firing?

FIGURE 7.7 Iranian banknotes

- *information.* Are statistics consistent when represented in standardized or simple formats? Was information that concerns the same issue consistent with the original source, when presented in different ways?
- *economic policies and actions.* Do policies and actions match the normal goals of commercial and economic endeavour? Why would a Minister provide money for a project that was bound to fail?
- *ethics and behaviour or policy.* Do rulers act in accord with their own ethical codes, and are those codes themselves consistent with the values of the ruler? Why, if Islamic Iran despises Israeli tradition, was stoning for adultery enshrined in Iranian law in 1983, which copies old Jewish Deuteronomic Law (Deut. 22: 13–21)?
- *equity across populations.* Do leaders treat their colleagues fairly? At a board meeting, why does the male chair ask women board members to make the tea?
- *the steps of lineage.* Are there unexplained gaps in lineage charts, when related to absolute chronologies (accurate calendars)? Do claims about the existence of ancestors fit with the evidence from objective sources such as portraits (C6.1.3)?
- *'coincidences of interest'.* Leaders, especially politicians, often try to make one policy serve the demands of a range of interest groups. A freedom of information law would please numerous activist groups who may agree about little else. Politicians joke, "Never waste a crisis". If an animal rights group kills a child with a bomb, this would provide the chance to please both conservative anti-terrorism groups and children's rights organizations with a firm response. Researching how consistent support can be achieved across disparate groups is a vital skill for political researchers.

In up-system research, identifying inconsistencies is essentially a focused form of comparison, and can be a distinct aim of mixed methods and triangulation (C6.3).

7.4 CONTRA-ARGUMENTS

Another characteristic of up-system research is that many studies are strongly contested or contradictory. This might be in the form of the denial of well-established facts about events such as the Nazi Holocaust, arguments based on definitions such as whether the mass killings of Armenians in the Ottoman Empire amounted to 'genocide', misplaced empathy for nationalistic heroes, or politicized bias and deliberate spin. Alternatively, a contra-perspective may appear flawed or biased because it is a new and unique insight, and previous mainstream views have been heavily politicized. Daikichi Irokawa's book, *The Age of Hirohito* (1995), gently questioned stereotypical western views of the Japanese wartime Emperor[39] which has led to a more balanced assessment and a greater understanding of why General MacArthur did not present the Emperor as a war criminal.

It can be very tempting for researchers to ignore contrary views because they are inconvenient and do not fit the findings. But, however extreme, contrary views provide a basis for critically testing analysis, which is likely to culminate in strengthened ontological and epistemological assumptions, clearer arguments, better presentation of data and more robust conclusions. The British intelligence agency MI5 tests draft intelligence reports by asking a 'red team' to deliberately challenge and demolish the findings of colleagues. All researchers need to deploy a method to challenge their conclusions.

Contra-arguments can be utilized through simple comparisons with similar studies, at different levels – comparing aims and focus, questions, data collection and testing, selection of findings, and the logic underpinning the analysis. Assessment might then take the form of looking for political or other biases – who funded the research, what is the identity of the researchers (political, religious, professional), and what are the affiliations of the researchers (commercial, governmental, familial)? Simple analytical frameworks can help to take account of different perspectives. In the field of diplomatic analysis, Boyd-Judson proposes assessing the 'moral universe' of leaders in other countries by asking if:

1 a variety of conflicting moral claims can be reasonably justified by different ethical norms.
2 an adversary is likely to hold a moral justification that is important to his or her strategic decision making.

And then to 'Acknowledge the enemy's moral universe within strategic parameters in order to reach strategic goals.'[40]

On the level of 'thought experiments', contra-arguments can be hypothetical. Counterfactual (contrary to the facts) analysis explores "what if … "."What if A had *not* happened, would B still have happened?", or "what if C had happened, would A still have happened?", for example, "What if politicians were not paid? Would they become more corrupt about claiming expenses? Would only those who genuinely wanted to serve the public become MPs? Would only wealthy people who want status and power, become MPs?" Counterfactual thinking is often used to test research about the evaluation of outcomes – "The UN head intervened, and the conflict ceased. What if the UN head had not intervened, would the conflict still have ceased?"

It is, of course, very hard for researchers to escape their own prejudices, values, professional perspectives and paymasters. In his book, *In Retrospect: The Tragedy and Lessons of Vietnam*, Robert McNamara was candid about his failures: 'We received no thoughtful analysis of the problem and no pros and cons regarding alternative ways to deal with it … We failed to analyse our assumptions critically, then or later. The foundations of our decision making were gravely flawed … '.[41] Remembering history is one way to keep in mind the value of contra-arguments. People such as

J.S. Bach, Gandhi, Martin Luther King, Nelson Mandela, Kim Dai-jung and Jesus share a common characteristic – they were all imprisoned for being judged as criminals.

7.5 COMMON SENSE

> **COMMON SENSE**
>
> Good sound practical sense. The general sense of mankind, or of a community. (*OED*)

> **PLAUSIBILITY**
>
> Having a show of truth, reasonableness, or worth; apparently acceptable; fair seeming, specious. (*OED*)

A general test of analysis is common sense – are the research outcomes *plausible*?[42] Simple errors can be detected by obvious questions that compare research findings with other facts – is it likely that MPs could have voted more times than the number of voting opportunities, could the number of a politician's educational qualifications have reduced as s/he got older? If a study finds that 90% of brain surgeons went to elite schools, does that support a conclusion that most of pupils at elite schools could be brain surgeons? Hazel Smith provides a neat common sense analysis in relation to the myths about North Korea:

> The 'common knowledge' on food aid is underpinned by assumptions that very often go unquestioned. The first is that there is systematic diversion of international food aid to the country's elite.
>
> The North Korean elite is a relatively small group of people close to Kim Jong-il and his family. Pyongyang's elites, like those elsewhere, have gastronomic choices. Their access to hard currency and contacts abroad means that they do not have to resort to surplus grain that is barely above the quality of animal feed to form any part of their diet.[43]

Often, the common sense view comes from putting oneself into the position of those who the research concerns, but that is more difficult when they are elites.

Discussions of causation in law provide relevant understandings about why arguing causation is ultimately based on common sense rather than factual evidence.[44] Hart and Honore ask, if a man hits a woman not knowing that she has a weak heart, and she dies from heart failure, is the cause that man's hit or the woman's weak heart? A common sense jury view is likely to conclude that it is wrong to hit anyone irrespective of their health status, so the assailant is guilty because the act was reckless and did not apply common sense precaution. If a government minister orders the police to stop a protest and they kill 100 protesters, is the cause of death the minister's orders, the behaviour of the police, or the behaviour of those protesting? Questions about the remit of managerial and operational responsibility must be asked, and the principles of law must be applied equally to all. In the end, there are no absolute rules, just plausible arguments.

In some forms of research, it is important that the outcomes are 'morally plausible', not just empirically accurate, because otherwise they can bias significant political and economic decisions. Pogge explains how indicators related to the international goal of 'halving world poverty by 2015' have been manipulated by moving from measuring the 'number' of people considered to be poor, to the 'proportion' (percent). Because of the likely world population increase of 20% between 2000 and 2015, a 'halving' (reduction of 50 per cent) of the *proportion* would be a reduction of less than half of the *number*. So politically it is more acceptable, and more deceitful, to use 'number'. The research and statistics may be perfect, but the moral plausibility of the presentation of the findings is questionable.[45]

Although the application of common sense is crucial in analysis, it creates a conundrum. One of the purposes of research is often to test and question supposed common sense views of the world. The most pertinent findings may therefore not fit prevailing views, and not be accepted by the academic community or for publication. The broader effect may be that researchers contrive research to fit, rather than question, prevailing models.[46] The early data about ozone depletion was ignored until 1985, because the computers used to analyse the satellite data from 1979 had been programmed to exclude ozone levels thought to be outside the expected norms.[47] Similarly, powerful people often exude a confidence that is difficult to question, and this 'halo effect' creates a common sense view of their integrity that is hard to challenge (C3.2).[48] That is why doctors who abused people with mental disabilities[49] and paedophile catholic priests,[50] were able to continue their activities unchallenged for so many years. The solution to the common sense conundrum is to compare (triangulate) differing perceptions of common sense, irrespective of power. Had researchers listened properly to patients in psychiatric hospitals, and to children in catholic orphanages, they might have found that the common sense view of these powerless groups was that "halos" are often a disguise not a symbol of virtue.

7.6 CRITICAL PROCESS ANALYSIS (CPA)

> **PROCESS**
>
> A continuous and regular action or succession of actions, taking place or carried out in a definite manner. (*OED*)

A distinctive aspect of up-system research is that powerful people often compile data about themselves and what they do, and about other powerful people. And they often create records of their methods (C1). If powerful people had a method for doing something, researchers have a source of data for researching them. This arises from critically analysing the process that they use to exercise their power. Much of the evidence for the Nuremburg trials came from the meticulous records of genocidal processes compiled by the Nazi leaders themselves.[51]

Critical Process Analysis (CPA) is based on an analytical framework for data collection and analysis, which addresses the possibility that any up-system process may lack validity – that it did not do what it claimed to do. It is often easier to identify improper processes than improper outcomes from the use of power, because processes and related methods have an intrinsic logic – consistency, sequences, scale, audit trails and information channels. CPA also accommodates the problem of access (C4.5), as it does not necessarily require direct contact and primary data.

CPA combines academic and investigatory approaches to research, and can utilize any research framework (C5). Policy analysis, network analysis and the counterfactual approaches of outcomes analysis are directly applicable, as are reconstruction frameworks, to fill gaps in the data about a process. In reconstructive frameworks (C5.2), understating the 'function' of one aspect – what did it do and why was it there? – can provide a basis for extrapolating how a whole process worked. If there was a budget line for a "lawyer", what were the aims and outcomes of the legal advice, and the implications for the whole process? If the information is not available, did the lawyer find something inconvenient – a risk of harm to local people, that a chemical was not tested for safety? Understanding 'underlying structures' is often more significant than analysing obvious outcomes (C5.2). If investigators wanted to understand why a school had collapsed during an earthquake, they would check-out those who planned, managed and regulated its construction, not look at its exam results.

Standard *process analysis* usually concerns efficiency in commercial settings,[52] and asks questions about the links between the steps within a process – "What is the core purpose of this step and how else could it be accomplished?"[53] Within this, *process tracing* uses any data[54] to trace causal links and mechanisms.[55] The term 'critical process analysis' is sometimes used to describe the analysis of processes that are particularly 'critical', vital, to a system.[56] But for up-system research, CPA is used to critically understand the use

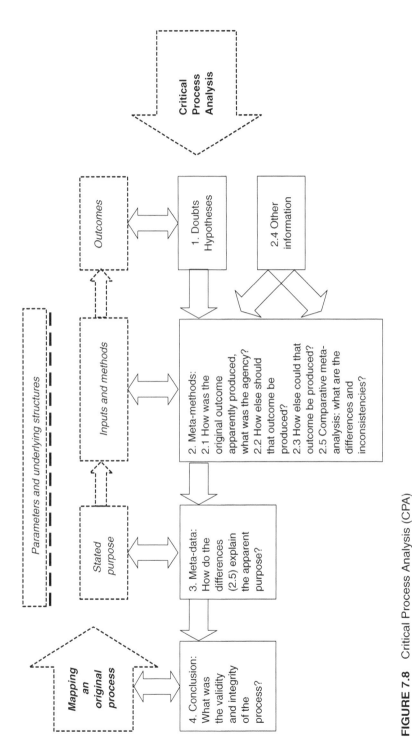

FIGURE 7.8 Critical Process Analysis (CPA)

of power within a process, not just to make a process more efficient, which reflects the tradition of 'critical theory' (C.2.5). Standard process analysis might ask, "How can disciplinary hearings be arranged more quickly?" But CPA is likely to ask, "The managers could and should have arranged the disciplinary hearings more quickly, so why did they not do this?"

Although CPA is distinct, the standard process model – input > process > output – provides a basis for first mapping an *original process* based on what those involved with the process claim had done (Figure 7.8). This process map comprises:

   i   the *stated purpose* – policies, aims, intended outcomes.
  ii   the *apparent inputs* and *methods* to make the process work – resources, personnel, information, meetings, research, communication systems, implementation procedures.
 iii   but both (i) and (ii) operate within *parameters* and *underlying structures* which shape and control the process – norms, regulations, resource constraints, time frames, ideologies, religious values, power structures, coercion.
 iv   *outcomes* ('outputs') – decisions, information, policies, actions.

This explanation of an original process is then critically questioned *backwards* – critically 'reverse engineered' (C5.2) – through the process:

1   *Doubts* raised about the *outcomes*, provide the starting point – media comment, profiling, informants, intuition, gossip. Doubts can create *hypotheses* about the causal links creating these doubts – "That pressure from the CEO caused omissions in the minutes of the meeting". These hypotheses provide the bases for then developing:
2   *Meta-methods* (methods to investigate methods) in relation to the 'doubts', to address three guiding questions:

    2.1   How *was* the outcome produced, according to the records? What was the *agency* – who or what made things happen? What was the underlying *function* of a specific aspect, in relation to aspects of the whole process which may be hidden?
    2.2   How else *should* that outcome have been produced – counterfactual scenarios based on standard practice, logic, efficiency, common sense, feasibility?
    2.3   How else *could* that outcome have been produced – counterfactual scenarios of other non-standard alternatives?
    2.4   *Other information* is introduced to investigate questions 2.2 and 2.3 – details about the methods usually used by others to produce similar outcomes, professional standards, procedural norms, legislation.
    2.5   *Comparative meta-analysis*[57] compares the answers to these questions to understand significant differences, and to discover and explain lack of *consistency* (above).

3   Any differences are then analysed in relation to the original *stated purpose*, to illuminate true motives.
4   *Conclusions* are then made about the validity and integrity of the *original process* – was this sound, complete, honest – "the truth, the whole truth, and nothing but the truth"?

CPA therefore entails questioning an original process by reconstructing that process in counterfactual ways that it *should* and *could* have been done, to compare and explain significant differences with the claims about what was done. It uses the question, "What if … " to interrogate what was claimed. This is easily implemented as a desk-based study, using tools such as flow charts and timelines.

One of the significant characteristics of powerful people is that they tend to create processes that 'import goods and export "bads"'.[58] Even in Plato's vision of his *Republic*, orphans, widows and criminals were to be exported to the 'colonies', while the "good" politicians and slaves would remain or be imported to build the state. Later versions of colonial power followed the tradition. This process can be spatial and temporal. Present-day politicians readily export 'bads' such as electronics waste to less wealthy countries where the toxins harm local people and pollute their country, and long-term threats such as nuclear waste are exported for future generations to cope with. And they happily import 'goods', for example rare earth elements, the products of scarce water such as flowers, and well-trained health-care workers, from other countries. This export–import trade occurs within all forms of the abuse of power, from nations to shops. CPA provides a way to identify and question this common but rarely recognized abuse of power.

7.7 CONCEPTUALIZATION

> **CONCEPT**
>
> An idea of a class of objects, a general notion. (*OED*)

Stephen Jay Gould explains the problem of transforming data into knowledge, discussed throughout this chapter:

> Facts do not "speak for themselves"; they are read in the light of theory. Creative thought, in science as much as in the arts, is the motor of changing opinion. Science is a quintessentially human activity, not a mechanized, robotlike accumulation of objective information, leading by laws of logic to inescapable interpretation.[59]

Most analysis will eventually be compared with theory (C2), to show how it fits within, and contributes to, broader conceptualizations.[60] "How might the use of ICT to organize a protest group fit within theories of 'leaderless groups'?"[61] "How does presidential enthusiasm for a war fit with theories of 'military Keynesianism'?"[62] Findings may support, contradict or modify existing theory, or occasionally construct a new theory.

Often theorization is in a practical, 'functional' way.[63] Formal theories derive from two sources: *empirical* research – a particularly robust piece of primary research, or a meta-analysis of a number of similar research studies, and/or *reason* – logical and consistent chains of evidence-based argument. Usually there is a combination of both. Theories can inform new research by suggesting *hypotheses* to test, or *research questions* to address (C4.3). Researchers often fear theorization, but valuable theoretical contributions can often be explained very simply – "The feminist view that there is a 'glass ceiling' preventing women from attaining leadership positions in companies is also true within environmental activist groups."

In a research design (C4), the use of theory can be *deductive* – existing theory is tested by observations and findings – or *inductive* – observations and findings are explained by existing or new theory. But in practice, research is often iterative – a mixture of the two.[64] Testing a theory is not necessarily a complex intellectual exercise (Figure 7.9). A *grounded theory* approach starts, without a theory or hypothesis, from data collection. Significant data is identified and coded, and codes are grouped into concepts. From these concepts categories are built, from which a new theory may emerge, and possibly a hypothesis.[65] Theory can support the *generalization* of research findings, and link isolated pieces of research to broader levels of thinking and discussion. In time, theory can create *concepts* (terms implying a distinct idea or meaning) and consensual *norms* or *moral values*, such as "corporate social responsibility".

'I spent a morning with a film crew on an industrial estate, crushing the carcass of a pig with a half tonne weight: the aim was to recreate the effect upon his body of Henry VIII's jousting accident of 24 January 1536, during which his horse rolled on top of him. We wanted to test the theory that his injuries that day included damage to his brain. Perhaps this later altered his personality, from kind and promising young prince to cruel and paranoid tyrant.'

Lucy Worsley, Chief Curator of Historic Royal Palaces, London.

FIGURE 7.9   Testing a theory – pig-crushing

Source: Worsley, L. (2010) 'Judicious razzle-dazzle can bring dry bones to life', *The Guardian*, 18 June: 34.

A common difficulty with theorization of up-system data is the scale-gap between the nature of the data, and the type of theorization. Interviews with a few Ministry officials may need to be theorized in terms of a century of tradition about the expectations of bureaucracies. A focus group of refugees displaced by dam building may need to be framed within international law that itself is seen as provisional, "soft" and unclear. Much as physicists try to relate theories about 'micro' systems such as quantum mechanics to 'macro' theories like relativity, using micro data, for example about torture, may need to inform macro theories, for example about state (Figure 7.10).

> Interviewing violence perpetrators and constructing their place within state hierarchies of violence requires inserting micro-level findings into macro-level theories of State, of social organization, of framing ideologies, and of work and career.
>
> Placing micro-level findings about Brazilian torturers into a macro-level framework captures State torture's systemic nature, with its five 'actor types' – "perpetrators", "facilitators", "framing ideologies", "bureaucratic organizations", and "bystanders". ... By studying only torturer's perpetrators, and not theorizing State, researchers bypass torture's systemic nature and can promote State torture system longevity.
>
> Martha Huggins, Sociology and Latin American Studies, Tulane University
> (Research on Brazilian police torturers, 1964–1985)
> *International State Crime Initiative* (ISCI), Research Methods Workshop: 'The State of State Crime Research', King's College, London, April 2011.

FIGURE 7.10   Interviewing perpetrators – theorizing State

The danger is that, because of this difficulty, theorization can become the creation of simplistic paradigms that are fuelled by 'utility' demands rather than evidence (C2.5). But whatever the pitfalls, trying to relate analysis to broader concepts is important if those findings are to live on and contribute to social change that cannot be achieved by lone researchers

Analysis is essentially a process of comparisons, explicit or implicit. This is true for any form of research, but for up-system studies there are distinct considerations:

- How can *causation* be established, and 'outcomes' assessed? Correlation (or coincidence) alone does not prove cause and effect, but it might indicate which factors might be worth further investigation. Arguably causation is virtually impossible to 'prove' and can only be inferred, and in the end it is a matter of 'common sense'.
- People who use power correctly are expected to be *consistent* in what they do. Analysis should ask whether policies match practice, stated values match demonstrated values, and public documents are consistent externally and internally.
- Ultimately, research findings are judged by the *plausibility* of claims, including their 'moral plausibility'. The conundrum is that sometimes the most significant research findings seem to challenge the common sense view, and do not initially seem plausible.
- The unique characteristic of researching powerful people is that they tend to document the processes that they use, and leave audit trails of their actions. Critical Process Analysis (CPA) is an analytical framework for 'reverse engineering' these processes, using counterfactual questions (what *should* and *could* have been done), to assess if the process happened as executants claimed.

Eventually analysis leads to the conceptualization of findings, to fit them within broader frameworks which can support significant academic progress, or movements for social change. A distinct problem of up-system research is that micro-data often needs to be fitted within macro-frameworks. But conceptualization is important because it addresses a question that journalists enjoy asking about the outcomes of a study, and researchers hate answering – "*What's the big idea?*"

KEY READING

Olofsson, P. (2005) *Probability, Statistics, and Stochastic Processes*. London Wiley-Interscience.

Ragin, C.C. (1987) *The Comparative Method: Moving Beyond Qualitative and Quantitative Strategies*. Berkeley: University of California Press.

Rossi, P.H. et al. (2004) *Evaluation: A Systematic Approach*. Thousand Oaks, CA: Sage.

Silverman, D. (1993) *Interpreting Qualitative Data: Methods for Analysing Talk, Text and Interaction*. London: Sage Publications.

Silverman, D. (2011) *Interpreting Qualitative Data*. London: Sage.

Somekh, B. (2011) *Theory and Methods in Social Research*. London: Sage.

8

OUTCOMES

8.1   REPORTING
8.2   PRESENTATION
8.3   INFLUENCING CHANGE

> Speak truth to power.
>
> *Eighteenth century Quaker duty*

Researchers often feel that their job has ended when data has been collected and findings produced (C6), and analysis completed and conclusions framed in relation to theory (C7). But social research is only a means to an end – the 'end' is the greater understanding of something, and perhaps social change. Academic research now requires a clear "contribution to knowledge", and professional research usually demands a 'problem-solving'[1] or 'solution-oriented'[2] outcome (C4.2). Research that takes a critical theory approach will go beyond discovering "what is" to assessing "what could be" (C2.5). In the past, researchers often assumed that their role was simply to record their findings, and the responsibility for understanding and making use of them was for others. The result was countless unreadable and unread academic papers. More recently, the responsibility for presenting research in a clear and accessible way, engaging in disseminating findings, and proposing implications for social change, has moved to the researcher. Sudhir Venkatesh, author of *Gang Leader for a Day*,[3] makes the point lucidly:

> My profession is dying. We generally assess value by our lack of accessibility: we think the more people who know about what we do, the less serious we must be. We have completely separated ourselves from the roots of our discipline, which used to be a public discipline. Academics don't appreciate the fact that we have tenure, a guaranteed income, based on participating in an institution that doesn't pay taxes. We have a responsibility to engage the public. Without that, sociology will continue to fester.[4]

Research funders now often want a description of likely outcomes, user engagement and likely impact, in funding proposals. They may require open notebook presentation of data throughout a project, interim findings, briefing papers for policy-makers and the press, and open access papers online. This requires a specific set of writing skills for researchers, and an ability to use different styles for different audiences.[5] Presenting up-system research also needs an acute sense of political contexts, a high level of clarity and accuracy (C4.6), and an awareness that knowledge might be 'comodified' and used as a source of power.[6] This chapter outlines the basics of academic and professional report writing, introduces effective presentation techniques and discusses how research outcomes might contribute to social change.

8.1 REPORTING

Academic reporting usually requires the researcher to describe the process of the research fully, but there is often confusion about style, particularly tenses. The present-day requirement is clear international English (or other language), rather than convoluted "academic language". The latter does not impress, and may be singled out by groups such as *PlainEnglish.UK* for ridicule, for example:

> While the literature on nonclassical measurement error traditionally relies on the availability of an auxiliary dataset containing correctly measured observations, this paper establishes that the availability of instruments enables the identification of a large class of nonclassical nonlinear errors-in-variables models with continuously distributed variables.[7]

Convoluted style may amuse, but it certainly will not contribute to social change. The style used by the international media, such as the BBC website, provides a good basic model, and books such as *Plain English Guide* provide sound advice.[8] Recent academic textbooks, from respectable university publishers, are also usually a useful guide to modern standards.

A text describing research is a report of something that has happened, and so it will generally be in the past tense ("The study found that ..."). But the literature and theoretical reviews usually use the present tense to indicate that the ideas remain current ("Marx claims that ..."), unless it seems appropriate to present an idea as clearly from a past era ("Hitler believed that ..."). Modern academic style is usually objective not personal, but the use of the first person ("I", "my", "me") is acceptable when it is the simplest and clearest way to phrase something – "The research" is better than "My research", but "My family ..." is better than "The family of the researcher ...".

In social science, the usual framework for an academic report (thesis or dissertation) is as follows, although sections may not always appear as separate chapters in this order.

1   INTRODUCTION (C4) – a short relevant *background*, which leads to a statement of the *problem* (practical or intellectual) that the study addresses. This supports the research *questions and/or hypothesis*. (But sometimes these come from, or are elaborated after, a literature or theoretical review.) The study is then focused in the form of *aim(s)* – the obvious goals of the study in single clear sentences – which have linked *objectives* – the ways those aims were achieved. *Definitions* and clarifications further focus the study, and explain the boundaries – what's in and what's out, and why? There is likely to be a *rationale*, which explains why the study was significant – what was new about it, what gaps did it fill? (This may be supported further by the literature and theoretical reviews.) There may be a short discussion of the *researcher's background*, strengths and weaknesses, and possible insights and biases that come from being either an 'outsider' or 'insider' in relation to the group being studied.[9] The *structure* of the rest of the study will be explained, and perhaps the main *outcomes* outlined so that the reader can follow the main arguments of the report easily.

2   LITERATURE REVIEW (C3)[10] – a critical examination of relevant key texts that relate to the study. ICT has made the old "review of all the literature" nonsensical. The review should start with the specific aims of the review ("to compare governmental and civil society views") and perhaps some questions ("How has the literature changed since 1989?"). It will explain the parameters ("European research since 1990"), how searches were made (databases, keywords, archives visited), and any problems with searches and how they were overcome ("In Korea there is no direct translation for 'international development', so …"). It will be organized under section headings, and the reasons for these headings explained ("From examining recent conference reports, four themes were evident …"). Sections may be chronological ("… from 1946–1989"), reflect sources ("NGO documents", "government reports"), or be thematic ("accountability", "corruption"). The main biases and omissions in the literature will be discussed, but there is no analysis in relation to the new research data. The aims are to demonstrate that the key literature is known and understood, explain the nature of the literature(s) as a whole ("… linked to government policies", "… reflects trends in social psychology"), provide a useful report for other researchers in the same field and identify the gaps in the literature which the new study filled. A short conclusion should address the questions and aims listed at the start of the review.

3   THEORETICAL FRAMEWORK (C2) – a critical review of the theories underpinning the study. A specific theoretical approach may be discussed in depth (reputation, reproduction), or a theoretical framework created from a number of theories to address a specific problem (Leadership, climate change and decision-making). It explains the assumptions of a study – what is taken for granted ("Elites are an inevitable part of any society"). Traditional theories may be tested and developed (deductive), theories may be identified which explain the data (inductive), or new theories constructed (C7.6).

4   METHODS (C4, 5, 6) – how the research aims and objectives were achieved. The *frameworks* (C5) are explained and linked to the *data collection methods* (C6). There are two aspects: *methodology* – a critical assessment of relevant existing frameworks and methods (crowdsourcing, how to interview elites), and *methods* – the methods that were chosen or adapted for the new study (how were the 'crowds' enrolled and managed, why were the interview questions chosen). Questions should clearly be linked to research questions. The overall *research design* might be shown as a diagram (Appendix 3). Shortcomings and biases are mentioned, and ethical considerations discussed (C4.6).

(Sections 5 and 6 may be separate chapters or sections, or an integrated discussion. The distinction is that findings (5) are "pure" and can easily be compared with similar findings from other studies. Analysis/discussion (6) provides arguments and opinions that are less easy to compare.)

5   FINDINGS and INITIAL ANALYSIS (C6) – the basic outcomes – data, statistics, quotes and descriptions. These may be grouped under general headings, often the main research questions. The data may be tested for reliability and validity, and initial analysis may indicate the most interesting outcomes and explain any strange findings or biases ("This may not reflect the views of all staff as senior managers were at a conference that week."). Findings are not related to the literature or theory at this stage, and there is no in-depth analysis. Findings might conclude with a list of key issues, charts or typologies which can then structure the further analysis. Large tables, long transcripts and lists can be put as appendices.

6   DISCUSSION and FURTHER ANALYSIS (C7) – findings are compared with the literature (including other research studies) and theory, to provide explanations that create new knowledge or solve specific problems. Further analysis may include discussion of cross-cutting themes or investigating aspects of the data that were not expected. Put, facts first – opinions last.

7   CONCLUSIONS and IMPLICATIONS – a brief overview of what was done and what was found which clearly addresses the initial research questions and aims, back-referenced to the evidence in the other sections ("See 4.5.6, 5.2"). Implications may include recommendations, policy proposals and ideas for further research. But these should be specific and clearly aimed at entities that could implement them (Law Commission – consider new legislation, Medical Council – amend code of practice, Police College – research into police training). Conclusions do not include any new data and usually no quotes unless there is something very apposite from a significant authority which sums up the study. Finally, the last few pages may promote the main message from the research and perhaps speculate further, but speculation must still relate in some way to the research ("Perhaps these ministerial positions should be abolished, because …").

An academic report may then be the basis for academic papers or books, but it is rare that a dissertation or thesis is simply published in its original form. Academic papers need to be framed in specific ways for specific journals,[11] and books need to appeal to a wide audience. Most book publishers want a structured proposal (usually explained in online 'guidance for submissions') and the most important section concerns sales and marketing. An initial research report may also be re-presented to form a funding proposal for further research.[12]

Unlike academic reports, professional research reports usually minimize the discussion of the research process, perhaps by describing it in an appendix or website. The emphasis is on clear evidence-based findings, and a logical discussion of the implications. The most important part is the executive summary, because this is all that most people will read. The Carnegie report *Researching Power and Influence* provides a relevant example of a professional research report, which aims to 'increase the ability of civil society associations to influence and affect change.'[13] One of the disheartening aspects of professional reports is that often the same things have been said many times before, and have changed nothing. *Late Lessons from Early Warnings* provides an example in the field of environmental hazards.[14] One way to deal with this is to present the history of failure as an aspect of the research. It can represent evidence of an ongoing failure of policy-makers to respond to sound evidence, and probably to follow their self-declared standards and claims.

8.2 PRESENTATION

Improved ICT provides increasingly diverse ways to present information, and 'visual research' presentation is now very sophisticated.[15] But being clear about what a presentation needs to communicate and matching the presentation style to the likely audience, are more important than impressive graphics.

Word processing software and PowerPoint provide the means for creating simple charts and graphs, and Excel for turning statistics into graphs and quantitative charts.[16] Many books explain specific techniques such as flowcharts[17] or process maps.[18] Experts such as Edward Tufte present more in-depth explanations about why certain forms of presentation may be effective. His *Envisioning Information* provides a general discussion with striking examples,[19] and his other books cover specific approaches such as PowerPoint[20] and quantitative information.[21] The rule is, do not use anything just for an effect. Does a graph provide better information if it is shown as 3D blocks or colour? If not, a basic format is better. A 3D block confuses which part of the top shows the actual number – the back or front. Colours and grey shades do not copy or print well, and distinctions may be lost. A diagram should always present something more effectively than a text, but be accompanied by an explanation. Figure 8.1 is an example of the effective use of a simple Venn diagram to explain the confusing terminology and power relationships associated with the 'British Isles'.

Specific audiences may respond best to specific forms of presentation. Experts will appreciate the concise use of technical terms, but a non-expert audience may respond best to analogies that present intangible ideas in familiar contexts, for example:

> The difficulty of understanding complexity and power in a large bureaucracy is like understanding football. Does the most power lie with star players, referees, managers, trainers, sponsors, advertisers, media, club owners, the rule-makers, or the crowd? The answer depends on what type of power is being analysed, and for what reason.

If research is to be used in a setting such as a law court, this may involve showing magnified examples of handwriting or printer outputs, known to be from a certain person, and compared with examples that are claimed to be from that person. Perhaps

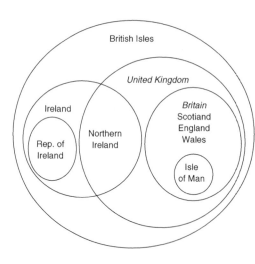

'British Isles' is a geographical term describing a group of islands, Within this, the geographical island, 'Ireland', comprises an independent EU country – the Republic of Ireland – and 'Northern Ireland' which is politically part of the 'United Kingdom' (UK). 'Britain' comprises the countries 'England', 'Scotland' and 'Wales', and is within the political region, 'United Kingdom'. The Isle of Man is a Crown Dependency – a British possession of the Crown – termed part of the 'British Islands'. It is governed by UK law, but also has democratic self-government. Its parliament, the 'Tynwald', is the oldest continuous ruling body in the world, dating from 979AD.

FIGURE 8.1   The use of a Venn diagram to explain the confusing terminology associated with the 'British Isles'

Source: Adapted from BBC/British Council Destination UK. Available at: www. teaching english.org.uk.

misalignments may disclose later insertions.[22] It is necessary to select clear examples, but not to select untypical examples just to prove an argument. Opposing lawyers can also examine the same documents, and can win simply by showing a biased presentation of data. It is also relevant to understand that judges and others may have ideological positions that will shape their interpretation of evidence,[23] and that evidence needs to be presented in a way that achieves a truthful outcome rather than fuelling, or fighting, prejudice. Presenting raw data of abuse of power, for example children's drawings (Figure 8.2), can be effective as both formal evidence, and as advocacy for change. The *International Criminal Court* (ICC) has used children's drawings of war crimes in Sudan.

As a basis for change, presentation converts data, findings and analysis into information. There are various 'public understanding' movements, which have analysed the techniques for presenting complicated research in an accessible way, and might provide a framework for presenting up-system research. The journal *Public Understanding of Science* provides ongoing discussion of this well-established area of endeavour.[24] The appointment of David Spiegelhalter as the Winton Professor of the Public Understanding of Risk, at Cambridge University shows the growing significance of risk communication.[25] Facilitating the understanding of up-system research is often done by advocacy groups such as *Amnesty International, Human Rights Watch* or *Corporate Watch*. Tombs and Whyte consider how research about the crimes of powerful people should be disseminated effectively.[26]

"Draw and tell" methods – 'The police they take us in the room, and two of them hit us on the back many times with a big belt.'

FIGURE 8.2   Researching abuse of power among South African street-working children

Source: Williams, C. (1990) 'Street children and education: A comparative study of European and third World approaches', unpublished PhD thesis, University of Birmingham. (British Library.)

8.3 INFLUENCING CHANGE

Research funders and organizations often want outcomes presented in a way that influences change and advocates a particular line of action. But it is rare that individual researchers can arrange to meet powerful decision-makers, and it is usually necessary to work though campaigning or other organizations. Advocates try to identify *agency* – what or who will make the difference to a situation? Environmental campaigners may change how CEOs behave by influencing their company insurers or investors. Politicians will respond to likely media coverage, and a newspaper can be brought down by per-suading advertisers to pull out. Retailers will change practice overnight if they fear consumer boycotts. Research might also achieve change by presenting it formally to relevant organizations – professional or investigatory bodies, prosecution services or the police, and public inquiries – or less formally through films, poems, songs and art. It can be useful to address correspondence to a high profile person – police chief, politician, judge – because any subsequent attempts to bury or misuse the research would attract more media attention if the addressee is well-known.

For professional researchers in advocacy organizations such as *Amnesty International*, the whole research process will reflect the need for appropriate and effective outputs (Figure 8.3). The aim of achieving social change is sometimes intrinsic to a research design and strategy. From 1995, *Transparency International* has implemented a survey methodology[27] which has an integral dissemination and impact element. Elites – such as the *Asian Development Bank*, *Economist Intelligence Unit*, *World Economic Forum* and busi-ness leaders resident in the countries concerned – are invited to assess the corruption levels in specific countries. The result is a score and ranking of most countries in the world. Having "invested" in the process, these elites are then likely to take notice of the results. They have an interest in seeing corruption reduced, as generally do the politicians in those countries because of impacts on inward investment, tourism and their personal status among world leaders.

Decision-makers, journalists and others who can implement change, are busy peo-ple who do not have the time to read long research reports. Using research to achieve change therefore needs smart strategies for gaining the attention and interest of busy people. Often short 'findings'[28] or 'briefings'[29] papers may present key outcomes in a few bullet points on a front page, with elaborations and sources of further informa-tion later.[30] These should contain clear, and if necessary simplified, descriptions of the research outcomes, but not political rhetoric or simplistic sound bites. Project websites can contain further information, resources and full reports. Free online repositories such as the *Social Science Research Network*[31] and *Scribd* can be used to provide open access to long reports.[32] The *Ranking Web of World Repositories* provides details of hun-dreds of similar sites.[33] An internet site, like the examples on pp. 254-60, could be

Producing good quality written material from research not only requires the ability to assess and analyse the information gathered, it requires the ability to think strategically and to devise effective actions. Having devised such actions and written such reports the researcher must be able to play a role in communicating them to governments, to the media and – often – to the contacts who contributed to the research in the first place. It is an ongoing process and all the activities, the techniques used and the skills required are interdependent.

Source: *Amnesty International*, Research Policy Manual (internal).

FIGURE 8.3   Effective use of research

the result of a research project. Support and dissemination comes from sites such as *Dkosopedia,* and many wiki sites provide the chance for findings to be presented alongside the original data. To avoid overdependence on ICT, tactics like *Wikileaks* 'Operation Paperstorm' distribute versions of their material – data and analysis – through posters and flyers.[34]

Press and other media receive many press releases about immediate news stories (Appendix 13), and the major outlets usually respond better when they come from known press officers. A 'letter to the editor' may be picked up by journalists on that paper or elsewhere. Investigatory journalists, such as those at India's *Tehelka,*[35] appreciate good evidence of relevant abuses of power, although they may take all the credit for revealing the story. To get a longer factual article accepted entails a brief email to a relevant editor, asking if s/he would be interested to see a full draft. Opportunistic dissemination can come from using radio phone-ins or programmes that put public questions to high profile panellists, and contributing to blogs and other online discussions with political leaders.[36]

Another strategy is to present information to relevant organizations that use research-based evidence to achieve accountability. At an international level, this might include the *International Criminal Court* (ICC) which would make use of evidence about significant abuses of power amounting to crimes against humanity. Similarly, at a national level evidence might be submitted to the police or prosecution service, or to formal complaints agencies such as the UK *Office for Judicial Complaints.*[37] Formal Inquiries often accept evidence from the experts and organizations,[38] and may eventually present it online. Shadow sites may accept other material and analysis.[39] Professional bodies – medical, social work, teaching – will usually consider evidence in the form of complaints. NGOs such as *Public Concern at Work* help employees and the public to 'whistleblow' about abuses of power, anonymously.[40] Many organizations specialize in redressing specific forms of abuse of power.[41]

Alternatively, questionable entities can be directly challenged and presented with the evidence of wrongdoing. If their activities seem potentially hazardous – for example likely to cause harm to workers or the public – a formal approach can be made using the "on legal notice" principal. This simply means that if a responsible person has been told in writing about actual or potential hazards, and they or their organization continue with that hazardous activity and cause harm, the law will consider their action more serious because they have been warned that it is potentially harmful. Mangers often respond very quickly to legal notice, if it is pointed out that they personally will be held to account if things go wrong.

Face-to-face meetings with decision-makers may be difficult to organize, and they may have many such meetings in a day. Providing a very clear indication of the content of any meeting will mean they can get other relevant staff to attend, and leaving well written briefing papers (with contact details) for possible follow-up is essential. The most effective approach to briefing powerful people privately is usually to avoid confrontation and anger, and to treat the meeting as a chance to enlighten and educate those concerned. Senior people are often shielded from the truth about their actions and responsibilities, by sub-elites and gatekeepers who have their own personal interests to promote. A briefing from a well-informed representative of a well-respected organization is often very welcome, particularly if it comes at an apposite moment. Government officials will appreciate good evidence if they need to attend an inquiry or international meeting on that topic. CEOs may enjoy hearing of the corrupt practice of their competitors, before a TV appearance. Finding the "windows of opportunity" is crucial – approaching the right person at the right time with the right information. The *Oxford Research Group* provides useful advice about engaging with decision-makers (Figure 8.4).

Approaches to achieving accountability can be categorized in terms of *strategies* (questioning and dialogue, evidence gathering and advocacy, whistle-blowing) and *sanctions*

Oxford Research Group

Step 1: Three principles – Change happens through individuals, dialogue is different from lobbying, think in new ways.

Step 2: Identify the right decision-makers – Research and understand relevant organizational structures.

Step 3: Be aware of assumptions – Decision-makers operate on the basis of deep-rooted beliefs – what are they – how can they be changed?

Step 4: Make contact – Use letters to get face-to-face meetings. Demonstrate knowledge and serious intent, avoid aggression, gain the interest of the decision-maker.

Step 5: Manage anger – Genuine anger can be effective, but counterproductive if it creates fear and resentment. Match means to ends.

Step 6: Plan alternative strategies – Predict a range of scenarios, and formulate appropriate responses to them.

Step 7: Non-confrontational communication – Develop a dialogue, not monologue.

Step 8: Prepare for meetings – What is to be achieved? What are the questions? What should be said first, etc?

Step 9: Follow-ups – Be ready for media interest and other publicity.

Step 10: Change is possible – Don't be overwhelmed by the magnitude of world problems.

FIGURE 8.4   Achieving change – dialogue with decision-makers

Source: ORG (2000) *Everyone's Guide to Achieving Change: A Step-by-Step Approach to Dialogue with Decision-makers.* Oxford: Oxford Research Group.

(naming and shaming, public apology, hearings *in absentia*).[42] But there is little consideration of more sophisticated psychological approaches, such as trying to change the self-perception of leaders.[43] The sustainability NGO *Forum for the Future* uses a 'solution-oriented' approach, which reflects the fact that politicians usually know the problems, and respond better if problems are presented together with potential strategies for addressing them.[44]

Conceptual tools are available to help professional and public researchers to analyse power and influence change through participatory activities.[45] The idea of finding 'spaces' for change is central.[46] Gavanta provides a model for power analysis, and finding opportunities for change, based on identifying the 'spaces for participation' (closed, invited, claimed/created), in relation to visible, hidden and invisible forms of power, at local, national and global levels.[47] Vermeulen encourages analysts to identify 'sources, structures, positions, relationships and mechanisms, and outcomes of power'.[48] Tools can be categorized into tools for understanding, organizing, and ensuring action and sustainability.[49] These approaches recognize that bringing about change means engaging with powerful people, and therefore understanding the nature of power.[50]

Advocacy groups often use public meetings and conferences to promote their research, and use simple strategies such as asking the first question before others have the courage to speak. Contributing to law reform and policy development is another approach.[51] Organizations wait for opportunities, such as when a government is planning new legislation, likely to have a 'Public consultation', or needs to respond to a major problem or news story. They will check if other organizations are trying to influence developments in a similar way, and collaborate. Finally, one of the strongest levers of change is to publicize the impact of how research has been used. A reduction in crime in the US has been attributed not only to the new forensic technologies,[52] but also to the TV programmes based on these methods which create an impression that microscopic and CCTV evidence can lead to criminals being arrested and convicted easily. Daily reports from the ICC and other tribunals probably have a similar influence on potential state despots.

The effective dissemination of up-system research is therefore not very different from disseminating research about other social issues, except in one way. It often focuses on named individuals, and those individuals are, by definition, powerful and unlikely to welcome research that presents them in a negative way. Researchers need to be clear about libel and other laws in the countries they are working in (C4.6). The internet can help to avoid some of these problems, but the country where the evidence came from will nearly always be identifiable, and that can make people in those countries, who may be associated with the research, very vulnerable.

Social research is now expected to produce significant new understandings, and/or contribute to social change. This needs to be considered at the planning stage (C4) so that data is collected in the right format for presentation to entities that can help to bring about change. If research is for a TV documentary, it would be foolish not to have visual data. If it is for a public inquiry or court, it must provide evidence in relation to relevant laws or the remit of the inquiry. In general, effective presentation requires consideration of:

- an appropriate *style* of writing. A text should always be clear and straightforward, but an academic report for experts will include technical details to provide convincing testable evidence, whereas a professional report to influence generic readers and the public will minimize technical language.
- effective *presentation* techniques. This usually requires professional help, because researchers often cannot see clearly what is most significant about their research, and how it is best presented to specific audiences. Information officers and editors will be aware of current trends in communications and publishing, and of the overuse of gimmicks such as bullet points, formatting and colour.
- using a *solution-oriented* style. Politicians and other decision-makers are usually very aware of the problems in their field, but they need the problems packaged with proposals for solving them – "MPs are claiming expenses corruptly, and so a new expenses policy should cover … "
- the '*spaces*' for achieving change. Who might listen, who might help, and where and when might change be achieved? Research outcomes may need to be prepared in readiness for opportunistic dissemination in response to a major news event, government consultation, political change, or natural or human disaster.
- the laws of *libel* and related hazards. Powerful people can react very fiercely when criticized, and the safety of researchers and others involved in a piece of research needs to be ensured when significant findings are made public.

Using research findings to achieve social change can be a very rewarding aspect of any study. But Voltaire (1694–1778) provides a wise warning[53] – *It is dangerous to be right, when those with power are wrong.*

KEY READING

Cornwall, A. and Coehlo, V. (eds) (2006) *Spaces for Change? The Politics of Citizen Participation in New Democratic Arenas.* London: Zed Books.

Cutts, M. (1999) *Plain English Guide: How to Write Clearly and Communicate Better.* Oxford: Oxford University Press.

Denicolo, P. and Becker, L. (2011) *Success in Publishing Journal Articles.* Sage: London.

Few, S. (2004) *Show Me the Numbers: Designing Tables and Graphs to Enlighten.* Oakland: Analytics Press.

Hunjan, R. and Keophilavong, S. (2010) *Power and Making Change Happen.* Dunfermline: Carnegie UK Trust.

Knight, D. (2006) *Public Understanding of Science: A History of Communicating Scientific Ideas.* London: Routledge.

Richardson, L. (1990) *Writing Strategies.* London: Sage.

Tufte, E.R. (1990) *Envisioning Information.* Cheshire: Graphics Press.

Appendices

TOOLS AND TEMPLATES FOR RESEARCH PLANNING

1 MAPPING A CASE STUDY WITHIN A CONCEPTUAL FRAMEWORK
2 LINKING THE ELEMENTS OF A RESEARCH STUDY
3 A BASIC RESEARCH DESIGN
4 A BASIC GANTT CHART
5 ACHIEVING FOCUS AT, OR ACROSS, SPECIFIC LEVELS
6 SYSTEMATIC LINKS FROM TOPIC TO DATA COLLECTION
7 MAKING DISTINCTIONS BETWEEN ELITE AND LEADERSHIP ROLES
8 EXPLAINING THE FOCUS OF A STUDY
9 STANDARD RESEARCH FRAMEWORKS
10 RELATING BASIC QUESTIONS TO FRAMEWORKS AND INFORMATION SOURCES
11 COMPARING JOURNALISTIC AND ACADEMIC APPROACHES TO ACCESS
12 INSTRUMENTS TO IMPLEMENT POWER
13 THE STRUCTURE OF A PRESS RELEASE

Appendix 1

MAPPING A CASE STUDY WITHIN A CONCEPTUAL FRAMEWORK

CASE STUDY – GRAND AYATOLLAH KHOMEINI (1902–1989)

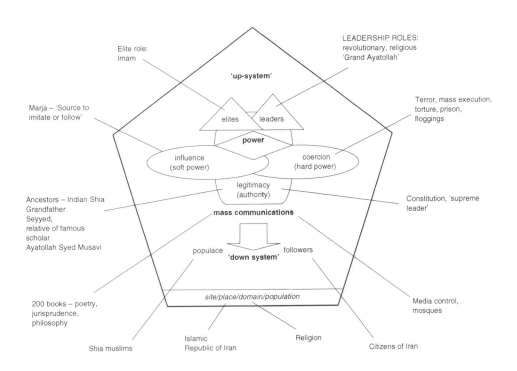

Appendix 2

LINKING THE ELEMENTS OF A RESEARCH STUDY

EXAMPLE: "LEGITIMACY AND ICT AMONG AFRICAN CHIEFTAINCIES"

Historical background (C1)	Theory (C2)
Anthropology: lineage, chieftaincy.	Legitimacy. Reputation.

Literature (C3)	Design (C4)
Colonial and post independence history. ICT and elites.	Focus: - How has legitimacy changed? - Has ICT influenced legitimacy? - How is this relevant for international development experts? Ethics: Avoiding harm to positive local traditions.

Frameworks (C5)	Data (C6)	Instruments	Tests	Findings	Analysis (C7)	Theoretical relevance
Genealogy. Power structure. Biography. Legitimacy.	Ritual objects . Life history interviews. Government records. Observation of ICT use.	Genealogy templates. Interview, documentary analysis, & observation schedules. Video camera/ editor.	Triangulation – chiefs, elders, tribe members, texts on ritual objects. Paper analysis.	Genealogy charts and corroborative evidence. Videos of ICT use.	Comparing colonial and current records. Critical Process Analysis (CPA) to test the relevance of traditional chiefing ceremonies.	Post colonial power structures. ICT and power.

Outcomes (C8)
ICT use is a significant new aspect of legitimizing chieftaincies in African villages. International development experts, such as health education managers, can influence change in villages by recognizing how ICT is used by chiefs.

Appendix 3

A BASIC RESEARCH DESIGN

EXAMPLE: MISUNDERSTANDINGS IN POLITICAL COMMUNICATION

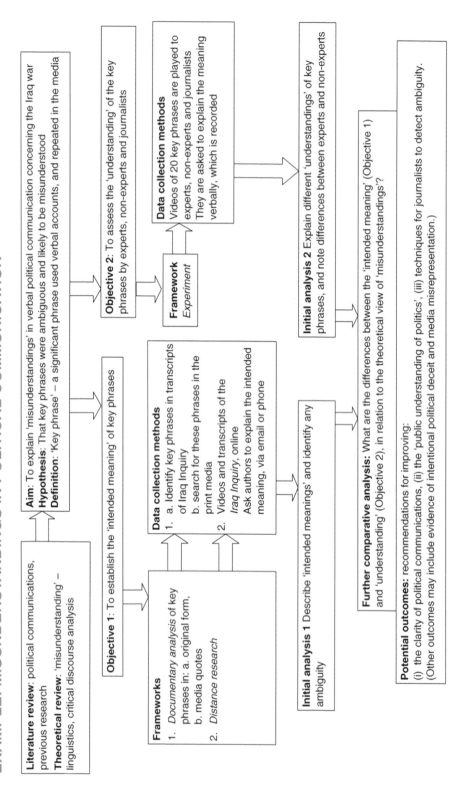

Literature review: political communications, previous research

Theoretical review: 'misunderstanding' – linguistics, critical discourse analysis

Aim: To explain 'misunderstandings' in verbal political communication concerning the Iraq war

Hypothesis: That key phrases were ambiguous and likely to be misunderstood

Definition: 'Key phrase' – a significant phrase used verbal accounts, and repeated in the media

Objective 1: To establish the 'intended meaning' of key phrases

Objective 2: To assess the 'understanding' of the key phrases by experts, non-experts and journalists

Frameworks
1. *Documentary analysis* of key phrases in: a. original form, b. media quotes
2. *Distance research*

Data collection methods
1. a. Identify key phrases in transcripts of Iraq Inquiry
   b. search for these phrases in the print media
2. Videos and transcripts of the *Iraq Inquiry*, online
   Ask authors to explain the intended meaning, via email or phone

Framework
Experiment

Data collection methods
Videos of 20 key phrases are played to experts, non-experts and journalists
They are asked to explain the meaning verbally, which is recorded

Initial analysis 1 Describe 'intended meanings' and identify any ambiguity

Initial analysis 2 Explain different 'understandings' of key phrases, and note differences between experts and non-experts

Further comparative analysis: What are the differences between the 'intended meaning' (Objective 1) and 'understanding' (Objective 2), in relation to the theoretical view of 'misunderstandings'?

Potential outcomes: recommendations for improving:
(i) the clarity of political communications, (ii) the 'public understanding of politics', (iii) techniques for journalists to detect ambiguity.
(Other outcomes may include evidence of intentional political deceit and media misrepresentation.)

Appendix 4

A BASIC GANTT CHART

	Task	Who?	Duration	Week 1	Week 2	Week 3	Week 4
1	Draft research design and identify interviewees	Whole team	5 days	▬▬			
2	Arrange access and permissions	Lynn	3 days		▬		
3	Document collection and analysis	Hiromi	6 days		▬▬		
4	Design questionnaires	Clive and Michele	3 days	▬			
5	Check interview dates and arrange substitutes	Lynn	2 days			▬	
6	Pilot study interviews	Whole team	2 weeks			▬▬▬	

Appendix 5

ACHIEVING FOCUS AT, OR ACROSS, SPECIFIC LEVELS

EXAMPLE: THE OUTCOMES OF INTERNATIONAL POLICIES

Level	Frameworks (C5)		Data collection methods (C6)
Individual	Biographical		*Interviews* with minister, and press officers
Small group	Ethnography (participant observation)		*Observation* of department meetings, and policy briefings
Organization	Context analysis Policy analysis	Cross-sectional study	*e-research* - websites and government reports
Region	Survey		*Opinion poll* - perceptions of regional influence
Nation	Observation		*Remote observation* - online parliamentary proceedings, media appearances
Global / International	Comparative		*Documentary* - International indicators of the outcomes of policies

Appendix 6

SYSTEMATIC LINKS FROM TOPIC TO DATA COLLECTION

Topic			
Purpose, rationale and problematization (From objective authorities)			
Initial hypotheses/research questions (From theory, literature, experience)			
Aim 1		Aim 2	
Objective 1.1	*Objective 1.2*	*Objective 2.1*	*Objective 2.2*
Specific hypotheses/ questions 1.1.1 … 1.1.2…	Specific hypotheses/ questions 1.2.1… 1.2.2…	Specific hypotheses/ questions 2.1.1… 2.1.2…	Specific hypotheses/ questions 2.2.1… 2.2.2…
Framework - Biography Methods - Interviews	Framework - Ethnography Methods - Observation	Framework - Ethnography Methods - Photography	Framework - Documentary analysis Methods - XYZ software
Interview questions 1.1.1.1-5… 1.1.2.1-7…	Observation schedule 1.2.2.1-8… 1.2.2.1-13…	Observation schedule 2.1.1.1-3… 2.1.2.1-7…	Documentary coding frame 2.2.1.1-7… 2.2.2.1-9…

(Continued)

(Continued)

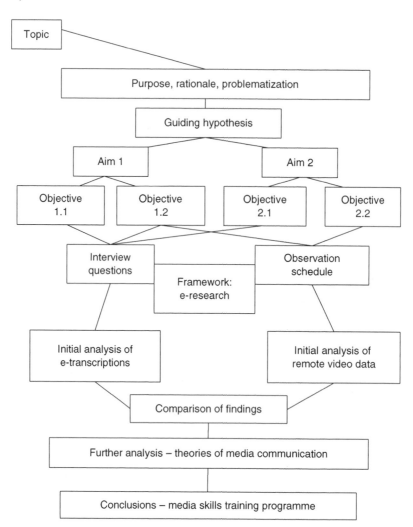

Appendix 7

MAKING DISTINCTIONS BETWEEN ELITE AND LEADERSHIP ROLES

	Elite role	Leadership role
Aim of study	*To explain how perceptions of Jordan's royal family influence the country's economic development.*	*To explain how the personality of military pilots influences loyalty among junior personnel*
1 Up-system role	*Constitutional monarchy (Group)*	*Air force officers (Individuals)*
2 Down-system population	*Jordanian citizens (populace)*	*Lower ranking personnel (followers)*
3 Legitimacy	*Hereditary, tradition*	*Graduates of military academy*
4 Status	*Ascribed*	*Achieved*
5 Form of power	*Constitutional, law (coercion), charisma (influence)*	*Military hierarchy, rules and orders (coercion), charisma (influence)*
6 Place/domain	*Jordan*	*Military aviation*

Appendix 8

EXPLAINING THE FOCUS OF A STUDY

EXAMPLE: IMPROVING HEALTH SERVICE LEADERSHIP

Health service governance in Laos

The **purpose** of this **planning** study is to access the **problem** of how bilateral aid agencies might contribute to developing leadership within health service **systems**, at ministry and regional **levels** in Laos. The **rationale** is provided by the WHO assessment of Laos (WHO 2002: 77–9). The study therefore **aims** to:

1   *understand the influence of external intervention on health service management in Laos*
2   *assess how future external assistance could benefit health service leadership*

Specific objectives are elaborated in Table 7.6.

From Cheong's theoretical account of health provision in developing countries (2003) (see Chapter 3.7), this study **assumes** that good *local* leadership is essential to improve health services, but the literature suggests that this is not the case in Laos (see Chapter 3.2). The guiding **hypothesis** is therefore that

> *indigenous cultural views are significant to understanding the effectiveness of leadership in Laotian health services, but have been ignored.*

From the **literature** (Chapter 3), four **initial questions** have been identified: How did external intervention:

 (i) influence the conceptualization of health care by Laotian elites during the Siamese suzerainty,
 (ii) affect health service management during the French protectorate eras and Japanese occupation,
(iii) influence and support health service leadership since 1954, and
(iv) appear contrary to indigenous views of health?

The main **concepts** and **definitions** are explained in Appendix 2.

[Bold words link to the discussion in Chapter 4, but might be used similarly in a report.]

Appendix 9

STANDARD RESEARCH FRAMEWORKS

Framework	Characteristics	Difficulties	Advantages	General methodology	Up-system examples
Action research (see 'Systematic correspondence' C5.2)	Cycles of interventions and evaluations to understand and change a situation	Powerful people do not welcome interventions. Study may collapse before the cycles of planned interventions are complete	Provides a clear focus. Applicable to leadership training	Lewin, Kurt (1958) *Group Decision and Social Change.* Hollingsworth, S. (1997) *International Action Research.* Coghlan, D. & Brannick, T. (2010) *Doing Action Research in Your Own Organisation*	McNiff, J. & Whitehead, J. (2000) *Action Research in Organisations*
Case studies	A study of something because it is either typical (common) or atypical (unique)	If selection of the case is opportunistic or convenience, the academic rationale may be poor	Clear boundaries. Typical cases can be generalized	Yin, R.K. (2002) *Case Study Research: Design and Methods*	Herzog, H. (1995) 'Research as a communication act: A study on Israeli women in local politics', in R. Hertz and J.B. Imber, *Studying Elites Using Qualitative Methods*, pp. 171–186
Comparative	Analysis of similarities and differences in relation to common factors	Ensuring that terms and concepts in different settings mean the same thing, e.g. 'government committee', 'company'	Provides persuasive evidence for change – "They are better than you."	Sica, A. (2006) *Comparative Methods in the Social Sciences.* Oyen, E. (1990) *Comparative Methodology: Theory and Practice in International Social Research*	Lasswell, H. (1952) *The Comparative Study of Elites.* Engelstad, F (ed.) (2006) *Comparative Studies of Social and Political Elites.* Sasaki, M. (ed.) (2007) 'Elites – new comparative perspectives', *Comparative Sociology*, 6(1–2)
Cross-sectional (Appendix 5)	A study of the same thing at different levels of a population or organization	Difficult to ensure that the same things are being studied	Multiple perspectives which increase validity	Bryman, A. (2001) *Social Research Methods*	Sooryamoorthy, R. & Gangrade, K.D. (2001) *NGOs in India: A Cross-Sectional Study*

Framework	Characteristics	Difficulties	Advantages	General methodology	Up-system examples
e-research (see 'remote observation' C6.1.2)	Internet as: - object of analysis - data collection tool - online focus group - means to interview - survey tool	Information overload. Ensuring sources are credible	Cheap and quick. Often produces surprising, new or hidden data	Jankowski, N.W. (2009) *E-Research: Transformation in Scholarly Practice*	Workman, J.P. (1995) 'Using electronic media to support fieldwork in a corporate setting' in R. Hertz and J.B. Imber, *Studying Elites Using Qualitative Methods*, 65–71
Ethnography (see also 'critical ethnography', C2.5)	Describes and explains social and cultural interaction through methods such as participant observation	Hard to gain unobtrusive access without deceit	Can reveal informal dynamics, and leader-follower interaction	Hamersley, M. and Atkinson, P. (2007) *Ethnography: Principles in Practice.* Thomas, J. (1993) *Doing Critical Ethnography*	Ortner, S.B. (2010) 'Access: Reflections on studying up in Hollywood', *Ethnography*, 11(2): 211–233 Gains, F. (2011) 'Elite ethnographies: Potential, pitfalls and prospects for getting "up close and personal"', *Public Administration*, 89: 156–166
Experimental (see 'natural experiment' C5.1)	An intervention is tested, perhaps on one group, and comparisons are made with another similar 'control' group that did not experience the intervention	Powerful people are unlikely to cooperate. Role play and simulation do not reflect real world circumstances	Useful for informing and evaluating leadership training	Christensen, L.B. (2006) *Experimental Methodology.*	Lammers, J., Stapel, D.A. and Galinsky, A.D. (2010) 'Power increases hypocrisy: Moralizing in reasoning, immorality in behavior'. *Psych. Science.*, 21: 737–744

(Continued)

Framework	Characteristics	Difficulties	Advantages	General methodology	Up-system examples
Longitudinal (see '*systematic correspondence*' C5.2)	Repeated observations of the same things over a long time period, compared with 'base-line data'. 'Cohort studies' track the same people; 'panel studies' survey a sample of a population at each stage	High attrition rate of cohort subjects. Base-line data cannot be amended. Context changes can confound results	Indicates effects of major policy changes. Can track career development of cohorts experiencing leadership training	Menard, S. (2007) *Handbook of Longitudinal Research: Design, Measurement, and Analysis.* British Cohort Study, *Centre for Longitudinal Studies*	Freeman, J. (2001) *Gifted Children Grown up.* Almquist, Y. (2009) 'Peer status in school and adult disease risk: A 30-year follow-up study of disease specific morbidity in a Stockholm cohort', *Journal of Epidemiology and Community Health*, 10:11
Psychological	Assessments of the minds of powerful people – personality, cognitive style, mental health	Difficult to get data directly from actual leaders/ elites, 'distance psychology' is problematic, and simulations are hard to generalize	Insights can inform international intelligence analysis, decision-making, negotiation and conflict resolution	Hermann, M.G. (1977) *A Psychological Examination of Political Leaders.* – Content analysis (27–61); Non-verbal and paralinguistic analysis (62–79)	Hermann, M.G. (ed.) (1977) *A Psychological Examination of Political Leaders*
Surveys	Large scale interviews, or postal/ e-questionnaires across a populace or sample. More often used to research the public or followers, but occasionally for leaders and elites	Powerful people rarely respond to postal/e-surveys or get staff to provide standard responses	Secondary elites, populace or followers may be keen to give anonymous views about powerful people	Groves, R.M. (2004) *Survey Methodology*	Useem, M. (1995) 'Researching corporate executives', in R. Hertz and J.B. Imber, *Studying Elites Using Qualitative Methods*, pp. 83–93. Wiatr, J.J. (2003) 'Polish local elites and democratic change, 1990–2002', *Communist and Post Communist Studies*, 36: 373–383

Appendix 10

RELATING BASIC QUESTIONS TO FRAMEWORKS AND INFORMATION SOURCES

EXAMPLE: THE FUTURE OF CEOS IN THE EXFAIL COMPANY

Basic questions (Figure 2.8)	Frameworks (C5)			
	Documentary	Crowdsourcing	Remote observation	Investigative
How have they been studied previously?	Media searches			Criminal / complaint records
Who are they?	Online Cvs			e-searches
What are they like?		Employee perceptions	Media appearances	
What is their legitimacy?	Who's Who			Family background
Who, and what, do they have power over?	Job descriptions			Other affiliations
What is their power/ organizational structure?	Management structures (company reports)			

(Continued)

(Continued)

Basic questions (Figure 2.8)	Frameworks (C5)			
How do they exercise their power?	Media reports	Employees' views		
What are their aims?	Mission statements			Other goal-oriented affiliations
How do they make decisions?	Management structures	Employees' views		
What are the outcomes?	Company reports		Shareholders' meeting	Personal benefits
How did, or might, their power decline and end?		Rumours	Media mistakes	Corrupt practice

Appendix 11

COMPARING JOURNALISTIC AND ACADEMIC APPROACHES TO ACCESS

	Journalistic	Academic
Where	Over a meal, in a bar.	Office setting
Funding the interview	Hospitality expense account	Formal research grant. Self.
When	Anytime, especially "now". After interviews with subordinates	Office hours, planned in advance
Payback	Wide publicity	Limited publication
Opening explanation	Brief	Long, ethical, technical
Style	Listener, modest, naive	Expert
Questions	2-3 key questions	Long interview schedule
Technique	Perhaps a notebook, sometimes a voice recorder. Maybe covert and under-cover	Voice recorder, laptop questionnaire. Open and upfront
Expectations	Affirm hunches. Binary 'yes' 'no' answers	Extensive data that will be transcribed
Presentation	Will wrap a story around brief highly significant answers	Coded transcripts and long findings
Checking, validity	Previously checked other sources. Uses interviewee to check other sources	Check later
Sharing	Will store all data, including access details and 'irrelevant' information on a central database	Sharing only through formal publication

Appendix 12

INSTRUMENTS TO IMPLEMENT POWER

Violence, force or tradition

Diktat – harsh rules imposed upon the losers of a war by the winners.

Edict – law created by a monarch.

Proclamation – a formal announcement by a monarch that is binding on subjects.

Doctrine – beliefs, teachings or instructions presented as law.

Charter – a grant of powers or rights to a subordinate entity.

International law

Treaties – international agreements or "contracts", in the form of protocols, covenants, conventions or exchange of letters.

Declaration – a non–binding assertion by a group of experts.

Frameworks for action – international agreements that are not binding.

National law

Constitution – principles or precedents providing the basis for governance.

Decree – a law created by a head of state (theoretically) in accord with specific procedures such as those in a constitution.

Statute – a government order commanding or prohibiting something, with enforceable sanctions.

Executive order – instructions from presidents, governors, or mayors which do not have the full force of law.

Regulations – administrative rules that create or restrict rights or responsibilities.

Memorandums, instructions, advice usually clarify the implementation of specific legislation and regulations. No criminal punishments, but employees who do not comply may face sanctions, especially if things go wrong, and breaches could provide evidence for civil claims.

Enabling acts – permission, based on statute, that entities may take certain relevant actions, e.g. health minister using emergency powers to counter a pandemic.

Contracts – mutual agreements between two or more parties, which can be enforced through national courts.

Civil law – regulates how compensation is paid for wrongful acts or omissions.

Organizations

Rules – mutually-agreed standards, which may be enforced by fines, loss of privileges or rank, or exclusion (e.g. OECD, UN, trade unions, societies, professional codes of conduct).

Religious and traditional ideologies

Edict – a law created by the head of a church.

Decree – a law created by the head of a church (e.g. a papal bull or brief).

Fatwa – a religious opinion about Islamic law by an Islamic scholar. (For Sunnis, not binding; for Shias, may be binding on individuals who follow a particular scholar.)

Ruling – a Fatwa that clarifies but does not develop Islamic law.

Moral values – codes enforced through social sanctions, e.g. arranged marriage, filial piety.

Myth – an idea that has no, or a spurious, legal basis, but is enforced by pressure, e.g. gay relationships are wrong, there will be punishment in an afterlife for disobeying a ruler, disability is a punishment for wrongdoing in a previous life.

Budgets

Budgets implement policy through permitting and deterring specific activities, and therefore provide tangible data of the use of power in specific circumstances.

Appendix 13

THE STRUCTURE OF A PRESS RELEASE

	Sudo University
21.12.2012	Press Office

PRESS RELEASE

Leaders are better at cheating ——————————————— | Clear factual title |

New research finds that 90 percent of men with high —— leadership skills are also good at cheating.

| The story in the first sentence (with statistics if possible) |

Last month many MPs were found to have misused their expense accounts. Yesterday Professor Ivan Ego from the *Centre for the Psychology of Power* (CPP), Sudo University, —— provided an explanation. His recent study found that male students who are above average on the Leadership Potential Scale were also better at deception skills…

| The 'pegs' – the related big news, people, organizations |

Ms Constance de Seat MP, who took part, concluded, "I was shocked at how well I did in the cheating." …

| Quotes and human interest |

But similar research, carried out in 2003 found the opposite effect…

| Contrasting views |

A full report, photos, and news about a follow up study, are available at…

| More sources |

Contact details… ——————————————

Further information available from…

Dates of release, embargo details…

| *…and make sure they work and respondents are available at the right time!* |

GLOSSARY

absolute chronologies	lists showing who existed (or what happened) in relation to an objective dating system (calendar)
abuse of power	harm caused 'through acts or omissions that do not yet constitute violations of national criminal laws but of internationally recognized norms relating to human rights' (1985 UN Declaration)
access	a way or means of approach (to researching powerful people)
accountable	required to answer questions about actions
acephalous	'headless' – a society without political leaders or hierarchies
achieved status	a social position gained through personal endeavour
anarchy	'without ruler' – the absence of a hierarchical system of government
androcracy	rule by men
aristocracy	'rule of the best' – a hereditary elite
ascribed status	a social position allocated at birth by family background
authoritarian	a system of rule through dominance and submission
autocracy	'one who rules by himself' – rule with unlimited authority
bureaucracy	impartial, rule-based, hierarchical administration (Weber – rational-legal authority)
caste	an ascribed and fixed position within a stratified social system, which often does not permit relations between such groups
census	an enumeration and/or demographic assessment of a population

characteristic	an individualistic feature, ability or attribute (see 'trait')
chiefdom/chieftaincy	centralized power based mainly on allegiance
class	a position within stratified social system
coercion	the use or threat of physical or other force for a purpose
collapse	the decline of complete societies
community of practice	a group who share a profession or trade
consciousness	mass awareness
conspiracy theories	beliefs that certain activities of groups can exert harmful power
contingent	dependent on circumstances
control	the encouragement of conformity and sanction of deviance
corporatism	state control of significant corporations to enhance government power
cosmopolitanism	an undivided view of humanity and power
cumulative lock-in	a process of belief-based decisions and other factors that make reversing a course of action increasingly difficult
decentralization	the transfer of power and/or responsibility from central to local administrations
decline	downward trend
decree	a law created by the head of a church (e.g. a papal bull or brief)
degeneracy	the decline of societies through biological weakness
democracy	'rule by the people'
despotism	rule by an entity (individual or group) with absolute power
dictatorship	unrestricted absolute rule
digerati	cyber elites

digital governance	the enhancement of political power through ICT
diktat	harsh rules imposed upon the losers of a war by the winners
doctrine	beliefs, teachings or instructions presented as law
domain	a specific field of expertise or area of power
domination	the likelihood that a command will be obeyed by subordinates
down-system	entities that have less power than up-system entities
dystopia	imperfect society with dysfunctional governance
echelon	rank
edict	law created by a monarch or head of a church
elite education	formal learning and teaching for select groups
elite roles	rights and responsibilities that someone in an elite position is expected to perform
elite spaces	places that elites inhabit
elites	select groups at the top of a hierarchical relationship with a generalized down-system populace
empathy	understanding the emotions and feelings
empowerment	the process of increasing the power of powerless people
epistemic communities	groups who believe a particular narrative of events, or share a knowledge source
epistemology	the study of theories of knowledge
ethnocracy	rule by a dominant ethnic group
eugenics	a study of human heredity, often leading to beliefs about genetic superiority
evolutionary theories	explanations of human characteristics derived from understandings of biological adaptation

fascism	rule by a totalitarian, nationalist government
fatwa	a religious opinion about Islamic law by an Islamic scholar
feudalism	government by landowners through control of labour
followers	a specific group that will serve a particular leader
gatekeepers	staff who protect access to powerful people
genealogy	genetic lineage chart
genius	exceptionally high mental ability
gerontocracy	rule by elders
global elites	elites that function within networks that operate outside nation states or similar geographical units
global leadership	leadership with implications for global systems
groupthink	the exclusion of information that challenges the view of a powerful group
halo effect	when the perception of one particular above-average trait generates a perception that other qualities are above average
hegemonic	the power of one group over another
hereditary	inherited from ancestors
hierarchical	organized according to greater and lesser power
hierarchies	lists ranking people or thing from high to low status
ideology	a system of ideas
influence	the use of persuasion to achieve something, an ability to bring about change without violence
inner circle	elites within elites
intelligence	information gathered to gain strategic advantage
isocracy	rule through the equal power of citizens

khakistocracy	military rule supported by business and other elites
kinship	lineage defined by descent or affinity
kleptocracy	'rule by thieves'
kratocracy	rule by those who are strong
leader	someone who organizes and controls specific followers
leadership	abilities or behaviour associated with the role of a leader; office or position of leaders
leadership ethics	moral rules of using power over others
leadership roles	rights and responsibilities that someone in a leadership position is expected to perform
leadership studies	research and scholarship about leadership
leadership training	development of the skills of a leader
legalism	rule by severe laws that punish and reward (Chinese, *Fa*)
legitimate authority	an accepted and/or successful claim to power
lineage	a line of common descent
lists	catalogues
logocracy	rule through words
Machiavellian	deceitful and underhand political behaviour, usually by powerful people
Marxian	Deriving from the work of Karl Marx
mass communication	a system for elites to communicate with the masses
masses	a general non-specific and unorganized population
massification	the use of modern communications which give elites greater control
matriarchy	leadership by females, particularly mothers

meritocracy	rule by those who achieve power through merit
monarchy	a system of government in which political power is inherited by specific individuals (kings, queens, emperors)
necrocracy	a government still working according to the rules of a dead former leader
nobility	the upper class
ochlocracy	rule by a mob or mass
oligarchy	'rule by the few'
ontology	the study of how we know that something exists
opposition	a group that is opposed to or against a prevailing power group
outcome	the consequence of an action
panarchism	a system of government which any individual can freely leave without moving from their home
patriarchy	leadership by males, particularly fathers
pedigree	a lineage of (usually elite) ancestors
peer	a person of the same rank
place	an area with boundaries
plural	diverse and competing
pluralism	a situation in which power is shared among different entities
plutocracy	rule by the wealthy
political	pertaining to the process of influencing the creation and implementation of group goals
polyarchy	rule by more than three entities
populace	the mass of people of a community, as distinct from the elites

population	all the people or other entities within a certain place or category
poverty	a lack of resources because of a lack of power
power	ability to affect others strongly
power elite	a group of controlling elites from different organizations
power structure	a network of organizations and roles within a population through which power operates
powerlessness	a lack of power deriving from physical weakness, isolation and vulnerability
proclamation	a formal announcement by a monarch that is binding on subjects
propaganda	doctrines propagated by an organization or movement to increase its power
provenance	the origin and history of the ownership of an object
rank	the relative power, status or authority of a person within a system
regime	a form of government, or the rules or ideology that frames a government
relative chronologies	lists showing who existed (or what happened) before or after who, but not linked to an objective dating system
reproduction of elites	the process of elites creating more elites like themselves
republic	a system within which the government is controlled by most of the people
reputation	socially recognized status
royalism	the ideology that elites of the nobility have an intrinsic right to power
site	place or location

situated	the two-way relationship between leader and situation
situation	circumstances, context
situational	arising from circumstances
social change	the difference between the present and previous (and possible future) condition of an aspect of society
social movement	non-government action group
spokespeople	staff who speak on behalf of powerful people
state crime	'state organizational deviance resulting in human rights violations, including crimes committed, instigated or condoned by state agencies or by non-state entities that control substantial territory' (ISCI)
status	position within a group
strategy	a plan, method or series of moves for achieving a specific outcome
stratification	hierarchical structures of social power
stratified	layered hierarchically
stratocracy	lawful government by military chiefs
subordinate	a lower level of person, according to ability, status, age, etc.
subsidiarity	enabling decisions to be made at the lowest possible level in a system
sultanism	rule by a Muslim despot
superior	a higher level of person, according to ability, status, age, etc.
surveillance	observation in order to control
technocentric	centred on technology
technocracy	rule by technical experts

thalassocracy	rule through the sea
theocracy	rule by officials who claim to be guided by gods
timocracy	government by elites, particularly property owners
totalitarian	unrestricted rule by a single entity which controls all aspects of society
toxic leaders	those who make relationships and circumstances progressively worse
trait	distinctive personal characteristic
transactional	the negotiated relationship between leaders and followers
transformational	a relationship in which leaders motivate followers to achieve change
transition	a large-scale socio-political change, usually of countries
tribal	a system of government, outside of states, organized through kinship or other close bonds
typologies	lists organized into types
tyrannicide	the killing of tyrants
tyrant	a ruler who uses coercion without law
up-system	entities that have power over down-system entities
utopia	ideal society with perfect governance
victims	'persons who, individually or collectively, have suffered harm, including physical or mental injury, emotional suffering, economic loss or substantial impairment of their fundamental rights' (1985 UN Declaration)

INTERNET SOURCES

International		
UN Databases	Lists all UN and related databases	www.un.org/databases/index.html
UN Information Centres (UNIC)	A network of 63 centres	http://unic.un.org/
UN Documents	Access to all UN documents	www.un.org/en/documents/index.shtml
UN Documentation: Research Guide	Documentation about disarmament, environment, human rights, international law, peacekeeping, the UN regular budget and treaties	www.un.org/Depts/dhl/resguide/quick.htm
Globalex. UN Research	An electronic publication for international law research	www.nyulawglobal.org/globalex/United_Nations_Research1.htm
UN Audio Visual Library Of International Law	Archives covering aspects of international law	http://untreaty.un.org/cod/avl/intro.html
World Federation of Exchanges	List of the main stock exchanges and members	www.world-exchanges.org
Yahoo Business and Economy Directory	Wide range of lists and links	http://dir.yahoo.com/Business_and_Economy/?skw=dir+yahoo%21+business
Researching companies online	Links to free resources	www.learnwebskills.com/company/
BBC country profiles	Reliable political and other information	http://news.bbc.co.uk/1/hi/country_profiles/default.stm
Elections by country (Wiki)	Information on the way the head of state and the parliament or legislature is elected, with links to latest country data	http://en.wikipedia.org/wiki/Elections_by_country
Political Instability Task Force	Academic site with data sets and discussion, funded by the CIA	http://globalpolicy.gmu.edu/pitf/
Political Resources	Lists of political sites, parties, media	www.political resources.net
Institute for Democracy and Electoral Assistance	Interactive databases, networks, research resources	www.idea.int

Rulers	Lists of heads of state and heads of government etc. going back 300 years	www.rulers.org
Rotary International	A worldwide organization of more than 1.2 million business, professional and community leaders	www.rotary.org
Interaction Council	Independent international organization of former heads of state and others	www.interactioncouncil.org

Accountability organizations		
Human Rights Watch	Resources to 'hold oppressors accountable for their crimes'	www.hrw.org
Amnesty International	Data about human rights investigations	www.amnesty.org.uk
Transparency International	International corruption indexes	www.transparency.org
International State Crime Initiative, Kings' College, London	A community of scholars working to further the understanding of state crime	http://statecrime.org
Nato Watch	Newsletter and observatory	www.natowatch.org
Corporate Watch	Corporate accountability UK	www.corporatewatch.org.uk
CorpWatch US	US corporate accountability. (Not related to Corporate Watch)	www.corpwatch.org
Corporate Europe Observatory	EU corporate accountability	www.xs4all.nl/~ceo
Spinwatch	Monitors PR and spin	www.spinwatch.org
The Propaganda Project	Tools for identifying and understanding propaganda techniques	www.propagandaproject.org
Open Government	A journal on freedom of information	www.opengovjournal.org
Tax Justice Network	Research and advocacy about tax evasion by elites	www.taxjustice.net
Investor Research and Responsibility Centre	Resources for investigating US investment sources	www.irrc.org
Essential information	Lists anti-corporate US NGOs	www.essential.org
Search	Online research for justice and public decision-makers	www.search.org/about/
Who owns whom	Large database of company networks, directors etc.	www.whoownswhom.co.za/
Essential	Lists anti-corporate sites	www.essential.org
Paywizard	Details of elite salaries	www.paywizard.co.uk/main/vip-celebrity-salary/politician-salary

(Continued)

(Continued)

Investigative journalism		
Power Reporting	Resources for computer-assisted reporting, including people finders	http://powerreporting.com
iwatch	*The Centre for Public Integrity and International Consortium of Investigative Journalists*	www.iwatchnews.org
Investigative Reporters and Editors, Inc.	Database and resources	www.ire.org
The virtual chase	Tools for investigative research and many relevant websites	http://archive.virtualchase.justia.com/tir/
Center for Media and Democracy	Investigative reporting group, which exposes corporate spin and government propaganda (PRWatch, SourceWatch, and BanksterUSA)	www.prwatch.org/cmd
The Schuster Institute for Investigative Journalism	*Brandies University*	www.brandeis.edu/investigate
JournalismNet	Access to public records, people finder and other tools	www.peoplesearchpro.com/journalism
Reuters	Business briefing (not free)	www.briefing.reuters.com

Finding individuals		
Webuser	How to find people online	www.webuser.co.uk/help-and-advice/guides/371224/how-to-find-people-online
Who's Who?	List of elites worldwide, who may be relevant to UK	www.ukwhoswho.com
123People	Name search. Scans web for press articles, photos, phone numbers, networks and other data	www.123people.com
192.com	People finder	www.192.com/people
LinkedIn	Social network of professionals	www.linkedin.com/home?trk=hb_home
People search *White pages* *Mashable*	Many similar sites under 'find people', 'people search' etc Discusses merits of these sites	www.peoplesearch-uk.co.uk www.whitepages.com/person?site_id=10583 http://mashable.com/2007/07/18/people-search
Facebook *Myspace*	Social network sites, with free searches	www.facebook.com/find-friends www.myspace.com/browse/people

tweetscan	Public messages and user profiles on Twitter	http://tweetscan.com
yoname	People search across social networks and blogs	www.yoname.com
Yasni	Free people check	www.yasni.com
Whois.net	Domain-based research services	www.whois.net
Forbes	Rich Lists, by country, 'world's billionaires', companies, people, celebrities	www.forbes.com/lists

Methodology		
Society for Political Methodology	Portal for publications, news and *The Political Methodologist*	http://polmeth.wustl.edu
Sage	Research methods online	http://srmo.sagepub.com
Endgame research	Manuals and resources for researching companies	www.endgame.org/siteindex.html
Corporate Watch	Manual - *How to Research Companies*	www.corporatewatch.org.uk
Who rules America?	Bill Domhoff's guide to power structure research, including links and theoretical discussions	http://sociology.ucsc.edu/whorulesamerica
Paul Hensel's Political Methodology page	Online resources and relevant books for statistical methodology	www.paulhensel.org/methods.html
Global Integrity	Open-source metrics, indicators, and techniques for assessing transparent and accountable government	www.globalintegrity.org
Quality of Governance Institute	Methods for assessing governments	www.qog.pol.gu.se/
World Bank	Methods from the International Comparison programme	http://web.worldbank.org/WBSITE/EXTERNAL/DATASTATISTICS/ICPEXT/0,,contentMDK:20117138~menuPK:299204~pagePK:60002244~piPK:62002388~theSitePK:270065,00.html
Transparency International	Indexes etc include methodology discussions	www.transparency.org

(Continued)

(Continued)

Sites that facilitate 'distance research'		
International		
International Court of Justice (ICJ)	Press room. Video and audio clips	www.icj-cij.org/presscom/multimedia.php?p1=6&PHPSESSID=71d7e13734814d7a77014390c3a063f0
UN Security Council	Webcasts and documentation	www.unmultimedia.org/tv/webcast/index.html
International Criminal Court (ICC)	Webcasts and documentation	www.icc-cpi.int/Menus/ICC
International Criminal Tribunal for the former Yugoslavia (ICTY)	Webcasts and documentation	www.icty.org/
International Criminal Tribunal for Rwanda	ICTR by satellite	www.unictr.org/Portals/0/English/News/Satellite/ictr_by_Satellite.pdf
Global Policy Forum	Ongoing links to UN tribunals and courts	www.globalpolicy.org/international-justice/international-criminal-tribunals-and-special-courts.html
Open countries		
BBC Democracy Live	A range of tools to observe and track British parliamentarians	http://news.bbc.co.uk/democracylive/hi/default.stm
BBC 'follow'	Shadowing	http://news.bbc.co.uk/democracylive/hi/follow
Write To Them	Contact with British parliamentarians	www.writetothem.com
Sceptical voter	Contact details, voting and other data for British parliamentarians	http://skeptical-voter.org/wiki/index.php?title=Main_Page
Theyworkforyou	Contact details, voting and other data for British parliamentarians	www.theyworkforyou.com
Number 10	British Prime Minister's Office	www.number10.gov.uk/footer/contact-us
National Archives	British government records going back 1000 years	www.nationalarchives.gov.uk

Holyrood House	Scottish Parliament	www.holyrood.tv/popup.asp?stream=http://vr-bng. lbwa.verio.net/main_chamber
New Zealand Parliament TV	Realtime video, archives	www.parliament.nz/en-NZ/AboutParl/SeeHear/ PTV
New Zealand Green Party blog	Daily perspectives from an influential minority party	http://blog.greens.org.nz
Goodlaw	Gateway to track South Korean politicians. No English	www.goodlaw.org
US Government	Official site	www.usa.gov
Washington Post	Votes database	http://projects.washingtonpost.com/congress
US Government Watch FactCheck eHOW Politifact	Independent monitors Voting records of US politicians General data	www.dojgov.net/US_Government_Watch.htm http://factcheck.org/ www.ehow.com/how_2071209_check-politicians-voting-record.html www.politifact.com/
OpenCongress	Sources and links for researching the US Congress	www.opencongress.org/wiki/Wiki_Home
GovSpot	US politics and government	www.govspot.com/shortcuts/votingrecords.htm
Closed countries		
North Korea Leadership Watch	Tracks leaders' activities. Archives and details of Kim family	http://nkleadershipwatch.wordpress.com
North Korea Watch	Daily reports	http://northkoreawatch.blogspot.com
North Korea Economy Watch	Reports, statistics, academic/business resources	www.nkeconwatch.com
Uriminzokkiri	North Korean government site in English. (It is illegal to use the twitter link from South Korea)	www.stumbleupon.com/su/1z72lb/www.uriminzokkiri.com/Newspaper/English/main.php
YouTube uriminzokkiri	North Korean government videos. (YouTube also has many private and undercover videos of NK)	www.youtube.com/user/uriminzokkiri

(Continued)

(Continued)

Google Earth	Pictures of elite districts in Pyongyang, and other sites	www.nkeconwatch.com/north-korea-uncovered-google-earth
Iran Twazzup	Gateway to Iranian civil society communications. List of twitter sites	http://iran.twazzup
Voice of Balatatin	A popular independent Iranian English site	http://en.balatarin.com
Press TV	Iranian government agency in English	www.presstv.ir
Democratic Voice of Burma	Independent media site.	www.dvb.no
Mizzima (Burma)	Independent news and multimedia	www.mizzima.com
Congo News Agency	Official news site	http://congonewsagency.com
Congo Planet	Commercial news site	www.congoplanet.com
My Wage	Elite salaries in Zimbabwe and elsewhere	www.mywage.org/zimbabwe/main

REFERENCES

INTRODUCTION

1   Nader, L. (1972) 'Up the anthropologist', in D.H. Hymes (ed.), *Reinventing Anthropology.* New York: Pantheon Books. pp. 284–311.
2   Hertz, R. and Imber, J.B. (eds) (1995) *Studying Elites Using Qualitative Methods.* London: Sage. p.viii.
3   Nader, L. (1972) 'Up the anthropologist', in D.H. Hymes (ed.), *Reinventing Anthropology.* New York: Pantheon Books. pp. 284–311.
4   Rhodes, R.A.W., Hart, P.T. and Noordegraaf, M. (eds) (2010) 'Observing government elites: Up close and personal', *Public Administration,* 88(1): 269–272.
5   Rodgers, D. and Jones, G.A. (2009) 'Introduction: Youth violence in Latin America – an overview and agenda for research', in G.A Jones. and D. Rodgers (eds), *Youth Violence in Latin America: Gangs and Juvenile Justice in Perspective.* New York: Palgrave Macmillan. See also: D. Rogers, 'An anthropologist in a Managua gang', *Envio digital.* Available at: www.envio.org.ni/articulo/2033
6   Venkatesh, S. (2008) *A Gang Leader for a Day: A Rogue Sociologist Takes to the Streets.* London: Penguin Press.
7   Price, D.H. (2004) *Threatening Anthropology.* Durham: Duke University Press. p. xv.
8   Williams, C. and Yazdani, F. (2009) 'The rehabilitation paradox: Street working children in Afghanistan', *Diaspora, Indigenous, and Minority Education,* 3(1): 4–20.
9   Jost, J.T. and Major, B. (eds) (2001) *The Psychology of Legitimacy: Emerging Perspectives on Ideology, Justice, and Intergroup Relations.* New York: Cambridge University Press.
10 Williams, C. (2006) *Leadership Accountability in a Globalizing World.* London: Palgrave Macmillan.
11 Jackson, P. (2013) *Intelligence Studies.* London: Sage.
12 Sun Tzu (1910/2005) *The Art of War* (trans. L. Giles). New York: Project Gutenberg.
13 Boesche, R. (2002) *The First Great Political Realist: Kautilya and his Arthashastra.* Lanham: Lexington Books.
14 Cooper, J. (2011) *The Queen's Agent: Francis Walsingham at the Court of Elizabeth I.* London: Faber and Faber.
15 de Garzia, A. (1954) *Discovering National Elites: A Manual of Methods for Discovering the Leadership of a Society and its Vulnerabilities to Propaganda.* Stanford: Institute for Journalistic Studies, Stanford University. ('Media analysis', p. xxvii). Available at: www.grazian-archive.com/governing/Elite/Table%20of%20Contents.html
16 Gardener, H. (1995) *Leading Minds: An Anatomy of Leadership.* New York: Basic Books.
17 Gardener, H. (1993) *Creating Minds: An Anatomy of Creativity Seen Through the Lives of Freud, Einstein, Picasso, Stravinsky, Eliot, Graham and Gandhi.* New York: Basic Books.

18 Taylor, P. (2011) *Talking to Terrorists: A Personal Journey from the IRA to Al Qaeda*. London: Harper Press.

19 Boyd-Judson, L. (2011) *Strategic Moral Diplomacy: Understanding the Enemy's Moral Position*. Sterling, VA: Kumarian Press.

20 *The Guardian, MPs Expenses*. Available at: http://mps-expenses2.guardian.co.uk/

21 Williams, C. (2011) 'Are leadership studies the oldest form of research? A history of "studying up"'. *Journal of Leadership Studies*.

22 Parry, G. (1971) *Political Elites*. London: George Allen and Unwin. p. 68.

23 Carroll, W.K. and Carson, C. (2003) 'Forging a new hegemony? The role of transnational policy groups in the network and discourses of global corporate governance', *Journal of World Systems Research*, IX(I): 67–102.

24 Harrison, L. (2001) *Political Research: An Introduction*. London: Routledge.

25 Davis, T.R. (1984) 'Defining and researching leadership as a behavioural construct: An idiographic approach', *Journal of Applied Behavioural Sciences*, 20(3): 237–251; Desmond. M. (2004) 'Methodological challenges posed in studying an elite in the field', *Area*, 36(3): 262–269.

26 Goldsmith, M., Greenberg, C., Robertson, A. and Hu-Chan, M. (2003) *Global Leadership: The Next Generation*. New York: Prentice Hall.

27 Pumain, D. (2006) *Hierarchy in Natural and Social Sciences*. New York: Springer-Verlag.

28 Gardener, H. (1993) *Creating Minds: An Anatomy of Creativity Seen Through the Lives of Freud, Einstein, Picasso, Stravinsky, Eliot, Graham and Gandhi*. New York: Basic Books. p. 11; Fishman, N. and Harwood, R. (2007) 'Evaluating advocates' spheres of influence with domain leaders', *The Evaluation Exchange (Harvard Graduate School of Education)*, XIII(1&2): 30.

29 Robinson, A. (2011) *Genius: A Very Short Introduction*. Oxford: Oxford University Press.

30 Weber, M. (1922/1978) *Economy and Society*. California: University of California Press. p. 21; Diamond, J. and Robinson, J.A. (eds) (2010) *Natural Experiments of History*. Cambridge, MA: Belknap Press of Harvard University Press.

31 Lachmann, R. (2009) *States and Power*. Cambridge: Polity Press; Jessop, B. (2007) *State Power*. Cambridge: Polity Press; Coleman, R. et al. (2009) *State, Power, Crime*. London: Sage.

32 Hanhimaki, J.M. (2008) *The United Nations: A Very Short Introduction*. Oxford: Oxford University Press.

33 Beck, U. (2008) *Power in the Global Age*. Cambridge: Polity Press.

34 Bourdieu, P. (2002) *Masculine Domination*. Stanford: Stanford University Press; Hester, M., Kelly, L. and Radford, J. (eds) (1999) *Women, Violence and Male Power: Feminist Research, Activism and Practice*. Milton Keynes: Open University Press; Neal, S. (1995) 'Researching powerful people from a feminist and anti-racist perspective: A note on gender collusion and marginality', *British Educational Research Journal*, 21(4): 517–531.

35 Shakespeare, T. (2006) *Disability Rights and Wrongs*. London: Routledge.

36 Graham, K. and Williams. C. (2002) 'Through the eyes of people: An interview with Juan Somavia, Director General of the International Labour Organization (ILO)'; 'Freedom is a Universal Value: and interview with Mike Moore, Director General of the World Trade Organization (WTO)'; 'Healthy people, healthy planet: An interview with Gro Harlem Brundtland, Director-General of the World Health Organization (WHO)'; 'Be able to hope: An interview with Thorvald Stoltenberg, former Director-General of the UNHCR'. Amman: UN University Leadership Academy.

37 Oberdorfer, D. (1997) *The Two Koreas: A Contemporary History*. London: Basic Books.

38 Williams, C. (2009) 'Can restoration of rivers solve recession?', *The Korea Herald*, 31 March: 4.
39 Roehrig, T. (2002) *The Prosecution of Former Military Leaders in Newly Democratic Nations: The Cases of Argentina, Greece, and South Korea*. London: McFarland.
40 *K Pop news*. Available at: www.allkpop.com/.
41 Lee, Y.-J. (2011) 'Leadership and development in South Korea and Egypt: The significance of "cultural shifts"'. Unpublished PhD thesis, University of London (SOAS).

CHAPTER 1: ORIGINS

1 Nader, L. (1977) 'Studying up', *Psychology Today*, 11: 132.
2 Peck, E. and Dickenson, H. (2009) *Performing Leadership*. London: Palgrave Macmillan.
3 Gowdy, J. (2006) 'Hunter-gatherers and the mythology of the market', in R.B. Lee and R.H. Daly (eds), *The Cambridge Encyclopedia of Hunters and Gatherers*. New York: Cambridge University Press. p. 391.
4 Woodcock, G. (1962) *Anarchism*. Harmondsworth: Penguin Books.
5 Atran, S. (2010) *Talking to the Enemy: Violent Extremism, Sacred Values and What it Means to be Human*. London: Allen Lane. p. 473.
6 Whittam Smith, A. (2011) 'Protest movements don't need a spearhead to be successful', *The Independent* (*Viewspaper*), 20 January: 5.
7 Evans-Pritchard, E.E. (1940) 'The Nuer of the Southern Sudan', in M. Fortes and E.E. Evans-Pritchard (eds), *African Political Systems*. London: Oxford University Press. pp. 272–296.
8 Leeson, P.T. (n.d.) 'Better off stateless: Somalia before and after government collapse', unpublished paper, Dept. of Economics, West Virginia University. Available at: www.peterleeson.com/Better_Off_Stateless.pdf
9 Kulish, V.V. (2002) *Hierarchical Methods: Hierarchy and Hierarchical Asymptotic Methods in Electrodynamics*. New York: Springer. pp. xvii–xx; 49–71.
10 Fried, M. H. (1975) *The Notion of Tribe*. Reading, MA: Cummings Publishing Company.
11 Thomas, E.A. (1960) *The Harmless People*. London: Secker & Warburg. ('Toma the leader': Chapter XI.)
12 Spencer, P. (1965/2003) *The Samburu: A Study of Gerontocracy*. London: Routledge.
13 Arden, H. and Wall, S. (1900) *Wisdomkeepers: Meetings with Native American Spiritual Elders*. New York: Beyond Words Publishing.
14 Mead, M. (1977) *Culture and Commitment: A Study of the Generation Gap*. St Albans: Panther.
15 Doyle, W. (2010) *Aristocracy: A Very Short Introduction*. Oxford: Oxford University Press.
16 Turnbull, C.M. (1976) *Man in Africa*. Harmondsworth: Penguin. ('Government without Kings': 67.)
17 Dubois, A.J.A. (1905/2007) *Hindu Manners, Customs, and Ceremonies*. New York: Cosimo Classics.
18 Engels, F. (1884) *The Origin of the Family, Private Property, and the State*. Zurich: Hottingen.
19 Pasternak, B., Ember, M. and Ember, C. (1997) *Sex, Gender, and Kinship: A Cross-cultural Perspective*. New Jersey: Prentice-Hall.

20 Ranger, T. (1982) 'Tradition and travesty: Chiefs and the administration in Makoni district, Zimbabwe', *Africa*, 52(3): 20–41.

21 Carneiro, R.L. (1981) 'The chiefdom: Precursor of the state', in G.D. Jones and R.R. Kautz (eds), *The Transition to Statehood in the New World*. Cambridge, MA: Cambridge University Press. pp. 37–79.

22 Mair, L.P. (1936) 'Chieftainship in modern Africa', *Journal of the International African Institute*, 9(3): 307; Ogot, B. (1963) 'From chief to president', *Transition*, 10: 26.

23 Vansina, J. (1962) 'A comparison of African kingdoms', *Journal of the International African Institute*, 32(4): 325.

24 Eire, C. (2010) *A Very Brief History of Eternity*. Princeton: Princeton University Press.

25 Mair, L.P. (1936) 'Chieftainship in modern Africa', *Journal of the International African Institute*, 9(3): 312.

26 Feeley-Harnik, G. (1985) 'Issues in divine kingship', *Annual Review of Anthropology*, 14; Richards, I.A. (1968) 'Keeping the king divine', *Proceedings of the Royal Anthropological Institute of Great Britain and Ireland*: 23.

27 Ranger, T. (1982) 'Tradition and travesty: Chiefs and the administration in Makoni district, Zimbabwe', *Africa*, 52(3): 20–41.

28 Richards, I.A. (1968) 'Keeping the king divine', *Proceedings of the Royal Anthropological Institute of Great Britain and Ireland*: 23.

29 Vansina, J. (1962) 'A comparison of African kingdoms', *Journal of the International African Institute*, 32(4): 325.

30 Burns, J.M. (1978) *Leadership*. New York: Harper & Row.

31 Kaberry, P.M. (1950) 'Land tenure among the Nsaw of the British Cameroons', *Africa*, 20(4): 307–323.

32 Williams, J.M. (2004) 'Leading from behind: Democratic consolidation and the chieftaincy in South Africa', *Journal of African Studies*, 42(1):113–135.

33 Meyerowitz, E.L.R. (1962) *At the Court of an African king*. London: Faber and Faber; Obeng, E.E. (1986) *Ancient Ashanti Chieftaincy*. Accra: Tema.

34 Akbar, S.A. (1984) 'Al-Beruni: The first anthropologist', *RAIN*, 60: 9–10.

35 Tapper, R. (1995) 'Islamic anthropology and the anthropology of Islam', *Anthropological Quarterly*, 68(3):185–193.

36 Alam, M. and Subrahmanyam, S. (2007) *Indo-Persian Travels in the Age of Discoveries, 1400–1800*. Cambridge: Cambridge University Press. Chapter 1.

37 Lane, E.W. (1973) *An Account of the Manners and Customs of the Modern Egyptians*. New York: Dover Publications. p. 175.

38 Thompson, J. (1996) 'Edward William Lane's "Description of Egypt"', *International Journal of Middle East Studies*, 28(4): 574.

39 Brown, R. (1890) *The World: its Cities and Peoples*. London: Cassell.

40 Ranger, T. (1982) 'Tradition and travesty: Chiefs and the administration in Makoni district, Zimbabwe', *Africa*, 52(3): 20–41.

41 Dennet, R.E. (1906) *At the Back of the Black Man's Mind or Notes on the Kingly Office in West Africa*. Available at: www sacred-texts.com

42 Smith, H.S. (c.1911) *Yakusu: The Very Heart of Africa*. London: Marshall. pp. 24–29, 299. Available at: www.archive.org/details/yakusuveryhearto00smit

43 Hochschild, A. (1998) *King Leopold's Ghost: A Story of Greed, Terror, and Heroism in Colonial Africa*. London: Pan Macmillan.

44 Smith, H.S. (c.1911) *Yakusu: The Very Heart of Africa*. London: Marshall. pp. 24–29, 299. Available at: www.archive.org/details/yakusuveryhearto00smit

45 Nader, L. (1977) 'Studying up', *Psychology Today*, 11: 132.

46 Cheater, A. (1999) *The Anthropology of Power*. London: Routledge.

47 Marcus, G.E. (1979) 'Ethnographic research among elites in the Kingdom of Tonga: Some methodological considerations', *Anthropological Quarterly*, 52(3): 135–151; Nugent, S. and Shore, C. (eds) (2002) *Elite Cultures: Anthropological Perspectives*. London: Routledge.

48 Burns, K.R. (2006) *The Forensic Anthropology Training Manual*. London: Pearson Education.

49 Kelly, J. (2010) *Rape in War: Motives of Militia in DRC*. Washington: US Institute of Peace.

50 Khaldun, Ibn (1967/2004) *The Muqaddimah: An Introduction to History* (F. Rosenthal, trans.; N.J. Dawood and B. Lawrence, eds). New Jersey: Princeton University Press. (Bk.1: Preliminary Remarks.)

51 Available at: www.bbc.co.uk/ahistoryoftheworld/

52 Brier, B. (2008) *Daily Life of the Ancient Egyptians*. Santa Barbara: Greenwood. p. 202.

53 British Museum (2010) *The History of the World in 100 Objects*. Available at: www.bbc.co.uk/ahistoryoftheworld/

54 Early writing tablet, British Museum. Available at: www.bbc.co.uk/programmes/b00qb5y1

55 Shaw, I. (2003) *The Oxford History of Ancient Egypt*. Oxford: Oxford University Press. p. 5.

56 Paton, D. (1918) *Early Egyptian Records of Travel*. London: Princeton University Press. p. 36.

57 Sima Qian (1993), *Records of the Grand Historian of China. Qin Dynasty* (B. Watson, trans.). New York: Columbia University Press.

58 Norwich, J.J. (2011) *The Popes: A History*. London: Chatto & Windus.

59 Lorenz, E. (2007) *The Harivamsa: The Dynasty of Krishna*. Oxford: Oxford University Press.

60 Graham, W.A. (1993) 'Traditionalism in Islam: An essay in interpretation', *Journal of Interdisciplinary History*, 23(3): 495–522.

61 Burke, J.A. (1832) *A General and Heraldic Dictionary of the Peerage and Baronetage of the British Empire*. London: Colburn and Bentley. Available at: www.burkespeerage.com

62 Edwin, A. (1998) *The 21st Century Pedigree Handbook*. London: Edwin Anthony.

63 Cantrell, R. (2003) *Understanding Sun Tzu on the Art of War*. Arlington: Centre for Advantage.

64 Sun Tzu (1910/2005) *The Art of War* (L. Giles, trans.). New York: Project Gutenberg. (Chapter 1: Laying plans, paras 13, 14.)

65 Simpson, R.S. (trans.) (1996) *Demotic Grammar in the Ptolemaic Sacerdotal Decrees*. Oxford: Griffith Institute. pp. 258–271. Available at: www.britishmuseum.org/explore/highlights/article_index/r/the_rosetta_stone_translation.aspx

66 Wallis Budge, E.A. (1893/2008) *The Rosetta Stone: Key to the Decipherment of the Ancient Egyptian Writing System*. Ohio: Forgotten Books. Available at: www.forgotten-books.org

67 Woods, M. and Woods, M.B. (2008) *Seven Wonders of the Ancient Middle East*. Colorado: Twenty-First Century Books. p. 28.

68 Schulz, M. (2008) 'Falling for ancient propaganda: UN treasure honors Persian despot', *Spiegel online*, July 15. Available at: www.spiegel.de/international/world/0,1518,566027,00.html

69 Shanks, H. (1995) *Jerusalem: An Archaeological Biography*. New York: Random House; Khalsa, O.K. (1998) *The Debate Over the Historicity and Chronology of the United Monarchy in Jerusalem,* UCLA Archaeology. Available at: www.mediasense.com/athena/jerusalem.htm

70 Shanks, H. (1997) 'Face to face: Biblical minimalists meet their challengers', *Biblical Archaeology Review*, 23(4): 26–42, 66.

71 Finkelstein, I. and Silberman, N.A. (2001) *The Bible Unearthed: Archaeology's New Vision of Ancient Israel and the Origin of its Sacred Texts*. New York: Simon and Schuster. p. 23.

72 Soueif, A. (2010) 'The dig dividing Jerusalem', *The Guardian* (Supp.), 27 May: 10–13.

73 Freisenbruch, A. (2010) *The First Ladies of Rome: The Women Behind the Caesars*. London: Jonathan Cape.

74 Dever, W.G. (2005) *Did God Have a Wife?: Archaeology and Folk Religion in Ancient Israel*. Grand Rapids, MI: Eerdmans.

75 Asirifi-Danquah (2007) *The Struggle Between Two Great Queens, 1900-1901: Yaa Asantewaa of Edweso, Asante and Victoria of Great Britain*. Ghana: Asirifi-Danquah.

76 Terrill, R. (1984) *The White-boned Demon: A Biography of Madame Mao Zedong*. New York: William Morrow.

77 Pitts, M. (2010) 'How CSI methods are rewriting our past', *The Guardian 2*, 18 June: 14.

78 Genovese, M.A. (1992) *Women as National Leaders*. London: Sage.

79 Chamberlain, B.H. (trans.) (1919/2005) *The Kojiki, Records of Ancient Matters*. North Clarendon: Charles E. Tuttle.

80 Akima, T. (1993) 'The myth of the goddess of the undersea world and the tale of Empress Jingǒ's subjugation of Silla', *Japanese Journal of Religious Studies*: 202–3.

81 Duff, T.E. (2002) *Plutarch's Lives: Exploring Virtue and Vice*. Oxford: Oxford University Press. ('Life of Alexander' and 'Life of Julius Caesar'.)

82 Khaldun, Ibn (1967/2004) *The Muqaddimah: An Introduction to History* (F. Rosenthal, trans.; N.J. Dawood and B. Lawrence, eds). New Jersey: Princeton University Press. (Bk.1: Preliminary Remarks.)

83 Khaldun, Ibn (1967/2004) *The Muqaddimah: An Introduction to History* (F. Rosenthal, trans.; N.J. Dawood and B. Lawrence, eds). New Jersey: Princeton University Press. (Bk.1: Preliminary Remarks.) p. 106.

84 Baali, F. (1988) *Society, State, and Urbanism: Ibn Khaldun's Sociological Thought*. New York: State University of New York Press. p. 47.

85 Ismail Serageldin, El Mongy bo Senena, Mosh`el bin Jassim Al Thani (eds) (2010) *The Mediterranean in the 14th Century: The Rise and Fall of Empires*. Alexandria: Bibliotheca Alexandria Publications.

86 Shaw, S.J. and Shaw, E.K. (1976) *History of the Ottoman Empire and Modern Turkey, Vol. 1: Empire of the Gazis: the rise and decline of the Ottoman Empire, 1280–1808*. Cambridge: Cambridge University Press.

87 Lee, P.H. (1996) *Sources of Korean Tradition*. Columbia: Columbia University Press. p. 302.

88 Fook, J. (1999) 'Reflexivity as method'. *Health Sociology Review*, 9(1): 11–20.

89 Lee, *Sources of Korean Tradition*, p. 304.

90 Bernheim, E. (1894) *Lehrbuch Der Historischen Methode*. Chicago: Kessinger Publishing.

91 Garraghan, G.J. (1946) *A Guide to Historical Methods*. New York: Fordham University Press. p. 168; Shafer, R.J. (1974) *A Guide to Historical Method*. Illinois: The Dorsey Press.

92 Renfrew, C. and Bahn, P. (2008) *Archaeology: Theories, Methods and Practice*. London: Thames & Hudson; Evzen, N. (1993) *Archaeological Method*. Cambridge: Cambridge University Press.

93 *Prehistoric temples of Malta*. Available at: www.art-and-archaeology.com/malta/malta.html

94 Cuvier, G. (1798) *Tableau élémentaire de l'histoire naturelle des animaux*. Paris: Baudouin.

95 Ross, A. (2005) 'Better DNA out of fossil bones', *BBC News Online*. Available at: http://news.bbc.co.uk/1/hi/sci/tech/4260334.stm

96 Cox, M. and Hunter, J. (2005) *Forensic Archaeology*. London: Routledge.

97 Burns, J.F. (2006) 'Uncovering Iraq's horrors in desert graves', *New York Times*, 6 May.

98 Charlier, P. (2010) 'Multidisciplinary medical identification of a French king's head (Henry IV)', *British Medical Journal*, 341, 14 December.

99 Miller, D. and Tilley, C. (1984) *Ideology, Power and Prehistory*. Cambridge: Cambridge University Press; Routledge, B. (2011*) Archaeology and State Theory: Subjects and Objects of Power*. Bristol: Duckworth.

100 UNESCO (1999) *Disarming History. Conclusions and Recommendations*. Available at: www.unesco.org/cpp/uk/news/visby.htm

101 Chahin, M. (1987) *The Kingdom of Armenia*. New York: Dorset Press.

102 Chomsky, N. (2011) 'Noam Chomsky warns against intervention in Libya', *News night* (online), 9 March.

103 Stroud, B. (1984) *The Significance of Philosophical Scepticism*. Oxford: Oxford University Press.

104 BBC (2010) 'Reith lectures – The scientific citizen', 1 June, Radio 4. Available at: www. bbc.co.uk/programmes/b00sj9lh

105 Bagini, J. and Fosl, P.S. (2010) *The Philosopher's Toolkit: A Compendium of Philosophical Concepts and Methods*. London: Wiley.

106 Lao Tzu (2006) *Tao Teh Ching* (J.C.H. Wu, trans.). Boston, MA: Shambhala. p. 35.

107 Confucius (*K'ung-fu-tzu*) (1979) *The Analects* (D.C. Lau, trans.). Harmondsworth: Penguin Books. Book XII, 17 XIV.9.

108 Confucius (*K'ung-fu-tzu*) (1979) *The Analects* (D.C. Lau, trans.). Harmondsworth: Penguin Books. Book XII, 17.

109 Glenn, H.P. (2000) *Legal Traditions of the World*. Oxford: Oxford University Press. p. 282.

110 Yuan, Zheng (1994) 'Local government schools in Sung China: A reassessment', *History of Education Quarterly*, 34(2), Summer: 193–213.

111 Elman, B. (2002) *A Cultural History of Civil Examinations in Late Imperial China*. Berkeley: University of California Press.

112 Wen Kui (trans.) (1939) *The Complete Works of Han Fei Tz with Collected Commentaries*. Hong Kong. Chapters. XXVIII, LIV, XV.

113 Plato (1955) *Plato and The Republic* (H.D.P. Lee, trans.). Harmondsworth: Penguin. Part 7.

114 Book 3.5.

115 Plato (1955) *Plato and The Republic* (H.D.P. Lee, trans.). Harmondsworth: Penguin. p. 145.

116 Aristotle (1999) *Politics* (B. Jowlett, trans.). Kitchener: Batoche Books. Available at: http://socserv2.mcmaster.ca/~econ/ugcm/3ll3/aristotle/Politics.pdf

117 Boesche, R. (2002) *The First Great Political Realist: Kautilya and his Arthashastra*. Lanham: Lexington Books. p. 1.

118 Polybius (1889/1962) *Histories* (E.S. Shuckburgh, trans.). London: Macmillan.

119 Chapters 6.47, 6.40, 6.45

120 Eliot, J. (1628/1882) *De Jure Maiestatis*. London: Chiswick Press.

121 Weber, M. (1919/2000) *Politics as a Vocation*. Minneapolis: Fortress Press.

122 Machiavelli, N. (1984) *The Prince* (D. Donno, trans.). London: Bantam Classics.

123 Williams, C. (2006) *Leadership Accountability in a Globalizing World*. London: Palgrave Macmillan. pp. 132–138.

124 Smith, M.J. (1998) *Social Science in Question*. London: Sage. p. 27.

125 Ostrander, S.A. (1993) 'Surely you're not in this just to be helpful. Access, rapport, and interviews in three studies of elites', *Journal of Contemporary Ethnography*, 22(1): 7–27.

126 Williams, C. (2011) 'Are leadership studies the oldest form of research? A history of "studying up"'. *Journal of Leadership Studies*, being reviewed.

127 Chahin, M. (1987) *The Kingdom of Armenia*. New York: Dorset Press. p. 275.

CHAPTER 2: THEORY

1   Mao, Tse-tung (1927) 'On practice', *Marxist Documentation Project*. Available at: www.marxists.org/reference/archive/mao/selected-works/volume-1/mswv1_16.htm

2   Schram, S.R. (1967) *Quotations from Chairman Mao Zedong*. London: Bantam Books.

3   Pojman, L.P. (2008) *Philosophy: The Quest for Truth*. Oxford: Oxford University Press.

4   Deutsch, D. (2011) *The Beginning of Infinity: Explanations that Transform the World*. London: Allen Lane. pp. 1–33.

5   Joseph Berger, J. and Zelditch, M. (1993) *Theoretical Research Programs: Studies in Theory Growth*. Stanford: Stanford University Press.

6   Jacquette, D. (2003) *Ontology*. Montreal: McGill-Queen's University Press.

7   Bostrom, N. (2009) 'The simulation argument: some explanations', *Analysis*, 69(3): 458–461.

8   Searle, J.R. (2006) 'Social ontology: some basic principles', *Anthropological Theory*, 6(1): 12–29; Searle, J.R. (1995) *The Construction of Social Reality*. New York: Free Press.

9   Searle, J.R. (2010) *Making the Social World*. Oxford: Oxford University Press; Searle, J.R. (2003) 'Social ontology and political power', *Berkeley Law School*: 3. Available at: www.law.berkeley.edu/centers/kadish/searle.pdf

10 Searle, J.R. (2003) 'Social ontology and political power', *Berkeley Law School*: 3: 1. Available at: www.law.berkeley.edu/centers/kadish/searle.pdf

11 Morten, L. (2008) *The Pleasure Centre: Trust Your Animal Instincts*. Oxford: Oxford University Press.

12 Morse, S. (2006) 'Brain overclaim syndrome and criminal responsibility: A diagnostic note', *Ohio State Journal of Criminal Law*, 3: 397.

13 Dick, P.K. (1978) 'How to build a universe that doesn't fall apart two days later' (public speech). Available at: http://deoxy.org/pkd_how2build.htm

14 Audi, R. (1997) *Epistemology: A Contemporary Introduction to the Theory of Knowledge*. London: Routledge.

15 Blackburn, S. (1996) *Dictionary of Philosophy*. Oxford: Oxford University Press.

16 Rumsfeld, D.H. (2002) Press conference at NATO HQ in Brussels (February 12), *Department of Defence* news briefing. Available at: http://transcripts.cnn.com/TRANSCRIPTS/0312/05/ltm.09.html

17 Bhaskar, R.A. (1997/1975) *A Realist Theory of Science*. London: Version.

18 Hand, R.J. (2006) *Terror on the Air!: Horror Radio in America, 1931–1952*. Jefferson, NC: Macfarland & Company. p. 7.

19 Bartholomew, R.E. (2001) *Little Green Men, Meowing Nuns and Head-Hunting Panics: A Study of Mass Psychogenic Illness and Social Delusion*. Jefferson, NC: Macfarland & Company. p. 217.

20 Thatcher, M. (1987) Interview for *Woman's Own* ("No such thing as society"), *Margaret Thatcher Foundation*. Available at: www.margaretthatcher.org/speeches/displaydocment.asp?docid=106689

21 Shively, W.P. (2005) *The Craft of Political Research*. London: Prentice-Hall.

22 Scott, J. (2001) *Power.* Cambridge: Polity Press.

23 Mann, M. (1986) *The Sources of Social Power: Volume 1, A History of Power from the Beginning to AD 1760.* Cambridge: Cambridge University Press; Mann, M. (1993) *The Sources of Social Power: Volume 2, The Rise of Classes and Nation States 1760– 1914.* Cambridge: Cambridge University Press.

24 Mann, M. (2011) *Power in the 21st Century.* Cambridge: Polity Press.

25 Weber, M. (1922) *Economy and Society: An Outline of Interpretive Sociology* (G. Roth and G. Wittich, trans.). New York: Bedminster Press.

26 Dobratz, B., Buzzell, T.L. and Waldner, L. (2010) *Political Sociology: Debates in the Sociology of Power.* New Jersey: Pearson Education.

27 Draper, A. and Kesselman, M. (2010) *Politics of Power.* London: W. W. Norton.

28 Glenn, H.P. (2000) *Legal Traditions of the World.* Oxford: Oxford University Press. pp. 282–291.

29 Baali, F. (1988) *Society, State, and Urbanism: Ibn Khaldun's Sociological Thought.* New York: State University of New York Press. p. 88.

30 Plato, *Laws*, Book 3.5.

31 Machiavelli, N. (1984) *The Prince* (D. Donno, trans.). London: Bantam Classics.

32 Pareto, V. (1963) *A Treatise on General Sociology.* New York: Dover Publications.

33 Gramsci, A. (1971) *Selections from the Prison Notebooks* (Q. Hoare and G. Smith, eds and trans.). London: Lawrence and Wishart.

34 Nye, J.S. (2004) *Soft Power: The Means to Success in World Politics.* Jackson: Public Affairs.

35 Radkau, J. (2009) *Max Weber: A Biography.* Cambridge: Polity Press.

36 Weber, M. (1922/1978) *Economy and Society.* California: University of California Press. p. 212.

37 Pye, L.W. and Pye, M.W. (1985) *Asian Power and Politics: The Cultural Dimensions of Authority.* London: Belknap Press.

38 Wittfogel, K. (1957) *Oriental Despotism: A Comparative Study of Total Power.* New Haven, CT: Yale University Press.

39 Ladkin, D and Taylor, S.S. (2010) 'Enacting the "true self": Towards a theory of embodied authentic leadership', *Leadership Quarterly*, 21: 64–74.

40 Gilley, B. (2006) 'The meaning and measure of state legitimacy: Results for 72 countries', *European Journal of Political Research*, 45(3): 499–525.

41 Ankerl, G. (1980) *Toward a Social Contract on a Worldwide Scale.* Geneva: ILO.

42 Suchman, M.C. (1995) 'Managing legitimacy: Strategic and institutional approaches', *Academy of Management Journal*, 20(3): 571–610.

43 Weber, M. (1958) *The Protestant Ethic and the Spirit of Capitalism.* New York: Charles Scribner's Sons.

44 Weber, M. (1947) *The Theory of Social and Economic Organization* (A.M. Henderson and T. Parsons, trans.). London: Collier Macmillan.

45 Sharp, R. and Green, A. (1975) *Education and Social Control.* London: Routledge.

46 Walford, G. (1994) *Researching the Powerful in Education.* London: UCL Press.

47 Harber, C. (2004) *Schooling as Violence: How Schools Harm Pupils and Societies.* London: Routledge.

48 Weber, M. (1922/1978) *Economy and Society.* California: University of California Press.

49 Marx, K. and Engels, F. (1848/1998) *The Communist Manifesto.* New York: Penguin.

50 Marx, K. (1859/1979) *A Contribution to the Critique of Political Economy.* New York: International Publishers. Preface.

51 Parsons, T. (1969) *Politics and Social Structure.* New York: The Free Press.

52 Foucault, M. (1988) *Madness and Civilisation: A History of Insanity in the Age of Reason*. London: Vintage.

53 Lassman, P. (2010) *Pluralism*. Cambridge: Polity Press.

54 Dahl, R.A. (1961) *Who Governs?* New Haven: Yale University Press.

55 Peterson, M. (2009) *An Introduction to Decision Theory*. Cambridge: Cambridge University Press.

56 Vroom, V.H. and Yetton, P.W. (1973) *Leadership and Decision Making*. Pittsburgh, PA: University of Pittsburgh Press.

57 Dunleavy, P. (1991) *Democracy, Bureaucracy and Public Choice: Economic Models in Political Science*. London: Pearson.

58 Urry, J. and Waleford, J. (eds) (1973) *Power in Britain*. London: Heinemann.

59 MacMillan, I.C. (1978) *Strategy Formulation: Political Concepts*. T Paul, MN: West Publishing.

60 Smith, J.M. (2003) *Seeds of Deception*. IA: Yes! Books.

61 Grek, S. (2010) 'International organisations and the shared constructions of policy "problems": Problematisation and change in education governance in Europe', *European Educational Research Journal*, 9(3): 396–406.

62 Forgacs, D. and Hobsbawm, E.J. (eds) (2000) *The Antonio Gramsci Reader: Selected Writings 1916–1935*. New York: New York University Press.

63 Lukes, S. (1974) *Power: A Radical View*. London: Macmillan.

64 Quigley, C. (1981) *The Anglo-American Establishment: From Rhodes to Cliveden*. New York: Books in Focus; Quigley, C. (1966/1975) *Tragedy and Hope: A History of the World in our Time*. New York: Macmillan.

65 Aaronovitch, D. (2009) *Voodoo Histories: The Role of the Conspiracy Theory in Shaping Modern History*. London: Jonathan Cape.

66 Westergaard, J. and Resler, H. (1976) *Class in a Capitalist Society*. Harmondsworth: Penguin.

67 *Iraq Body Count*. Available at: www.iraqbodycount.org/

68 Morrell, K. (2009) 'Governance and the public good,' *Public Administration,* 87(3): 538–556.

69 Harper, C.L. (1993*) Exploring Social Change*. Engelwood Cliffs, NJ: Prentice-Hall.

70 Kynaston, D. (2010) 'Prime minister's questions', in *The Guardian (Review),* 8 May: 4.

71 Gaventa, J. (2006) 'Finding the spaces for change: A power analysis', *IBS Bulletin*, 27(6): 23–33.

72 Shackman, G., Liu, Ya-Lin and Wang, G. (Xun) (2002) *Why Does a Society Develop the Way it Does?* Available at: http://gsociology.icaap.org/report/summary2.htm

73 Nagel, T. (2005) 'The problem of global justice', *Philosophy & Public Affairs*, 33(2): 113–147.

74 Appiah, K.A. (2006) *Cosmopolitanism: Ethics in a World of Strangers*. New York: W.W. Norton.

75 Held, D. and McGrew, A. (eds) (2007) *Globalization Theory: Approaches and Controversies*. Cambridge: Cambridge University Press.

76 Williams, C. (2010) 'Global justice and education: from nation to neuron' *Educational Review*, 62(3): 343–356.

77 Kallinikos, J. (2011) *Governing Through Technology: Information Artefacts and Social Practice*. London: Palgrave Macmillan; Homburg, V. (2008) *Understanding E-Government: Information Systems in Public Administration*. London: Routledge.

78 *Digital Governance*. Available at: www.cddc.vt.edu/digitalgov/gov-menu.html

79 BBC (2011) 'LulSec hackers claim CIA website shutdown', *BBC News Online*, 16 June.

80 Nye, J. (2011) *The Future of Power*. New York: Public Affairs.

81 O'Rioden, T. (1981) 'Ecocentrism and technocentrism', in M.J. Smith (ed.), *Thinking Through the Environment: A Reader*. Milton Keynes: Open University. pp. 32–40.

82 Kirilenko, A., Samadi, M., Kyle, A.S. and Tuzun, T. (2011) 'The flash crash: The impact of High Frequency Trading on an electronic market', working paper. Available at: http://papers.ssrn.com/sol3/papers.cfm?abstract_id=1686004

83 US Army research contracts. Available at: www.dodsbir.net/selections/abs2011-1/armyabs111.htm

84 Weinberger, S. (2011) 'Terrorist "pre-crime" detector field tested in United States Screening system aims to pinpoint passengers with malicious intentions', *Nature News*. Available at: www.nature.com/news/2011/110527/full/news.2011.323.html

85 Bottomore, T.B. (1993) *Elites and Society*. London: Routledge.

86 Ward, L.F. (1907) 'Social Darwinism', *American Journal of Sociology*, 12: 709–710.

87 Galton, F. (1869) *Hereditary Genius*. London: Macmillan.

88 Engs, R.C. (2005) *The Eugenics Movement: An Encyclopedia*. Westport, CT: Greenwood Publishing Group.

89 Mills, C.W. (1956) *White Collar: The American Middle Classes*. New York: Oxford University Press.

90 Parry, G. (1971) *Political Elites*. London: George Allen and Unwin. pp. 95, 97.

91 Crewe, I. (1974) 'Introduction: Studying elites in Britain', in I. Crewe (ed.), *British Sociology Yearbook: Elites in Western Democracy*. London: Croom Helm.

92 Moysner, G. (1988) 'Non-standard interviewing in elite research', in R.G. Burgess (ed.), *Studies in Qualitative Methodology*. Greenwich: JAI Press. p. 111.

93 Menges, C.C. (n.d.) *Ruling Elite Theories and Research Methods: An Evaluation*. Santa Monica: RAND Corporation.

94 Kerbo, H.R. and Della Fave, L.R. (1979) 'The empirical side of the power elite debate: An assessment and critique of recent research', *The Sociological Quarterly*, 20: 5–22.

95 Domhoff, G.W. (1980) *Power Structure Research*. London: Sage.

96 Moysner, G. and Wagstaffe, M. (eds) (1987) *Research Methods for Elite Studies*. London: Allen & Unwin; Moysner, G. (1988) 'Non-standard interviewing in elite research', in R.G. Burgess (ed.), *Studies in Qualitative Methodology*. Greenwich: JAI Press.

97 Hertz, R. and Imber, J.B. (1993) 'Fieldwork in elite settings', *Journal of Contemporary Ethnography*, 22 (3): 3–122.

98 Hertz, R. and Imber, J.B. (1995) *Studying Elites Using Qualitative Methods*. London: Sage.

99 Walford, G. (1994) 'Reflexions on researching the powerful', in G. Walford, *Researching the Powerful in Education*. London: UCL Press.

100 Lasswell, H.D., Lerner, D. and Rothwell, C.E. (1952) *The Comparative Study of Elites*. Stanford: Stanford University Press.

101 Conniff, M.L. and McCann, F.D. (1991) *Modern Brazil: Elites and Masses in Historical Perspective*. Nebraska: University of Nebraska Press.

102 Farmer, K.C. (1992) *The Soviet Administrative Elite*. Santa Barbara: Greenwood Press.

103 Walden, G. (2000) *The New Elites: Making a Career in the Masses*. London: Allen Lane.

104 Kerbo, H.K and McKinsky, J.A. (1995) *Who Rules Japan: The Inner Circles of Economic and Political Power*. Santa Barbara: Greenwood Press; Scalapino, R.A. (1972) *Elites in the People's Republic of China*. Washington: University of Washington Press.

105 Schattschneider, E.E. (1960) *The Semi-Sovereign People*. New York: Holt, Reinhart and Winston. p. 35.

106 Dahl, R.A. (1972) *Polyarchy: Participation and Opposition*. Connecticut: Yale University Press.

107 Keller, S. (1991) *Beyond the Ruling Class: Strategic Elites in Modern Society*. New Brunswick: Transaction Publishers.

108 Best, H. and Higley, J. (2010) *Democratic Elites: New Theoretical and Comparative Perspectives*. Boston: Brill Academic Publishers; Bealey, F. (1996) 'Democratic elitism and the autonomy of elites', *International Political Science Review*, 17(3): 319–331.

109 Eldersveld, S. (1991) *Political Elites in Modern Societies*. Michigan: Michigan University Press.

110 Robinson, A. (2011) *Genius: A Very Short Introduction*. Oxford: Oxford University Press.

111 Parry, G. (1971) *Political Elites*. London: George Allen and Unwin. pp. 95,120.

112 Bottomore, T.B. (1993) *Elites and Society*. London: Routledge.

113 Walden, G. (2001) *The New Elites*. London: Penguin.

114 Grupp, J. (2007) *Corporatism: The Secret Government of the New World Order*. California: Progressive Press.

115 Michels, R. (1915) *Political Parties: A Sociological Study of the Oligarchical Tendencies of Modern Democracy* (E. Paul and C. Paul, trans.) New York: The Free Press.

116 Mills, C. W. (1956) *The Power Elite*. New York: Oxford University Press.

117 Porter, J. (1965) *The Vertical Mosaic: An Analysis of Social Class and Power in Canada*. Toronto: University of Toronto Press.

118 Porter, M. (1979) 'How competitive forces shape strategy', *Harvard Business Review*, March/April: 20.

119 Lawrence, B. and Glickman, L.B. (2009) *Buying Power: A History of Consumer Activism in America*. Chicago: University of Chicago Press.

120 *The Consumer Activism Project*. Available at: http://web.whittier.edu/academic/political science/tcap.htm

121 Corporate Watch (2002) *The Corporate Watch DIY Guide to How to Research Companies*. Available at: www.corporatewatch.org.uk

122 Hunter, F. (1953) *Community Power Structure: A Study of Decision Makers*. Chapel Hill, NC: University of North Carolina Press.

123 DiTomaso, N. (1980) 'Organizational analysis and power structure research', in G.W. Domhoff, *Power Structure Research*. London: Sage.

124 Burris, V. (1991) 'Director interlocks and the political behaviour of corporations and corporate elites', *Social Science Quarterly,* 72: 637–651.

125 Useem, M. (1984) *The Inner Circle*. Oxford: Oxford University Press.

126 Ostranda, S. (1984) *Women of the Upper Class*. Philadelphia: Temple University Press.

127 Carroll, W.K. (2010) *The Making of a Transnational Capitalist Class: Corporate Power in the 21st Century*. London: Zed Books.

128 Hambrick, D.C. and Mason, P.A. (1984) 'Upper echelons: The organisation as a reflection of its top managers,' *Academy of Management Review*, 9(2): 193–206.

129 Cormode, L. and Hughes, A. (eds) (1999) 'Networks, cultures and elite research: The economic geographer as situated researcher', *Geoforum*, 30: 299–363.

130 Lee, J. (2010) 'The significance of reputational risk: New evidence in small island offshore financial centres', working paper. Available at: http://ssrn.com/abstract=1647414

131 Harquail, C.V. (2011) 'Action branding: Using activity streams to authenticate identity claims', *Authentic Organizations*. Available at: http://authenticorganizations.com/harquail/2011/03/23/action-branding-using-activity-streams-to-authenticate-identity-claims/

132 Bourdieu, P. (1984) *Distinction*. London: Routledge; Bourdieu, P. (1991) *Language and Symbolic Power*. Cambridge: Polity Press; Bourdieu, P. (1993) *The Field of Cultural Production*. Cambridge: Polity Press.

133 Bourdieu, P. (1998) *The State of the Nobility: Elite Schools in the Field of Power*. Cambridge: Polity Press.

134 Bourdieu, P. and Passeron, J.C. (1990) *Reproduction in Education and Culture*. London: Sage. p. 5; Harker, R. (1990) 'Education and cultural capital' in R. Harker, C. Mahar and C. Wilkes (eds), *An Introduction to the Work of Pierre Bourdieu: The Practice of Theory*. London: Macmillan Press.

135 Bowles, S. and Gintis, H. (1976) *Schooling in Capitalist America*. Routledge: London.

136 Cookson, P.W. and Hodges Persell, C. (1985) *Preparing for Power: America's Elite Boarding Schools*. New York: Basic Books.

137 Haas, P.M. (1992) 'Introduction. Epistemic communities and international policy coordination', *International Organization*, 46(1): 1–35.

138 Wenger, E. (1998) *Communities of Practice: Learning, Meaning and Identity*. Cambridge: Cambridge University Press.

139 Wagner, C.S. (2008) *The New Invisible College: Science for Development*. Washington DC: Brooking Press.

140 Knorr-Cetina, K.D. (eds) (1983) *Science Observed: Perspectives on the Social Study of Science*. London: Sage. pp. 132–133.

141 Hughes, A. and Cormode, L. (1998) 'Researching elites and elite spaces', *Environment and Planning*, 30: 2098–2100; Woods, M. (1998) 'Rethinking elites: Networks, space, and local politics', *Environment and Planning*, 30: 2101–2119; Desmond, M. (2004) 'Methodological challenges posed in studying an elite in the field', *Area*, 36 (3): 262–269.

142 Ward, K.G. and Jones, M. (1999) 'Researching local elites: Reflexivity, "situatedness" and political-temporal contingency', *Geoforum*, 30: 301–312.

143 Desmond, M. (2004) 'Methodological challenges posed in studying an elite in the field', *Area*, 36(3): 262–269.

144 *Global Nomadic Leaders*. Available at: www.mkbconseil.ch/

145 Greenberg, B. (1947) 'Some relations between territory, social hierarchies, and leadership in the Green Sunfish', *Physiological Zoology*, 20(3): 267–299.

146 Young, M. (1958/1994) *The Rise of the Meritocracy*. New Jersey: Transaction Publishers.

147 Lee, Y.-J. (2010) 'Leadership and development in South Korea and Egypt: The significance of cultural shifts', unpublished PhD thesis, School of Oriental and Asian Studies, University of London. p. 254.

148 O'Donnell, G. (1986) *Transitions from Authoritarian Rule*. Baltimore: Johns Hopkins University Press; Higley, J. and Burton, M.G. (1989) 'The elite variable in democratic transitions and breakdowns', *American Sociology Review*, 54: 17–32; Lengyel, G. and Tholen, J. (eds) (2007) *Restructuring of the Economic Elites After State Socialism: Recruitment, Institutions and Attitudes*. Stuttgart: Ibidem.

149 Perthes, V. (ed.) (2004) *Arab Elites: Negotiating the Politics of Change*. Boulder, CO: Lynne Rienner Publishers.

150 Burton, M.G. and Higley, J. (2001) 'The study of political elite transformations', *International Review of Sociology*, 11(2): 181–199.

151 Rothkopf, D. (2008) *Superclass: The Global Power Elite and the World They Are Making*. London: Farrar, Straus and Giroux.

152 Dorling, D. (2010) *Injustice: Why Social Inequality Persists*. Bristol: Policy Press.

153 Pilger, J. (2002) *The New Rulers of the World*. London: Verso.

154 Pinker, S. (1997) *How the Mind Works*. London: Allen Lane. p. 494–502.

155 Smith, K.B. (2004) 'Evolutionary theory and political leadership: Why certain people do not trust decision-makers', *Midwest Political Science Association*, Chicago, April 2004.

156 Alford, J.R., Funk, C.L. and Hibbing, J.R. (2005) 'Are political orientations genetically transmitted?', *American Political Science Review*, 99(2): 153–167.

157 Oxley, R.D. et al. (2008) 'Political attitudes vary with physiological traits', *Science*, 321: 1667–1670; Balzer, A. et al. (2010) 'Liberals roll with the good; conservatives confront the bad: Physiological and cognitive differences across the political spectrum', *Midwest Political Science Association*, Chicago, April 2010.

158 Marx, K. and Engels, F. (1848/1998) *The Communist Manifesto*. New York: Penguin.

159 Toynbee, A.J. (1934–1961) *A Study of History* (Volumes I–XII). Oxford: Oxford University Press.

160 Lotter, S. (2004) 'Studying-up those who fell down: Elite transformation in Nepal', *Anthropology Matters*, 6(2).

161 Mosca, G. (1939) *The Ruling Class*. New York: McGraw Hill.

162 Williams, C. (2006) *Leadership Accountability in a Globalizing World*. London: Palgrave Macmillan. pp. 138–149.

163 Shirky, C. (2011) 'Political power and social media: Technology, the public sphere, and political change', *Foreign Affairs*, February.

164 Whittam Smith, A. (2011) 'Protest movements don't need a spearhead to be successful', *The Independent* (Viewspaper), 20 January: 5.

165 *Edge Foundation*. Available at: www.edge.org/about_edge.html

166 Tainter, J. (1990) *The Collapse of Complex Societies*. Cambridge: Cambridge University Press.

167 Quigley, C. (1966/1975) *Tragedy and Hope: A History of the World in our Time*. New York: Macmillan.

168 Tainter, J. (1990) *The Collapse of Complex Societies*. Cambridge: Cambridge University Press.

169 Diamond, J. (2005) *Collapse: How Societies Choose to Fail or Survive*. London: Allen Lane.

170 McAnany, P.A. and Yoffee, N. (eds) (2009) *Questioning Collapse: Human Resilience, Ecological Vulnerability, and the Aftermath of Empire*. Cambridge: Cambridge University Press.

171 Laslo, E. and Seidel P. (eds) (2006) *Global Survival: The Challenge and its Implications for Thinking and Acting*. New York: Club of Budapest/Select Books. See Chapter 16 – Williams, C. 'Educating world leaders'; Chapter 14 – Lamm, R.D. 'Governance barriers to sustainability'.

172 Khaldun, Ibn (1967/2004) *The Muqaddimah: An Introduction to History* (F. Rosenthal, trans., N.J. Dawood and B. Lawrence, eds). New Jersey: Princeton University Press. p. 106.

173 Warhol, A. (1968) Comment in catalogue for Andy Warhol's exhibition at the Moderna Museet, Stockholm, February–March.

174 Bass, B.M. and Stodgill, R.M. (1990) *Bass & Stogdill's Handbook of Leadership: Theory, Research and Management Applications*. New York: The Free Press. p. 3.

175 Ciulla, J.B. (1998) *Ethics: The Heart of Leadership*. London: Praeger. p. 10.

176 Bass, B.M. and Stodgill, R.M. (1990) *Bass & Stogdill's Handbook of Leadership: Theory, Research and Management Applications*. New York: The Free Press. p. 3.

177 Bass, B.M. and Bass, R. (2008) *The Bass Handbook of Leadership: Theory, Research, and Managerial Applications*, 4th edn. New York: Free Press.

178 Stogdill, R.M. (1948) 'Personal factors associated with leadership: A survey of the literature', *Journal of Psychology*, 25: 35–71.

179 Northouse, P.G. (2009) *Leadership: Theory and Practice*. London: Sage.

180 Bryman, A. et al. (2011) *The Sage Handbook of Leadership*. London: Sage.

181 Chemers, M.M. (2000) 'Leadership research and theory: A functional integration', *Group Dynamics: Theory, Research, and Practice*, 4(1): 27–43.

182 Northouse, P.G. (2011) *Introduction to Leadership: Interactive eBook*. New York: Sage.

183 Zaccaro, S. J. (2007) 'Trait-based perspectives of leadership', *American Psychologist*, 62: 6–16.

184 Hegel, G.W. (1820/1896) *Philosophy of Right* (F.S.W. Dyde, trans.). Available at: www.marxists.org/reference/archive/hegel/works/pr/preface.htm

185 Bryman, A. (1992) *Charisma and Leadership in Organizations*. London: Sage.

186 Lasswell, H. (1930/1986) *Psychopathology and Politics*. London: University of Chicago Press.

187 Lasswell, H. (1948/1967) *Power and Personality*. London: Viking.

188 Chemers, M.M. (2000) 'Leadership research and theory: A functional integration', *Group Dynamics: Theory, Research, and Practice*, 4(1): 33–34.

189 Morrison, A.M., White, R.P and van Velsor, E. (1994) *Breaking the Glass Ceiling: Can Women Reach the Top of America's Largest Corporations?* New York: Basic Books.

190 Coughlin, L., Wingard, E. and Hollihan, K. (2005) *Enlightened Power: How Women are Transforming the Practice of Leadership*. New York: Jossey-Bass.

191 Eagly, A.H. and Karau, S.J. (1991) 'Gender and the emergence of leaders: A meta-analysis', *Journal of Personality and Social Psychology*, 60: 685–710; Eagly, A.H. and Karau, S.J. (2002) 'Role congruity theory of prejudice toward female leaders', *Psychological Review*, 109: 573–598.

192 Spencer, H. (1841) *The Study of Sociology*. New York: D.A. Appleton.

193 Fiedler, F.E. (1967) *A Theory of Leadership Effectiveness*. New York: McGraw-Hill.

194 Hall, M.L. (2007) 'Communicating subjectivity: Leadership as situated construction', *Atlantic Journal of Communication*, 15(3): 194–213.

195 Bligh, M.C. et al. (2004) 'Charisma under crisis: Presidential leadership, rhetoric, and media responses before and after the September 11 terrorist attacks', *Leadership Quarterly*, 15: 211–239.

196 Mullin, G.H. (2001) *The Fourteen Dalai Lamas: A Sacred Legacy of Reincarnation*. Santa Fe, NM: Clear Light Publishers.

197 Kenny, D.A. and Zaccaro, S.J. (1983) 'An estimate of variance due to traits in leadership', *Journal of Applied Psychology*, 68: 678–685.

198 Mumford, M.D. et al. (2000) 'Leadership skills for a changing world solving complex social problems', *The Leadership Quarterly*, 11: 11–35.

199 Mumford, M.D. and Strange, J.M. (2002) 'Vision and mental models: The case of charismatic and ideological leadership', in B.J. Avolio and F.J. Yammarino (eds), *Charismatic and Transformational Leadership: The Road Ahead*. Oxford: Elsevier. pp. 109–142.

200 Zaccaro, S.J. (2007) 'Trait-based perspectives of leadership', *American Psychologist*, 62: 6–16.

201 Lewin, K., Lipitt, R. and White, R. (1939) 'Patterns of aggressive behaviour in experimentally created social climates', *Journal of Social Psychology*, 10: 272–301.

202 Avolio, B.J. et al. (1999) 'A funny thing happened on the way to the bottom line: Humor as a moderator of leadership style effects', *The Academy of Management Journal*, 42(2): 219–227.

203 Blake, R. and Mouton, J. (1964) *The Managerial Grid: The Key to Leadership Excellence*. Houston: Gulf Publishing.

204 Hackman, J.R. and Walton, R.E. (1986) 'Leading groups in organizations', in P.S. Goodman (ed.), *Designing Effective Work Groups*. San Francisco: Jossey-Bass.

205 George, J.M. (2000) 'Emotions and leadership: The role of emotional intelligence', *Human Relations,* 53: 1027–1055; Cote, S. and Saavedra, R. (2005) 'The contagious leader: Impact of the leader's mood on the mood of group members, group affective tone, and group processes', *Journal of Applied Psychology*, 90(2): 295–305.

206 Burns, J.M. (1978) *Leadership*. New York: Harper & Row.

207 Bass, B.M. (1990) 'From transactional to transformational leadership: Learning to share the vision', *Organizational Dynamics*, 18(3): 19–31. Bass, B.M. (1997) 'Does the transactional–transformational leadership paradigm transcend organizational and national borders?' *American Psychologist*, 52(2): 130–139.

208 Haslam, S.A. et al (2010) *The New Psychology of Leadership: Identity, Influence and Power*. London: Psychology Press.

209 Terry, R.W. (1993) *Authentic Leadership: Courage in Action*. San Francisco: Jossey-Bass; Ladkin, D. and Taylor, S.S. (2010) 'Enacting the "true self": Towards a theory of embodied authentic leadership', *Leadership Quarterly*, 21: 64–74.

210 Williams, C. and Lee, Y.-J. (2005) 'The minds of leaders', in B. Walker (ed.), *Preparing for Peace*. Westmorland: General meeting. (3.1 'self-perception'.)

211 Gardener, H. (1995) *Leading Minds: An Anatomy of Leadership*. New York: Basic Books. p. 6.

212 Grint, K. (2000) *The Arts of Leadership*. Oxford: Oxford University Press.

213 Peck, E. (2009) *Performing Leadership*. London: Palgrave Macmillan.

214 Ladkin, D. (2008) 'Leading beautifully: How mastery, congruence and purpose create the aesthetic of embodied leadership practice', *Leadership Quarterly*, 19: 31–41.

215 Stumpf, S. and Mullen, T. (1991) 'Strategic leadership: Concepts, skills, style, and process', *Journal of Management Development*, 10(1): 42–53.

216 Bryman, A. et al. (2011) *The Sage Handbook of Leadership*. London: Sage.

217 Pearce, C.L. and Conger, J.A. (2003) *Shared Leadership: Reframing the Hows and Whys of Leadership*. Thousand Oaks, CA: Sage.

218 Chrislip, D. (2002), *The Collaborative Leadership Fieldbook – A Guide for Citizens and Civic Leaders*. Hobokem: Jossey-Bass.

219 Gronn, P. (2002) 'Distributed leadership as a unit of analysis', *Leadership Quarterly*, 13: 423–451; Spillane, J.P. (2006) *Distributed Leadership*. Hoboken: Jossey-Bass Library/Wiley.

220 Greenleaf, R. (2002) *Servant Leadership*. Mahwa, NJ: Paulist Press.

221 Hughes, R.L., Ginnet, R.C. and Curphy, G.J. (2008) *Leadership: Enhancing the Lessons of Experience*. Maidenhead: McGrawHill. pp. 109, 124, 138.

222 Kaiser, R.B., Hogan, R. and Craig, S.B. (2008) 'Leadership and the fate of Organizations', *American Psychologist*, 63: 96–110.

223 Cattell, R.B. and Stice, G.F. (1954) 'Four formula for selecting leaders on the basis of personality', *Human Relations*, 7: 493–507.

224 Browne, C.G. and Cohn, T.S. (eds) (1958) *The Study of Leadership*. Illinois: Interstate. (Part 2 – Identifying leaders and leadership behaviour, pp. 87–224.); Fiedler, F.E. (1996) 'Research on leadership selection and training: One view of the future', *Administrative Science*, 41: 241–250.

225 Bass, B.M. (1949) 'An analysis of the leaderless group discussion', *Journal of Applied Psychiatry*, 33: 527–533.

226 Adair, J. (1988) *Effective Leadership*. London: Pan Books.

227 Tannenbaum, R. and Schmidt, W.H. (1958) 'How to choose a leadership pattern', *Harvard Business Review*, 36: 95–101.

228 House, R. and Podsakoff, P.M (1994) 'Leadership effectiveness: Past perspectives and future directions for research', in J. Greenberg (ed.), *Organizational Behavior: The State of the Science*. Hillsdale, NJ: Erlbaum Associates. pp. 45–82.

229 Stout, L. (2006) *Ideal Leadership: Time for a Change*. Shippensburg: Destiny Image Publishing.

230 Carmazzi, A.F. (2002) *Identity Intelligence: The Force for Making the Right Decisions for Personal and Professional Success*. Scotts Valley: Create space; 'Identity intelligence'. Available at: http://directivecommunication.com/products_page/identity_intelligence.php

231 Blondel, J. (1987) *Political Leadership*. London: Sage.

232 Sartori, G. (1987) *Democratic Theory Revisited*. New Jersey: Chatham House Publishers.

233 Paige, G.D. (1977) *The Scientific Study of Political Leadership*. London: The Free Press. p. 11.

234 Suh, D-s and Lee, Chea-jin (1976) *Political Leadership in Korea*. Washington: University of Washington Press.

235 Elcock, H. (2001) *Political Leadership*. Cheltenham: Edward Elgar. p. 16.

236 Korosenyi, A., Slomp, G. and Femia, J. (2009) *Political Leadership in Liberal and Democratic Theory*. Charlottesville: Imprint Academic.

237 Kellerman, B. (1984) *Political Leadership: A Source Book*. Pittsburgh: University of Pittsburgh Press; Ludwig, A.M. (2002) *King of the Mountain: The Nature of Political Leadership*. Lexington: University Press of Kentucky.

238 Morrell, K. and Hartley, J. (2006) 'A model of political leadership', *Human Relations*, 59: 483–504.

239 Post, J.M. (2003) *The Psychological Assessment of Political Leaders*. Michigan: University of Michigan Press.

240 Ward, K.G. and Jones, M. (1999) 'Researching local elites: Reflexivity, situatedness and political–temporal contingency', *Geoforum*, 30: 301–312.

241 Berg, R. and Rao, N. (2006) *Transforming Local Political Leadership*. London: Palgrave; Gains, F., Greasley, S.J. and Stoker, G. (2009) 'The impact of political leadership on organisational performance: Evidence from English urban government', *Local Government Studies*, 35(1): 75–94.

242 Collinge, C., Gibney, J. and Mabey, C. (2010) 'Leadership and place', special issue, *Policy Studies*, 31(4): 367–378.

243 Barker, C., Johnson, A. and Lavalette, M. (eds) (2001) *Leadership and Social Movements*. Manchester: Manchester University Press.

244 Whicker, M.L. (1996) *Toxic Leaders: When Organizations go Bad*. Westport, CT: Quorum Books.

245 Lipman-Blumen, J. (2004) *The Allure of Toxic Leaders: Why We Follow Destructive Bosses and Corrupt Politicians – and How We Can Survive Them*. New York: Oxford University Press.

246 Kellerman, B. (2004) *Bad Leadership: What it is, How it Happens, Why it Matters*. Cambridge, MA: Harvard Business School Press.

247 Turknett, R.L. and Turknett, C.N. (2005) *Decent People, Decent Company: How to Lead with Character in Work and in Life*. Boston: Intercultural Press.

248 Price, T.L. (2005) *Understanding Ethical Failures in Leadership*. Cambridge: Cambridge University Press.

249 Janis, I.L. (1972) *Victims of Groupthink*. Orlando: Houghton Mifflin Harcourt.

250 Johnson, D. (2005) *Overconfidence and War: The Havoc and Glory of Positive Illusions*. Harvard: Harvard University Press.

251 Lammers, J. and Stapel, D.A. (2010) 'Power increases hypocrisy: Moralizing in reasoning, immorality in behaviour', *Psychological Science*, 21: 737–744.

252 Anderson, C. and Galinsky, A.D. (2006) 'Power, optimism, and risk-taking', *European Journal of Social Psychology*, 36: 511–536.

253 Belsky, G. and Gilovich, T. (2000) *Why Smart People Make Big Money Mistakes – and How to Correct Them: Lessons from the New Science of Behavioural Economics*. New York: Fireside Books.

254 Bullock, A. (1990) *Hitler: A study in tyranny*. London: Penguin.

255 Baron-Cohen, S. (2011) *Zero Degrees of Empathy: A new theory of human cruelty*. London: Allen Lane.

256 Lammers, J. and Stapel, D.A. (2010) 'Power increases dehumanization', *Group Processes & Intergroup Relations,* DOI: 10.1177/1368430210370042

257 Robertson, Geoffrey (2005) *The tyrannicide brief.* London Chatto & Windus.

258 Banks, S.P. (2008) *Dissent and the Failure of Leadership.* Cheltenham: Edward Elgar.

259 Williams, C. (2006) *Leadership Accountability in a Globalizing World.* London: Palgrave Macmillan. pp. 110–119.

260 Ciulla, J.B. (ed.) (1998) *Ethics at the Heart of Leadership.* Westport: Praeger.

261 Lammers, J. and Stapel, D.A. (2009) 'How power influences moral thinking', *Journal of Personality and Social Psychology,* 97: 279–289.

262 Jonker, J. and de Witte, M. (eds) (2006) *Management Models for Corporate Social Responsibility.* New York: Springer.; Horrigan, B. (2010) *Corporate Social Responsibility in the 21st Century.* Cheltenham: Edward Elgar.

263 Williams, C. (2006) *Leadership Accountability in a Globalizing World.* London: Palgrave Macmillan.

264 Krieck, E. (1938) *Nationalpolitische Erzeihung.* Armanen Verlag: Leipzig.

265 Martin, M. (2002) *Leadership in a Globalizing World: Addressing the Challenges.* Geneva: University of Geneva. (Working paper series.)

266 Dickson, M.W., Den Hartog, D.N. and Mitchelson, J.K. (2003) 'Research on leadership in a cross-cultural context: Making progress, and raising new questions', *The Leadership Quarterly,* 14: 729–768.

267 Mendenhall, M., Osland, J., Bird, A., Oddou, G.R. and Maznevski, M.L. (2007) *Global Leadership: Research, Practice and Development.* London: Routledge.

268 House, R.J. (2010) *Global Leadership and Organizational Behavior Effectiveness Research Project.* Wharton School of Business, University of Pennsylvania. Available at: http://knowledge.wharton.upenn.edu/paper.cfm?paperid=660

269 Beck, U. (2008) *World at Risk.* Cambridge: Polity.

270 Amerasinghe, C.F. (1994) *The Law of the International Civil Service.* Oxford: Oxford University Press.

271 Williams, C. (2001) *Leaders of Integrity: Ethics and a Code for Global Leadership.* Amman: UN University Leadership Academy.

272 Hutchings, K. (2010) *Global Ethics: An Introduction.* Cambridge: Polity.

273 Knickerbocker, I. (1958) 'The analysis of leadership', in C.G. Browne and T.S. Cohn (eds), *The Study of Leadership.* Illinois: Interstate. pp. 3–11.

274 Lord, R.G. and Emrich, C.G. (2001) 'Thinking outside the box: Extending the cognitive revolution in leadership research,' *The Leadership Quarterly,* 11(4): 551–579.

275 Hughes, R.L., Ginnett, R.C. and Curphy, G.J. (1999) *Leadership: Enhancing the Lessons of Experience.* Boston: McGraw-Hill. p. 12.

276 Gamson, J. (1995) 'Stopping the spin and becoming a prop: Fieldwork on Hollywood elites', in R. Hertz and J.B. Imber (1995), *Studying Elites Using Qualitative Methods.* London: Sage. p. 86.

277 Bass, B.M. (2005) *Transformational Leadership.* Hillsdale: Lawrence Erlbaum Associates.

278 Lee, Y.-J. (2010) 'Leadership and development in South Korea and Egypt: The significance of "cultural shifts"', unpublished PhD, School of Oriental and African Studies (SOAS), University of London.

279 Browne, C.G and Cohn, T.S. (eds) (1958) *The Study of Leadership.* Illinois: Interstate. pp. 417–481.

280 Williams, C. (2006) 'Educating world leaders' in E. Laszlo and P. Seidel (eds), *Global Survival.* New York: Club of Budapest/Select Books.

281 Kelly, J. (2011) 'How do you spot a future world leader?', *BBC News Online*, 29 March.

282 Prince II, H. (2010) *Teaching Leadership: A Journey into the Unknown.* Available at: www.utexas.edu/lbj/research/leadership/publications/teaching_leadership.pdf

283 Browne, C.G and Cohn, T.S. (eds) (1958) *The Study of Leadership.* Illinois: Interstate.

284 Grint, K. (2000) *The Arts of Leadership.* Oxford: Oxford University Press.

285 Paige, G.D. (1977) *The Scientific Study of Political Leadership.* London: The Free Press. p. 13.

286 Mill, J.S. (1859) 'On liberty', *Library of Liberal Arts.* Available at: www.serendipity.li/jsmill/jsmill.htm.

287 Hegel, G.W. (1820/1896) *Philosophy of Right* (F.S.W. Dyde, trans.). Available at: www.marxists.org/reference/archive/hegel/works/pr/preface.htm

288 Mackay, C. (1841) *Extraordinary Popular Delusions and the Madness of Crowds.* London: Wordsworth Editions.

289 Le Bon, G. (1896/2002) *The Crowd: A Study of the Popular Mind.* London: Dover Publications.

290 Trotter, W. (1914/19) *Instincts of the Herd in Peace and War.* New York: MacMillan.

291 McDougall, W. (1920/2009) *The Group Mind.* Charleston: Bibliobazaar.

292 Ortega y Gasset, J. (1930/1994) *The Revolt of the Masses.* London: W.W. Norton & Company.

293 Campbell, S. (1943) *The Menace of the Herd.* Milwaukee: The Bruce Publishing Company.

294 Lippitt, R. et al (1952) 'The dynamics of power', *Human Relations*, 5: 37–64.

295 Redl, F.(1958) 'Group emotion and leadership', in *The Study of Leadership.* Illinois: Interstate. pp. 26–30.

296 Herman, A. (1997) *The Idea of Decline in Western History.* New York: The Free Press.

297 Gray, J. (2007) *Black Mass: Apocalyptic Religion and the Death of Utopia.* London: Allen Lane.

298 Reich, W.(1933/1946/1980) *The Mass Psychology of Fascism.* New York: Farrar, Strauss and Giroux.

299 Milgram, S. (1974) *Obedience to Authority: An Experimental View.* New York: HarperCollins.

300 Moscovici, S. (1979) *Psychologie des Minorités Actives.* Paris: P.U.F.

301 Canetti, E. (1960) *Crowds and Power.* London: Viking.

302 Berk, R.A. (1974) *Collective Behavior.* Dubuque, IA: Wm. C. Brown; Turner, R. and Killian, L.M. (1993) *Collective Behavior.* Englewood Cliffs, NJ: Prentice Hall; Moscovici, S. (1981) *L'Age des Foules: Un Traité Historique de Psychologie des Masses.* Paris: Fayard.

303 Buford, B. (1991) *Among the Thugs: The Experience, and the Seduction, of Crowd Violence.* New York: W.W. Norton; Rheingold, H. (2003) *Smart Mobs: The Next Social Revolution.* London: Perseus Books.

304 McPhail, C.(1991) *The Myth of the Madding Crowd.* New York: Aldine de Gruyter; Surowiecki, J.(2004) *The Wisdom of Crowds: Why the Many are Smarter than the Few and How Collective Wisdom Shapes Business, Economies, Societies and Nations.* London: Doubleday.

305 Griffin, E. (1997) *A First Look at Communication Theory.* New York: McGraw-Hill. pp. 34–42.

306 Bormann, E.G., Cragan, J.F. and Shields, D.C. (1994) 'In defense of symbolic convergence theory: A look at the theory and its criticisms after two decades', *Communication Theory*, 4: 259–294.

307 Reicher, S.D. (1987) 'Crowd behaviour as social action', in J.C. Turner (ed.), *Rediscovering the Social Group: A Self-Categorisation Theory.* Oxford: Blackwell.

308 Suri, J. (2003) *Power and Protest: Global Revolution and the Rise of Détente.* Cambridge, MA: Harvard University Press.
309 Johnston, H. and Klandermans, B. (1995) *Social Movements and Culture: Social Movements, Protest and Contention.* Minnesota: University of Minnesota Press.
310 Beck, U. (1999) *What is Globalization?* Cambridge: Polity Press.
311 Williams, C. (2006) *Leadership Accountability in a Globalizing World.* London: Palgrave Macmillan.
312 Chomsky, N. (1999/2003) *Profit Over People: Neoliberalism and Global Order.* New York: Seven Stories Press.
313 Pilger, J. (2003) *The New Rulers of the World.* London: Verso.
314 Idle, N. and Nunns, A. (2011) *Tweets from Tahrir.* New York: OR Books.
315 Blumer, H.G. (1969) 'Collective behavior', in A. Lee (ed.), *Principles of Sociology.* New York: Barnes and Noble Books. pp. 65–121; Mauss, A.L. (1975) *Social Problems of Social Movements.* Philadelphia: Lippincott; Tilly, C. (1978) *From Mobilization to Revolution.* Reading, MA: Addison-Wesley.
316 Mayhew, H. (1951/1968) *London Labour and the London Poor* (3 vols). London: Dover Publications.
317 Chambers, R. (1983) *Rural Development: Putting the Last First.* London: Wiley.
318 Wilkinson, A. (1998) 'Empowerment: theory and practice', *Personnel Review,* 27(1): 40–56.
319 Sumner, A. and Tribe, M. (2008) *International Development Studies: Theories and Methods in Research and Practice.* London: Sage.
320 Sen, S. (1999) *Development as Freedom.* New York: Knopf.
321 Wilkinson, R. and Pickett, K. (2009) *The Spirit Level: Why More Equal Societies Almost Always Do Better.* London: Allen Lane.
322 UN (1985) *Declaration of Basic Principles of Justice for Victims of Crime and Abuse of Power* (Resolution 40/34 of 29 November). New York: UN General Assembly.
323 Williams, C. (1998) *Environmental Victims: New Risks, New Injustice.* London: Earthscan.
324 Williams, C. (1995) *Invisible Victims: Crime and Abuse Against People with Learning Disabilities.* London: Jessica Kingsley.
325 HRW (2000) *The Pinochet Precedent: How Victims Can Pursue Human Rights Criminals Abroad.* New York: Human Rights Watch.
326 Berry, J. and Renner, G. (2004) *Vows of Silence: The Abuse of Power in the Papacy of John Paul II.* New York: Free Press.
327 Demick, B. (2010) *Nothing to Envy: Real Lives in North Korea.* London: Granta.
328 Arnison, N. (1991) *Medical Testimony on Victims Of Torture: A Physicians' Guide to Political Asylum Cases.* London: Physicians for Human Rights.
329 Davis, A. (2010) *Political Communication and Social Theory.* London: Routledge.
330 Marvick, D. (ed.) (1977) *Harold D. Lasswell on Political Sociology.* Chicago: University of Chicago Press.
331 Lasswell, H. (1927/1971) *Propaganda Technique in the World War.* Cambridge MA: MIT Press.
332 Bernays, E. (1928) *Propaganda.* New York: Liveright.
333 Runciman, D. (2008) *Political Hypocrisy: The Mask of Power, from Hobbes to Orwell and Beyond.* Princeton, NJ: Princeton University Press; Williams, C. (2006) *Leadership Accountability in a Globalizing World.* London: Palgrave Macmillan.
334 *The Propaganda Project.* Available at: www.propagandaproject.org
335 Roberts, A.S. (2005) 'Spin control and freedom of information: Lessons for the United Kingdom from Canada', *Public Administration,* 83: 1.

336 Williams, C. (2011) 'Learning to redress pre-emptive deceit: The Iraq Dossier', *SAGE Open*, 1: 3; *Spinwatch*. Available at: www.spinwatch.org/

337 Mills, C.W. (1956) *The Power Elite*. New York: Oxford University Press. Chapter 13.

338 Williams, C. (2006) *Leadership Accountability in a Globalizing World*. London: Palgrave Macmillan. p. 138.

339 Bronner, S.E. (2011) *Critical Theory: A Very Short Introduction*. Oxford: Oxford University Press.

340 Geuss, R. (1981) *The Idea of a Critical Theory. Habermas and the Frankfurt School*. Cambridge: Cambridge University Press; Held, D. (1980) *Introduction to Critical Theory: Horkheimer to Habermas*. Berkeley: University of California Press.

341 Thomas, J. (1993) *Doing Critical Ethnography*. London: Sage.

342 Kuhn, T.S. (1962) *The Structure of Scientific Revolutions*. Chicago: University of Chicago Press.

343 Beg, D., Fisher, S. and Rudiger, D. (1984) *Economics*. Maidenhead: McGraw-Hill.

344 Goodall, A. (2010) 'Room at the top for improvement', *Times Higher Education*, 9 December: 52–53.

345 Peter, L.J. and Hull, R. (1969) *The Peter Principle: Why Things Always Go Wrong*. New York: William Morrow and Company.

346 Hargrove, R. (2001) *E-Leader: Reinventing Leadership in a Connected Economy*. New York: Perseus Book Group.

347 Johnson, D. (2005) *Overconfidence and War: The Havoc and Glory of Positive Illusions*. Harvard University Press.

348 Peck, E. (2009) *Performing Leadership*. London: Palgrave Macmillan. p. 14.

349 Lasswell, H.D., Lerner, D. and Rothwell, C.E. (1952) *The Comparative Study of Elites*. Stanford: Stanford University Press.

350 Hunter, F. (1953) *Community Power Structure: A Study of Decision Makers*. Chapel Hill, NC: University of North Carolina Press.

CHAPTER 3: LITERATURE

1 Schirmer, J. (2011) 'Elite perpetrators', unpublished paper presented at the International State Crime Initiative (ISCI) research methods workshop: 'The state of state crime research'. ISCI, King's College, London. (Based on Schirmer, J. (1999) *The Guatemalan Military Project: A Violence Called Democracy*. Philadelphia: University of Pennsylvania Press.)

2 Colossus. Available at: www.searchenginecolossus.com

3 Fouchard, G. and Young, R. (2001) *A Simple Guide to Searching the Internet*. New Jersey: Prentice Hall.

4 Lane, C. (2002) *Naked in Cyberspace*. Medford, NJ: Cyber Age Books.

5 CIA. Available at: www.foia.cia.gov/

6 Dikotter, F. (2005) *Mao's Great Famine: The Story of Mao's Most Devastating Catastrophe, 1958–62*. London: Bloomsbury.

7 UCB libraries. Available at: http://ucblibraries.colorado.edu/govpubs/us/declassified.htm

8 Glynn, S. and Booth, A. (1979) 'The public records office and recent British economic historiography', *The Economic History Review*, 23(3): 303–315.

9 Keller, B. (2011) *Open Secrets*. New York: New York Times; *Wikileaks*. Available at: www.wikileaks.org

10 Operation Northwoods. Available at: www.smeggys.co.uk/operation_northwoods. php?image=01#tt

11 Chapman, R.A. and Hunt, M. (2010) *Freedom of Information: Local Government and Accountability*. Abingdon: Ashgate.

12 Canada FOI resource website. Available at: www3.telus.net/index100/indextorulings

13 *Open Government: A Journal on Freedom of Information*. Available at: www.open govjournal.org

14 MRS (2006) *Freedom of Information Act 2000: Guidance*. London: Market Research Society; CIA FOI. Available at: www.foia.cia.gov

15 Howden, D. (2010) 'I'll close down Twitter, says ridiculed ANC leader', *The Independent*, 5 November: 35.

16 Hart, C. (1998) *Doing a Literature Review: Releasing the Social Science Research Imagination*. London: Sage.

17 Lee, Y.-J. (2004) *Leadership and International Understanding: Linking Korea and the Middle East. A Historical and Literature Review*. Amman: United Nations University: International Leadership Institute. p. 83.

18 Glasziou, P., Irwig, L., Bain, C. and Colldiz, G. (2001) *Systematic Reviews in Health Care: A Practical Guide*. Cambridge: Cambridge University Press.

19 Snider, L. (2003) 'Researching corporate crime', in S. Tombs and D. Whyte, *Unmasking the Crimes of the Powerful*. New York: Peter Lang. pp. 49–68.

20 Cooper, H., Hedges, L.V. and Valentine, J.C. (eds) (2009) *The Handbook of Research Synthesis and Meta-Analysis*. New York: Russell Sage Foundation.

21 Nisbett, R.E. and Wilson, T.D. (1977) 'The halo effect: Evidence for unconscious alteration of judgments', *Journal of Personality and Social Psychology* (American Psychological Association), 35(4): 250–256.

22 Khaldun Ibn (2004) *The Muqaddimah: An Introduction to History* (F. Rosenthal, trans.; N.J. Dawood and B. Lawrence, eds). New Jersey: Princeton University Press. (Bk.1, Preliminary Remarks.)

23 Howard, M. (2005) *We Know What You Want: How They Change Your Mind*. New York: The Disinformation Company.

24 Fake news. Available at: www.prwatch.org/fakenews3/summary

25 Monbiot, G. (2010) 'These Astroturf libertarians are the real threat to democracy', *The Guardian,* 14 December: 29.

26 Smith, H. (2004) 'Improving intelligence on North Korea', *Jane's Intelligence Review*, April: 48–51.

27 MoFA (2009) *The Operation in Gaza – Factual and Legal Aspects* [29 July], Israeli Ministry of Foreign Affairs. Available at: www.mfa.gov.il/MFA/Terrorism-+Obstacle+to+Peace/Terrorism+and+Islamic+Fundamentalism-/Operation_in_Gaza-Factual_and_Legal_Aspects.htm

28 Israeli Embassy (2010) *Gaza Facts – the Israeli Perspective* [18 June]. Available at: www.mfa.gov.il/GazaFacts/; Tokyo [21 September]. Available at: http://tokyo.mfa.gov.il/mfm/web/main/document.asp?SubjectID=5802&MissionID=43&LanguageID=0&StatusID=1&DocumentID=-1

29 Devenny, P. (2006) 'Hezbollah's strategic threat to Israel', *Middle East Quarterly,* Winter: 31–38. Available at: www.meforum.org/806/hezbollahs-strategic-threat-to-israel#_ftnref2 (reporting: Associated Press, 25 May 2005).

30 Le Bon, G. (1896/2002) *The Crowd: A Study of the Popular Mind*. London: Dover Publications.

31 Pearson, D. (1998) *Provenance Research in Book History: A Handbook*. London: British Library.

32   Cooper, J. (2011) *The Queen's Agent: Francis Walsingham at the Court of Elizabeth I.* London: Faber and Faber.

33   www.Mahalo.com

34   Chemers, M.M. and Ayman, R. (1993) *Leadership Theory and Research: Perspectives and Directions.* London: Academic Press.

35   Bellamy, R. and Palumbo, A. (2010) *Political Accountability.* Abingdon: Ashgate.

36   Williams, C. (2006) *Leadership Accountability in a Globalizing World.* London: Palgrave Macmillan.

37   Green, P. and Ward, T. (2004) *State Crime: Governments, Violence and Corruption.* Pluto Press. (*International State Crime Initiative,* Kings College, London. Available at: www.statecrime.org)

38   Thornton, R. (2006) *Asymmetric Warfare: Threat and Response in the 21st Century.* London: Polity Press.

39   McCauley, C. (ed.) (2011) *Dynamics of Asymmetric Conflict.* London: Routledge.

40   Madsen, D.L. (1998) *American Exceptionalism.* Mississippi: University Press of Mississippi.

41   Chen, Hon-Fai (2009) 'Reflexive exceptionalism: On the relevance of Tocqueville's America for modern China', *Journal of Classical Sociology,* 9(1): 79–95.

42   Tezcur, G.M., Azadarmaki, T. and Bahar, M. (2006) 'Religious participation among Muslims: Iranian exceptionalism', *Middle East Critique,* 15(3): 217–232.

43   Oh, Kongdan and Hassig, R.C. (2000) *North Korea Through the Looking Glass.* Washington: Brookings Institution Press.

44   Bellin, E. (2004) 'The robustness of authoritarianism in the Middle East: Exceptionalism in the comparative perspective', *Comparative Politics,* 36(2): 139–157.

45   Wassim, T. (2009) 'Islamic exceptionalism? The role of religion in the civic and political lives of American Muslims', unpublished paper presented at the annual meeting of the *Southern Political Science Association,* 26 September 2010.

46   Alam, M.S. (2009) *Israeli Exceptionalism: The Destabilizing Logic of Zionism.* London: Palgrave Macmillan.

47   Diamond, J. (1997) *Guns, Germs and Steel: The Fates of Human Societies.* New York: W.W. Norton.

48   Adams, J. (1999) 'The social implications of hypermobility', in OECD, *The Economic and Social Implications of Sustainable Transportation.* Paris: OECD.

49   *List of Famous People with Disabilities.* Available at: www.disabled-world.com; Wiki: *List of People with Epilepsy, List of People Affected by Bipolar Disorder.*

50   Hawass, Z. et al. (2010) 'Ancestry and pathology in King Tutankhamun's family', *Journal of the American Medical Association,* 303(7): 638–647.

51   Hooper-Greenhill, E. (2007) *Museums and Education: Purpose, Pedagogy, Performance.* London: Routledge.

52   Williams, C. (2009) 'Could small nations lead the way to peace?', *The Korea Herald,* 8 September: 4.

53   Nath, S. et al. (2010) *Saving Small Island Developing States.* London: Commonwealth Secretariat.

54   James, M. (2002) *Encyclopaedia of Stateless Nations: Ethnic and National Groups Around the World.* Westport: Greenwood Press.

55   Gruenbaum, E. (2000) *The Female Circumcision Controversy: An Anthropological Perspective.* Philadelphia: University Of Pennsylvania Press.

56   Yalop, D. (2010) *Beyond Belief: The Catholic Church and the Child Abuse Scandal.* London: Constable.

57   Khumri, Pul-E. (2007) 'Afghan boy dancers sexually abused by former warlords', *Reuters Online,* 18 November.

58 Temple, B. and Moran, R. (2006) *Doing Research with Refugees: Issues and Guidelines.* London: The Policy Press.

59 Williams, C. (1990) 'Street children and education: A comparative study of European and Third World approaches', unpublished PhD thesis, School of Education, University of Birmingham. p. 244.

60 Williams, C. (1995) *Coping with Crime – A Skills Book for People with Learning Difficulties.* Brighton: Pavilion; Walmsley, J. and Johnson, K. (2003) *Inclusive Research with People with Learning Disabilities: Past, Present and Futures.* London: Jessica Kingsley.

61 Hinton, R. (1995) 'Trades in different worlds: Listening to refugee voices', *PLA Notes*, 24: 21–26.

62 Williams, C. (2006) *Leadership Accountability in a Globalizing World.* London: Palgrave Macmillan.

63 Marshall, P.D. (ed.) (2006) *The Celebrity Culture Reader.* London: Routledge.

64 Rojek, C. (2004) *Celebrity.* London: Teaktion Books.

65 Palmer, C. (2000) 'Spin doctors and sports brokers. Researching elites in contemporary sport – A research note on the Tour de France', *International Review for the Sociology of Sport*, 35(3): 364–377.

66 Pickering, M. and Griffin, G. (2008) *Research Methods for Cultural Studies.* Edinburgh: Edinburgh University Press.

67 Inglis, F. (2010) *A Short History of Celebrity.* Princeton: Princeton University Press.

68 Harvey, R. (2010) 'Burma's youth rapping for change', *BBC News Online*, 24 February.

69 Redl, F. (1958) 'Group emotion and leadership', in C.G. Browne and T.S. Cohn, (eds), *The Study of Leadership.* Illinois: Interstate.

70 Parten, M.B. (1933) 'Leadership among preschool children', *Journal of Abnormal and Social Psychology*, 27: 430–440.

71 ABC (2005) 'Girls saves tourists after raising tsunami warning', *ABC Online*, 3 January. Available at: www.abc.net.au/news/newsitems/200501/s1275521.htm

72 Barnes, P. (2002) *Leadership with Young People.* Lyme Regis: Russell House Publishing; Fertig, C. (2005) *Help Your Children Become Good Leaders.* Available at:www.associatedcontent.com/article/3262/help_your_children_become_good_leaders.html?cat=25

73 Winner, E. (1997) *Gifted Children: Myths and Realities.* New York: Basic Books; Webb, J.T. (2005) *Misdiagnosis and Dual Diagnoses of Gifted Children and Adults: ADHD, Bipolar, Ocd, Asperger's, Depression, and Other Disorders.* Scottsdale: Great Potential Press.

74 Freeman, J. (2001) *Gifted Children Grown Up.* London: David Fulton Publishers.

75 Almquist. Y. (2009) 'Peer status in school and adult disease risk: A 30-year follow-up study of disease specific morbidity in a Stockholm cohort', *Journal of Epidemiology and Community Health*, 10: 11.

76 Bourdieu, P. and Passeron, J.C. (1990) *Reproduction in Education and Culture.* London: Sage. p. 5; Bowles, S and Gintis, H. (1976) *Schooling in Capitalist America.* Routledge: London.

77 Wintrobe, R. (2006) *Rational Extremism: The Political Economy of Radicalism.* Cambridge: Cambridge University Press.

78 Zaeef, A.S. (2010) *My Life with the Taliban.* London: C. Hurst.

79 Young, M. (2004) *Terrorist Leaders (Profiles in History).* San Diego, CA: Greenhaven Press.

80 Davies, L. (2008) *Educating Against Extremism.* Stoke-on-Trent: Tretham.

81 Oakes, L. (1997) *Prophetic Charisma: The Psychology of Revolutionary Religious Personalities.* Syracuse, NY: Syracuse University Press.

82   Mumford, M. et al. (2007) 'The sources of leader violence: A comparison of ideological and non-ideological leaders', *The Leadership Quarterly*, 18: 217–235.

83   Green, P. and Ward, T. (2004) *State Crime: Governments, Violence and Corruption.* Pluto Press. (*International State Crime Initiative,* Kings College, London. Available at: www.statecrime.org)

84   Mukadam, M. et al. (2010) *The Training and Development of Muslim Faith Leaders: Current Practice and Future Possibilities.* London: Communities and Local Government.

85   Boucek, C. (2008) *Saudi Arabia's 'Soft' Counterterrorism Strategy: Prevention, and Aftercare.* Washington: Carnegie Endowment for International Peace.

86   Olshansky, B. (2002) *Secret Trials and Executions: Military Tribunals and the Threat to Democracy.* New York: Sven Stories Press.

87   Dodge, M. and Geis, G. (2006) 'Fieldwork with the elite: Interviewing white-collar criminals' in D. Hobbs and R. Wright, *The Sage Handbook of Fieldwork.* pp. 80–91.

88   Sereny, G. (1996) *Albert Speer: His Battle with the Truth.* London: Vintage.

89   Kim Dae Jung (1987) *Prison Writings.* California: University of California Press.

90   Whitehorn, L. (2003) 'Fighting to get them out', *Social Justice*, 30(2): 51.

91   *Secret Societies Research Project.* Available at: www.abovetopsectret.com

92   Atkinson, R. and Flint, J. (2003) 'Sampling, snowball: Accessing hidden and hard-to-reach populations', in R.L. Miller and J.D. Brewer, *The A–Z of Social Research.* London: Sage. pp. 275–280.

93   Human Rights Watch (2010) *Our Research Methodology.* Available at: www.hrw.org/en/node/75141

94   Stewart, P.D. (1977) 'Attitudes of regional Soviet political leaders: Toward understanding the potential for change', in M.G. Hermann (ed.), *The Psychological Examination of Political Leaders.* New York: Free Press. pp. 237–273; Welsh, W.A. (1977) 'Effect of career and party affiliation on revolutionary behaviour among Latin American political elites', in M.G Hermann. (ed.), *The Psychological Examination of Political Leaders.* New York: Free Press. pp. 274–308; Higley, J. and Lengyel, G. (2000) *Elites after State Socialism: Theories and Analysis.* Maryland: Rowman & Littlefield.

95   *North Korea LeadershipWatch.* Available at: NKleadershipwatch.wordpress.com

96   Sekunda, N. and Hook, R. (1998) *The Spartan Army.* London: Osprey Publishing.

97   Beaumont, R. (1976) *Military Elites.* London: Robert Hale; Couch, D. (2003) *The Warrior Elite.* London: Crown Publications.

98   McNab, C. (2002) *How to Pass the SAS Selection Course (SAS training manual).* London: Sidgwick & Jackson.

99   Williams, K. (1989) 'Researching the powerful: Problems and possibilities', *Crime, Law and Social Change,* 13(3): 253–274.

100 Williams, C. and Lee, Y.-J. (2005) 'The minds of leaders', in B. Walker (ed.), *Preparing for Peace.* Westmorland: General Meeting.

101 Sampson, A. (2004) *Who Runs this Place? The Anatomy of Britain in the 21st Century.* London: John Murray.

102 AMEInfo (2008) *Global Environment and Energy Elites Meet in Dubai',* AMEInfo. Available at: www.ameinfo.com/179475.html

103 Owen, R. (2004) *State, Power and Politics in the Making of the Modern Middle East.* London: Routledge; Rugh, A.B. (2007) *The Political Culture of Leadership in the United Arab Emirates.* New York: Palgrave Macmillan.

104 Okonta, I. (2009) *When Citizens Revolt: Nigerian Elites, Big Oil, and the Ogoni Struggle for Self Determination.* Trenton: Africa World Press.

105 Lane, D. (2000) 'Russia: The oil elite's evolution, divisions and outlooks', in J. Higley and L. György (eds), *Elites after State Socialism: Theories and analysis.* Maryland: Rowman & Littlefield. p. 179.

106 Hirsch, A. (2010) 'Vote trading "leading to unqualified ICC judges"', *The Guardian*, 9 September: 17.
107 Lichter, S.R. et al. (1986) *The Media Elite: America's New Powerbrokers*. New York: Hastings House.
108 Quinn, B. (2011) 'Egyptian web activist freed after protests tells TV station: "I am no hero"', *The Guardian*, 8 February: 23.
109 Taylor, J. (2011) 'Inside the secret world of the geeks with the power to unleash anarchy', *The Independent*, 25 June: 16–17.
110 Greenfield, S. (2003) *Tomorrow's People: How 21st Century Technology is Changing the Way We Think*. London: Allen Lane; Carr, N. (2010) *The Shallows: What the Internet is Doing to our Brains*. New York: W.W. Norton & Company; Brockman, J. (2011) *Is the Internet Changing the Way you Think? The Net's Impact on Our Minds and Future*. London: Harper Perennial.
111 Nicolle, D. (1993) *The Mamluks 1250–1517*. London: Osprey.
112 Eade, J. (2002) 'How far can you go? English Catholic elites and the erosion of ethnic boundaries', in C. Shore and S. Nugent, *Elite Cultures: Anthropological Perspectives*. London: Routledge.
113 Yalop, D. (2010) *Beyond Belief: The Catholic Church and the Child Abuse Scandal*. London: Constable.
114 Olsson, P.A. (2005) *Malignant Pied Pipers of Our Time: A Psychological Study of Destructive Cult Leaders from Rev. Jim Jones to Osama bin Laden*. Frederick, MD: Publish America.
115 Lindsay, D.M. (2007) *Faith in the Halls of Power: How Evangelicals Joined the American Elite*. New York: Oxford University Press.
116 Lindsay, D.M. (2007) *Faith in the Halls of Power: How Evangelicals Joined the American Elite*. New York: Oxford University Press.
117 Williams, C. (2006) *Leadership Accountability in a Globalizing World*. London: Palgrave Macmillan. pp. 59–127.
118 Haas, P.M. (1992) 'Introduction. Epistemic communities and international policy coordination', *International Organization*, 46(1): 1–35.
119 Taylor, J. (2008) *The New Elite: Inside the Minds of the Truly Wealthy*. New York: AMACOM.
120 Cahill, K. (2011) *Who Owns the World: The Hidden Facts Behind Land Ownership*. London: Mainstream.
121 Mallaby, S. (2010) *More Money Than God: Hedge Funds and the Making of the New Elite*. London: Bloomsbury.
122 Williams, C. (2006) *Leadership Accountability in a Globalizing World*. London: Palgrave Macmillan. pp. 25–36.
123 Wilkinson, R. and Pickett, K. (2009) *The Spirit Level: Why More Equal Societies Almost Always Do Better*. London: Allen Lane.
124 Greenberg, B. (1947) 'Some relations between territory, social hierarchies, and leadership in the Green Sunfish', *Physiological Zoology*, 20(3): 267–299.
125 Harcourt, J.L. et al. (2009) 'Social feedback and the emergence of leaders and followers', *Current Biology*, 19: 248–252.
126 Beauchamp, G. (2000) 'Individual differences in activity and exploration influence leaders in pairs of foraging zebra finches', *Behaviour*, 137: 301–314.
127 Dumont, B. et al. (2005) 'Consistency of animal order in spontaneous group movements allows the measurement of leadership in a group of grazing heifers', *Applied. Animal Behaviour Science*, 95: 55–56.
128 Biro, D. et al. (2006) 'From compromise to leadership in pigeon homing', *Current Biology*, 16: 2123–2128.

129 de Waal, F. (2000) *Chimpanzee Politics: Power and Sex among Apes*. Baltimore: Johns Hopkins University Press.

130 Johnson, D. (2005) *Overconfidence and War: The Havoc and Glory of Positive Illusions*. Harvard University Press.

131 Goodall, A. (2010) 'Room at the top for improvement', *Times Higher Education*, 9 December: 52–53.

132 Mitani, J.C. et al. (2010) 'Lethal intergroup aggression leads to territorial expansion in wild chimpanzees', *Current Biology*, 20(12): R507–R508.

133 Kelsey, A. (2009) *Does the Size of Your Group Matter?*, Leading Leaders. Available at: www.leadingleaders.net/articles/

134 Leca, J.-B. et al. (2003) 'Distributed leadership in semi-free-ranging white-faced capauchin monkeys', *Animal Behaviour*, 6: 1045–1052.

135 Pinker, S. (1997) *How the Mind Works*. London: Allen Lane. p. 514.

136 Davies, E. (2011) 'Ravens Stressed by "Gang Life"', *BBC News Online*, 9 February. Available at: http://news.bbc.co.uk/earth/hi/earth_news/newsid_9390000/9390840.stm

137 van Vugt, M. (2006) 'Evolutionary origins of leadership and followership', *Personality and Social Psychology Review*, 10: 354–371.

138 Tooby, J. and Cosmides, L. (1992) 'Psychological foundations of culture', in J.H. Barkow., L. Cosmides and J. Tooby (eds), *The Adapted Mind: Evolutionary Psychology and the Generation of Culture*. New York: Oxford University Press.

139 Singer, P. (2000) *A Darwinian Left: Evolution and Cooperation*. London: Yale University Press.

140 Alford, J.R. et al. (2005) 'Are political orientations genetically transmitted?', *American Political Science Review*, 99(2): 153–167.

141 Oxley, D.R. et al. (2008) 'Political attitudes vary with physiological traits', *Science*, 321: 1667–1670; Balzer, A. et al. (2010) 'Liberals roll with the good; conservatives confront the bad: Physiological and cognitive differences across the political spectrum', unpublished paper presented at the annual meeting of the Midwest Political Science Association, April, Chicago.

142 Smith, K.B. et al. (2007) 'Evolutionary theory and political leadership: Why certain people do not trust decision-makers', *Journal of Politics*, 69(2): 285–299.

143 Churcher, J. (2010) 'Right wing brains different', *The Independent*, 29 December: 15.

144 Williams, C. (2002) 'New security risks and public educating: The relevance of recent evolutionary brain science', *Journal of Risk Research*, 5(3): 225–248.

145 Woodcock, G. (1962) *Anarchism*. Harmondsworth: Penguin Books.

146 Whittam Smith, A. (2011) 'Protest movements don't need a spearhead to be successful', *The Independent* (Viewspaper), 20 January: 5.

147 Shirky, C. (2011) 'Political power and social media: Technology, the public sphere, and political change', *Foreign Affairs*, February.

148 Atran, S. (2010) *Talking to the Enemy: Violent Extremism, Sacred Values and What it Means to be Human*. London: Allen Lane.

149 Beck, U. (1999) *World Risk Society*. Cambridge: Polity.

150 Uhl-Bien, M. et al. (2007) 'Complexity leadership theory: Shifting leadership from the industrial age to the knowledge era', *The Leadership Quarterly*, 18 (4): 298–318.

151 White, R. (2002) *Leadership and Uncertainty: Embracing the Unknown*. London: FT Press.

152 Charan, R. (2008) *Leadership in the Era of Economic Uncertainty: Managing a Downturn*. New York: McGraw-Hill.

153 Post, J.M. (2004) *Leaders and their Followers in a Dangerous World: The Psychology of Political Behaviour*. Ithaca, NY: Cornell University Press.

154 Bartz, D. (2010) 'Toyota sees robotic nurses in your lonely final years', *Wired*, 19 January.

155 BBC (2003) 'Robot Attends Czech State Dinner', *BBC News Online*, 21 August.

156 *The Ethical Robot*. Available at: http://ieet.org/index.php/IEET/more/ter20101127

157 BBC (2006) '"Move to New Planet", Says Hawking', *BBC News Online*, 30 November. Available at: http://news.bbc.co.uk/1/hi/uk/61588855.stm

158 Williams, C. (2010) 'Global justice and education: from nation to neuron', *Educational Review*, 62(3): 343–356.

CHAPTER 4: PLANNING

1 Ahrens, T. (2004) 'Refining research questions in the course of negotiating access for fieldwork,' in C. Humphrey (ed.), *The Real Life Guide to Accounting Research*. Oxford: Elsevier. pp. 295–307.

2 Blaikie, N. (2009) *Designing Social Research*. London: Sage; de Vaus, D. (2001) *Research Design in Social Research*. London: Sage; Maxwell, J.A. (2005) *Qualitative Research Design: An Interactive Approach*. London: Sage.

3 Cresswell, J.W. (2009) *Research Design: Qualitative, Quantitative, and Mixed Methods Approaches*. London: Sage.

4 *Types of Research Designs*. Available at: www.experiment-resources.com/research-designs.html

5 *Gantt Chart Templates*. Available at: www.ganttcharttemplate.com

6 Morris, P.W.G. (1994) *The Management of Projects*. London: Thomas Telford.

7 Coleman, R. (2003) 'CCTV surveillance, power, and social order', in S. Tombs and D. Whyte (eds), *Unmasking the Crimes of the Powerful*. New York: Peter Lang. p. 96. (Who are the powerful?)

8 Davis, T.R. (1984) 'Defining and researching leadership as a behavioural construct: An idiographic approach', *Journal of Applied Behavioural Sciences*, 20(3): 237–251.

9 Schirmer, J. (1999) *The Guatemalan Military Project: A Violence Called Democracy*. Philadelphia: University of Pennsylvania Press.

10 Wood, P. (2010) 'Karzai's office blames British for Taliban imposter', *BBC News Online*, 26 November.

11 Schirmer, J. (2011) 'Elite perpetrators', unpublished paper presented at the International State Crime Initiative (ISCI) research methods workshop: 'The state of state crime research'. ISCI, King's College, London. (Based on Schirmer, J. (1999) *The Guatemalan Military Project: A Violence Called Democracy*. Philadelphia: University of Pennsylvania Press.)

12 Stodgill, R.M. (1963) *Manual for the Leadership Behavior Description Questionnaire-Form: An Experimental Approach*. Columbus, OH: The Ohio State University.

13 Crotty, M.J. (1998) *Foundations of Social Research: Meaning and Perspective in the Research Process*. London: Sage.

14 Collier, D. and Mahoney, J. (1996) 'Insights and pitfalls: Selection bias in qualitative research', *World Politics*, 49: 1.

15 Holmes, B. (1985) 'The problem (solving) approach', in A. Watson and R. Wilson (eds), *Contemporary Issues in Comparative Education*. New Hampshire: Croom Helm.

16 Parkin, S. (2010) *The Positive Deviant: Sustainability Leadership in a Perverse World*. London: Earthscan.

17 Thomas, R.M. (1990) *International Comparative Education: Practices Issues and Prospects*. Oxford: Pergamon.

18 Rossi, P.H. et al. (2004) *Evaluation: A Systematic Approach*. Thousand Oaks, CA: Sage.

19 Yeager, P.C. and Kram, K.E. (1990) 'Fielding hot topics in cool settings: The study of corporate ethics', *Qualitative Sociology*, 13(2): 127–148.

20 Sereny, G. (1996) *Albert Speer: His Battle with the Truth*. London: Vintage.

21 Roehrig, T. (2002) *The Prosecution of Former Military Leaders in Newly Democratic Nations: Argentina, Greece and South Korea*. London: McFarland & Co.

22 Yeager, P.C. and Kram, K.E. (1995) 'Fielding hot topics in cool settings', in R. Hertz and J.B. Imber (eds), *Studying Elites Using Qualitative Methods*. London: Sage. p. 42.

23 Crotty, M.J. (1998) *Foundations of Social Research: Meaning and Perspective in the Research Process*. London: Sage.

24 Club of Rome (1991) *The First Global Revolution*. London: Pantheon.

25 Holmes, B. (1985) 'The problem (solving) approach', in A. Watson and R. Wilson, *Contemporary Issues in Comparative Education*. New Hampshire: Croom Helm.

26 Prins, G. et al. (2010) *The Hartwell Paper: A New Direction for Climate Policy After the Crash of 2009*. London: LSE/McKinder Programme. p. 16–17.

27 Blackburn, S. (1996) *Dictionary of Philosophy*. Oxford: Oxford University Press.

28 Bedell-Avers, K.E. et al. (2008) 'Conditions of problem-solving and the performance of charismatic, ideological, and pragmatic leaders: A comparative experimental study', *Leadership Quarterly*, 19: 89–106.

29 Onwuegbuzie, A.J. (2006) 'Linking research questions to mixed methods data analysis procedures', *The Qualitative Report*, 11(3): 474–498.

30 *Wordle*. Available at: www.wordle.net

31 Odendahl, T. and Shaw, A.M. (2002) 'Interviewing elites', in J.F. Gubrium and J.A. Holstein (eds), *Handbook of Interview Research: Context and Method*. Thousand Oaks: Sage. pp. 299–316; Ostrander, S.A. (1993) 'Surely you're not in this just to be helpful. Access, rapport, and interviews in three studies of elites', *Journal of Contemporary Ethnography*, 22(1): 7–27.

32 Horwood, J. and Moon, G. (2003) 'Accessing the research setting: The politics of research and the limits to inquiry', *Area*, 35: 106–109.

33 Buchanan, D., Boddy, D. and McCalman, J. (1988) 'Getting in, getting on, getting out, and getting back', in A. Bryman (ed.), *Doing Research in Organizations*. London: Routledge. pp. 53–67.

34 Schirmer, J. (2011) *The Guatemalan Military Project: A Violence Called Democracy*. Philadelphia: University of Pennsylvania Press.

35 Holstein, J.A. and Gubrium, J.F. (2003) *Inside Interviewing*. London: Sage. ('The reluctant respondent', pp. 153–169.)

36 Hornsby-Smith, M. (1993) 'Gaining access', in M. Gilbert (ed.), *Researching Social Life*. London: Sage.

37 Walford, G. (1994) *Researching the Powerful in Education*. London: UCL Press. p. 222.

38 Conti, J.A. and O'Neil, M. (2007) 'Studying power: Qualitative methods and the global elite', *Qualitative Research*, 7(1): 70.

39 Lilleker, D.G. (2003) 'Interviewing the political elite: Navigating a potential minefield', *Politics*, 23(3): 207–214; Smart, D. and Higley, J. (1977) 'Why not ask them? Interviewing Australian elites about national power structure', *Australian and New Zealand Journal of Sociology*, 13: 250.

40 Biernacki, P. and Waldord, D. (1981) 'Snowball sampling: Problems and techniques of chain referral sampling', *Sociological Methods and Research*, 10(2); Farquharson, K.

(2005) 'A different kind of snowball: Identifying key policymakers', *International Journal of Social Research Methodology*, 8(4).

41 Sereny, G. (1996) *Albert Speer: His Battle with the Truth*. London: Vintage.

42 Rushe, D. (2011) '"They must have known": Madoff accuses banks from his prison cell', *The Guardian*, 17 February: 29.

43 Gilding, M. (2010) 'Motives of the rich and powerful in doing interviews with social scientists', *International Sociology*, 25(6): 755–777.

44 Broadhead, R. and Rist, R. (1976) 'Gatekeepers and the social control of social research', *Social Problems*, 21: 52–64; Undheim, T.A. (2006) 'Getting connected: How sociologists can access the high tech elite', in S. Nagy et al. (eds), *Emergent Methods in Social Research*. London: Sage. pp. 13–36.

45 Tombs, S. and Whyte, D. (2003) 'Scrutinizing the powerful', in S. Tombs and D. Whyte, *Unmasking the Crimes of the Powerful*. New York: Peter Lang. pp. 32–36.

46 Gamson, J. (1995) 'Stopping the spin and becoming a prop: Fieldwork on Hollywood elites', in R. Hertz and J.B. Imber (eds), *Studying Elites Using Qualitative Methods*. London: Sage. pp. 83–93.

47 Lotter, S. (2004) 'Studying-up those who fell down: Elite transformation in Nepal', *Anthropology Matters*, 6(2).

48 Unpublished personal correspondence with *Vodafone*, September 2010, ref. no. CS00005305348.

49 Unpublished personal correspondence with *Barclays*, July 2011, ref. no. 100G0M9T.

50 McEvoy, J. (2006) 'Elite interviewing in a divided society: Lessons from Northern Ireland', *Politics*, 26(3): 184–191.

51 Undheim, T.A. (2006) 'Getting connected: How sociologists can access the high tech elite', in S. Nagy. et al. (eds), *Emergent Methods in Social Research*. London: Sage. pp. 13–36.

52 Mullings, B. (1999) 'Insider or outsider, both or neither: some dilemmas of interviewing in a cross-cultural setting', *Geoforum*, 30: 337–350; Gamson, J. (1995) 'Stopping the spin and becoming a prop: Fieldwork on Hollywood elites', in R. Hertz and J.B. Imber (eds), *Studying Elites Using Qualitative Methods*. London: Sage.

53 Herod, A. (1999) 'Reflections on interviewing foreign elites: Praxis, positionality, validity, and the cult of the insider', *Geoforum*, 30: 313–327.

54 Mitchell, R.G. (1993) *Secrecy and Fieldwork*. London: Sage. pp. 12–22.

55 Marcus, G. (2001) 'From rapport under erasure to theatres of complicit reflexivity', *Qualitative Inquiry*, 7: 519–528.

56 Gilding, M. (2010) 'Motives of the rich and powerful in doing interviews with social scientists', *International Sociology*, 25(6): 762.

57 Ortner, S.B. (2010) 'Access: Reflections on studying up in Hollywood', *Ethnography*, 11(2): 211–233.

58 Conti, J.A. and O'Neil, M. (2007) 'Studying power: Qualitative methods and the global elite', *Qualitative Research*, 7(1): 63–82.

59 England, K.V.L. (2002) 'Interviewing elites: Cautionary tales about researching women managers in Canada's banking industry', in P.J. Moss (ed.), *Feminist Geography in Practice: Research and Methods*. Oxford: Blackwell. pp. 200–213.

60 Dexter, L.A. (1970) *Elite and Specialized Interviewing*. Evanston, IL: Northwestern University Press.

61 Schirmer, J. (2011) *The Guatemalan Military Project: A Violence Called Democracy*. Philadelphia: University of Pennsylvania Press.

62 Welch, C. et al. (2002) 'Corporate elites as informants in qualitative international business research', *International Business Review*, 11: 611–628.

63 Cookson, P.W. (1994) 'The power discourse: Elite narratives and educational policy formation', in G. Walford (ed.), *Researching the Powerful in Education*. London: UCL Press. pp. 127–128.

64 Alton, Lord and Cox, Baroness (2010) *Building Bridges Not Walls: The Case for Constructive, Critical Engagement with North Korea* (All Party Parliamentary Group for North Korea October). Available at: www.scribd.com/doc/40523738/Building-Bridges-Not-Walls-Final-Report

65 HHI (2009) *Characterizing Sexual Violence in the Democratic Republic of the Congo*. Cambridge, MA: Harvard Humanitarian Initiative. p. 13.

66 Undheim, T.A. (2006) 'Getting connected: How sociologists can access the high tech elite', in S. Nagy et al., *Emergent Methods in Social Research*. London: Sage. pp. 13–36.

67 Useem, M. (1995) 'Researching corporate executives', in R. Hertz and J.B. Imber (eds), *Studying Elites Using Qualitative Methods*. London: Sage. p. 31.

68 Hammersley, H. and Traianou, A. (2011) *Ethics in Qualitative Research*. London: Sage.

69 Denscombe, M. (2002) *Ground Rules for Social Research*. Milton Keynes: Open University Press.

70 Welch, C., Marschan-Piekkari, R., Penttinen, H. and Tahvanainen, M. (2002) 'Corporate elites as informants in qualitative international business research', *International Business Review*, 11: 611–628.

71 Godin, M., Kishan, J., Muraskin, D. and Newhouse, L. (2006) *The Medium of Testimony: Testimony as Re-presentation* (RSC Working Paper No. 37). Oxford: Refugee Studies Centre.

72 Pogge, T. (2009) '*Developing morally plausible indices of poverty and gender equity: A research program*', *Philosophical Topics*, 2(37): 199–221.

73 Czarniawska, B. (2009) *Organizing in the Face of Risk and Threat*. Cheltenham: Edward Elgar.

74 Israel, M. and Hay, I. (2006) *Research Ethics for Social Scientists*. London: Sage; Iphofen, R. (2011) *Ethical Decision Making in Social Research*. London: Palgrave Macmillan.

75 Nader, L. (1972) 'Up the anthropologist', in D.H. Hymes (ed.), *Reinventing Anthology*. New York: Pantheon Books. pp. 284–311.

76 Forth, J. et al. (2008) *Methodological Review of Research with Large Businesses. Paper 4: Confidentiality and disclosure*. London: HM Revenue and Customs.

77 Barendt, E. (2010) *Academic Freedom and the Law: A Comparative Study*. Oxford: Hart Publishing.

78 BBC (2010) 'Gordon Brown mortified by his bigoted woman slur', *BBC News Online*, 28 April.

79 Lilleker, D.G. (2003) 'Interviewing the political elite: Navigating a potential minefield', *Politics*, 23(3): 212–213.

80 Corporate Watch (2010) *How to Research Companies*. Available at: www.corporatewatch.org.uk

81 Gilding, M. (2010) 'Motives of the rich and powerful in doing interviews with social scientists', *International Sociology*, 25(6): 765.

82 Ward, S.J.A. (2010) *Global Journalism Ethics*. Quebec: McGill-Queen's University Press.

83 Dalton, M. (1959) *Men who Manage*. New York: John Wiley.

84 Frankel, M.S. and Siang, S. (1999) *Ethical and Legal Aspects of Human Subjects Research on the Internet.* Washington DC: Scientific Freedom, Responsibility and Law Program, Directorate of Science and Policy Programs, American Association for the Advancement of Science. Available at: www.aaas.org/spp/sfrl/projects/intres/report.pdf

85 Milmo, C. (2011) 'Lloyd's insurer sues Saudi Arabia for "funding 9/11 attacks"', *The Independent,* 19 September: 25.

86 Alston, P. (1994) *The Best Interests of the Child: Reconciling Culture and Human Rights.* London: Clarendon Press.

87 *Public Concern at Work.* Available at: www.pcaw.co.uk; Dehn, G. and Calland, R. (2010) *Whistle Blowing Around the World: Law Culture and Practice.* London: ODAC/PCAW.

88 Emanuel, E. and Emanuel, L. (1992) 'Proxy decision making for incompetent patients: An ethical and empirical analysis', *Journal of the American Medical Association,* 267(15): 2067–2071.

89 Rogers, C. and Corwin, M. (2006) *Undercover.* London: Authentic.

90 Dawson, J. and Peart, N.S. (2003) *The Law of Research: A Guide.* Dunedin: University of Otago Press.

91 *Index on Censorship.* Available at: www.indexoncensorship.org

92 *World Association of Professional Investigators.* Available at: www.wapi.com/; *Institute of Professional Investigators.* Available at: www.ipi.org.uk/

93 Williams, C. (1995) *Invisible Victims: Crime and Abuse Against People with Learning Disabilities.* London: Jessica Kingsley. pp. 60–64.

94 Fitzgerald, D.G. (2007) *Informants and Undercover Investigations: A Practical Guide to Law, Policy, and Procedure.* New York: CRC.

95 *The Regulation of Investigatory Powers Act* 2000 (UK). Available at: www.statutelaw.gov.uk/content.aspx?activeTextDocId=1757378

96 *Photography and the Law (UK).* Available at: www.urban75.org/photos/photographers-rights-street-shooting.html

97 Pratt, B. and Loizos, P. (1992) *Choosing Research Methods.* Oxford: Oxfam. p. 13.

CHAPTER 5: FRAMEWORKS

1 Beissel-Durrant, G. (2004) 'A typology of research methods within the social sciences', unpublished working paper. ESRC National Centre for Research Methods. Available at: http://eprints.ncrm.ac.uk/115/

2 Denscombe, M. (1998) *The Good Research Guide.* Buckingham: The Open University Press.

3 Cresswell, J.W. (2009) *Research Design: Qualitative, Quantitative, and Mixed Methods Approaches.* London: Sage.

4 Bryman, A. (2008) *Social Research Methods.* Oxford: Oxford University Press. p. 35.

5 Berger, J. and Zelditch, M. (1993) *Theoretical Research Programs: Studies in Theory Growth.* Stanford: Stanford University Press.

6 Cresswell, J.W. (2009) *Research Design: Qualitative, Quantitative, and Mixed Methods Approaches.* London: Sage. p. 13; Denscombe, M. (1998) *The Good Research Guide.* Buckingham: The Open University Press. p. 3.

7 *Sage Research Methods Online* (SRMO). Available at: http://srmo.sagepub.com

8 Douglas, J.D. (1976) *Investigative Social Research.* Beverly Hills, CA: Sage.

9 Northmore, D. (1996) *Lifting the Lid: A Guide to Investigative Research.* London: Continuum.

10 Morgan, J.B. (1990) *The Police Function and the Investigation of Crime*. London: Avebury.

11 Innes, M. (1985) *Investigating Murder*. London: Police Foundation.

12 Fredrickson, D.D. (2004) *Street Drug Investigation: A Practical Guide for Plainclothes and Uniformed Personnel*. New York: Charles C. Thomas.

13 Viaene, S. et al. (2002) 'A comparison of state-of-the-art classification techniques for expert automobile insurance claim fraud detection', *Journal of Risk and Insurance*, 69(3): 373–421.

14 Bolton, R.J. and Hand, D.J. (2002) 'Statistical fraud detection: A review', *Statistical Science*, 17(3): 235–249.

15 Beers, D.A. (2011) *Practical Methods for Legal Investigations: Concepts and Protocols in Civil and Criminal Cases*. New York: CRC Press.

16 Nissan, E. (2010) *Computer Applications for Handling Legal Evidence, Police Investigation and Case Argumentation*. New York: Springer.

17 De Burgh, H. (2008) *Investigative Journalism*. London: Routledge.

18 Hunter, L. (2011) *Story-Based Inquiry: A Manual for Investigative Journalists*. Paris: UNESCO.

19 Willard, R.J. (1997) *PI: A Self-Study Guide on Becoming a Private Detective*. London: Paladin Press; Rapp, B. (1992) *Serious Surveillance for the Private Investigator*. London: Paladin.

20 Eftimiades, N. (1994) *Chinese Intelligence Operations*. London: Frank Cass.

21 Buckwalter, A. (1983) *Surveillance and Undercover Investigation*. London: Butterworth-Heinemann; Volkman, E. (2007) *The History of Espionage*. London: Carlton.

22 Dalton, M. (1959) *Men who Manage*. New York: Wiley; Ho, K. (2010) *Liquidated: An Ethnography of Wall Street*. North Carolina: Duke University Press.

23 *Hidden Cameras and Voice Recorders*. Available at: www.lightinthebox.com; www.kgbcameras.co.uk/cameras/

24 Posey, B. (2004) *How Spyware and the Weapons Against it are Evolving*. Available at: www.WindowsSecurity.com

25 *Spying and Surveillance Manuals*. Available at: www.spygadgets.org.uk/surveillance-and-spy-books

26 Treham, M. (2008) *Tehelka as Metaphor*. New Delhi: Roli Books.

27 Stogdill, R.M. (1948) 'Personal factors associated with leadership: A survey of the literature', *Journal of Psychology*, 25: 35–71.

28 Beach, L.R. (1993) 'Four revolutions in behavioural decision theory', in M.M. Chemers and R. Ayman (eds), *Leadership Theory and Research*. New York: San Diego. pp. 272–289.

29 Parten, M.B. (1933) 'Leadership among preschool children', *Journal of Abnormal and Social Psychology*, 27: 430–440.

30 Diamond, J. and Robinson, J.A. (eds) (2010) *Natural Experiments of History*. Cambridge, MA: Belknap Press of Harvard University Press.

31 *BBC News Online* 'Have your say'. Available at: www.bbc.co.uk/news/

32 Hermann, M.G. (1977) *A Psychological Examination of Political Leaders*. London: The Free Press.

33 Browne, C.G. and Cohn, T.S. (eds) (1958) *The Study of Leadership*. Illinois: Interstate.

34 Christensen, L.B. (2006) *Experimental Methodology*. Boston, MA: Allyn & Bacon.

35 Lewin, K. et al. (1939) 'Patterns of aggressive behaviour in experimentally created "social climates"', *Journal of Social Psychology,* 10: 271–299.

36 Lammers, J., Stapel, D.A. and Galinsky, A.D. (2010) 'Power increases hypocrisy: Moralizing in reasoning, immorality in behavior', *Psychological Science*, 21: 737–744.

37 Redl, F. (1958) 'Group emotion and leadership', in C.G. Browne and T.S. Cohn (eds), *The Study of Leadership*. Illinois: Interstate.

38 Anderson, C. and Galinsky, A.D. (2006) 'Power, optimism, and risk-taking', *European Journal of Social Psychology*, 36: 511–536.

39 Parten, M.B. (1933) 'Leadership among preschool children', *Journal of Abnormal and Social Psychology*, 27: 430–440.

40 Galinsky, A.D., Gruenfeld, D.H. and Magee, J.C. (2003) 'From power to action', *Journal of Personality and Social Psychology*, 85: 453–466.

41 Miller, R.L. (2005) *Biographical Research Methods*. London: Sage; Lee, H. (2009) *Biography: A Very Short Introduction*. Oxford: Oxford University Press.

42 Logan, R. (2002) *100 Most Popular Business Leaders for Young Adults: Biographical Sketches and Professional Paths*. Greenwood Press.

43 Seldon, A. and Pappworth, J. (1983) *By Word of Mouth: Elite Oral History*. London: Methuen.

44 Gardner, H. (1995) *Leading Minds*. New York: Basic Books.

45 Wipperman, W. (2010) *Skandal im Jagdschloss Grunewald* (Scandal in Hunting Lodge Grunewald). Darmstadt: Primus Verlag; Rogers, J.A. (1996) *World's Great Men of Color*. New York: Touchstone.

46 Alaszewski, A. (2006) *Using Diaries for Social Research*. London: Sage. ('Researching diaries', pp. 24–25.)

47 *Fiction by Politicians*. Available at: www.booksbypoliticians.co.uk/Fiction

48 Mumford, M. et al. (2007) 'The sources of leader violence: A comparison of ideological and non-ideological leaders', *The Leadership Quarterly*, 18: 217–235.

49 *Ushahidi* crowdsourcing tools. Available at: www.ushahidi.com/

50 *Portable Antiquities Scheme*. Available at: http://finds.org.uk

51 *Big Garden Birdwatch*, RSPB. Available at: www.rspb.org.uk/birdwatch/?gclid=CJmCk 4agiqcCFc0f4QodLmsqdg

52 Hewitt, D. (2010) 'The march of netizens', *BBC News Online*. Available at: www.bbc. co.uk/news/world-asia-pacific-11576592

53 *The Guardian* (2009) 'Investigate your MP's expenses'. Available at: http://mps-expenses.guardian.co.uk/

54 *Iraq Body Count*. Available at: www.iraqbodycount.org

55 *Wikileaks*. Available at: www.wikileaks.org

56 *OpenNotebookScience*. Available at: www.makeuseof.com/tag/started-open-notebook-science/

57 Mead, M. and Metraux, R. (eds) (1953) *The Study of Culture at a Distance*. Chicago, IL: University of Chicago Press.

58 Hermann, M.G. (1977) *A Psychological Examination of Political Leaders*. London: The Free Press. ('Political leaders at a distance – problems of assessment', pp. 27–146.)

59 Morrell, K. (2006) 'Aphorisms and leaders' rhetoric: A new analytical approach', *Leadership*, 2(3): 367–382

60 Scott, J.C. (1990) *A Matter of Record: Documentary Sources in Social Research*. Cambridge: Polity Press; Prior, L. (2003) *Using Documents in Social Research*. London: Sage; Scott, J. (2006) *Documentary Research*. London: Sage.

61 de Garzia, A. (1954) *Discovering National Elites: A Manual of Methods for Discovering the Leadership of a Society and its Vulnerabilities to Propaganda*. Stanford: Institute for Journalistic Studies, Stanford University. ('Media analysis' xxvii). Available at: www. grazian-archive.com/governing/Elite/Table%20of%20Contents.html

62 Ciulla, J.B. (ed.) (1998) *Ethics at the Heart of Leadership*. Westport: Praeger.

63 Williams, C. (2001) *Leaders of Integrity: Ethics and a Code for Global Leadership.* Amman: UN University Leadership Academy.

64 Bowen, S.H. (2002) 'Elite issues is ethics management: The role of ethical paradigms in decision making', *Journal of Public Affairs*, 2(4): 270–283.

65 Miller, R.L. (1999) *Researching Life Stories and Family Histories.* London: Sage.

66 *Lineage Chart.* Available at: http://dkwilde.com/Genealogy/Dent/genmain/chart_descrip. html; *Chart Generator.* Available at: www.lineagecharts.com/ChartLayoutGenerator/ LayoutInput.htm

67 Burke, J.A. (1832) *A General and Heraldic Dictionary of the Peerage and Baronetage of the British Empire.* London: Colburn and Bentley. Available at: www.burkespeerage.com

68 Edwin, A. (1998) *The 21st Century Pedigree Handbook.* London: Edwin Anthony.

69 Pearson, D. (1998) *Provenance Research in Book History: A Handbook.* London: British Library; Shaw, D.J. (ed.) (2005) *Books and Their Owners: Provenance Information and the European Cultural Heritage.* London: Consortium of European Research Libraries.

70 George, A.L. and Bennett, A. (2005) *Case Studies and Theory Development in the Social Sciences.* Boston: MIT Press. p. 96.

71 *World Oil Pipelines.* Available at: www.theodora.com/pipelines/world_oil_gas_and_ products_pipelines.html

72 Habermas, J. (1979) *Communication and the Evolution of Society.* Toronto: Beacon Press. pp. 8–14.

73 Bhimji, W. (2009) *Guidance on the Use of Strategic Futures Analysis for Policy Development in Government.* London: Government Office for Science.

74 Pinker, S. (1997) *How the Mind Works.* London: Allen Lane. pp. 21–24.

75 Thomann, J. (1973) 'Meta-methodology: An overview of what it is and how it was developed', unpublished paper presented at the American Educational Research Association Annual Meeting, New Orleans, 26 February–1 March.

76 Cooper, H., Hedges, L.V. and Valentine, J.C. (eds) (2009) *The Handbook of Research Synthesis and Meta-analysis.* New York: Russell Sage Foundation.

77 Wolf, F.M. (1986) *Meta-analysis: Qualitative Methods for Research Synthesis.* Beverly Hills, CA: Sage.

78 Reis, S., Hermoni, D., Van-Raalte, R., Dahan, R. and Borkan, J. (2003) 'Meta-synthesis of qualitative studies: From theory to practice', in *The Domain of Patient Priorities and Evaluations of General Practice/Family Medicine.* Providence: ProvideBrown University.

79 Jackson, P. (2013) *Intelligence Studies.* London: Sage.

80 *International Journal of Intelligence and Counterintelligence.*

81 *Carne Ross.* Available at: www.carneross.com/writings

82 Ross, C. (2007) *Independent Diplomat: Dispatches from an Unaccountable Elite.* Ithaca, NY: Cornell University Press.

83 de Garzia, A. (1954) *Discovering National Elites: A Manual of Methods for Discovering the Leadership of a Society and its Vulnerabilities to Propaganda.* Stanford: Institute for Journalistic Studies, Stanford University. ('Media analysis' xxvii.) Available at: www. grazian-archive.com/governing/Elite/Table%20of%20Contents.html

84 Smith, H. (2004) 'Improving intelligence on North Korea', *Jane's Intelligence Review*, April: 48–51.

85 BBC (2010) 'White House welcomes: State dinner to cold shoulder', *BBC News Online.* Available at: www.bbc.co.uk/news/world-us-canada-10470615

86 *International Association of Protocol Consultants and Officers.* Available at: www.protocol consultants.org/; www.ediplomat.com/nd/protocol/diplomatic_protocol.htm; www.dev. diplomacy.edu/edu/protocol.old/protocol_b.htm

87 McCaffree, M.J., Innis, P. and Sand, R.M. (2002) *Protocol: The Complete Handbook of Diplomatic, Official and Social Usage*. Dallas: Durban House Press.

88 MoD (2009) *Security and Stabilisation: The Military Contribution*. Joint Doctrine Publications 3–40: Chapter 9, Political and social analysis. Available at: www.mod.uk/ DefenceInternet/microsite/dcdc

89 De Smith, M.J. et al. (2006) *Geospatial Analysis: A Comprehensive Guide to Principles, Techniques and Software Tools*. London: Matador.

90 Judd, T. (2011) 'Police and military trial 3D tracking technology', *The Independent*, 12 May: 9.

91 Marchetti, V. and Marks, J.D. (1974) *The CIA and the Cult of Intelligence*. Washington: Knopf.

92 Buchana, D. and Bryman, A. (2009) *The Sage Handbook of Organizational Research Methods*. London: Sage; *Organisational Research Methods* journal. London: Sage.

93 Punnett, B.J. and Shenkar, O. (2004) *Handbook for International Management Research*. London: Wiley. (Part 2, Designing effective research.)

94 Farquhar, J. (2011) *Case Study Research for Business*. London: Sage.

95 Czarniawska-Joerges, B. (2004) *Narratives in Social Science Research*. Thousand Oaks, CA: Sage; Boje, D.M. (2001) *Narrative Methods for Organizational and Communication Research*. London: Sage.

96 Froud, J., Johal, S., Leaver, A. and Williams, K. (2006) *Financialization and Strategy: Narrative and Numbers*. London: Routledge. pp. 122–137.

97 Yorozu, C. (2011) 'Narrative management in Japan: The complexities of large scale organizational change'. Unpublished PhD thesis, Manchester University.

98 Merrill, J. et al. (2006) 'Description of a method to support public health information management: Organizational network analysis', *Journal of Biomedical Informatics*, 40(4): 422–428.

99 Ward, J. and Peppard, J. (2002) 'Situation analysis', in J. Ward and J. Peppard, *Strategic Planning for Information Technology*. London: Wiley.

100 Corporate Watch (2010) *How to Research Companies*. Available at: www.corporate watch.org.uk

101 Tweedale, G. (2003) 'Researching corporate crime: A business historian's perspective', in S. Tombs and D. Whyte (eds), *Unmasking the Crimes of the Powerful: Scrutinizing States and Corporations*. New York: Peter Lang.

102 Westergaard, J. and Resler, H. (1976) *Class in a Capitalist Society*. Harmondsworth: Penguin.

103 Harper, C.L. (1993) *Exploring Social Change*. Engelwood Cliffs: New Jersey.

104 Rossi, P.H. et al. (2004) *Evaluation: A Systematic Approach*. Thousand Oaks, CA: Sage.

105 White, H. (2006) *Impact Evaluation: The Experience of the Independent Evaluation Group of the World Bank*. Washington: World Bank.

106 *Political Instability Task Force*. Available at: http://globalpolicy.gmu.edu/pitf/

107 Rossi, P.H. et al. (2004) *Evaluation: A Systematic Approach*. Thousand Oaks, CA: Sage. p. 273.

108 Leeuw, F. and Vaessen, J. (2009) *Impact Evaluations and Development: NONIE Guidance on Impact Evaluation*. Washington: World Bank.

109 Nagel, S.S. (1999) *Policy Analysis Methods*. New York: New Science Publishers; Fischer, F. and Miller, G.J. (2006) *Handbook of Policy Analysis: Theory, Politics and Methods*. London: CRC Press/Taylor & Francis; Fischer, F., Miller, G.J. and Sidney, M.S. (eds) (2006) *Handbook of Public Policy Analysis: Theory, Methods, and Politics*. New York: Marcel Dekker.

110 Ozga, J. (2011) 'Researching the powerful: Seeking knowledge about policy', *European Educational Research Journal*, 10(2): 218–224.

111 Dutta, P. K. (1999) *Strategies and Games: Theory and Practice*. Cambridge, MA: MIT Press.

112 'Game theory', *Stanford Encyclopaedia of Philosophy*. Available at: http://plato.stanford. edu/entries/game-theory/.

113 Darnton, G. and Darnton, M. (1997) *Business Process Analysis*. Andover: Thomson Business Press; Flynn, B., Sakakibara, S., Schroeder, R.G. and Bates, K.A. (1990) 'Empirical research methods in operations management', *Journal of Operations Management*, 9(2): 250–284.

114 Tansey, O. (2007) 'Process tracing and elite interviewing: A case for non-probability sampling', *Political Science and Politics*, 40(4).

115 George, A.L. and Bennett, A. (2005) *Case Studies and Theory Development in the Social Sciences*. Boston: MIT Press. pp. 6, 206.

116 Smart, D. and Higley, J. (1977) 'Why not ask them? Interviewing Australian elites about national power structure', *Australian and New Zealand Journal of Sociology*, 13: 248–253; *Who Rules America?* Theoretical, methodological and other resources. Available at: www.whois.net

117 Domhoff, G.W. (1980) *Power Structure Research*. London: Sage.

118 Morgan, J. (2011) 'The name says it all (Reputational Rankings)', *Times Higher Education*, 10 March: 33–39.

119 Lee, J. (2010) 'The significance of reputational risk: New evidence in small island off-shore financial centres', working paper. Available at: http://ssrn.com/abstract=1647414

120 Bartelson, J. (1995) *A Genealogy of Sovereignty*. Cambridge: Cambridge University Press; Brint, M. (1991) *A Genealogy of Political Culture*. Boulder, CO: Westview Press.

121 *Genealogy Methods*. Available at: www.bbc.co.uk/history/familyhistory/get_started/; *Lineage Chart*. Available at: http://dkwilde.com/Genealogy/Dent/genmain/chart_descrip.html; *Chart Generator*. Available at: www.lineagecharts.com/ChartLayout Generator/LayoutInput.htm

122 Burke, J.A. (1832) *A General and Heraldic Dictionary of the Peerage and Baronetage of the British Empire*. London: Colburn and Bentley. Available at: www.burkespeerage. com; www.ancestry.co.uk

123 Wellman, B. and Berkowitz, S.D. (eds) (1988) *Social Structures: A Network Approach*. Cambridge: Cambridge University Press; Brandes, U. and Erlebah, T. (eds) (2005) *Network Analysis: Methodological Foundations*. Berlin: Springer-Verlag; Freeman, L. (2006) *The Development of Social Network Analysis*. Vancouver: Empirical Press.

124 For updated lists, see *Wiki*, 'Social network analysis software'.

125 Savage, M. (2010) 'The story so far: A blame game with one politician in the frame', in *The Independent,* 23 January: 13.

126 Burris, V. (1991) 'Director interlocks and the political behaviour of corporations and corporate elites', *Social Science Quarterly,* 72: 637–651.

127 Parry, B. (1998) 'Hunting the gene-hunters: The role of hybrid networks, status, and chance in conceptualizing and assessing corporate elites', *Environment and Planning*, 30: 2147–2162.

128 Boyes, R. (2009) 'Dear leaders Kim Jong-il's successor Kim Jong-un is a Schwarzenegger fan', *The Times*, 8 June. Available at: www.timesonline.co.uk/tol/news/world/asia/article6451519.ece

129 Alba, R.D. (1978) 'Elite social circles', *Sociological Methods & Research*, 7(2): 167–188.

130 Griffiths, D.P. (2008) 'The social networks of the public elite', unpublished thesis, University of Manchester, Faculty of Humanities. Available at: www.staff.stir.ac.uk/david.griffiths/research/thesis.pdf

131 Carroll, W.K. and Carson, C. (2003) 'Forging a New Hegemony? The role of transnational policy groups in the network and discourses of global corporate governance', *Journal of World-Systems Research*, ix(1): 67–102.

132 Howden, D. (2011) 'Fears for food supply as radioactive water pours from stricken reactor', *The Independent*, 29 March, p. 23.

133 Bowles, S. and Gintis, H. (1976) *Schooling in Capitalist America*. Routledge: London.

134 Banakar, R. and Travers, M. (2005) *Theory and Method in Socio-legal Research*. Oxford: Hart Publishing.

135 Sidgwick, H. (1907/1981) *The Methods of Ethics*. Indianapolis: Hackett.

136 Lee, Jae-min (2011) 'Making more laws available in English', *The Korea Herald*, 19 May: 15.

137 Radin, B. (2000) *Beyond Machiavelli: Policy Analysis Comes of Age*. Washington: Georgetown University Press.

138 Ackoff, R.L. (1970) *Redesigning the Future: A Systems Approach to Societal Problems*. New York: Wiley.

139 Checkland, P. (1981) *Systems Thinking, Systems Practice*. New York: Wiley.

140 Iles, V. (2010) *Briefing Paper One: Systems Thinking*. Available at: www.reallylearning.com/Free_Resources/Systems_Thinking/systems_thinking.html

CHAPTER 6: DATA

1 Nelson, M. (1992) Unpublished discussion at the Third International Workshop on closed ecological systems 24–27 April. Available at: www.biospherics.org/hist3rdwkshopintro.html

2 Jupp, V. (2006) *The Sage Dictionary of Social Science Research Methods*. London: Sage; Denscombe, M. (2001) *The Good Research Guide*. Buckingham: Open University Press.

3 Beissel-Durrant, G. (2004) *A Typology of Research Methods Within Social Sciences*, ESRC/NCRM. Available at: www.ncrm.ac.uk/publications/documents/NCRMResearchMethodsTypology.pdf

4 *Sage Research Methods Online* (SRMO). Available at: http://srmo.sagepub.com.

5 Olsen, W. (2011) *Data Collection*. London: Sage.

6 Klenke, K. (2008) *Qualitative Research in the Study of Leadership*. London: Elsevier.

7 Moyser, G. and Wagstaffe, M. (eds) (1987) *Research Methods for Elite Studies*. London: Allen & Unwin.

8 Shively, W.P. (1980) *The Craft of Political Research*. New Jersey: Prentice-Hall.

9 Paige, G.D. (1977) *The Scientific Study of Political Leadership*. New York: The Free Press.

10 Northmore, D. (1996) *Lifting the Lid: A Guide to Investigative Research*. London: Continuum.

11 Marcus, G.E. (1998) 'Ethnography in/of the world system: The emergence of multisited ethnography', in G.E. Marcus, *Ethnography Through Thick and Thin*. Princeton, NJ: Princeton University Press. pp. 79–104.

12 Desmond, M. (2004) 'Methodological challenges posed in studying an elite in the field', *Area*, 36(3): 262–269; Hirsch, P.M. (1995) 'Tales from the field: Learning from

researchers' accounts', in R. Hertz and J.B. Imber (eds), *Studying Elites Using Qualitative Methods*. London: Sage. p. 73.

13   Blasius, J. and Thiessen, V. (2011) *A Guide to Using and Understanding Secondary Data*. London: Sage.

14   Salkind, N. (ed.) (2007) *Encyclopedia of Measurement and Statistics*. Thousand Oaks, CA: Sage.

15   Conti, J.A. and O'Neil, M. (2007) 'Studying power: Qualitative methods and the global elite', *Qualitative Research*, 7(1): 70; Klenke, K. (2008) *Qualitative Research in the Study of Leadership*. London: Elsevier.

16   Yanow, D. and Schwartz-Shea, P. (2006) *Interpretation and Method: Empirical Research Methods and the Interpretive Turn*. New York: M.E. Sharpe.

17   Shively, W.P. (1980) *The Craft of Political Research*. New Jersey: Prentice-Hall. p. 21.

18   Ragin, C.C. (1987) *The Comparative Method: Moving Beyond Qualitative and Quantitative Strategies*. Berkeley: University of California Press.

19   Cresswell, J.W. (2009) *Research Design: Qualitative, Quantitative, and Mixed Methods Approaches*. London: Sage.

20   Charlier, P. (2010) 'Multidisciplinary medical identification of a French king's head (Henry IV)', *British Medical Journal*, 341, 14 December.

21   Whyte, D. (2009) 'Using expert interviews to unmask the crimes of the powerful', paper presented at the annual meeting of the American Society of Criminology (ASC). Available at: www.allacademic.com/meta/p126854_index.html

22   Onwuegbuzie, A.J. and Leech, N.L. (2006) 'Linking research questions to mixed methods data analysis procedures', *The Qualitative Report,* 11(3).

23   Lieberman, E.S. (2003) 'Nested analysis as mixed-method strategy for comparative research', *American Political Science Review*, 99(3): 435–452.

24   Munck, G.L. and Snyder, R. (2007) 'Debating the direction of comparative politics: An analysis of leading journals', *Comparative Political Studies*, 40(5): 5–31.

25   *Software for Online Surveys*. Available at: www.surveymonkey.com/pricing/

26   Robson, C. (1993) *Real World Research*. Oxford: Blackwell. pp. 255–266; Cole, R.L. (1980) *Introduction to Political Inquiry*. London: Collier Macmillan. pp. 72–82. (Indexes and scales.)

27   Kress, G. and van Leeuwen, T. (1996) *Reading Images: The Grammar of Visual Design*. London: Routledge.

28   Scott, J.C. (1990) *A Matter of Record: Documentary Sources in Social Research*. Cambridge: Polity Press; Prior, L. (2003) *Using Documents in Social Research*. London: Sage; Scott, J. (2006) *Documentary Research*. London: Sage.

29   *Media by Milosevic*. Available at: www.pbs.org/wnet/wideangle/episodes/media-by-milosevic/photo-essay-how-milosevic-controlled-the-media/874/

30   *Independent* (2010) 'Spot the difference – Egyptian paper put leader in front', *Independent*, 17 September: 45.

31   Ford, N. (2011) *The Essential Guide to Using the Web for Research*. London: Sage.

32   *Iraq Inquiry Digest* (2011) 'New early drafts of Iraq Dossier published'. Available at: www.iraqinquirydigest.org/?p=11636

33   *Wikileaks*. Available at: www.wikileaks.org

34   BBC (2010) *A History of the World. Empire builders*. Available at: www.bbc.co.uk/ahistoryoftheworld/

35   Assar, G.R.F. (2004) 'Genealogy and coinage of the early Parthian rulers. I', *Parthica*, 6: 69–93; Assar, G.R.F. (2005) 'Genealogy and coinage of the early Parthian rulers, II: A revised stemma', *Parthica*, 7: 29–63.

36 Sarhandi, D. and Boboc, A. (2001) *Evil Doesn't Live Here: Posters from the Bosnian War.* New York: Princeton Architectural Press.

37 Scott, J.P. (2006) *Documentary Research.* London: Sage.

38 Ellen, D. (1989) *The Scientific Examination of Documents.* New York: Wiley.

39 Michel, L. and Baier, P.E. (1985) 'The diaries of Adolf Hitler: Implications for document examination', *Journal of the Forensic Science Society,* 25: 167.

40 Krippendorff, K. (2004) *Content Analysis: An Introduction to its Methodology.* Thousand Oaks, CA: Sage; Winter, D.G. and Stewart, A.J. (1977) 'Content analysis as a technique for assessing political leaders', in M.G. Hermann, *A Psychological Examination of Political Leaders.* London: The Free Press; Bligh, M.C. et al. (2004) 'Charisma under crisis: Presidential leadership, rhetoric and media responses before and after the September 11th terrorist attacks', *Leadership Quarterly,* 15(2): 211–239; Insch, G.S. et al. (2002) 'Content analysis in leadership research: Examples, procedures, and suggestions for future use', *Leadership Quarterly,* 8(1): 1–25.

41 Garraghan, G.J. (1946) *A Guide to Historical Methods.* New York: Fordham University Press. p. 168; Shafer, R.J. (1974) *A Guide to Historical Method.* Illinois: The Dorsey Press.

42 Morrell, K. (2010) 'Leadership, rhetoric, and formalist literary theory', *Journal of Leadership Studies,* 3(4): 86–90.

43 Williams, C. and Yazdani, F. (2009) 'The rehabilitation paradox: Street working children in Afghanistan', *Diaspora, Indigenous, and Minority Education,* 3(1): 4–20.

44 Gee, J.P. (2005) *An Introduction to Discourse Analysis: Theory and Method.* London: Routledge; van Dijk, T. A. (ed.) (1997) *Discourse Studies.* London: Sage.

45 www.discourseanalysis.net; Discourse analysis software. Available at: http://source-forge.net/projects/datool/

46 Cookson, P.W. (1994) 'The power discourse: Elite narratives and educational policy formation', in G. Walford (ed.), *Researching the Powerful in Education.* London: UCL Press. pp. 127–128.

47 Fowler, R. (1979). *Language and Control.* London: Routledge; Fairclough, N. (2001) *Language and Power.* London: Longman; Holes, C. (1995) *Critical Discourse Analysis: The Critical Study of Language.* London: Longman; Bloor, M. and Bloor, T.B. (2007) *The Practice of Critical Discourse Analysis.* London: Hodder Arnold; van Dijk, T.A. (1998) *Ideology: A Multidisciplinary Approach.* London: Sage.

48 Fairclough, N. (2001) *Language and Power.* London: Longman.

49 van Dijk, T.A. (2008) *Discourse, Knowledge, Power and Politics: Towards Critical Epistemic Discourse Analysis,* Lecture CADAAD, Hertfordshire, 10–12 July. Available at: www.discourses.org/UnpublishedArticles/Discourse,%20knowledge,%20power%20and%20politics.pdf

50 Hansen, A. (2009) *Mass Communication Research Methods.* London: Sage.

51 Arber, P. and Harper, T. (2010) *Magnificent Maps: Power, Propaganda and Art.* London: British Library.

52 Monmonier, M. (1996) *How to Lie with Maps.* Chicago: University of Chicago Press.

53 British Library maps, 188.t.1 (1).

54 *Palestinian Maps Omitting Israel.* Available at: www.jewishvirtuallibrary.org/jsource/History/palmatoc1.html

55 Connery, B.A. and Combe, K. (eds) (1994) *Theorizing Satire: Essays in Literary Criticism.* London: Palgrave.

56 Mohassess, M. (1973) *Ardeshir and Stormy Winds.* Tehran: Tus Publications.

57 Calogero, R.M and Mullen, B. (2008) 'About face: Facial prominence of George W. Bush in political cartoons as a function of war', *Leadership Quarterly,* 19: 107–116.

58 Murdoch, B. (1990) *Fighting Songs and Warring Words: Popular Lyrics of Two World Wars*. London: Routledge.

59 BBC (2010) 'Favourite political songs', *BBC World Service*. Available at: www.bbc.co.uk/worldservice/programmes/pol_song.shtml

60 Robertson, G. (2010) *The Case of the Pope: Vatican Accountability for Human Rights Abuse*. London: Penguin.

61 Richards, D. (1996) 'Elite interviewing: Approaches and pitfalls', *Politics*, 16(3): 199–204; Dexter, L.A. (1970) *Elite and specialized interviewing*. Evanston, IL: Northwestern University Press; Morris, Z.S. (2009) 'The truth about interviewing elites', *Politics*, 29(3): 209–217; Kezar, A. (2003) 'Transformational elite interviews: Principles and problems', *Qualitative Inquiry*, 9(3): 395–415; Odendahl, T. and Shaw, A.M. (2002) 'Interviewing elites', in J.F. Gubrium and J.A. Holstein (eds), *Handbook of Interview Research*. Thousand Oaks, CA: Sage. pp. 299–316; Moyser, G. (2006) 'Elite interviewing' in V. Jupp, *The Sage Dictionary of Social Science Research Methods*. London: Sage; Whyte, D. (2009) 'Using expert interviews to unmask the crimes of the powerful', paper presented at the annual meeting of the American Society of Criminology (ASC). Available at: www.allacademic.com/meta/p126854_index.html

62 Holstein, J.A. and Gubrium, J.F. (2003) *Inside Interviewing*. London: Sage. ('The reluctant respondent', pp. 153–169.)

63 Harvey, W.S. (2011) 'Strategies for conducting elite interviews', *Qualitative Research*, 11(4): 431–441.

64 Harvey, W.S. (2010) 'Methods for junior researchers interviewing elites: An interdisciplinary approach', *Geography Compass*, 4(3): 193–205.

65 Welch. C. et al. (2002) 'Corporate elites as informants in qualitative international business research', *International Business Review*, 11: 611–628.

66 Smith, K.E. (2006) 'Problematizing power relations in elite interviews', *Geoforum* 37: 643–653; Morris, Z.S. (2009) 'The truth about interviewing elites', *Politics*, 29(3): 209–217.

67 Neal, S. (1995) 'Researching powerful people from a feminist and anti-racist perspective: A note on gender collusion and marginality', *British Educational Research Journal*, 21(4): 517–531.

68 Ozga, J. (2011) 'Researching the powerful: Seeking knowledge about policy', *European Educational Research Journal*, 10(2): 218–224.

69 Schirmer, J. (1999) *The Guatemalan Military Project: A Violence Called Democracy*. Philadelphia: University of Pennsylvania Press.

70 Moyser, G. (1988) 'Non-standard interviewing in elite research', in R.G. Burgess (ed.), *Studies in Qualitative Methodology*. Greenwich: JAI Press; Dexter, L.A. (1970) *Elite and Specialized Interviewing*. Evanston, IL: Northwestern University Press.

71 Hirsch, P.M. (1995) 'Tales from the field: Learning from researchers' accounts', in R. Hertz and J.B. Imber (eds), *Studying Elites Using Qualitative Methods*. London: Sage. p. 73.

72 Lilleker, D.G. (2003) 'Interviewing the political elites: Navigating a potential minefield', *Politics*, 23(3): 207–224.

73 Lilleker, D.G. (2003) 'Interviewing the political elites: Navigating a potential minefield', *Politics*, 23(3): 207–224.

74 Welch, C. (2007) *Interviewing Elites in International Organisations*. Sydney: University of Western Sydney.

75 Thomas, R.J. (1993) 'Interviewing important people in big companies', *Journal of Contemporary Ethnography'*, 22(1): 80–96.

76 Peabody, R.L. et al. (1990) 'Interviewing political elites', *Political Science and Politics*, 23: 451–455; Lilleker, D.G. (2003) 'Interviewing the political elites: Navigating a

potential minefield', *Politics*, 23(3): 207–224; Williams, P.M. (1980) 'Interviewing politicians: The life of Hugh Gaitskill', *Political Quarterly*, 18(3): 303–316.

77 Rivera, S.W. et al. (2002) 'Interviewing political elites: Lessons from Russia', *Political Science and Politics*, 35(4); Czudnowski, M.M. (1987) 'Interviewing political elites in Taiwan', in G. Moyser and M. Wagstaffe (eds), *Research Methods for Elite Studies*. London: Allen & Unwin. pp. 232–263; Smart, D. and Higley, J. (1977) 'Why not ask them? Interviewing Australian elites about national power structure', *Australian and New Zealand Journal of Sociology*, 13: 248–253.

78 Suh Dae-sook and Lee Chea-jin (eds) (1976) *Political Leadership in Korea*. Seattle: University of Washington Press.

79 Dodge, M. and Geis, G. (2006) 'Fieldwork with the elite: Interviewing white-collar criminals' in D. Hobbs and R. Wright, *The Sage Handbook of Fieldwork*. pp. 80–91.

80 McDowell, L. (1998) 'Elites in the City of London: Some methodological considerations', *Environment and Planning*, 30: 2133–2146.

81 Undheim, T.A. (2006) 'Getting connected: How sociologists can access the high tech elite', in S. Nagy et al. (eds), *Emergent Methods in Social Research*. London: Sage. pp. 13–36.

82 Davies, P.H.J (2001) 'Spies as informants: Triangulation and the interpretation of elite interview data in the study of the intelligence and security services', *Politics*, 21(1): 73–80.

83 Davies, P.H.J. (2000) 'MI6's requirements directorate: Integrating intelligence into the machinery of government', *Public Administration*, 78(1): 29–49; Eftimiades, N. (1994) *Chinese Intelligence Operations*. London: Frank Cass.

84 Schoenberger, E. (1991) 'The corporate interview as a research method in economic geography', *The Professional Geographer*, 43(2): 180–189.

85 Czudnowski, M.M. (1987) 'Interviewing political elites in Taiwan', in G. Moyser and M. Wagstaffe (eds), *Research Methods for Elite Studies*. London: Allen & Unwin. pp. 232–263; Rivera, S.W. et al. (2002) 'Interviewing political elites: Lessons from Russia', *Political Science and Politics*, 35(4); Denitch, B. (1972) 'Elite interviewing and social structure: An example from Yugoslavia', *Public Opinion Quarterly*, 36: 143–158.

86 Scheyvens, R. et al. (2003) 'Working with marginalised, vulnerable or privileged groups', in R. Scheyvens and D. Storey, *Development Fieldwork*. London: Sage. pp. 168–192.

87 Stephens, N. (2007) 'Collecting data from elites and ultra elites: Telephone and face-to-face interviews with macroeconomists', *Qualitative Research*, 7(2): 203–216.

88 Walford, G. (1994) 'Reflections on researching the powerful', in G. Walford (ed.), *Researching the Powerful in Education*. London: UCL Press; Czudnowski, M.M. (1987) 'Interviewing political elites in Taiwan', in G. Moyser and M. Wagstaffe (eds), *Research Methods for Elite Studies*. London: Allen & Unwin. pp. 232–263.

89 Gamble, A. (1994) 'Political memoires', *Politics*, 14(1).

90 Peabody, R.L. et al. (1990) 'Interviewing political elites', *Political Science and Politics*, 23(3): 451–455.

91 Leech, B. (2002) 'Interview methods in political science', *Political Science and Politics,* 35(4): 665–668.

92 Davies, P.H.J. (2001) 'Spies as informants: Triangulation and the interpretation of elite interview data in the study of the intelligence and security services', *Politics*, 21(1): 76–77.

93 Undheim, T.A. (2006) 'Getting connected: How sociologists can access the high tech elite', in S. Nagy et al., *Emergent Methods in Social Research*. London: Sage. pp. 13–36.

94   Kinkaid, H.V. and Bright, M. (1957) '"The tandem interview": A trial of the two-interviewer team', *Public Opinion Quarterly*, 21(2): 304–312; Kinkaid, H.V. and Bright, M. (1957) 'Interviewing the business elite', *American Journal of Sociology*, 63(3): 304–311.

95   HHI (2009) *Characterizing Sexual Violence in the Democratic Republic of the Congo.* Cambridge, MA: Harvard Humanitarian Initiative. p. 10.

96   Peabody, R.L. et al. (1990) 'Interviewing political elites', *Political Science and Politics*, 23(3): 451–455; Byron, M. (1993) 'Using audio-visual aids in geography research: Questions of access and responsibility', *Area*, 25: 379–385.

97   Berkeley, B. (2001) *The Graves are Not Yet Full: Race, Tribe and Power in the Heart of Africa.* New York: Basic Books. p. 188.

98   Czudnowski, M.M. (1987) 'Interviewing political elites in Taiwan', in G. Moyser and M. Wagstaffe (eds), *Research Methods for Elite Studies*. London: Allen & Unwin.

99   Conti, J.A. and O'Neil, M. (2007) 'Studying power: Qualitative methods and the global elite', *Qualitative Research*, 7(1): 70.

100 Thomas, R.J. (1995) 'Interviewing important people in big business', in R. Hertz, and J.B. Imber, *Studying Elites Using Qualitative Methods*. London: Sage. pp. 83–93.

101 Lilleker, 'Interviewing the political elite: Navigating a potential minefield', p. 210.

102 *Bigthink*, interviews with famous thinkers. Available at: http://bigthink.com

103 *Ali G Interviews, the Beckhams*. Available at: www.youtube.com/watch?v=P842Tmi6lrc; *Chomsky*. Available at: www.youtube.com/0watch?v=fOIM1_xOSro

104 BBC, 'Five minutes with … '. Available at: http://news.bbc.co.uk/1/hi/programmes/five_minutes_with/default.stm

105 Graham, K. and Williams, C. (2002) Series – *Through the Eyes of People: An Interview with Juan Somavia, Director General of the International Labour Organization (ILO); Freedom is a Universal Value: An interview with Mike Moore, Director General of the World Trade Organization (WTO); Healthy People, Healthy Planet: An Interview with Gro Harlem Brundtland, Director-General of the World Health Organization (WHO); Be Able to Hope: An Interview with Thorvald Stoltenberg, Former Director-General of the UNHCR.* UN University Leadership Academy: Amman.

106 *How I Cross Examine a Cop.* Available at: www.youtube.com/watch?v=-oQOdV21d6M

107 Memon, A. and Bull, R. (eds) (1999) *Handbook of the Psychology of Interviewing.* Chichester: Wiley; Milne, R. and Bull, R. (1999) *Investigative Interviewing: Psychology and Practice.* London: Wiley; Campos, I. (1999) 'The cognitive interview', *Psychology, Crime and Law*, 5: 1–2.

108 Raskin, D.C. (1989) *Psychological Methods in Criminal Investigation and Evidence.* New York: Springer. (Chapter 6, The cognitive interview.)

109 Thomas, R.J. (1995) 'Interviewing important people in big companies', in R. Hertz and J.B. Imber (eds), *Studying Elites Using Qualitative Methods*. London: Sage. p. 9.

110 Thomas, R.J. (1993) 'Interviewing important people in big companies', *Journal of Contemporary Ethnography*, 22(1): 9.

111 Waldman, M. (2010) *The Sun in the Sky: The Relationship Between Pakistan's ISI and Afghan Insurgents (Discussion Paper 18).* London: LSE/DESTIN. p. 3.

112 Thomas, R.J. (1995) 'Interviewing important people in big business', in R. Hertz and J.B. Imber, *Studying Elites Using Qualitative Methods*. London: Sage. pp. 83–93.

113 Stewart, D.W. and Shamdasani, N. (1990) *Focus Groups: Theory and Practice.* London: Sage.

114 Gaiser, T.J. (1997) 'Conducting on-line focus groups: A methodological discussion', *Social Science Computer Review*, 15(2): 135–144; Schneider, S.J. et al. (2002) 'Characteristics of the discussion in online and face-to-face focus groups', *Social Science Computer Review*, 20(1): 31–42.

115 Morgan, D. and Krueger, R.A. (1997) *The Focus Group Kit*. London: Sage.

116 Atkinson, J.M. (1984) *Our Masters' Voices: The Language and Body Language of Politics*. London: Methuen.

117 Winter, D.G. and Stewart, A.J. (1977) 'Content analysis', in M.G. Hermann (ed.), *A Psychological Examination of Political Leaders*. New York: The Free Press. pp. 27–62.

118 Winter, D.G. and Stewart, A.J. (1977) 'Non-verbal and paralinguistic analysis', in M.G. Hermann (ed.), *A Psychological Examination of Political Leaders*. New York: The Free Press. pp. 62–79.

119 Browne, C.G. and Thomas, S.C. (1958) 'Observation and evaluation methods', in *The study of leadership*, pp. 87–122.

120 Gillham, B. (2008) *Observation Techniques: Structured and Unstructured Approaches*. London: Continuum.

121 Rhodes, R.A.W., Hart, P.T. and Noordegraaf, M. (eds) (2010) 'Observing government elites: Up close and personal', *Public Administration*, 88(1): 269–272.

122 Jorgensen, D.L. (1989) *Participant Observation: A Methodology for Human Studies*. London: Sage.

123 Venkatesh, S. (2008) *A Gang Leader for a Day: A Rogue Sociologist Takes to the Streets*. London: Penguin Press.

124 Ortner, S.B. (2010) 'Access: Reflections on studying up in Hollywood', *Ethnography*, 11(2): 211–233.

125 Gains, F. (2011) 'Elite ethnographies: Potential, pitfalls and prospects for getting "up close and personal"', *Public Administration*, 89: 156–166.

126 Margolis, E. and Pauwels, L. (eds) (2011) *The Sage Handbook of Visual Research Methods*. London: Sage.

127 Williams, C. and Lee, Y.-J. (2005) 'The minds of leaders', in B. Walker (ed.), *Preparing for Peace*. Westmorland: General Meeting. p. 242.

128 Tosh, J. (2006) *The Pursuit of History: Aims, Methods and New Directions in the Study of Modern History*. Longman.

129 Renfrew, C. and Bahn, P. (2008) *Archaeology: Theories, Methods and Practice*. London: Thames & Hudson.

130 Pearson, D. (1998) *Provenance Research in Book History: A Handbook*. London: British Library.

131 Margolis, E. and Pauwels, L. (eds) (2011) *The Sage Handbook of Visual Research Methods*. London: Sage.

132 Hatt, M. and Klonk, C. (2006) *Art History: A Critical Introduction to its Methods*. Manchester: Manchester University Press.

133 Lee, Y.-J. (2010) 'Leadership and development in South Korea and Egypt: The significance of cultural shifts', unpublished PhD thesis, School of Oriental and Asian Studies, University of London.

134 Yamek, S. (2010) 'Turkish business elites', unpublished paper presented at the ESRC Seminar: Studying elites, 16–17 September, CRESC, University of Manchester.

135 Lee, Y.-J. (2011) 'Leadership and development in South Korea and Egypt: The significance of "cultural shifts"', unpublished PhD thesis, University of London (SOAS).

136 Lewis, J. (2009) *Scientology*. New York: Oxford University Press. p. 235.

137 Worsley, L. (2010) *Courtiers: The Secret History of Kensington Palace*. London: Faber and Faber.

138 Arber, S. (1993) 'Designing samples', in N. Gilbert (ed.), *Researching Social Life*. London: Sage; Goldstein, K. (2002) 'Getting in the door: Sampling and completing elite interviews', *Political Science and Politics*, 35(4): 669–672.

139 Wengraf, T. (2001) *Qualitative Research Interviewing: Biographic, Narrative and Semi-Structured Methods*. London: Sage.

140 Wiatr, J.J. (2003) 'Polish local elites and democratic change, 1990–2002', *Communist and Post Communist Studies*, 36: 373–383.

141 Riemer, J. (1977) 'Varieties of opportunistic research', *Urban Life*, 5: 467–477.

142 Biernacki, P. and Waldord, D. (1981) 'Snowball sampling: Problems and techniques of chain referral sampling', *Sociological Methods and Research*, 10(2).

143 Atkinson, R. and Flint, J. (2003) 'Sampling, snowball: Accessing hidden and hard-to-reach populations', in R.L. Miller and J.D. Brewer (eds), *The A–Z of Social Research*. London: Sage. pp. 275–280.

144 Denitch, B. (1972) 'Elite interviewing and social structure: An example from Yugoslavia', *Public Opinion Quarterly*, 36: 143–158; Rivera, S.W. et al. (2002) 'Interviewing political elites: Lessons from Russia', *Political Science and Politics*, 35(4).

145 Farquharson, K. (2005) 'A different kind of snowball: Identifying key policymakers', *International Journal of Social Research Methodology*, 8(4).

146 Coleman, R. (2003) 'CCTV surveillance, power, and social order', in S. Tombs and D. Whyte (eds), *Unmasking the Crimes of the Powerful*. New York: Peter Lang. p. 97.

147 Tansey, O. (2007) 'Process tracing and elite interviewing: A case for non-probability sampling', *Political Science and Politics*, 40(4).

148 Lammers, J., Stapel, D.A. and Galinsky, A.D. (2010) 'Power increases hypocrisy: Moralizing in reasoning, immorality in behavior', *Psychological Science*, 21: 737–744.

149 Aberbach, J.D. and Rockman, B.A. (2002) 'Conducting and coding elite interviews', *Political Science and Politics*, 35(4): 673–676; Saldana, J. (2009) *The Coding Manual for Qualitative Researchers*. London: Sage.

150 HHI (2009) *Characterizing Sexual Violence in the Democratic Republic of the Congo*. Cambridge, MA: Harvard Humanitarian Initiative. p. 14.

151 Robson, C. (1993) *Real World Research*. Oxford: Blackwell. pp. 385–389; 311–313; 252–253; 206–225 (Observation).

152 George, A.L. and Bennett, A. (2005) *Case Studies and Theory Development in the Social Sciences*. Cambridge, MA: MIT Press. p. 32.

153 Dexter, L.A. (1970) *Elite and Specialized Interviewing*. Evanston, IL: Northwestern University Press. p. 7.

154 Davies, P.H.J (2001) 'Spies as informants: Triangulation and the interpretation of elite interview data in the study of the intelligence and security services', *Politics*, 21(1): 73–80.

155 Slawner, K. (2006) *Interpreting Victim Testimony: Survivor Discourse and the Narration of History*. Available at: www.yendor.com/vanished/karenhead.html

156 Smith, H. (2004) 'Improving intelligence on North Korea', *Jane's Intelligence Review*, April: 48–51.

157 Godin, M., Kishan, J., Muraskin, D. and Newhouse, L. (2006) *The Medium of Testimony: Testimony as Re-presentation* (RSC Working Paper No. 37). Oxford: Refugee Studies Centre.

158 Chulov, M. (2011) 'Defector who triggered war on Iraq admits: "I lied about WMD"', *The Guardian*, 16 February: 1–5.

159 Demick, B. (2010) *Nothing to Envy: Real Lives in North Korea*. London: Granta.

160 Swetz, F.J. (1992) *The Sea Island Mathematical Manual: Surveying and Mathematics in Ancient China*. Pennsylvania: The Pennsylvania State University Press. p. 63.

161 Webb, E.J. et al. (1966) *Unobtrusive Measures: Nonreactive Research in the Social Sciences*. Chicago: Rand Macnally.

162 Denzin, N. (2006) *Sociological Methods: A Sourcebook.* Piscataway, NJ: Aldine Transaction.

163 Davies, P.H.J (2001) 'Spies as informants: Triangulation and the interpretation of elite interview data in the study of the intelligence and security services', *Politics*, 21(1): 73–80.

164 Eftimiades, N. (1994) *Chinese Intelligence Operations.* London: Frank Cass.

165 Davies, P.H.J (2001) 'Spies as informants: Triangulation and the interpretation of elite interview data in the study of the intelligence and security services', *Politics*, 21(1): 73–80.

166 Shively, W.P. (1980) *The Craft of Political Research.* New Jersey: Prentice-Hall. pp. 50–63.

167 Demick, *Nothing to Envy: Real Lives in North Korea.*

168 Campbell, D.T. and Fiske, D.W. (1959) 'Convergent and discriminant validation by the multitrait-multimethod matrix', *Psychological Bulletin*, 56(2): 465–476.

169 Berry, J.M. (2002) 'Validity and reliability issues in elite interviewing', *Political Science and Politics*, 35(4).

170 Cole, R.L. (1980) *Introduction to Political Inquiry.* New York: Macmillan. p. 83.

171 Stigler, S. (2008) 'Fisher and the 5% level', *Chance*, 21(4): 12.

CHAPTER 7: ANALYSIS

1 Gould, S.J. (1998) *Full House: The Spread of Excellence from Plato to Darwin.* New York: Random House.

2 Silverman, D. (2011) *Interpreting Qualitative Data.* London: Sage.

3 Locke, J. (1690) *Essay Concerning Human Understanding.* London.

4 Deutsch, D. (2011) *The Beginning of Infinity: Explanations that Transform the World.* London: Allen Lane. pp. 1–33.

5 Ragin, C.C. (1987) *The Comparative Method: Moving Beyond Qualitative and Quantitative Strategies.* Berkeley: University of California Press.

6 Morse, S. (2004) *Indices and Indicators in Development: An Unhealthy Obsession with Numbers.* London: Earthscan.

7 Bollen, K.A. and Lennox, R. (1991) 'Conventional wisdom on measurement: A structural equation perspective', *Psychological Bulletin*, 110: 305–314.

8 Gilley, B. (2006) 'The meaning and measure of state legitimacy: Results for 72 countries', *European Journal of Political Research*, 45(3): 499–525.

9 Morrell, K. (2006) 'Aphorisms and leaders' rhetoric: A new analytical approach', *Leadership*, 2(3): 367–382.

10 MoD (2009) *Security and Stabilisation: The Military Contribution.* Joint Doctrine Publications 3-40: Chapter 9, Political and social analysis. Available at: www.mod.uk/DefenceInternet/microsite/dcdc

11 Lindley, T.F. (1987) 'David Hume and necessary connections', *Philosophy*, 62(239): 49–58.

12 Barker, C. (2005) *Cultural Studies: Theory and Practice.* London: Sage. p. 448; Giddens, A. (1984) *The Constitution of Society.* Cambridge: Polity Press.

13 Shively, W.P. (1980) *The Craft of Political Research.* New Jersey: Prentice-Hall. pp. 14–15.

14 Boaduo, N. A-P. (2010) 'Epistemological analysis: Conflict and resolution in Africa', *The Journal of Pan African Studies*, 3(10).

15 Fricker, M. (2009) *Epistemic Injustice: Power and the Ethics of Knowing*. Oxford: Oxford University Press.

16 Almquist, Y. (2009) 'Peer status in school and adult disease risk: A 30-year follow-up study of disease specific morbidity in a Stockholm cohort', *Journal of Epidemiology and Community Health*, 10: 11.

17 Lewin, K. et al. (1939) 'Patterns of aggressive behaviour in experimentally created "social climates"', *Journal of Social Psychology*, (10): 271–299.

18 Rossi, P.H. et al. (2004) *Evaluation: A Systematic Approach*. Thousand Oaks, CA: Sage.

19 White, H. (2009) *Theory-based Impact Evaluation: Principles and Practice* (Working paper 3). New Delhi: International Initiative for Impact Evaluation.

20 Shively, W.P. (2005) *The Craft of Political Research*. London: Prentice-Hall. pp. 108–131.

21 Bazeley, P. (2007) *Qualitative Data Analysis with NVIVO*. London: Sage.

22 Garner, R. (2011) 'Cable desperate to stop fees stampede', *The Independent*, 7 April: 9. (UK Office of National Statistics, study.)

23 Olofsson, P. (2005) *Probability, Statistics, and Stochastic Processes*. London Wiley-Interscience.

24 Popper, K. (1959/2002) *The Logic of Scientific Discovery*. London: Routledge.

25 Andreas, P. (2010) *Sex, Drugs, and Body Counts: The Politics of Numbers in Global Crime and Conflict*. New York: Cornell University Press.

26 Cho, Ji-Hyun (2011) 'Listed firms change CEO every 31 months: Data', *Korea Herald*, 30 May: 6. (www.chaebul.com)

27 Hari, J. (2011) 'What Trump tells us about America', *The Independent* (Viewspaper), 29 April: 3.

28 Sterne, L. (1996) *Tristram Shandy*. Wordsworth Editions: London. p. 105.

29 BBC (2002) 'Iran president in NY campus row', *BBC News Online*, 25 September. Available at: http://news.bbc.co.uk/1/hi/7010962.stm

30 Taylor, J. (2011) 'Three men hanged for sodomy in Iran – where "gay people don't exist"', *The Independent*, 8 September: 32.

31 UNEP (2006) *Consistency in Laws and Regulations* (46), manual on compliance with and enforcement of multilateral environmental agreements. Nairobi: UNEP.

32 Thornton, G.C. (1996) *Legislative Drafting*. London: LexisNexis. pp. 72, 113.

33 Volokh, A. (2008) 'Choosing interpretive methods: A positive theory of judges and everyone else', *New York University Literary Review*, 83: 769.

34 Davis, M. and Stark, A. (2001) *Conflict of Interest in the Professions*. Oxford: Oxford University Press.

35 Cabinet Office (2010) *Ministerial Code (UK)*. Available at: www.cabinetoffice.gov.uk/resource-library/ministerial-code

36 Eagly, A.H. and Karau, S.J. (2002) 'Role congruity theory of prejudice toward female leaders', *Psychological Review*, 109: 573–598.

37 Festinger, L. (1956) *When Prophecy Fails: A Social and Psychological Study of a Modern Group that Predicted the Destruction of the World*. New York: Harper-Torchbooks.

38 Adam, B. (1998) *Timescapes Of Modernity: The Environment and Invisible Hazards*. London: Routledge. pp. 110–116.

39 Irokawa, D. (1995) *The Age of Hirohito: In Search of Modern Japan*. London: The Free Press.

40 Boyd-Judson, L. (2011) *Strategic Moral Diplomacy: Understanding the Enemy's Moral Position*. Sterling, VA: Kumarian Press.

41 McNamara, R.R.S. (1995) *In Retrospect: The Tragedy and Lessons of Vietnam.* London: Times Books. Preface, p. 39.

42 Marschan-Piekkari, R. and Welch, C.A. (eds) (2004) *Handbook of Qualitative Research Methods for International Business.* London: Edward Elgar.

43 Smith, H. (2004) 'Improving intelligence on North Korea', *Jane's Intelligence Review,* April: 48–51.

44 Hart, H.L.A. and Honore, A.M. (1985) *Causation in the Law.* Oxford: Oxford University Press.

45 Pogge, T. (2009) 'Developing morally plausible indices of poverty and gender equity: A research program', *Philosophical Topics,* (37)2: 199–221.

46 Silverman, D. (1993) *Interpreting Qualitative Data. Methods for Analysing Talk, Text and Interaction.* London: Sage Publications.

47 WMO (2003) *Climate in the 21st Century.* Cambridge: Cambridge University Press.

48 Nisbett, R.E. and Wilson, T.D. (1977) 'The halo effect: Evidence for unconscious alteration of judgments', *Journal of Personality and Social Psychology,* 35(4): 250–256.

49 Williams, C. (1995) *Invisible Victims: Crime and Abuse against People with Learning Disabilities.* London: Jessica Kingsley.

50 Yalop, D. (2010) *Beyond Belief: The Catholic Church and the Child Abuse Scandal.* London: Constable.

51 The Stationery Office (1999) *The Judgment of Nuremberg 1946.* London: The Stationery Office.

52 Darnton, G. and Darnton, M. (1997) *Business Process Analysis.* Andover: Thomson Business Press.

53 Lynch, F. (1994) *Reengineering Business Processes and People Systems.* Pagosa Springs, CO : QualTeam, Inc.

54 Tansey, O. (2007) 'Process tracing and elite interviewing: A case for non-probability sampling', *Political Science and Politics,* 40(4).

55 George, A.L. and Bennett, A. (2005) *Case Studies and Theory Development in the Social Sciences.* Boston: MIT Press. pp. 6, 206.

56 Levine, H.L. (2007) 'The use of critical process analysis to reduce risk and increase biologics product quality', unpublished presentation at the FIP Quality International 2007 Conference, Acton, MA: BioProcess Technology Consultants.

57 Guzzetti, B.J., Snyder, T.E., Glass, G.V. and Gamas, W.S. (1993) 'Promoting conceptual change in science: A comparative meta-analysis of instructional interventions from reading education and science education', *Reading Research Quarterly,* 28(2): 116–159.

58 Williams, C. (2010) 'Global justice and education: from nation to neuron', *Education Review,* 62(3): 343–356.

59 Gould, S.J. (1979) *Ever Since Darwin.* New York: W.W. Norton & Co. pp.161–162.

60 Somekh, B. (2011*) Theory and Methods in Social Research.* London: Sage.

61 Atran, S. (2010) *Talking to the Enemy: Violent Extremism, Sacred Values and What it Means to be Human.* London: Allen Lane. p. 473.

62 Custers, P. (2010) 'Military Keynesianism today: an innovative discourse', *Institute of Race Relations,* 51(4): 79–94.

63 Chemers, M.M. (2000) 'Leadership research and theory: A functional integration', *Group Dynamics: Theory, Research, and Practice,* 4(1): 27–43.

64 Bryman, A. (2001) *Social Research Methods.* Oxford: Oxford University Press. pp. 8–11.

65 Glaser, B. (1992) *Basics of Grounded Theory Analysis.* Mill Valley, CA: Sociology Press; Strauss, A. and Corbin, J. (1990) *Basics of Qualitative Research: Grounded Theory Procedures and Techniques.* London: Sage; Parry, K.P. (2002) 'Grounded theory and social process: A new direction for leadership research', *Leadership Quarterly,* 9(1): 85–105; Yeager, P.C. and Kram, K.E. (1995) 'Fielding hot topics in cool settings', in R. Hertz and J.B. Imber, *Studying Elites Using Qualitative Methods.* London: Sage. p. 43.

CHAPTER 8: OUTCOMES

1   Holmes, B. (1985) 'The problem (solving) approach', in A. Watson and R. Wilson (eds), *Contemporary Issues in Comparative Education*. New Hampshire: Croom Helm.

2   Parkin, S. (2010) *The Positive Deviant: Sustainability Leadership in a Perverse World*. London: Earthscan.

3   Venkatesh, S. (2008) *A Gang Leader for a Day: A Rogue Sociologist Takes to the Streets*. London: Penguin Press.

4   Appleyard, B. (2008) 'Hanging out with the ghetto's Gordon Gekkos', *The Sunday Times,* 17 February.

5   Richardson, L. (1990) *Writing Strategies*. London: Sage.

6   Tombs, A. and Whyte, D. (2002) 'Unmasking the crimes of the powerful', *Critical Criminology*, 11: 217–236.

7   *Plain English Campaign*. Available at: www.plainenglish.co.uk/index.htm

8   Cutts, M. (1999) *Plain English Guide: How to Write Clearly and Communicate Better*. Oxford: Oxford University Press.

9   Mullings, B. (1999) 'Insider or outsider, both or neither: Some dilemmas of interviewing in a cross-cultural setting', *Geoforum*, 30: 337–350.

10 Hart, C. (1998) *Doing a Literature Review: Releasing the Social Science Research Imagination*. London: Sage.

11 Denicolo, P. and Becker, L. (2011) *Success in Publishing Journal Articles*. London: Sage.

12 Denicolo, P. and Becker, L. (2011) *Success in Research Proposals*. London: Sage.

13 Keophilavong, S. (2008) *The Democracy Initiative: Researching Power and Influence*. London: Carnegie Trust.

14 EEA (2002) *Late Lessons from Early Warnings: The Precautionary Principle 1896–2000*. Copenhagen: European Environment Agency.

15 Margolis, E. and Pauwels, L. (eds) (2011) *The Sage Handbook of Visual Research Methods*. London: Sage.

16 Few, S. (2004) *Show Me the Numbers: Designing Tables and Graphs to Enlighten*. Oakland: Analytics Press.

17 Joiner Associates Staff (1995) *Flowcharts: Plain & Simple Learning & Application Guide.* Greenwood: Oriel Inc.

18 Damelio, R. (1996) *The Basics of Process Mapping*. New York: Productivity Press.

19 Tufte, E.R. (1990) *Envisioning Information*. Cheshire: Graphics Press.

20 Tufte, E.R. (2003) *The Cognitive Style of PowerPoint*. Cheshire: Graphics Press.

21 Tufte, E.R. (2001) *The Visual Display of Quantitative Information*. Cheshire: Graphics Press.

22 Ellen, D. (1989) *The Scientific Examination of Documents*. New York: Wiley. (Chapter 11 – Document examination in court.)

23 Volokh, A. (2008) 'Choosing interpretive methods: A positive theory of judges and everyone else', *New York University Literary Review*, 83: 769.

24 Knight, D. (2006) *Public Understanding of Science: A History of Communicating Scientific Ideas.* London: Routledge.

25 David Spiegelhalter's personal home page. Available at: www.statslab.cam.ac.uk/Dept/People/Spiegelhalter/davids.html

26 Tombs, S. and Whyte, D. (2003) 'Scrutinizing the powerful', in S. Tombs and D. Whyte, *Unmasking the Crimes of the Powerful*. New York: Peter Lang. pp. 36–39.

27 *Transparency International,* Policy and research. Available at: www.transparency.org/policy_research_surveys_indices/cpi/2008

28 Williams, C. (1995) *Crime and Abuse Against People with Learning Disabilities*, Findings. Available at: www.jrf.org.uk/sites/files/jrf/sc70.pdf

29 *ESRC 'Evidence Briefings'*. Available at: www.esrc.ac.uk/publications/evidence-briefings/default.aspx

30 Stephens, C. et al. (2001) *Environmental Justice*, ESRC Global Environmental Change Programme. Available at: www.foe.co.uk/resource/reports/environmental_justice.pdf

31 *Social Science Research Network*. Available at: www.ssrn.com

32 *Scribd*. Available at: www.scribd.com

33 *Ranking Web of World Repositories*. Available at: http://repositories.webometrics.info

34 BBC (2010) 'Anonymous Wikileaks activists move to analogue tactics', *BBC News Online*, 16 December.

35 TEHELKA. Available at: www.tehelka.com

36 *Online Questions to MPs*. Available at: www.38degrees.org.uk/choose-the-issues

37 http://judicialcomplaints.judiciary.gov.uk

38 www.the-hutton-inquiry.org.uk/content/evidence.htm#full

39 www.iraqinquirydigest.org/?p=5355

40 www.pcaw.co.uk

41 *Abuse of Power Organizations*. Available at: www.datehookup.com/content-organizations-dedicated-to-fighting-abuse.htm

42 Williams, C. (2006) *Leadership Accountability in a Globalizing World*. London: Palgrave Macmillan. pp. 157–176.

43 Williams, C. and Lee, Y.-J. (2005) 'The mind of leaders: De-linking war and violence', in B. Walker (ed.), *Preparing for Peace*. Kendal: Westmorland General Meeting. Available at: www.preparingforpeace.org

44 Parkin, S. (2010) *The Positive Deviant: Sustainability Leadership in a Perverse World*. London: Earthscan.

45 VeneKlasen, L. and Miller, V. (eds) (2002) *A New Weave of Power, People & Politics: The Action Guide for Advocacy and Citizen Participation*. London: Practical Action Publishing.

46 Cornwall, A. and Coehlo, V. (eds) (2006) *Spaces for Change? The Politics of Citizen Participation in New Democratic Arenas*. London: Zed Books.

47 Gavanta, J. (2006) 'Finding the spaces for change: A power analysis', *IDS Bulletin*, 37(6): 23–33.

48 Vermeulen, S. (2005) *Power Tools: Handbook to Tools and Resources for Policy Influence in Natural Resource Management*. London: IIED.

49 Keophilavong, S. (2008) *The Democracy Initiative: Researching Power and Influence*. London: Carnegie Trust.

50 Hunjan, R. and Keophilavong, S. (2010) *Power and Making Change Happen*. Dunfermline: Carnegie UK Trust.

51 Clark, J. (1992) 'Policy influence, lobbying and advocacy' in M. Edwards and D. Hulme (eds), *Making a Difference: NGOs and Development in a Changing World*. London: Earthscan.

52 Prentice, C. (2009) 'Major US cities hail crime reduction', *BBC News Online*, 12 August.

53 Voltaire (1752) *The Age of Louis XIV*. Translated from the French. London: R. Dodsley. (Introduction.)

INDEX

abuse of power, 3, 67, 80, 100, 102, 129, 159,
    216–217, 219
    traditional, 101
access, 6, 8, 16, 25, 27, 33, 52, 62, 93–5, 99, 103, 109,
    117, 124–127, 131, 134, 137, 139, 141, 152, 154,
    156, 157, 161, 163, 166, 169, 171, 175, 204, 212,
    216, Appendix 11
accountability, 3, 4, 6, 40, 45, 48, 52, 64, 65, 74, 75, 79,
    81, 82, 83, 84, 85, 86, 99, 106, 119, 117, 140, 177,
    213, 219, 220, 255
accuracy, 179
achieved status, 11, 23, 69
action research, Appendix 9
action-oriented, 115, 116, 141, 154
advocacy, 40, 80, 85, 86, 103, 113, 115, 134, 140, 154,
    169, 216, 218, 220, 221, 255
affiliations, 149
Afghanistan, 101, 113, 146, 158
Africa, 22, 24, 27, 106, 191, 217
agency, 113, 143, 191, 206, 217
agenda setting, 61
aggregate, 114, 155, 179, 187, 188
Ahmadinajad, Mahmoud, 195
aims, 11, 27, 95, 109, 121–122, 137, 152, 162,
    180, 212, 200, 204, 206, 213–214, Appendices 3,
    6, 7, 8, 10
airbrushing, 36, 156
al-Azhar University, 126
al-Janabi, Rafid, 57, 177
al-Sulayhi, Arwa (the little Queen of Sheba), 36
Althusser, Louis, 120
American Majority, 97
Amnesty International, 3, 76, 116, 127, 128, 131, 140,
    141, 151, 162, 177, 178, 179, 216, 218, 255
analysis, 185–210
    centre of gravity, 146
    content, 141, 158
    context, 147
    counterfactual, 147, 192, 201, 204, 207
    documentary, 40, 44, 95, 156
    meta, 95
    network, 149

analysis *cont.*
    organizational, 147
    policy, 148, 204
    process, 148
    secondary, 95, 144, 155
    situation, 147
    statistical, 154, 192
    systems, 145–152
analytical frameworks, 155, 187, 189, 190
anarchical, 22
animal studies, 106–107
anthropology, 22–30
aphorisms, 187, 189
approach, 137
Arab, 123
    Spring, 1
archaeology, 40, 140, 143, 170
    forensic, 7, 36, 41
aristocracy, 23, 66
Aristotle, 44
Armenia, 47, 116, 200
art, 170
Art of War, The, 34
Arthashasta, 4, 44
Asantewaa, Yaa, 36
ascribed status, 11, 23, 69
Ashanti, 36, 51
Ashera (Queen of Heaven), 36
Ashoka, 33, 34, 52, 103
assumptions, 28, 46, 58, 61, 80, 81, 112, 113, 121, 134,
    147, 192, 201, 202, 213, 220
asymmetrical power, 100
Ataturk, M.K., 173
Augustus, Caesar, 31, 157
authentic leadership, 60, 71
authority, 12, 13, 21, 23, 28, 30, 37, 38, 42, 58, 59, 72,
    79, 97, 99, 101, 157, 198, Appendix 1
    moral, 84
    autocracy, 44, 52

Babylon, 35
Bach, J.S., 202

backcasting, 144
backdrop, 2, 7, 17, 156, 163, 173
bad leaders, 73, 74, 82
bads, 207
bankers, 124
banknotes, 9, 157, 199
Bass, B.M., 69, 71
BBC, 7, 92, 114, 126,139, 163, 165, 212, 216
behaviour, 34, 42, 45, 52, 58, 60–61, 69, 71–76, 78–79,
     84, 107, 114, 131, 138–139, 142, 146, 148, 150,
     155, 178, 195–196, 200, 203
Belgium, 28
best interests, 132
bias, 128
biography, 95, 118, 139, 140, 156
Biruni, 24
Bivings Group, 97
blagging, 133
Blair, Tony, 157
blogs, 219
body language, 141, 142, 162, 169
born or made, 37, 69, 70, 77, 107
borrowed power, 1, 127
Bosnia, 186
Bottomore, T.B., 63, 65
Boudica, 36
bourgeois, 60, 67, 79
Brazil, 103, 209
briefings, 218
Britain, 58, 80, 120, 216
buildings, 173–174
bureaucracy, 60, 64
Burkes Peerage, 33
Burma, 103
Burns, J.M., 71

Cameroon, 24
Canada, 65, 161
carbon dating, 36, 157
Carlyle, Thomas, 5, 69
carrot and stick, 43, 59
case study, Appendix 1, 9
caste, 23
Catalonia, 22, 108
causal direction, 193, 194
causation, 59, 120, 190–195
celebrity, 4, 5, 14, 103, 130, 132, 139, 191
census, 31, 175
centre of gravity analysis, 146
CEOs, 94, 112, 117, 118, 120, 147, 149, 179, 194, 217
chain referral, 166, 176
Chanakya, 44
change, 217
   social, 81, 147, 209, 217

characteristics, 5, 69, 138
Charles I, 24, 74
chieftaincy, 23
children, 103–105, 109, 138, 139, 151, 191, 216
China, 11, 12, 31, 33, 34, 42, 66, 71, 74, 92, 97, 100,
     109, 146, 156, 157, 174
Chomsky, Noam, 41, 79
chronologies, 32
Chung Ju-yung, 9
CIA, 62, 91, 92, 93
civil society, 79, 140
closed regimes, 106, 259
coding, 154, 176
coercion, 12
cognitive dissonance, 196
cohort, 139, 193
coincidence, 192, 194
coins, 157
collaborative research, 141
collapse, 67
     see also decline
College of Arms, 33
colonial regimes, 25, 27, 66, 207
common sense, 202–203
Comoros Islands, 25
community of practice, 66, 150
comparison, 34, 37, 44, 45, 64, 147, 178, 186–190,
     Appendix 9
concept, 52, 120, 121, 122, 179, 187, 207, 208
     framework, 13
confidentiality, 130, 131
confounders, 191, 193–194
Confucius, 42
Congo, 27–29
     Democratic Republic of, 127
consent, 129, 131
consequences, 61
consistency, 143, 177, 178, 187, 195–200, 204
conspiracy, 61, 65
constitutive leadership, 71
content analysis, 141, 158
context analysis, 147
contingency, 37, 45, 70
contra-arguments, 200–202
control, 12, 27, 45, 46, 58, 59, 60, 61, 62, 65, 66, 73,
     74, 76, 78, 80, 85, 86, 100, 113, 139, 144, 159,
     161, 163, 185, 192, 193, Appendix 1
convenience samples, 176
Corporate Watch, 65, 130, 216
corporate, 65
     crime, 147, 155
     elite, 150
     ethics, 117
     social responsibility, 75

correlation, 192, 193, 194
corroboration, 179
    see also triangulation
Corruption Convention (UN), 3
cosmopolitanism, 62
counterfactual analysis, 132, 147, 192, 201, 204, 206,
        207, 209
court, 137, 142, 154, 180, 215, 221
Crete, 22
crime, 137
    state, 99, 100, 103
Critical Process Analysis, 17, 94, 96, 144, 148, 158,
        186, 204–207, Appendix 2
critical, 42, 81–84
    process analysis, 204–207
    theory, 81, 206, 209
cross-cultural, 123
cross-sectional, 118, Appendix 9
crowd, 77, 78–79, 99, 140, 215
    psychology, 43, 51, 79, 95, 178
crowdsourcing, 6, 40, 47, 52, 110, 140, 157
Cuba, 93
cults, 103
culture, 8, 123
cumulative lock-in, 74–5
customer services, 125
Czech Republic, 108

da Silva, Lula, 103
da Vinci, Leonardo, 103
Dalai Lama, 70
Darwin, Charles, 153
data, 153–181
    meta, 133, 154
    primary, 154, 158, 204
    protection, 133
    raw, 154, 216
    secondary, 95, 139, 154
    selection, 175, 176
    testing, 176
David, King, 35
de Klerk, F.W., 70, 103
deceit, 25, 30, 45, 57, 74, 130, 133, 166, 203, Appendix 3
    pre-emptive, 80
decision-making, 61, 64, 67, 73–74, 138, 147, 154,
        180, 185, 220
    belief-based, 74
    evidence-based, 74
decisive groups, 146
decline, 38, 39, 43, 44, 45, 48, 50, 51, 52, 67, 78, 83,
        86, 185, 246
    see also collapse
defamation, 134, 159, 161
defector, 57, 177

definition, 121–124
degeneracy, 78
democracy, 13, 14, 44, 45, 50, 52, 62, 64, 73, 78, 101,
        106, 120, 121,197, 174
design, 112–114, 228, Appendix 3
    emergent, 112
despots, 103
Deutsch, David, 186
Diamond, Jared, 68
diaries, 139, 158
Dickens, Charles, 79
dictatorship, 14, 113
digerati, 67
digital governance, 62
diplomacy, 5, 173
disability rights, 12, 80, 198, 203
discourse analysis, 142, 158
dissertation, 212–214
distance research, 8, 141
distributed leadership, 72, 107
DNA, 33, 41, 178
documentary analysis, 40, 44, 95, 141, 156, 158
domain, 12, 64, 156
domination, 59, 67, 85, 158
down-system, 1, 46, 76, 78
drawings, 104–105, 133, 177, 217
drones, 62
dynasties, 2, 30, 32, 47, 51, 144

Eadgyth, 36
East Asia, 64, 99
echelon theory, 65
education systems, 150
Egypt, 1, 2, 8, 22, 25, 30, 32, 36, 38, 44, 80, 108, 144,
        156, 157, 168, 169, 194
Eichman, Adolf, 29
elite, 42
    interlocking, 65
    memory, 66
    reproduction, 44, 66, 103, 117, 180
    spaces, 66
    studies, 11, 28
    theory, 23, 63–68
elites, 26, 63–68
    global, 76, 150
    legal, 106
    media, 106
    new, 106
    wealthy, 106
Elizabeth I, Queen, 5, 99
Elyiot, Thomas, 45, 46
empathy, 5
empowerment, 80, 141
Engels, Friedrich, 23, 60, 79

England, 36, 45, 151, 159
entrapment, 133
environmental victims, 80
epistemic, 56
    communities, 66, 81, 106, 150
    injustice, 191
epistemology, 37, 56–58, 121, 158, 177
e-research, 92, Appendix 9
Eritrea, 36
ethics, 41–42, 47, 124, 142, 150, 185, 200
    global, 76
    leadership, 74
    reciprocal, 132
    research, 25, 128
Ethiopia, 36
ethnography, 26, Appendix 9
eugenics, 64
Europe, 23–25, 27–28, 35–36, 40, 45–46, 61–62, 64,
    74, 92, 78–79, 101, 173, 176, 255
evaluation, 147, 186
evolutionary psychology, 46, 61, 67, 74, 107, 144, 194
exceptionalism, 100
experiments, 139, Appendix 9
    natural, 138, 143
extending interviews, 163
extremism, 103

Facebook, 108, 141, 176
field of power, 66
fieldwork, 154, 155
findings, 178, 180, 218
focus, 114–119, Appendix 5, 8
    group, 112, 159
followers, 11, 30, 68, 71, 76, 107
    accepting, 76
    fish, 106
    questioning, 76
Fon, 24
forensic, 143, 163
Foucault, Michel, 61
Foxe, 40
frameworks, 136–152, Appendix 9, 10
France, 78, 79, 159, 171, 174
fraud, 7, 137, 196
Freedom of Information, 6, 94
Freud, Sigmund, 78

Gaddafi, Muammar, 38
Gallup, 166
Galton, Francis, 64, 69
game theory, 148
Gandhi, 202
gang leaders, 1, 123, 107, 209

Gantt charts, 112, Appendix 4
Gardener, Howard, 5, 71
gatekeepers, 125, 220
genealogy, 23, 27, 32, 33, 47, 49, 51, 84, 149, 159
generalization, 175, 208
Geneva, 12
genius, 12, 65
genocide, 56, 74, 197, 200
Germany, 11, 57, 74, 76, 100, 160
gerontocracy, 23, 66
Ghana, 24, 36, 123
gifted, 103
glass ceiling, 69
global, 75–76
    elites, 57, 76, 101, 150
    ethics, 76
    leadership, 74, 76, 187, 188
    nomadic leaders, 66
Global Leadership Responsibility Index, 188
god, 23, 28, 55, 56, 68, 174
    kings, 24, 35, 45
goods, 207
Gorbachev, Mikhail, 103
Goya, 170
Gramsci, Antonio, 61, 151
graphs, 187
Gray, John, 55
Great Men, 30, 69, 78
Great Women, 36
Greece, 35, 37, 78, 144, 157, 173
grid, 173
Grint, Keith, 73, 77
group-think, 74
Guatemala, 113, 161

Habermas, Jurgen, 81, 144
hacking, 62
Haiti, 5, 103
halo effect, 37, 96, 97, 98, 163, 203
Hammurabi, 35
Han Fei, 43
hard power, 43
Hatshepsut, 36
Hawking, Stephen, 108
Hawthorn effect, 141
Hebrew law, 34, 35
Hegel, 69, 78
hegemony, 11, 61
heredity, 23, 43, 69
hero, 5, 6, 11, 69, 78, 103, 113
Herodotus, 32, 51
Hezbollah, 97
hierarchy, 12, 47, 51

Himiko, 36
Hindu, 4, 44
Hirohito, Emperor, 5, 200
history, 30–41, 170
Hitler, Adolf, 74, 76, 78, 99, 113, 158
Hollywood, 170, Appendix 9
Huggins, Martha, 209
human rights, 128
Human Rights Watch, 3, 40, 76, 127, 216
Hume, David, 191
Hunter, Floyd, 65, 148
Hypermobility, 101
hypothesis, 119, 120, 191, 195, 208
    null, 56, 193
    ontological, 56
Hyundi, 9

Iceland, 101
ICT, 8, 67, 80–82, 92, 95, 106–107, 129, 140–141,
    149, 170, 207, 215, 219
ideological leaders, 103, 216
ideology, 34, 41, 60, 61
impact, 212
    assessment, 147
impartiality, 128
Imperial College, 66
index, 114
    Corruption Perceptions, 154–155, 166
    Global Leadership Responsibility, 187–188
    Human Development, 187
Index on Censorship, 133
India, 4, 23, 24, 33, 34, 44, 52, 103
Indica, 25
indicators, 114, 120, 144, 154, 179, 187
indirect research, 127
inference, 193
influence, 12
information, 216
inner circles, 65
instruments, 114, 155
    of power, 151, Appendix 12
integrity, 128, 147
intelligence, 3, 145, 146, 149, 189, 201
    officers, 162
interlocks, 149
International Committee of the Red Cross, 127, 128
International Criminal Court, 3, 8, 188, 216, 219, 221
international leadership, 76
International State Crime Initiative, 3, 100, 209
interview, 8, 114, 161, 162, 169, 209
    cognitive, 163
    schedules, 155
investigation, 126, 137, 154, 162, 163, 176

invisible colleges, 66
Iran, 25, 58, 100, 120, 134, 141, 157, 159, 195, 199,
    196, 198–199, 200
    Shah of, 198–9
    see also Persia
Iraq, 28, 57, 62, 157, 159, 177
    Body Count, 140
    dossier, 157
    Inquiry, 5, 12, Appendix 3
Islam, 100, 134, 173, 198
Isle of Man, 101, 216
Israel, 34, 35, 36, 97, 98, 100, 108, 157, 159, 163, 164
Italy, 33, 45, 61

Japan, 33, 34, 36, 49, 100, 101, 108, 125, 149, 150, 192
Jepson School of Leadership Studies, 77
Jerusalem, 35
Jewish *see* Israel
Jiang Qing, 36
Jingu, Empress, 36
Jordan, 163, 167
journalistic, 126, 131, 137, 138, 162, 170, Appendix 11
judge, 195, 216, 219
Jung, Karl, 165
justification, 116

Karnac, 32
Kellerman Barbara, 73
Kensington Palace, 174
keywords, 122
Khaldun, Ibn, 30, 37, 67, 68, 96
Khentykaues, 36
Khomeini, Ayatollah, 12, 157, 198–199, Appendix 1
Kim Dae-jung, 13, 104, 202
Kim Il-sung, 24, 104, 146, 157
king, 45
    god, 24, 35, 45
    lists, 1, 2, 32, 47, 48, 144, 174
King's Speech, The, 6, 7
kinship, 23, 149
knowledge, 186
knowns, 57
Korea, 36, 38, 103, 123, 171–172, 174, 192
    North, 24, 38, 80, 97, 100, 120, 127, 134, 141, 146,
        149, 157, 170, 177
    South, 9, 12, 13, 14, 66, 73, 79, 101, 102, 104–105,
        126, 151, 167, 173
Kuwait, 4, 159
Kwan Sun Yu, 14, 37

Lao Tzu, 42
Laos, Appendix 8
Lasswell, Harold, 69, 80, Appendix 9

le Bon, Gustav, 78, 99
leaderless, 22
leaders, 68–77
  bad, 73, 74, 82
  direct, 71
  gang, 1, 123, 209
  indirect, 71
  military, 106, 113, 117, 123, 148
  religious, 23, 33, 35, 40, 101, 174, 191
  toxic, 73
leadership, 30, 68–77
  authentic, 60, 71
  constitutive, 71
  distributed, 72, 107
  education, 43, 139, 163, 164
  international, 76
  performing, 22, 47
  political, 73, 106, 154, 219
  servant, 42, 72
  situated, 70
  studies, 11, 28, 106
  theory, 43, 68–77, 82
  training, 5, 66, 71, 72, 76, 107, 117
  transactional, 71, 76, 85
  transformational, 76
Lee, Yun-joo, 2, 8, 14, 66, 77, 96, 105, 123, 126, 169, 173
legal elites, 106
legal issues, 133
legitimacy, 1, 12, 30, 35, 38, 59, 71, 106, 117, 143, 157, 159, 160, 170, 174, 187, 194
lens, 115
levels, 118, Appendix 5
Libya, 38
lineage, 23, 32, 33, 47, 143, 200
LinkedIn, 176
lists, 1, 2, 32, 36, 47, 48, 144, 174
literature, 91–110, 141, 213
Locke, John, 186
Lokele, 27–29
longitudinal, Appendix 9
Lorenz, Conrad, 153
Lukes, Steven, 61

MacGregor, Neil, 157
Machiavelli, 45
Madoff, Bernard, 124
mafia, 123, 133
Majali, Abdul Salam, 163–165
Malaysia, 160
Malta, 40
Mamlukes, 106
management, 82
Mandela, Nelson, 70, 151
Manderins, 171

Manetho, 32, 51, 144
Mann, Michael, 59
Mannheim, Karl, 61
Mao Zedong, 36, 54, 92, 157, 158
maps, 159
Martelly, Michel (Sweet Micky), 103
Marx, Karl, 23, 54, 60, 64, 67, 79, 107, 122, 209
mass, 11, 60, 61, 77, 78
  communications, 12, 34, 35, 80, 159, 191
massification, 80
Mayhew, Henry, 79
McNamara, Robert, 151, 201
Mead, Margaret, 23
media elites, 106
medical conditions, 101
memoires, 140, 162
memorials, 101, 102
memory elite, 66
meritocracy, 43, 66
  distorted, 66
Mesopotamia, 31
meta, 145
  analysis, 95, 145, 150
  data, 145, 171
  methods, 145, 171
  synthesis, 145
method, 10, 213
  interpretive, 170
Michels, Robert, 65
Middle East, 100, 106, 108
Milgram, S., 79
military, 106
  intelligence, 189
  leaders, 106, 113, 117, 123, 148
Mills, C. Wright, 65, 80
mixed methods, 155, 179
Mohilla, 24, 27
monopolists, 159, 160
moral, 84
  plausibility, 129, 203
  authority, 84, 198
  universe, 201
  values, 208
morally plausible, 129
Mosca, Gaetano, 63
Mubarak, Hosni, 1, 38, 156
Mugabe, Robert, 144
museums, 30, 101, 133, 157, 170
Mussolini, Benito, 33, 99, 158

Nader, Laura, 1, 28
Napoleon, 170
Narmer Palette, 31

Nath, Vikas, 62
Native Americans, 23
Nazi, 64, 74, 78, 79, 100, 118, 192, 200, 204
necessary connections, 191
network, 143, 145–152, 166, 176
    analysis, 149
new elites, 106
new social movements, 79
New Zealand, 101
Nigeria, 103
no comment, 130
nobility, 23
nominal fallacy, 112
non-nation states, 101
non-verbal language, 141
Norman, Sam Hinga, 142
Notre Dame, 174
Nuremberg trials, 204

Obama, President, 156
objects, 170–173
observation, 169
    charts, 155
    remote, 170
ochlocracy, 45, 78
off the record, 130
oligarchy, 44, 65
ontology, 42, 55, 121, 177, 178, 191
open notebook, 140, 212
Operation Northwoods, 93
opinion poll, 166
opportunism, 168, 170, 175, 219
oppositional power, 79
organizational analysis, 147
origins, 21–53
Ottoman, 200
outcome-oriented, 113, 211–222
outcomes, 61, 147, 190, 204, 211–222
Oxford Research Group, 220

Pakistan, 12, 113
Palestine, 159
paradigms, 72, 81
Parallel Lives, 37
Pareto, Vilfredo, 63
Peck, Edward, 72, 82
pedigree, 33
people, 161–170
perception, 104–105, 166, 169
    self, 71
performing leadership, 22, 47, 72
permissions, 113
Persia, 24, 32, 44, 62, 157
    see also Iran

persona, 25, 125, 126, 131, 138
Peter principle, 82
pheets, 95
Philippines, 161
philosophy, 41–46
photos, 133
Picasso, 170
pig crushing, 208
Pilger, John, 67, 79
pilot study, 114
Pinker, Steven, 67
place, 12, 73, 101, 106, 108
plain English, 212
planet, 109
planning, 111–135
    surgical, 113
Plato, 44, 45, 108, 207
plausibility, 202–203
pluralist, 45, 61, 64, 174
Plutarch, 37, 69
police, 1, 123, 137, 217, 219
policy analysis, 148, 204
Political Instability Task Force, 147
political leadership, 73, 106, 154, 219
political prisoners, 103, 129,
        163, 187
polyarchy, 64
Polybius, 45, 67, 78
Ponet, John, 45
Pope, 33, 161, 169
    Joan, 33
Popper, Karl, 193
populace, 11, 77–81
population, 12, 77–81, 175
portraits, 171
positive illusions, 74, 82
posters, 157
poverty, 79, 187
power, 12, 58–63
    analysis, 221
    asymmetrical, 100
    elite, 65
    field of, 66
    hard, 43
    oppositional, 79
    soft, 43
    structure, 65, 148
    technocentric, 62
powerless, 80
    groups, 101
press release, Appendix 13
Prins, Gwyn, 119
privacy, 130
probability, 55, 120, 175, 193

problem, 116, 119–121
    oriented, 117
    solving, 115, 209
process, 204
    analysis, 148, 198, 204
    critical analysis, 148
    tracing, 148, 204
proletariat, 60, 67
propaganda, 61, 80, 99, 134, 158, 159, 166, 191
proportionality, 132
prospective, 92, 147
protocol, 146
provenance, 33, 143, 170
proxy, 120, 154
psychological studies, 139, Appendix 9
public, 77
    domain, 132
    inquiries, 218, 221
    interest, 132
    investigation, 143
    understanding, 216
purpose, 6, 30, 95, 109, 114–119, 121, 129, 153
purposive sample, 175

Quakers, 22, 151, 211
qualitative, 154, 186
quantitative, 154, 186
questions, 52, 86
Quigley, Carroll, 61

radar chart, 190
rational choice theory, 61
rationale, 114, 116–118
reciprocal ethics, 132
reconstructive research, 32, 40, 140, 143, 204
reflexive, 38
refugees, 67, 80, 97, 102, 103, 116, 127–129, 163, 208
Regan, Ronald, 11
rehabilitation, 158
reliability, 178, 180
religious leaders, 23, 33, 35, 40, 101, 174, 191
remote observation, 127, 141, 170
reporting research, 212
repositories, 218
reproduction of elites, 44, 66, 103, 117, 180
reputation, 43, 65, 66, 148, 176, 179
research, 10
    design, 112–114
    direct, 137–139
    ethics, 25, 128, 112–114
    indirect, 139–145
    questions, 120, 191, 208, Appendix 10
    undercover, 133, 138
resources, 73

retrospective, 92, 147
reverse engineering, 144, 204–206
reviewing literature, 94–99
rhetoric, 158
risk, 74, 76, 106, 107, 108, 139, 216
robots, 62, 63, 108
roles, 11, 122, Appendix 7
Rome, 31, 37, 45, 62, 78, 159, 173
Roosevelt, F.D., 166
Rothkopf, D., 67
Rumsfeld, Donald, 57
Russia, 33, 64, 103, 106
    see also sources, Soviet Union
Rwanda, 28

Saddam Hussein, 4, 74, 159, 177
sample, 175
satire, 146, 159, 160, 171
Saudi Arabia, 11, 196, 198
sceptic, 42
scientific method, 44, 46
Scotland, 21, 160
Scott, John, 59
Schwarzenegger, Arnold, 11, 103, 149
search engines, 92
searching literature, 92–94
secondary analysis, 95, 144, 155
security, 146
Sejong the Great, King, 13, 174
self-perception, 71, 221
Sen, Amartya, 80
sensemaking, 71
servant leadership, 42, 72
shadowing, 133, 141, 170
Sheba, Queen of, 36
shills, 97
Sierra Leone, 142
significance, 179
site, 13, 156
situated leadership, 70
situational, 37, 69, 70–72, 83, 85
    analysis, 147
Siwan, 35
small states, 101
Smith, Hazel, 97, 177, 202
snowballing, 124, 148, 167, 176
social, 79
    change, 81, 147, 209, 217
    movements, 73, 107
    network, 79, 107
socio-legal research, 150
sociology, 46, 58, 59, 60, 107, 209
soft power, 43
solution-oriented, 115, 154, 209, 221

Somalia, 23
songs, 159
sources, 86
   internet, 254
   South Africa, 217
   Soviet Union, 156; *see also* Russia
space, 62, 101, 106, 109, 146, 221
Spain, 171, 198
speeches, 6, 7, 17, 51, 56, 64, 84–86, 134, 138, 158,
   169, 187, 189, 194
Speer, Albert, 118
Spencer, Herbert, 70
spidergram, 149
Spinwatch, 80
spy, 5, 138, 162
stamps, 157
standardization, 187
state crime, 99, 100, 103
statistical analysis, 154, 192
status, 1, 5, 11, 23, 25, 33, 36, 43, 47, 50, 51, 61, 66, 67,
   69, 70, 74, 80, 84, 102, 117, 120, 122, 127, 148,
   149, 151, 160, 171, 174, 192
stings, 131, 138
Stodgill, R.M., 69
story-based inquiry, 138
strategy, 3, 34, 64, 136, 141, 148
   research, 111
stratification, 12, 64
street-working children, 1, 79, 217
substituted judgment, 132
Sudan, 22, 30
Sun Tzu, 3, 7, 34
superclass, 67
superiors, 1
surgical questioning, 162
surveillance, 61, 131
survey, 77, 97, 112, 120, 124, 147, 166, 169, 175–178,
   186, 194, 218, Appendix 9
   questionnaires, 155
survival research, 68
Suu Kyi, Aung San, 151
Sweden, 191
Switzerland, 149
systematic, 47, Appendix 6
   correspondence, 125, 145
   review, 95, 144
systems analysis, 145–152

Taharqo, King, 30
Tainter, Joseph, 67–68
talented, 187
Taliban, 11, 113, 158, 166, 198
Tantawy, Grand Sheik Muhammad S., 126
Tehelka, 138, 219

Tepco, 150
terrorism, 103, 151
testimony, 80, 177, 178
text, 141, 156–161, 174
Thailand, 134, 191
Thatcher, Margaret, 58
theory, 54–87, 207–210, 213
   general, 55
   grand, 57
   meta, 55
   specific, 55
thesis, 212–214
Tibet, 70
titles, 160
toxic leaders, 73
traits, 52, 67, 69, 70, 71, 73, 74, 82, 84, 96, 107, 150, 187
transactional leadership, 24, 52, 71, 76, 85
transcript, 156, 158, 163
translators, 162
transformational leadership, 71, 76
Transparency International, 154, 155, 166, 218
triangulation, 33, 38, 125, 177, 179, 200
tribal, 11, 23, 24, 34, 38
tribunal, 8, 103, 141, 142, 154, 170, 221
Tristram Shandy, 195
Turkey, 173
Tuvalu, 5
tweets, 141
Twitter, 157
typologies, 47, 51, 187
tyranny, 44, 74, 78

undercover research, 133, 138
UNESCO, 138
United monarchy, 35
United Nations, 3, 80
   General Assembly, 197
   leaders, 163
United States of America, 11, 63, 64, 65, 66, 78, 79,
   80, 93, 100, 120, 171
upper echelon theory, 65
up-system, 1, 10, 46–53, 83, 129
Urry, John, 61
user engagement, 212
Ushahidi Project, 140
utility, 5, 82, 208
utopia, 78
U-turns, 103

validity, 40, 176, 178, 204
values, 143, 198, 208
variables, 120, 191
Venn diagram, 215–216
Victims of Abuse of Power (UN), 3, 80

Vietnam, 34, 151, 201
Voltaire, 222

Walsingham, Francis, 4, 99
war crimes, 34, 79, 118, 200
Warhol, Andy, 68
wealthy elites, 106
weapons of mass destruction, 57
Weber, Max, 59
white collar crime, 162
Wikileaks, 8, 93, 132, 139, 140,
    157, 219
Wikipedia, 92

witchcraft, 28
women, 12, 27, 36, 65, 69, 79, 80, 96,
    126, 161, 168, 196, 198
Wordle, 122
Worsley, Lucy, 208

Yasakuni Shrine, 5
Yemen, 36
Yi Sun-shin, 9
Young, Michael, 66
Yugoslavia, 28, 156

Zoroastrianism, 35

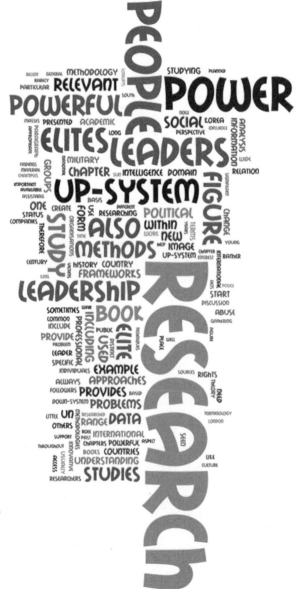

Graphic thanks to Wordle.net